Stan Lee PRESENTS

ESSENTIAL

THE TOMB OF DRACULA

VOL. 4

STORIES FROM TOMB OF DRACULA MAGAZINE #2-6, DRACULA LIVES! #1-13 & FRANKENSTEIN MONSTER #7-9

"SANCTUARY"
WRITER: ROGER MCKENZIE
PENCILER: GENE COLAN
INKER: DAVE SIMONS

"PAVANE FOR AN UNDEAD PRINCESS!"
WRITER: PETER GILLIS
PENCILER: JOHN BUSCEMA
INKER: BOB MCLEOD

"BLOODLINE"
FROM *TOMB OF DRACULA MAGAZINE #3*
WRITER: PETER GILLIS

1452

"THAT DRACULA MAY LIVE AGAIN!"
FROM *DRACULA LIVES #2*
WRITER: MARV WOLFMAN
ARTIST: NEAL ADAMS

1452

"LORD OF DEATH...LORD OF HELL!"
FROM *DRACULA LIVES #3*
WRITER: MARV WOLFMAN
PENCILER: JOHN BUSCEMA
INKER: SYD SHORES

1459

"LOOK HOMEWARD, VAMPIRE!"
FROM *DRACULA LIVES #4*
WRITER: GERRY CONWAY
ARTIST: VICENTE ALCAZAR

1459

"COURT OF THE DEAD!"
FROM *TOMB OF DRACULA MAGAZINE #2*
WRITER: MARV WOLFMAN
PENCILER: FRANK ROBBINS
INKERS: JOHN ROMITA SR. & JOHN TARTAGLIONE

1465

"THE SINS OF THE FATHERS"
FROM *DRACULA LIVES #12*
WRITER: GERRY CONWAY
ARTIST: TOM SUTTON

1471

"BLOOD OF MY BLOOD!"
FROM *DRACULA LIVES #13*
WRITER: **GERRY CONWAY**
ARTIST: **STEVE GAN**

1597

"PARCHMENTS OF THE DAMNED!"
FROM *DRACULA LIVES #12*
WRITER: **DOUG MOENCH**
ARTISTS: **SONNY TRINIDAD, YONG MONTANO & STEVE GAN**

1606

"THIS BLOOD IS MINE!"
FROM *DRACULA LIVES #4*
WRITER: **GARDNER FOX**
ARTIST: **DICK AYERS**

1691

"SUFFER NOT A WITCH!"
FROM *DRACULA LIVES #1*
WRITER: **ROY THOMAS**
PENCILER: **ALAN WEISS**
INKER: **DICK GIORDANO**

1762

"A DUEL OF DEMONS"
FROM *DRACULA LIVES #5*
WRITER: **GERRY CONWAY**
ARTIST: FRANK SPRINGER

1789

"SHADOW OVER VERSAILLES"
FROM *DRACULA LIVES #6*
WRITER: **TONY ISABELLA**
PENCILER: **JOHN BUSCEMA**
INKER: **PABLO MARCOS**

1700s

"ASSAULT OF THE SHE-PIRATE!"
FROM *DRACULA LIVES #7*
WRITER: **MIKE FRIEDRICH**
ARTIST: **GEORGE EVANS**

1809

"THE PIT OF DEATH"
FROM *DRACULA LIVES #10-11*
WRITER: **DOUG MOENCH**
ARTIST: **TONY DEZUNIGA**

1800s

"SCARLET IN GLORY!"
FROM *DRACULA LIVES #9*
WRITER: **DOUG MOENCH**
PENCILER: **PAUL GULACY**
INKER: **MIKE ESPOSITO**

1823

"DEATH VOW!"
FROM *TOMB OF DRACULA MAGAZINE #4*
WRITER: **ROGER MCKENZIE**
PENCILER: **JOHN BUSCEMA**
INKER: **KLAUS JANSON**

1862

"A HOUSE DIVIDED"
FROM *TOMB OF DRACULA MAGAZINE #6*
WRITER: **JIM SHOOTER**
PENCILER: **GENE COLAN**
INKER: **DAVE SIMONS**

1875

"BOUNTY FOR A VAMPIRE"
FROM *DRACULA LIVES #13*
WRITER: **TONY ISABELLA**
ARTIST: **TONY DEZUNIGA**

1800s

"TO WALK AGAIN IN DAYLIGHT"
FROM *DRACULA LIVES #1*
WRITER: **STEVE GERBER**
PENCILER: **RICH BUCKLER**
INKER: **PABLO MARCOS**

1890

STOKER'S DRACULA

1898

"THE FURY OF A FIEND!"
FROM *FRANKENSTEIN MONSTER #7*
WRITER: **MIKE FRIEDRICH**
PENCILER: **JOHN BUSCEMA**
INKER: **JOHN VERPOORTEN**
LETTERER: **CHARLOTTE JETTER**

1898

"MY NAME IS...DRACULA"
FROM *FRANKENSTEIN MONSTER #8*
WRITER: **MIKE FRIEDRICH**
PENCILER: **JOHN BUSCEMA**
INKER: **JOHN VERPOORTEN**
LETTERER: **JEAN IZZO**

1898

"THE VAMPIRE KILLERS"
FROM *FRANKENSTEIN MONSTER #9*
WRITER: **MIKE FRIEDRICH**
PENCILER: **JOHN BUSCEMA**
INKER: **JOHN VERPOORTEN**
LETTERER: **JOHN COSTANZA**

1903

"TWICE DIES THE VAMPIRE!"
FROM *DRACULA LIVES #9*
WRITER: **GERRY CONWAY**
ARTIST: **SONNY TRINIDAD**

1926

"BLACK HAND...BLACK DEATH!"
FROM *DRACULA LIVES #8*
WRITER: **LEN WEIN**
PENCILER: **GENE COLAN**
INKER: **ERNIE CHUA**

1944

"THE TERROR THAT STALKED CASTLE DRACULA!"
FROM *DRACULA LIVES #2*
PLOT: **STEVE GERBER**
SCRIPT: **TONY ISABELLA**
LAYOUTS: **JIM STARLIN**
FINISHES: **SYD SHORES**

TODAY

"POISON OF THE BLOOD"
FROM *DRACULA LIVES #1*
WRITER: **GERRY CONWAY**
PENCILER: **GENE COLAN**
INKER: **TOM PALMER**

TODAY

"THE VOODOO QUEEN OF NEW ORLEANS!"
FROM DRACULA LIVES #2
WRITER: **ROY THOMAS**
PENCILER: **GENE COLAN**
INKER: **DICK GIORDANO**

TODAY

"SHADOW IN THE CITY OF LIGHT!"
FROM *DRACULA LIVES #3*
WRITER: **GERRY CONWAY**
ARTIST: **ALFONSO FONT**

TODAY

"FEAR STALKER"
FROM *DRACULA LIVES #4*
WRITER: **MARV WOLFMAN**
PENCILER: **MIKE PLOOG**
INKER: **ERNIE CHUA**

"NIGHT FLIGHT TO TERROR!"
FROM *DRACULA LIVES #5*
WRITER: **TONY ISABELLA**
PENCILER: **GENE COLAN**
INKER: **PABLO MARCOS**

"A DEATH IN THE CHAPEL!"
FROM *DRACULA LIVES #6*
WRITER: **STEVE GERBER**
PENCILER: **GENE COLAN**
INKER: **ERNIE CHUA**

"HERE COMES THE DEATH MAN"
FROM *DRACULA LIVES #7*
WRITER: **GERRY CONWAY**
ARTIST: **VICENTE ALCAZAR**

"LAST WALK ON THE NIGHT SIDE"
FROM *DRACULA LIVES #8*
WRITER: **DOUG MOENCH**
ARTIST: **TONY DEZUNIGA**

"THE LADY WHO COLLECTED DRACULA"
FROM *DRACULA LIVES #9*
WRITER: **DOUG MOENCH**
PENCILER: **FRANK ROBBINS**
INKER: **FRANK SPRINGER**

"A NIGHT IN THE UNLIFE!"
FROM *DRACULA LIVES #9*
WRITER: **GERRY CONWAY**
ARTIST: **ALFREDO ALCALA**

"BLOODY MARY"
FROM *DRACULA LIVES #13*
WRITER: **RICK MARGOPOLOUS**
PENCILER: **GEORGE TUSKA**
INKER: **VIRGILIO REDONDO**

REPRINT CREDITS

MARVEL ESSENTIAL DESIGN:
JOHN "JG" ROSHELL OF COMICRAFT
FRONT COVER ART:
EARL NOREM
BACK COVER ART:
NEAL ADAMS
COVER COLORS:
AVALON'S ANDY TROY
SPECIAL THANKS TO:
POND SCUM, TOM PALMER, MARV WOLFMAN & RALPH MACCHIO
COLLECTION EDITOR:
MARK D. BEAZLEY
ASSISTANT EDITOR:
JENNIFER GRÜNWALD
SENIOR EDITOR, SPECIAL PROJECTS
JEFF YOUNGQUIST
DIRECTOR OF SALES:
DAVID GABRIEL
PRODUCTION:
JERRON QUALITY COLOR
BOOK DESIGNER:
TERNARD SOLOMON
CREATIVE DIRECTOR:
TOM MARVELLI
EDITOR IN CHIEF:
JOE QUESADA
PUBLISHER:
DAN BUCKLEY

ESSENTIAL

CC
02956
JUNE №5
$1.25

THE TOMB OF DRACULA

3 TERRIFYING TALES:

"SANCTUARY"

"LILITH: DAUGHTER OF DEATH"

"PAVANE FOR AN UN-DEAD PRINCESS"

PLUS! STEPHEN KING

PROLOGUE-- THE QUIET, RUSTIC VILLAGE OF POENARI LIES IN THE SHADOWS OF THE COLD ROMANIAN ALPS.
LIFE HAS NOT CHANGED MUCH, HERE, OVER THE YEARS.
NEITHER HAS DEATH...
HURRY, CHILD--! RUN!

JUST A LITTLE FURTHER AND WE WILL BE SAFE!
THE CHURCH IS OUR ONLY HOPE, NOW!

FIVE CENTURIES BEFORE, INVADING TURKISH HORDES PUSHED NORTH FROM CONSTANTINOPLE, WIDENING THE OTTOMAN EMPIRE ACROSS THE WAR-TORN FACE OF MEDIEVAL EUROPE.

IT WAS HERE THAT VLAD TEPES, SECOND SON OF VLAD DRACUL, RAISED AN ARMY AND BECAME A HERO TO HIS PEOPLE.

TONIGHT HIS ARMY RETURNS. BUT THEY ARE NO LONGER WARRIORS. AND VLAD TEPES IS ANYTHING BUT A HERO...

FATHER ALDEA, UNLOCK THIS DOOR!
BY ALL THAT'S HOLY, LET US IN!
MOMMA...

...LOOK!

AS ONE, THE DARK SWARM DROPS FROM THE NIGHT SKY, BLACK WINGS POUNDING LIKE A CHORUS OF INHUMAN HEARTBEATS.
THEIR SHARP, CRUEL FANGS GLEAM DEAD-WHITE IN THE MOONLIGHT AND THEIR EYES BURN RED...
RED AS THE BLOOD FOR WHICH THEY THIRST.
MOTHER AND CHILD SCREAM ONCE, LONG AND LOUD...

...ROUSING FATHER ALDEA FROM A TROUBLED SLEEP.
A MOMENT, PLEASE! I'M COMING!

BUT, BY THE TIME HE REACHES THE VESTRY DOORS, IT IS QUIET OUT-SIDE. OMINOUSLY QUIET.
THROWING BACK THE LATCH HE WONDERS IF, PERHAPS, HE HAS BEEN DREAMING.

BUT, IF SO, THEN HIS DREAMS HAVE JUST BECOME A NIGHTMARE...
BLESSED MOTHER OF MERCY-- NO!

NO!
PICKED CLEAN, STRIPPED OF FLESH AND BLOOD ALIKE, THEY STUMBLE FORWARD, ARMS OUTSTRETCHED, GROPING FOR THE STARTLED PRIEST...
...AS IF BLINDLY, SILENTLY PLEADING FOR--
SANCTUARY
BUT THERE IS NO SANCTUARY HERE.
THERE IS ONLY DEATH.

DEUS VOBISCUM!
GOD BE WITH YOU!

GOD BE WITH US ALL!

THE NOSFERATU HAVE RETURNED, DRAWN LIKE MAGGOTS...

"...TO THE ROTTING CORPSE OF CASTLE DRACULA!
"BUT WHY? WHAT UNHOLY PURPOSE GUIDES THEIR FLIGHT?"
SHIVERING, FATHER ALDEA BOWS, LIFTING HIS EYES TO HEAVEN.
BUT HE SEES ONLY THE RUINS OF HELL... THE ANCESTRAL HOME OF THE FAMILY DRACUL...
...THAT HAD BEEN SEVERLY DAMAGED WEEKS BEFORE BY AN EXPLOSION SET OFF BY THE RELENTLESS VAMPIRE HUNTER QUINCY HARKER, IN ONE FINAL, DESPERATE ATTEMPT TO RID THE WORLD OF DRACULA... WHICH FOR A TIME SUCCEEDED.

QUINCY HARKER IS DEAD, HAVING PERISHED IN THE HOLOCAUST. BUT DRACULA, THE EVIL PERSONIFICATION THE DUTCHMAN SPENT HIS LIFE OPPOSING STILL ENDURES... HAVING BEEN RETURNED TO LIFE BY A FOOLISH MORTAL WOMAN WHO CLAIMED SHE NEEDED THE VAMPIRE LORD'S HELP.
SUDDENLY, A FOUL, REEKING WIND SWIRLS DARK AND MENACING CLOUDS, LIKE A BLACK SHROUD, ACROSS THE BLOODLESS FACE OF THE MOON.
THEN...
...THE STORM BREAKS.
A COLD, RELENTLESS DELUGE...
...THAT OBSCURES CASTLE DRACULA AND ALL WITHIN...

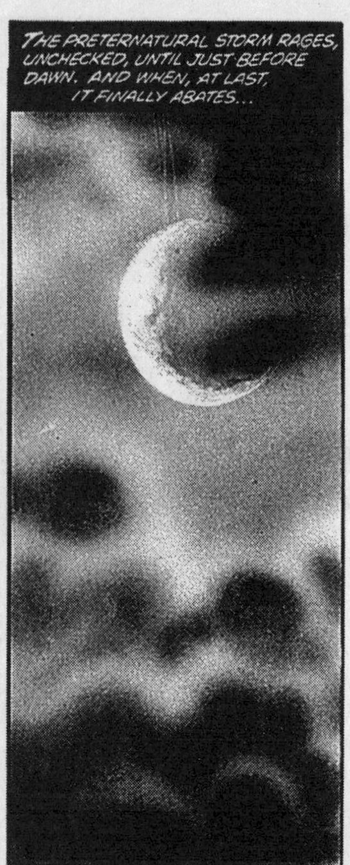

ONCE HE WOULD HAVE REVELED IN THEIR PLACATING CHANT, BUT NOW IT MERELY FILLS HIS UN-DEAD HEART WITH BOUNDLESS FURY...

ALL HAIL DRACULA, LORD OF THE UNDEAD!

HE WALKS AMONG US!
BOW TO HIM, OUR SAVIOR!

DRACULA! DRACULA!

AS YOU HAVE COMMANDED, OH, LORD, SO HAVE WE DONE!

HOW ELSE MAY WE PLEASE YOU?

YOU CAN-NOT!

ALL WE ARE, WE ARE BECAUSE OF YOU.
YOU ARE THE LIGHT. YOU ARE THE WAY. YOU GAVE US DEATH THAT WE MAY TASTE OF LIFE, NOW AND EVER MORE.
HOW HAVE WE OFFENDED YOU, MY LORD?

DID YOU THINK I HAD FORGOTTEN HOW YOU ALL SWORE ALLEGIANCE TO THE USURPER *TORGO*... WHO FOOLISHLY ATTEMPTED TO TAKE MY PLACE AFTER SATAN HAD TEMPOR-ARILY REMOVED MY VAMPIRIC POWERS?

AND UNTIL I DESTROYED HIM AFTER REGAINING MY MIGHT--YOU WERE HIS SLAVES, AND YOU SPAT UPON ME--DIDN'T YOU? DIDN'T YOU? SCUM! FILTH! YOU ALL OFFEND ME!

THERE WAS A TIME YOU FOUND ME ATTRAC-TIVE. TAKE ME, DRACULA! TAKE ME AS YOU DID THAT NIGHT!

YOU DARE OFFER YOURSELF TO ME...
...AGAIN?
YES, DRACULA! YES!

I WOULD DO ANYTHING FOR YOU!

WOULD YOU DIE FOR ME?
HAVE I NOT ALREADY DONE SO ONCE, MY LORD?

THEN DO SO ONCE MORE, SLUT!
I AM TIRED OF YOU.

I AM TIRED OF YOU ALL.
THE BLOOD!
THE HOLY BLOOD!

WE HAVE *LABORED* LONG AND HARD IN YOUR SERVICE!
WE THIRST, MY LORD! WE THIRST!

THEN *TAKE HER*, FOOLS!
TAKE HER AND BE DAMNED!

BUT ASK ME FOR NOTHING ELSE.
I AM A CRUEL MASTER.

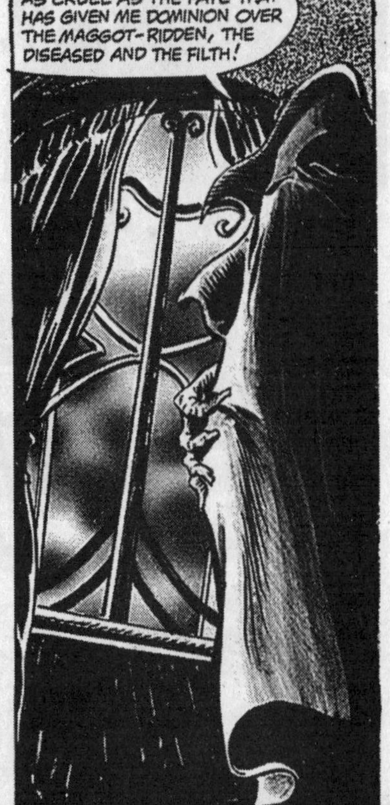
AS CRUEL AS THE FATE THAT HAS GIVEN ME DOMINION OVER THE MAGGOT-RIDDEN, THE DISEASED AND THE FILTH!

HOW COULD I EVER HAVE DREAMED OF FILLING THE WORLD WITH SUCH AS YOU?

HEAR ME, SCUM!
MARK MY WORDS WELL!
YOU CLAIM TO BE FLESH OF MY FLESH, BLOOD OF MY BLOOD! BUT YOU ARE NO MORE LIKE ME THAN MY OWN HATED DAUGHTER, LILITH!

I RENOUNCE YOU! I DESPISE YOU!
AND I WILL DEAL WITH YOU JUST AS SURELY AS I WILL DEAL WITH LILITH!
DRACULA'S THOUGHTS GO BACK, THEN, TO ANOTHER TIME, CENTURIES BEFORE...

...WHEN HE WAS STILL HUMAN, BUT NO LESS A MONSTER...
...AND WED TO A WOMAN, OUT OF POLITICAL EXPEDIENCY. ONE HE DID NOT LOVE...
COME, DINE WITH ME...
...ON THE TERRACE.
NO, VLAD, PLEASE. NOT AGAIN. ASK ANYTHING OF ME.
ANYTHING BUT THAT.

I ASK NOTHING.

I DEMAND IT!
YOU MAY BE WIFE IN NAME ONLY, BUT, BY GOD, YOU WILL STILL OBEY ME!

NOW, LIFT THE DAMNED CHILD HIGH. LET HER SEE THE DRACUL LEGACY.

LILITH MUST NEVER FORGET WHY I AM CALLED--

"--THE IMPALER!"

LATER, FOLLOWING THE DEATH OF HIS FATHER, DRACULA WOULD DRIVE WIFE AND DAUGHTER FROM HIM...

... AS SURELY AS HE HAD DRIVEN HIS TURKISH ENEMIES TO THEIR DEATH ON CRUDE WOODEN STAKES THAT STRETCHED ACROSS HIS DOMAIN AS FAR AS THE EYE COULD SEE.

BUT, THAT EVENING, DRACULA REMEMBERS, HE MERELY SAT DOWN TO SUPPER.

AND HE ATE WELL...

But then, Dracula's dark reverie is shattered by a cock's crow, somewhere in the distance, heralding the arrival of a new day.
And the beginning of the end...

MASTER, IT IS NEARLY DAWN! WE HAD NOT REALIZED!
SHELTER US FROM THE AWFUL TOUCH OF THE SUN! GIVE US SANCTUARY!
TAKE YOUR FILTHY HANDS OFF ME, FOOLS!

I TOLD YOU ONCE BEFORE TO ASK ME FOR NOTHING ELSE.
YOU WILL FIND NO SANCTUARY HERE!
And, smiling, Dracula settles back in deep, deep shadow, well away from the eastern-most window of his throne room...

...and the searing, damnable rays of the rising sun.
His cowering minions, however, are far less fortunate...
NO! THE SUN! IT BURNS! OH, LORD--! WHY HAVE YOU FORSAKEN US?

BECAUSE, AT LAST, I SEE YOU FOR WHAT YOU ARE!
YOU DO NOT DESERVE TO LIVE!
DENIED HEAVEN AND HELL ALIKE, MY DOMAIN IS EARTH--
--BUT I REFUSE TO RULE FILTH SUCH AS YOU!

THEN, ASSUMING THE FORM OF THE LESSER BEASTS...
...THE RAT AND THE WEASEL, THE WOLF AND THE BAT...

...DRACULA'S LEGIONS SPILL FROM THE CASTLE THAT HAS BECOME THEIR DEATH-TRAP...
...IN A MINDLESS ATTEMPT TO RETURN TO THEIR COFFINS...TO OUTRACE THE KILLING SUN.

BUT, ONE-BY-ONE, LIKE ICARUS, OF LEGEND, THEY FALL TO EARTH.

AND WHEN THEY CAN NO LONGER FLY, OR EVEN RUN ON ALL FOURS, THEY BEGIN TO CRAWL.
THEY DO ANYTHING TO ESCAPE THE UNHOLY YELLOW STAR THAT, LIKE THE EYE OF GOD, MELTS THE DEAD FLESH FROM THEIR DEAD BONES

AND YET, EVEN IN DEATH, THEY ARE NOT ALONE...
HELP... ME...

AND WHAT DO YOU WANT OF ME, YOU DISGUSTING WRETCH-- MERCY... TO SHIELD YOU FROM THE SEARING RAYS OF THE SUN? IF SO, THEN YOU KNOW LITTLE OF ME OR MY MOTIVES. FOR I AM--

--Lilith, Daughter of Death!

IT WILL SOON BE OVER BETWEEN US, FATHER. AS YOU'VE LAID WASTE TO YOUR MINDLESS LEGIONS -- SO SHALL I RETURN AND SEE YOU CRUMBLE BEFORE ME!
SHE STRIDES BOLDLY THROUGH THE HAZY MORNING MIST, HER PALE, UNDEAD FLESH INSENSITIVE TO THE CHILL... FOR IT IS COLDER THAN THE BRISK AIR... COLD AS THE GRAVE WHICH SHOULD HAVE CLAIMED IT NEARLY 500 YEARS AGO.
LILITH MOVES DEEPER INTO THE DANK FOREST, WHOSE ANCIENT EVERGREENS WERE MERE SEED-LINGS WHEN SHE FIRST TROD THE EARTH MANY CENTURIES GONE.
HER MIND IS ABLAZE WITH THOUGHTS OF THE PAST-- THOUGHTS OF HER FATHER AND THE CRUELTY HE VISITED UPON HER MOTHER AFTER LILITH'S BIRTH.
A MARRIAGE OF CONVENIENCE HE CALLED IT... ARRANGED FOR COURT PURPOSES ONLY, BY MY GRANDFATHER, VLAD DRACUL. WHEN VLAD DIED BARELY A YEAR AFTER THE CEREMONY...
...DRACULA WAS FREE TO RID HIMSELF OF THIS WOMAN HE SO DESPISED.
"HE WASTED LITTLE TIME IN EXPRESSING HIS CONTEMPT FOR MY MOTHER -- HIS FIRST WIFE.

"SEVERAL YEARS LATER DRACULA MURDERED GRETCHIN'S SON IN A SAVAGE ASSAULT ON THE GYPSIES, AND THE OLD WOMAN, MADDENED WITH GRIEF AND RAGE, BROKE HER PROMISE. THROUGH THE USE OF POTENT SPELLS, GRETCHIN TRANSFORMED ME FROM INNOCENT CHILD INTO AGELESS VAMPIRE!

"THE VERY MANNER OF MY CREATION ENDOWED ME WITH ALL THE POWERS OF THE UNDEAD --AND NONE OF THEIR MANY WEAKNESSES.

"FURTHER, GRETCHIN DEEMED IT MY DESTINY TO HAUNT MY FATHER THROUGHOUT ETERNITY... TO THWART HIS PLANS AND TO BE AN EVER-PRESENT GADFLY, REMINDING HIM ALWAYS OF THE HORROR OF HIS DEEDS!

"THEN, MORE THAN A CENTURY AGO, WE RECONCILED OUR DIFFERENCES IN AN UNEASY TRUCE. WE HAVE TAKEN SEPARATE PATHS WITH FEW ENCOUNTERS EVER SINCE.

"STILL, MY HATRED PERSISTED--EVEN BEYOND THE DAY I WAS SLAIN 30 YEARS AGO BY MY FATHER'S NEMESIS, QUINCY HARKER. FOR, SUCH WERE THE POWERS I HAD BEEN GRANTED, THAT IN DEATH, MY IMMORTAL ESSENCE WOULD SEEK OUT ANOTHER BODY...

"...THE BODY OF ONE WHO HATES HER FATHER AS GREATLY AS I HATE MINE! FOR YEARS MY LONELY SPIRIT WANDERED THE ENGLISH COUNTRYSIDE IN SEARCH OF SUCH A WOMAN.

"IT WASN'T UNTIL SEVERAL YEARS AGO THAT MY ENDLESS SEARCHING WAS REWARDED, WHEN I FELT COMPELLED TO PASS OVER AN OLD FARMHOUSE, WHERE INSIDE...
"...ITS OWNER, MARTIN O'HARA, HAD JUST STRUCK HIS DAUGHTER'S HUSBAND DURING A DISPUTE.
"ANGEL O'HARA DROPPED TENDERLY TO HIS SIDE, BUT HE NEITHER MOVED NOR BREATHED. WHILE FALLING, HE HAD STRUCK HIS HEAD AND NOW WAS DEAD.

"HATRED... HATRED OF HER FATHER SUCH AS ANGEL HAD NEVER KNOWN SWELLED IN HER BREAST. AT LAST, I HAD FOUND THE LIVING VESSEL SO LONG SOUGHT!

"MY PERSONA SLIPPED INSIDE HER YOUNG BODY, FEEDING ON THE EMOTIONAL INTENSITY SHE FELT. IT WAS I WHO TURNED TO FACE MARTIN O'HARA.

"I RIPPED HIS THROAT OPEN WITH A FEROCITY I HAD NOT KNOWN IN THREE DECADES.
"IT WAS GOOD.

"ONCE MORE--LILITH LIVED! ASSUMING THE FORM OF A BAT, I EMBRACED THE NIGHT, AND BEFORE IT ENDED, HAD MY VENGEANCE ON THAT AGED FOOL, QUINCY HARKER. IN THE DAYS THAT FOLLOWED, I WEARIED OF ENGLAND. I HAD PROWLED ITS ENVIRONS FOR TOO LONG AS A DIS-EMBODIED VAMPIRE. I LONGED FOR NEW SIGHTS, NEW SOUNDS, AND NEW BLOOD!
"IN THE GUISE OF ANGEL, WHOSE MIND I CONTROLLED ON SUCH OCCASIONS WHEN IT WAS NECESSARY, I MOVED TO AMERICA--TO NEW YORK'S GREENWICH VILLAGE. THERE, UNDER MY INFLUENCE, ANGEL MET A YOUNG MAN, MARTIN GOLD, WHO WAS JUST RE-COVERING FROM THE DEATH OF HIS WOMAN. HE CRAVED COMPANIONSHIP.

"ANGEL WAS THERE--AND AVAILABLE. IT WAS A RELATION-SHIP THAT WOULD PROVIDE STABILITY FOR BOTH PARTNERS...
BOO
"...AND ALLOW ME TO PURSUE MY OWN EXISTENCE IN A VIBRANT NEW WORLD WHERE NONE WERE AWARE OF MY PRESENCE.

"THEY SOON FELL IN LOVE, AND THOUGH MARTIN DISCOVERED ANGEL WAS PREGNANT BY HER FOR-MER HUSBAND, IT MEANT LITTLE TO HIM.
"ALL THE WHILE I DWELLED DEEPLY WITHIN HER--SECURE.

"BUT MY FATHER, WHO TRAVELED TO AMERICA AFTER SATAN HAD STOLEN HIS VAMPIRIC POWERS--DISCOVERED ME, WITH SOME UNCANNY SIXTH SENSE.
"HE NEEDED THE SHARP BITE OF A VAMPIRE TO RETURN TO HIM THAT WHICH HE HAD LOST.

"AND FOR DRACULA, ONLY THE FANGS OF A FAMILY MEMBER WOULD SATISFY HIS BLOATED EGO. I WAS ENRAGED. HE, WHO HAD DRIVEN MY MOTHER TO SUICIDE AND CAST ME OUT AS A BABE, NOW DEMANDED THAT I WILLINGLY HELP HIM!
"MY ANSWER TOOK THE FORM OF A TORRENTIAL STORM, WHICH I DIRECTED AT MY FATHER IN ALL ITS FURY... DRIVING HIM FROM ME, CURSING THE DAY I WAS BORN."

A FEW DAYS LATER, I LEARNED DRACULA HAD REGAINED HIS POWERS ONLY TO BE KILLED BY HIS ARCH-FOE QUINCY HARKER AS THEY STRUGGLED ON THE BATTLEMENTS OF CASTLE DRACULA.
BUT NOW DRACULA HAS AGAIN ARISEN FROM THE DEAD AND CLAIMED HIS THRONE. THE TRUCE BETWEEN US IS BROKEN. I WILL SEE HIM DESTROYED FOREVER BY MY HAND!

FIRST, THERE IS SOMEONE I MUST SEE, A MAN OF WHOSE EXISTENCE I KNEW NOTHING UNTIL RECENTLY.

THE GRAY OF A LATE AFTERNOON SKY HAS SETTLED OVER THE TRANSYLVANIAN VILLAGE WHEN LILITH ARRIVES AT A SMALL HOUSE ON ITS OUTSKIRTS.

VIKTOR BENZEL... MY NAME IS LILITH AND I WOULD LIKE TO SPEAK WITH YOU ABOUT A MATTER OF GREAT URGENCY. MAY I COME IN?
LILITH!
KNOWING WHO AND WHAT SHE IS, VIKTOR IS HESITANT ABOUT ALLOWING HER ENTRY, BUT HER DISARMING MANNER SETS HIM STRANGELY AT EASE.

I'M GLAD YOU KNOW OF ME VIKTOR--IT MAKES IT EASIER FOR ME TO ASK YOU FOR HELP. AS A GYPSY, AND GRETCHIN'S DIRECT DESCENDANT, YOU MAY BE THE ONLY ONE WHO CAN.
BUT I'VE PUT ALL THAT BEHIND ME NOW. I'M MERELY A MUSICIAN.
DON'T DENY ME, VIKTOR, HELP ME! SURELY YOU'RE IN POSSESSION OF THE KNOWLEDGE I NEED. YOU MUST HELP ME END THE CURSE THAT KEEPS ME UNDEAD.

CAN YOU IMAGINE WHAT IT'S LIKE TO LIVE ON AND ON--SEEING EVERYONE I'VE CARED FOR, AGE AND DIE AND DECAY? I'M AFRAID TO CARE ANYMORE...
I UNDERSTAND, BUT PERHAPS YOU DON'T. THE ONLY WAY TO HELP YOU IS TO DESTROY YOU!

IT'S TRUE THAT GRETCHIN WAS MY ANCESTOR, AND THAT MUCH OF HER KNOWLEDGE WAS PASSED ON TO ME AND MY BROTHER, KARL. BUT HE'S THE TRUE ADEPT--YOU SHOULD SEEK KARL OUT--
NO! THERE ISN'T TIME FOR THAT.
ALL RIGHT. THEN CONSIDER...KNOWING THE HORRORS DRACULA HAS BROUGHT TO SO MANY OF MY KIND, WHY SHOULD I NOW AID HIS FLESH AND BLOOD?

BECAUSE I DESIRE HIS DEATH EVEN MORE THAN YOU DO...

...AND NOW IS THE TIME TO STRIKE. DRACULA IS ALONE, HAVING TURNED ON THOSE HE MIGHT HAVE USED AGAINST ME. NOW, WILL YOU ASSIST ME, OR MUST I CARRY THE FIGHT MYSELF?
I... STAY FOR DINNER, AND I'LL THINK ABOUT IT.

AS THE HOURS PASS, VIKTOR BENZEL FEELS A GROWING AFFINITY FOR THIS BEAUTIFUL WOMAN BEFORE HIM-- AND TO HER SURPRISE, LILITH IS ATTRACTED TO HIM AS WELL.

AT LAST VIKTOR REACHES FOR LILITH'S HAND AND DRAWS HER WORDLESSLY TOWARD THE STAIRS. THAT SHE IS ONE OF THE UNDEAD HE KNOWS ALL TOO WELL, YET HE CAN NOT FIND IT IN HIS HEART TO FEAR HER; HE WANTS ONLY TO HOLD HER CLOSE, TO EASE HER ACHING LONELINESS...
AS THEY ASCEND THE CREAKING STAIRS, THE CLOCK IN THE FAR-OFF TOWN HALL SLOWLY STRIKES 12...

I CAN'T BELIEVE HOW INCREDIBLY LOVELY YOU ARE-- OR THAT YOU'RE REALLY HERE, LIKE THIS, WITH ME. LILITH, PLEASE... FORGET ABOUT YOUR FATHER, THE CURSE-- JUST STAY WITH ME.
HOW CAN I FORGET? HOW CAN I STAY WITH YOU, OR WITH ANYONE? ALL TOO SOON YOU WILL AGE, GROW SICK AND WEAK. HOW LONG WOULD IT BE THEN BEFORE YOU STARTED HATING ME...?!
I AM A VAMPIRE, VIKTOR! I HAVE SAVAGELY KILLED HUMAN BEINGS, AND ENJOYED IT!

DON'T TALK ABOUT YOURSELF THAT WAY!
WHY? IT'S ALL TRUE...!

BECAUSE IT ISN'T YOUR FAULT.
I AM A MONSTER...

DON'T!
WHAT DO YOU REALLY KNOW ABOUT ME, MORTAL! MUST I SHOW YOU WHAT I AM?!

KAAASSHHH

NO!
WHAT HAVE YOU DONE! -- SLASHED YOUR FACE WITH THAT GLASS -- WHY?

IT WILL HEAL, VIKTOR... IN SECONDS.
FOR I AM IN TRUTH UNDEAD!

YOU MUST HELP ME! I HAVE NO OTHER HOPE FOR RELEASE!
I...I'LL HELP YOU, LILITH. I'LL DO ANYTHING FOR YOU...

A FEW DAYS PREPARATION, AND VIKTOR IS READY TO BEGIN THE HIDEOUS RITUAL THAT WILL DIVORCE LILITH FROM THE HOST BODY IN WHICH SHE IS IMPRISONED. IN VIKTOR'S SHED THE NAKED VAMPIRE IS STRAPPED TO A COLD TABLE.
TREMBLING, VIKTOR KISSES LILITH ONE LAST TIME AND THEN STARTS THE NEARBY BUZZ SAW--
ON
heart
WHEN IT IS OVER, VIKTOR, SHAKING AND HORRIFIED, PLACES EACH SECTION OF HIS LOVER'S BODY INTO A SEPARATE CONTAINER, KNOWING THAT EVEN MANGLED AS SHE IS-- LILITH STILL LIVES...
...STILL FEELS--FOR SHE CANNOT TRULY DIE!
AT NIGHTFALL HE DRIVES TO A CROSSROADS AND BURIES THE CONTAINERS AT DIFFERENT POINTS OF THE COMPASS: NORTH, SOUTH, EAST, AND WEST... IN THE ARCANE MANNER DICTATED BY HIS ANCESTORS.

--WHICH, UNDER HIS GUIDANCE, SHEARS THROUGH THE BODY OF THE QUEEN OF THE UNDEAD. HE CUTS HER WRITHING FIGURE INTO BLOODY SECTIONS.
THE USE OF MODERN TOOLS MAKES THE AGONY NO LESS INTENSE. LILITH'S UNHOLY SCREAMS MINGLE WITH THE RAGGED WHIRRING OF THE SLICING BLADE... FORMING THE BACKGROUND OF A NIGHTMARE THAT SEEMS ENDLESS!
FOR TWENTY-FOUR HOURS HE WAITS, UNABLE TO EAT OR SLEEP. AT LAST THE HOUR ARRIVES: VIKTOR UNEARTHS THE CASEMENTS AND RETURNS HOME.
A HUGE CAULDRON IS RREPARED, INTO WHICH HE DEPOSITS THE BODY PARTS AS HE RECITES TIME-LOST CHANTS. WITHIN MOMENTS, THE STEAMING VAT BUBBLES WITH THE STUFF OF SORCERY. SUDDENLY, THE GHOSTLY FIGURES OF TWO WOMEN ARISE FROM THE CAULDRON, JOINED MOMENTARILY AS ONE... UNTIL MIRACULOUSLY--THEY SEPARATE AND SOLIDIFY.

BUT FOR YOU--WHAT HAS OCCURRED SO FAR IS ONLY *PART* OF THE RITUAL. I'LL HAVE TO GET IN TOUCH WITH KARL, ASK HIS HELP IN NEUTRALIZING THE VAMPIRE SPELL... TO TRULY FREE YOU OF YOUR CURSE.

IN THE MEANTIME, LILITH--STAY WITH ME... FORGET ABOUT YOUR FATHER. I CARE ABOUT YOU... I'M AFRAID FOR YOU. DON'T LEAVE.

I CAN'T STAY. DON'T YOU SEE, VIKTOR? I WILL HAVE NO PEACE UNTIL MY LIFE'S MISSION IS FULFILLED. TO STOP NOW WOULD MEAN MY ENTIRE EXISTENCE HAS BEEN IN *VAIN*. AND PERHAPS I OWE THIS AS WELL TO GRETCHIN, TO MY MOTHER, AND ALL THE MANY INNOCENTS DRACULA'S TOUCH HAS TAINTED.

ONCE I SOUGHT TO IGNORE HIS EVIL INFLUENCE--EVEN TO ASK THAT WE *SHARE* THE THRONE OF THE UNDEAD. BUT I KNOW DIFFERENTLY NOW. ONLY ONE COURSE IS OPEN TO ME...

CASTLE DRACULA BROODS OVER THE BORGO PASS, A MULTI-SPIRED MONUMENT TO THE UNSPEAKABLE DEPRAVITY OF ITS RECENTLY RETURNED MASTER. WITHIN ITS COLD, CLAMMY WALLS, UNRELENTING TERROR AND TORTURE HAVE HELD SWAY FOR AN AGE. AND WITHOUT--
--ITS MALEVOLENT, DEBILITATING INFLUENCE IS EVIDENT ON THE BLEAK COUNTRYSIDE WHICH SEEMS TO COWER IN THE CASTLE'S SHADOW.

TO THIS SINGULAR EDIFICE OF EVIL DRIFTS THE LEATHERY-WINGED INCARNATION OF LILITH... ONE OF THE FEW CREATURES, DAMNED OR DIVINE, ABLE TO APPROACH THESE SILENT STONE WALLS WITH SOMETHING LESS THAN UTTER LOATHING.

DRACULA ISN'T EVEN AWARE THAT I'VE COME TO TRANSYLVANIA--AND THAT LACK OF KNOWLEDGE MAY BE USED TO MY ADVANTAGE. UNLIKE OTHERS WHO'VE FALLEN BEFORE HIM IN THE PAST...
...I SHALL CHOOSE THE MOMENT AND MANNER OF OUR CONFRONTATION.
ELSEWHERE IN THE HELLISH ABODE, THE OBJECT OF LILITH'S INIMICAL THOUGHTS SURVEYS THE HANDIWORK OF HIS LATE SUBJECTS.

HOW PLEASURABLE TO PASS THROUGH SUCH PERFECTLY RESTORED SECTIONS OF THE CASTLE. THOSE WORTHLESS CRETINS WERE FORTUNATE THEY COMPLETED THE TASK TO MY SATISFACTION...
...OR THEIR GROTESQUE DEATHS WOULD HAVE BEEN ALL THE MORE UNBEARABLE.

STRANGE... THOUGH MUCH OF THE STRUCTURE SUFFERED DAMAGE--
--ONE WING REMAINED TOTALLY UNTOUCHED...

SAVE FOR THE LAYERS OF DUST, IT IS EXACTLY AS I REMEMBER, IN EVERY RICH AND BURNISHED DETAIL. THE YEARS HAVE DONE LITTLE TO DIMINISH ITS LUSTER. AND THE BED... THE BED...

...WHERE BEHIND THOSE LONG UNPARTED CURTAINS, MARIA AND I WOULD LIE-- CONSUMED IN THE FIRE OF A THOUSAND PASSIONS. IT WAS HERE WE CONCEIVED MY SON, VLAD TEPELUS...

...WHO EVENTUALLY GREW TO MANHOOD *HATING* ME WITH ALL HIS HEART--AS DOES HIS DESPICABLE HALF-SISTER, LILITH. IT WAS SHE WHO--NO... NO, I MUST BANISH SUCH DISTASTFUL REMEMBRANCES AND THINK ONLY OF MY MARIA.

SHE WOULD WAIT WHILE I DISROBED, AND WE WOULD SPEAK QUIETLY THROUGH THE SATIN SHROUD OF WHAT WAS TO COME.

I COULD SENSE HER MOVEMENTS, AS I KNEW SHE COULD MINE. I WOULD IMAGINE HER SOFT, WARM ARMS-- OUTSTRETCHED TO RECEIVE ME...
...THE HALF-LIDDED EYES AND LIQUID LIPS READY TO IMPART ECSTASY.

WITH THE SLIGHTEST TREMBLE, I WOULD DRAW THE RUFFLED DRAPE... AND EXACTLY AS I ENVISIONED...
...MARIA WOULD BE WAITING--ALWAYS.

FATHER... HAVE YOU COME TO TUCK ME IN--OR SHALL WE ADD INCEST TO YOUR MANY SINS?
LILITH!

YOU WOULD DARE!
YOU WOULD DARE TO PROFANE THIS PLACE--THIS VERY BED WITH YOUR PUTREFYING PRESENCE!
COME NOW, FATHER, THAT SLUT OF A WIFE YOU HAD...
...SHE MUST HAVE SHARED THIS BED WITH MANY A STRANGER WHEN YOU WERE AWAY. WHY SHOULD YOU DENY ITS COMFORT TO YOUR LOVING DAUGHTER?

I WILL PLUCK OUT YOUR LYING TONGUE AND STRANGLE YOU-- EH?!

YOU'LL DO NOTHING, FATHER...NOT WHEN I BECOME AS MIST AND SLIP FROM YOUR CLUMSY GRASP.

BUT DON'T FEAR ...I HAVE NO INTENTION OF VANISHING AFTER SUCH A SHORT STAY...
AAARRGGHH!! MY FACE! MY FACE!

...NOT UNTIL I'VE REDUCED YOU TO A MUTILATED MASS OF UNDEAD FLESH, BEGGING TO BE RELEASED IN FINAL DEATH!

DO YOU REMEMBER THE COUNTLESS INNOCENT VICTIMS BUTCHERED AT YOUR COMMAND... THE WOMEN AND CHILDREN BEHEADED OR IMPALED BECAUSE THEY FELL INTO DISFAVOR WITH YOU?
THEY SEEK REDRESS, LORD DRACULA! THEY REACH OUT FROM BEYOND THEIR GRAVES--THROUGH ME, TO HELP END YOUR FOUL EXISTENCE IN THE MOST TORTUROUS MANNER IMAGINABLE. I AM THEIR AVENGER!
FEEL THEM, FATHER--FEEL THEIR AWFUL STRENGTH WHICH SURGES THROUGH ME AT THIS MOMENT AS I CONSTRICT AROUND YOU!
UUULLLGGHH!

WEAKENING SO SOON, FATHER? YOU SEEM TO BE GOING LIMP IN MY GRIP.
BUT THIS IS FAR FROM OVER YET!
IT WOULD BE TOO MERCIFULLY EASY THIS WAY.
NO! THE HORROR HAS ONLY BEGUN IMPALER...
...OOONNNNULLYYYYY BBBEEEEGGGUN
COME BACK!!

SHE WAS TOYING WITH ME--WITH DRACULA, LORD OF THE UNDEAD! I THOUGHT ONLY SATAN HIMSELF CAPABLE OF SUCH A FEAT!
EVEN NOW, SHE CACKLES GLEEFULLY BELOW, KNOWING FULL WELL THE FINAL RECKONING APPROACHES.
LILITH!
ENTER, FATHER... ENTER FREELY, AND OF YOUR OWN WILL. IT SEEMS STOKER'S ACCOUNT OF YOU IN HIS NOVEL WAS MORE ACCURATE THAN I HAD EVER BELIEVED... THE VENEER OF BREEDING DISGUISING THE MURDEROUS BEAST BENEATH THE SKIN.
WHY HAVE YOU CHOSEN TO COME TO THIS CHAMBER? ANSWER ME!
I'M INTRIGUED BY THE SYMBOLISM OF DESTROYING YOU IN THIS THRONE ROOM... THE VERY PLACE FROM WHICH YOU ORDERED COUNTLESS EXECUTIONS YOURSELF.
AND WITH YOUR PENCHANT FOR IMPALING VICTIMS, YOU KNOW THE POWER OF SYMBOLS WELL... PARTICULARLY--
--CHRISTIAN SYMBOLS.
THE CROSS... THE DAMNABLE CRUCIFIX, HERE!?
YAAAAHHHH!!
PSSSSSSSS
PERHAPS YOU WISH A CLOSER LOOK. HERE, LET ME TOUCH YOU WITH IT... SUCH CONTACT IS SAID TO BE UPLIFTING FOR THE SOUL.
WHY DO YOU SHRINK FROM IT, DRACULA? CAN IT BE SOMETHING BEYOND EVEN YOUR ABILITY TO CORRUPT OR PERVERT?
AWAY WITH IT!

AS YOU WISH. IF YOU'RE HURT, AT LEAST ALLOW ME TO CLEANSE THE WOUND WITH-- HOLY WATER.
ENOUGH OF THIS. I DON'T NEED TRINKETS TO DOMINATE OUR ENCOUNTER, FATHER.
NO! NO!
WHAT I MUST ACCOMPLISH SHALL BE DONE WITH MY BARE HANDS.
THAT WAS YOUR MISTAKE, DAUGHTER. YOUR LAST FATAL MISTAKE.
THOUGH GYPSY SPELLS MAY ALLOW YOU IMMUNITY FROM VAMPIRIC WEAKNESSES... STILL IT IS DRACULA YOU CONTEND WITH! DRACULA, WHO IS THE GREATEST WARRIOR OF ALL!
MY ENEMIES-- ENDLESS IN NUMBER, HAVE EACH SOUGHT MY EXTINCTION THROUGHOUT THE CENTURIES. AND ALL OF THEM-- ALL OF THEM NOW ROT LIKE DOGS IN THEIR GRAVES!
BUT I LIVE ON-- I ENDURE-- I SURVIVE! BECAUSE I AM DRACULA...
...AND I AM SUPREME!

WHERE ARE YOUR TAUNTS NOW, DAUGHTER-- YOUR ACCUSATIONS AND INSULTS? HAVE YOU--
--UNINGGHH!
KRAKT!!
IS THIS ANSWER ENOUGH, DEAR FATHER? I HAVE REPELLED YOUR STUMBLING ATTACK... HUMILIATED YOU IN YOUR OWN STRONGHOLD... AND MADE LIES OF YOUR AUGHABLE CLAIMS TO GREATNESS!
BUAMP!
YET, STILL YOUR INSANE VANITY REFUSES TO ACCEPT THE INEVITABILITY OF DESTRUCTION THIS NIGHT!

YOU CANNOT DEFEAT ME, DRACULA. FOR I WAS CREATED TO BE YOUR SUPERIOR... YOUR MASTER. AND HOW-EVER LONG THE DELAY, YOU KNEW ONE DAY I WOULD COME FOR YOU LIKE THIS-- TO DESTROY YOU!
IT IS DESTINY, FATHER... AND NEITHER YOU NOR I MAY ALTER ITS DIRECTION.

BAH! YOU SPEAK OF DESTINY TO ME... OF WHAT IS WRITTEN OR DETERMINED AND CANNOT BE UNDONE!
WRAP!
NEVER, DAUGHTER! NEVER!

I HAVE NO USE FOR ANCIENT GYPSY DRIVEL MASQUERADING AS TRUTH!
I HAVE HURLED DOWN THE GAUNTLET OF CHALLENGE TO THE DEITIES OF HEAVEN AND HELL THEMSELVES--AND STILL I EXIST TO SPEAK OF IT! DRACULA BOWS TO NO FORCE... MOST ESPECIALLY NOT A SNIVELING SNIP OF A GIRL WHO PROFANES MY VERY BLOOD BY HAVING IT COURSE THROUGH HER VEINS.

MONSTER! MOVE ONE FURTHER STEP TOWARDS HER AND I WILL KILL YOU WHERE YOU STAND!
I COULDN'T LET LILITH FACE DRACULA ALONE, THOUGH I'D HOPED WHEN I GOT HERE SHE'D HAVE THE ADVANTAGE...
...AND I WOULD ONLY HAVE TO COMPLETE THE JOB. INSTEAD--

OHHH... VIKTOR--NO! HE MUST HAVE FOLLOWED ME FROM THE VILLAGE.
GET BACK! VIKTOR GET BACK!

SILENCE! I WILL RETURN TO YOU ONCE I HAVE FINISHED WITH THIS FOOL.

YOU BLACK-HEARTED BASTARD! IF SHE'S HURT I'LL--
YOUR CONCERN FOR MY DAUGHTER'S LIFE TOUCHES ME DEEPLY...

FOR YOU? OF COURSE, MY DEAR. I HAVE NO INTENTION OF NOURISHING MYSELF ON THIS ILL-MANNERED YOUNG INTERLOPER.

I MERELY WISH TO METE OUT THE *JUSTICE* DUE HIM FOR INVADING ANOTHER MAN'S HOME WITH THE INTENT TO KILL.

SHOULD YOU WIN OUR UNCOM-PLETED DUEL, DAUGHTER... YOU MAY SAVOR THE CORPSE YOURSELF!

VIKTOR... OH FATHER, DID YOU THINK THAT BY MURDERING HIM YOU WOULD SHOCK ME--SHATTER MY RESOLVE? NO... YOU HAVE ONLY STRENGTHENED ME. I CRAVE YOUR DEATH MORE NOW THAN WHEN I ENTERED THIS CASTLE.
THEN LET US TEST YOUR RESOLVE.

TAKE THESE, FOR I WEARY OF THE STRUGGLE.

YOUR FRIEND INTENDED THEM AS THE MEANS OF MY EXECUTION.
I WILL NOT DENY YOU.

SPLANK

USE THEM. I DEFY YOU TO DRIVE THAT STAKE THROUGH MY HEART WITH ALL THE FEROCITY THAT POSSESSES YOU. I OFFER YOU THE CHANCE TO PUT AN END TO THIS UNNATURAL HATRED WHICH HAS GNAWED AT YOU FOR AGES
DO WHAT YOU MUST, DAUGHTER. I SHALL NOT LIFT A FINGER TO STOP YOU.

IS IT DESPAIR WHICH MOVES YOU, FATHER... BECAUSE AT LONG LAST YOU KNOW DEEP INSIDE YOU COULD *NEVER* TRIUMPH OVER ME... OR IS IT SOMETHING LESS NOBLE, O'MASTER OF DECEIT? DO YOU EXPECT ME TO LOWER MY DEFENSES BECAUSE YOU OFFER NONE OF YOUR OWN? IF SO, BEWARE FOR--

AS I HAVE SAID, DAUGHTER, I WILL OFFER NO RESISTANCE. THE PRIZE IS NO LONGER WORTH THE PURSUIT. DO WITH ME AS YOU WILL.

THEN, MY DEAR FATHER, PREPARE... FOR THIS IS THE CULMINATION OF MY LIFE AND THE LAST MOMENT OF YOURS.

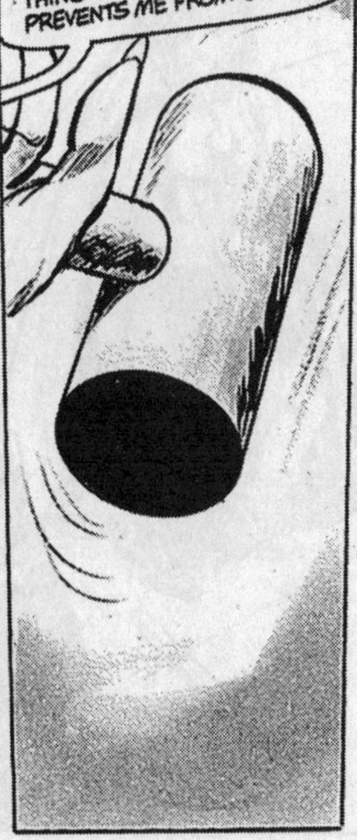

THE MOCKING ECHOES FADE, AND SOON, LILITH STANDS ALONE IN THE OPPRESSIVE SILENCE... ALONE TO PONDER THE PAINFUL LOSS OF A LOVER--PERHAPS THE ONLY MAN ON EARTH WHO COULD HAVE HELPED HER... AND THE LOSS OF A STRANGE INNOCENCE WHICH ALLOWED HER TO BELIEVE SHE WAS AN INSTRUMENT OF DESTINY ALL THESE CENTURIES.

THAT HAS ALTERED NOW. FATE HAS PLAYED ITS CRUEL JOKE IN THE FORM OF GRETCHIN'S OWN WORDS TO LILITH: "AND YOU SHALL EVER HAUNT HIS PRESENCE--BE HIS CONSTANT AGONY--" BUT SHE WILL NOT BRING HIS DEATH.

FOR LONG MOMENTS, SHE STANDS, UNTIL GOLDEN RAYS OF DAWN SPILL INTO THE DARK THRONE ROOM, HERALDING DAY'S APPROACH... A DAY FILLED WITH NEW HOPE AND THE PROMISE OF REDEMPTION FOR MOST OF HUMANITY.

BUT FOR THIS LOST QUEEN OF THE UNDEAD, WHO SO DESPERATELY DESIRES TO LOSE HER BLOODY CROWN... MORNING COMES ONLY WITH THE PROMISE OF ENDLESS EMPTINESS.

Writer: PETER GILLIS Art: JOHN BUSCEMA & BOB McLEOD

SHE HAS STAYED AS LONG AS POLITENESS REQUIRED. THERE IS NOTHING FOR HER HERE.

OR IS THERE?
LEAVING BEFORE WE HAVE BEEN INTRODUCED? HOW UNKIND.

MY NAME IS TEPESCH. VLADIMIR TEPESCH.
YOU DANCED WELL TONIGHT.

CAN I DROP YOU OFF SOMEWHERE, MR. TEPESCH? MY CAR IS JUST OUTSIDE--
HE NODS. THERE IS SOMETHING FASCINATING ABOUT THIS MAN: SOMETHING-- EXCITING.

LATER, AS ALL DESTINATIONS ARE FORGOTTEN...
AND I COME OUT HERE TO WATCH THE WATER DANCE. EVERYTHING DANCES, VLAD-- EVERYTHING!
AS YOU HAVE DANCED TOWARDS ME, ODETTE--

--AS YOU ARE NOW MINE.
YES, VLAD. OH Y--

YEEEEEEEEEEEEEEEEEEEEEEEEE

AND SOON THERE IS ONLY A PALE FIGURE AND A HUGE VAMPIRE BAT IN THE MOONLIGHT.

WHEN THE WAN FORM OF THE BALLERINA BESTIRS HERSELF MUCH LATER--
--ODETTE'S FIRST AND ONLY THOUGHT IS--

MY PERFORMANCE! I'LL MISS IT!

AND THAT PERVERT EVIDENTLY TOOK MY CAR, TOO!
BUT I CAN'T MISS A PERFORMANCE! I CAN'T!

AND SO, PROPELLED BY THE OBSESSION WHICH RULES HER LIFE, ODETTE JOGS INTO TOWN...
...ODDLY ENOUGH, NOT WORKING UP A SWEAT!

ODETTE! WHERE HAVE YOU BEEN THESE PAST THREE DAYS?
NEVER MIND THAT, GREG! I JUST HOPE I'M NOT TOO LATE TO GO ON TONIGHT.
STAGE DOOR

THE BALLET ITSELF PASSES AS IF A FAMILIAR DREAM. THEN, AFTERWARDS...
AND SO I HAD TO JUST JOG FROM SILVER LAKE TO THE THEATER, HELEN!
SILVER LAKE? BUT THAT'S OVER TWENTY MILES, ODETTE!

COFFEE, 'DETTA?
N-NO... I WANT...

HER THIRST IS FOR SOMETHING THICK, RED, AND HOT.
OH MY GOD--

BLOOD!
ODETTE? WHAT'S WRONG?

GOOD EVENING, MY DEAR. YOUR DANCE THIS EVENING SURPASSED EVEN MY EXPECTATIONS.
TEPESCH!!

DAMN YOU, WHAT'S GOING ON? WHAT HAVE YOU DONE TO ME? WHAT DID YOU DO?

I AM CALLED DRACULA, AND IT WAS MY INTENTION THAT YOU BECOME ONE OF MY IMMORTAL BRIDES--

--THAT YOU BECOME A VAMPIRE.
NO!!

YOU'RE LYING! I'LL RIP YOUR THROAT OUT FOR THAT, DRACULA! I'LL DESTROY YOU!

THAT YOU WILL NEVER DO, WOMAN--
FOR I AM LORD OF ALL VAMPIRES!
NO-- PLEASE--!

BUT--YOU CAN'T KEEP ME FROM DANCING! YOU JUST CAN'T!
DANCING... I-IT'S MY LIFE!

YOUR LIFE, AS YOU HAVE KNOWN IT, ENDED THREE DAYS AGO.
YOU ARE A DANCER NO LONGER--BUT A CREATURE OF MINE! OBSERVE!

REALITY DISSOLVES AS ODETTE BEGINS TO TRANSFORM INTO--A BAT!

NO!! I WILL REMAIN WHAT I AM! I WILL BE MYSELF!

I WILL BE A DANCER, DRACULA!
AND I WILL DEFY YOU!

VERY WELL. PERSIST IN YOUR FOND ILLUSION--FOR NOW!
BUT YOU ARE A VAMPIRE, ODETTE--AND I SHALL CLAIM YOU--SOON!
ODETTE BYELAI HOLDS HER SECRET FIRE WITHIN HER--AND TREMBLES.

IN THE NIGHTS THAT FOLLOW, ODETTE STRUGGLES TO REPRESS THE HORRIBLE CHANGES IN HER BODY.
'DETTA! NOW DON'T GO VANISHING LIKE YOU HAVE THESE PAST COUPLE OF NIGHTS!

LOOK, YOU KNOW HOW I FEEL ABOUT YOU. WHATEVER'S THE MATTER, YOU CAN TELL OLD FRIEND GREG!
THE THIRST IS SO STRONG--

'DETTA! PLEASE, I WANT TO HELP!
THERE ARE NO WORDS FOR FRIEND-SHIP ANY MORE.

ONLY DANCING--DANCING!
THE DAYS, SHE SPENDS CORPSE-LIKE IN HER BED...
...THE NIGHTS, PRACTICING AT HER PRIVATE BARRE, PLANNING THE SURVIVAL OF HER DREAM!

I HAVE TO TRY THIS AGAIN--!
SHE BECOMES A BAT.

THEN THROUGH FORCE OF WILL AND DESIRE--
--SEEKS TO MASTER THE TRANSFORMATION --NOT BAT--NOT WOLF-- BUT WHAT SHE WANTS!

I'VE DONE IT! I'VE DONE IT!
THE INCARNATION OF STRAVINSKY'S FIREBIRD STANDS IN HER APART-MENT, AND SHE KNOWS TRIUMPH!

BALLET AFTER BALLET PASSES, AND SHE EVEN DISCOVERS HER UNDEAD STRENGTH GIVING HER NEW GRACE AND EASE AND VIGOR.

SO IT IS A SERENE ODETTE WHO DANCES TO THE PROKOFIEV ON HER STEREO.

BUT SUDDENLY THE MUSIC IS ONLY A SCREECHING, GRATING NOISE!

SOMETHING WRONG WITH THE RECORD, NO DOUBT.
SHE PUTS ON HER BELOVED TCHAIKOVSKY.

BUT A VAMPIRE IS A SOULLESS THING. FEELING THE SENSATION OF MUSIC AS MUSIC IS FOREVER BEYOND IT! EVEN HER TCHAIKOVSKY IS JUST NOISE!

NOISE!
NOISE!
NOISE!!

SHE FLEES INTO THE NIGHT, BORNE ON THE WINGS OF MADNESS.

SHE DOES NOT CARE WHO THE MAN BELOW HER IS! SHE MUST HAVE HIM!

HE IS ONLY A HUMAN, AFTER ALL!

SPLAYED GROTESQUELY OVER HIM, ODETTE SLAKES THE THIRST SHE HAS REPRESSED FOR SO MANY NIGHTS.

IT IS GOOD.
IT IS ECSTASY.

THEN... THE UNSPEAKABLE HORROR OF IT...
GOD-- I DIDN'T. I COULDN'T HAVE!

I'M NOT A VAMPIRE! I'M A DANCER! I'M A DANCER!

I'M... I'M... I'M...

THE FOLLOWING NIGHT...

ODETTE! HOW IS MY COMPANY'S PRIMA BALLERINA? I HAVE HEARD YOU ARE TROUBLED!

ANATOLY, I NEED HELP. YOUR HELP!

MONTE BALLET

I? I AM BUT A CHOREOGRAPHER, ODETTE. BUT I WILL TRY!

ANATOLY, I'VE BEEN--CHANGED. I NOW HAVE--POWERS I DIDN'T HAVE BEFORE. BUT I MUST BE ABLE TO USE THESE POWERS IN THE DANCE, OR I'LL STOP DANCING--FOREVER!

I--SEE. AND WHAT ARE THESE POWERS?

I CAN *CHANGE*, ANATOLY! I CAN BECOME ANYTHING I DESIRE! ANYTHING--EXCEPT HUMAN!

I'VE GOT TO DANCE WITH MY WHOLE BEING, ANATOLY!

BUT YOU MUST GIVE ME DANCES... DANCES TO COMPLEMENT THIS THING THAT I'VE BECOME! WILL YOU DO IT? WILL YOU--?

YES, MY CHILD--WE SHALL USE THIS GIFT--TOGETHER.

Soon, there are new versions of classic ballets which use Odette's 'talents'!
SALAMMB
Giselle
Firebird
La Sylphide
DAMNATION

And then-- Swan Lake. When she was a child, it was the loveliest ballet in the world.
She forms herself from the mist of the lake.

Greg is dancing the prince. He has grown sadder, and cold toward her.
Not that it matters.

She leaps across the stage to him.

In mid-leap, she turns for the barest instant into a swan...

...then back to human form in Greg's arms.

The audience is awed by the seeming "effect." But one member knows the transformation was no mere stage trick... it was real.
Dracula has come to claim his due.

THE BEAUTY OF THE PERFORMANCE IS LOST ON THE UNDEAD PRINCE. HIS EYES BURN ONLY WITH A PRIMAL DESIRE FOR WHAT IS HIS... WHAT IS DRACULA'S. AND..
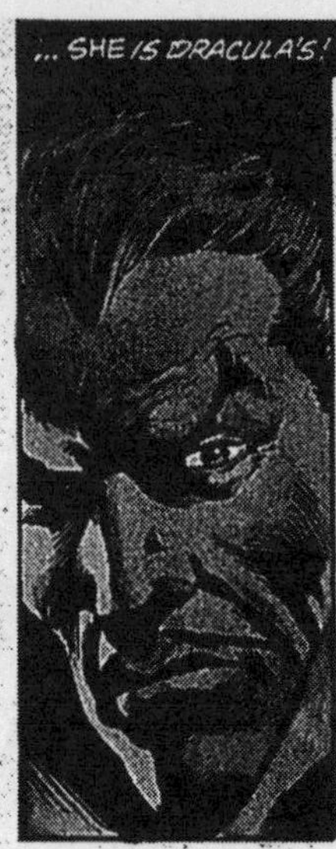
...SHE IS DRACULA'S!

ALL THAT MATTERS IS STRENGTH! ALL ELSE IS ONLY SHADOW!
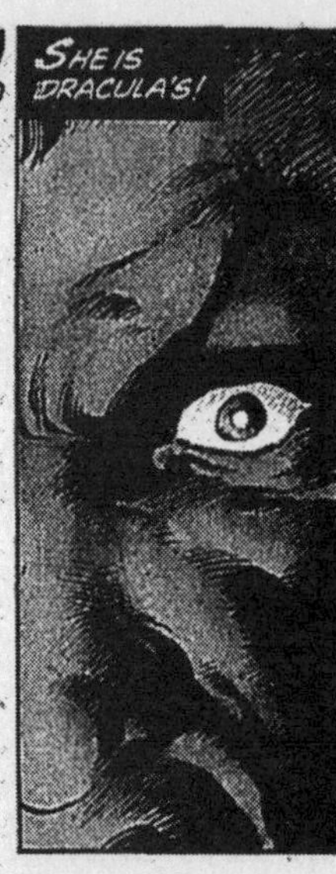
SHE IS DRACULA'S!

THE FINAL PARTING COMES! TENSELY, THE WHITE SWAN LEAPS AWAY FROM THE PRINCE...

...CHANGING TO THE BEAUTIFUL SWAN-FORM.

BUT HER PRACTICED CONTROL SUDDENLY FADES, AND DELICATE, FLUTTERING WINGS BECOME DARK, LEATHERY FOLDS.

SHE DROPS TO THE STAGE, AS THE DYING SWAN, THIS VAMPIRE-BALLERINA..

REMOVED FROM SIGHT, SHE GROPES FRANTICALLY, USING HER UNDEAD STRENGTH TO REND THE WOODEN FLOORBOARDS --SEEKING A MAKESHIFT STAKE...

...WHICH SHE PLUNGES THROUGH HER BREAKING HEART.

THE MUSIC ENDS AS DOES ODETTE'S UNDEAD "LIFE." THE AUDIENCE CONSIDERS IT A MARVELOUS PERFORMANCE.
IT WAS.

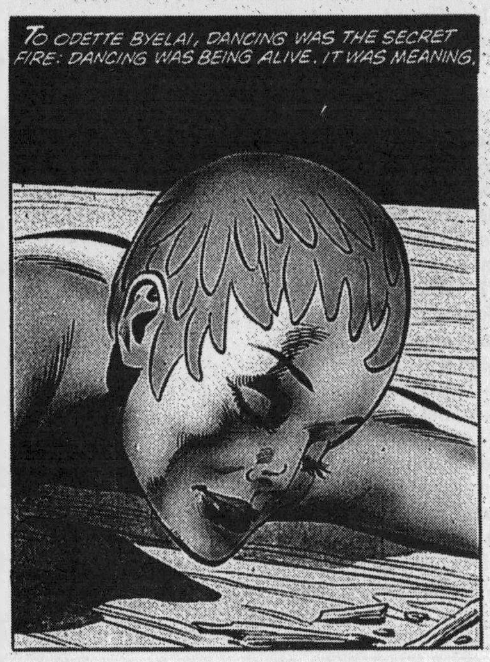
TO ODETTE BYELAI, DANCING WAS THE SECRET FIRE: DANCING WAS BEING ALIVE. IT WAS MEANING.

A FACT WHICH DRACULA, SLOWLY, IMPASSIVELY--
--APPLAUDS.

BLOODLINE:

A Probable Outline Of The Career Of Count Vlad Dracula

Compiled By Peter Gillis

To those for whom Count Dracula is only a figure in a few old movies, or perhaps a novel by Bram Stoker and an adaptation or two for the stage (and for whom *Tomb of Dracula* is a new experience), The Lord of Vampires seems to be a creature of the Victorian Era. He is inevitably attired in formal evening dress, hearkening back to the days when men "dressed for dinner", and his victims were always the painfully innocent and virginal women that typified the Victorian ideal of the "Lady of breeding." For some, Dracula was the symbol of the dark side of the age of Queen Victoria, the sexual, obsessive, evil aspect of the psyche that was so ruthlessly repressed, but which nevertheless could not be eliminated, and which surfaced from time to time in horrible forms. For others, Dracula has come to be no more than a period piece, an antique curiosity to be looked at through the wrong end of a telescope as nostalgia or camp.

But to those who have been long-time readers of Marvel Comics' Dracula (in both incarnations of *Dracula Lives!* and in *Tomb of Dracula*) a different picture presents itself; Count Dracula has been shown to have spread his cloak of fear over many eras, from the Late Middle Ages to our own present day. He is an immortal, ageless terror who tyrannized every age he lived through. Marvel readers have seen Vlad the Impaler preying on the citizens of France during the final years of the reign of Louis XVI, shortly before the French Revolution; they have seen him lay waste to Turk and Magyar during the Fifteenth and Sixteenth Centuries; they have seen him confront the urban technology of today. And through it all, he has remained Dracula: fearsome, implacable, utterly malevolent and utterly fascinating. In short, if you're unfamiliar with the Dracula of Marvel Comics, you've missed a great deal.

This, then, is a partial biography of that Dracula, from his birth to his death, and from his death to his fearsome 500-year death-in-life, as it has appeared within these pages. It is sketchy in many places, and totally obscure in others, and much of his career remains yet to be told; but it still presents an epic picture of the Lord of the Undead which is far removed from the narrow setting of bustles and corsets, white-tie-and-tails, and refined Victorian prose. This is the story of a Dracula who is the dark side of many eras: yes, and maybe ours as well.

1430

Vlad Dracula is born in the Transylvanian town of Schassburg (in modern Romanian, Sighisoara). He is the second son of Vlad Dracul, a Transylvanian nobleman. In 1431 the infant Vlad is taken by his father to the court of the Holy Roman Emperor Sigismund II in Nuremburg, where Dracul is invested with the Order of The Dragon, an anti-Turkish knightly order, and is named prince of Wallachia, a Romanian principality bordering Transylvania on the south. By 1437, Dracul has succeeded in ousting his half-brother Alexandru Aldea from the throne and assuming the rule himself.

Romania at this time is beset by the Ottoman Turks, under the Sultin Murad II. who had overrun Serbia and Bulgaria and were threatening all of Europe. Dracul, even though his membership in the Order of the Dragon forbids it, makes deals with the Turks, even going so far as to join, in 1438, a Turkish ravaging expedition into Transylvania. Dracula accompanies him.

1444

Dracul, Dracula and Dracula's younger brother Radu the Handsome are betrayed and captured by the Turks. Dracul protests his loyalty to the Sultan, and as proof offers Dracula and Radu as hostages to the court. It is here, in the court of Murad II, that Dracula is given his education, not only

in Turkish and in Greek philosophy, but in cruelty. Vlad Dracul and Mircea, Dracula's older brother, are murdered in 1447 by followers of John Hunyadi, the foremost crusader against the Turks of that age, while Dracula is still at the Turkish court.

1448

Dracula escapes the Turks, but relations between him and Murad II remain good enough to gain Dracula Turkish support when he ousts the Danestis from the throne of Wallachia, which he holds for eight months. Then, fearing the Transylvanians who killed his father, he flees to Moldavia, where he stays until 1451. In 1451, the friendly regime is overthrown and Dracula returns to Transylvania, throwing himself on the mercy of his father's and brother's murderer, John Hunyadi. It is Hunyadi, one of the greatest fighters and generals of that or any other age, who schools Dracula in the arts of war. In 1453 Constantinople falls to the Turks at last, and when, with Hunyadi's help, Dracula becomes again Prince of Wallachia in 1456, he is forced to use those arts of war against the powerful and unfriendly new Sultan, Mohammed II, called the Conqueror. It is between 1451 and 1456 that Dracula marries for the first time, a noblewoman of the Hungarian court, whom he despises. The marriage had been arranged by Dracula's father many years previously, and it lasts only one year, ending by Dracula throwing his wife out along with her infant daughter. She turns the daughter over to the gypsies and commits suicide. The daughter eventually becomes the vampiress Lilith, who seeks revenge on Dracula up until today.

1459

In pitched battle on the plains of Wallachia, in the very shadow of the Transylvanian Alps, Dracula is felled in battle by the Turkish Warlord Turac, who then takes Castle Dracula (near the present-day village of Snagov), and with it Dracula's second wife, Maria, and their infant son, Vlad Tepelus. Maria is raped by the Turkish soldiers, and, hearing of this, Dracula attacks Turac and is mortally wounded. Turac takes Dracula to the gypsy Lianda to have him healed. But Lianda is a vampire, and turns Dracula into one as well. Dracula then returns and kills Turac (his wife is now dead), and routs the Turks from the castle. Dracula then confronts Nimrod the First, Lord of all Vampires, and defeats him in battle, earning the title and powers of Lord of the Undead.

Turac, meanwhile, has also been turned into a vampire, and returns to his own castle, killing everyone within and draining their blood. His daughter, Elianne Turac, drives a stake through her father's heart and swears vengeance on Dracula. Through a pact with the powers of Darkness, she later gains immortality at the expense of her sight, and pursues Dracula until 1974, when he finally kills her. Subsequently Dracula expels the Turks from his borders, and sets up a kingdom ruled totally by fear — fear of the vampire. Vlad Tepelus is raised by gypsies, and grows up trying to destroy his father.

1465

Dracula is visited by ambassadors from other nations, including Spain, the Italian states, and Prussia, seeking agreements that he will stay within his boundaries in Transylvania. Infuriated by this, Dracula makes his first foray into the rest of Europe, heading north to Prussia. He depredates the countryside, gets bored, and returns. An assassin follows him back to Transylvania, and while there, falls in love with an innkeeper's daughter, Rache Van Helsing. The assassin is destroyed, and Rache vows vengeance. 400 years later, her descendant, Abraham Van Helsing, makes good on that vow.

1471

A Baron Hunyadi, one of the younger sons of John Hunyadi, starts making raids into Transylvania, looting and stealing serfs for use as slaves. Dracula confronts Hunyadi and tells him to stop, but Hunyadi refuses. Instead, he sends a woman to drive a stake through Dracula's heart. The ploy fails, and Dracula realizes the responsibility for his subjects is too much a nuisance, and so frees his serfs from alliegance to him. From this point forward, Transylvania remains under foreign rule, first Magyar, then Turkish, but none seek to interfere with Count Dracula's activities. (It is probably about this time that Dracula assumes the title "Count." Previously he had been called "Prince.")

1553-1566

For over a century Dracula inhabits his castle in South Transylvania, preying on the populace when he so desires, and instilling fear in a wide area. It is between the two dates mentioned above that Count Dracula has his two encounters with the English Puritan adventurer Solomon Kane. In the first encounter, Kane is searching for the daughter of a friend, whom Dracula has turned into one of

his vampire brides. The two duel, and Kane is forced to honor an oath and spare Dracula's "life" even though Dracula is at Kane's mercy. In the second encounter, Kane does kill Dracula by burying a cross in Dracula's heart. This is the first time Dracula is "killed", but he evidently does not stay dead for long, since his reign of terror is scarcely interrupted.

1597

A peasant named Durenyi invades Castle Dracula in Snagov. There he steals Dracula's diary and makes the discovery that vampires can be repulsed by the cross. (Previously, this knowledge was available only to a few, mainly clergymen). Durenyi makes this widely known, and so Dracula, for the first time, is foiled by the populace. Durenyi seeks to capitalize on his success, but is shunned by others and is ultimately killed by Dracula's subject vampires. He sells Dracula's diary to a bookseller in Biastritiz who ships it to England, where, 300 years later, Bram Stoker finds it, and, together with reports of contemporary events, fashions the novel *Dracula* out of it. It is at this point that Dracula quits his ancestral castle near Snagov and moves north to the castle near the Borgo Pass which remains his sometime home until the present day, though he now begins to rove more over the countryside and the continent, as the difficulty in obtaining victims increases.

1606

Dracula encounters Elizabeth Bathory, mother of Zsigmond Bathory, nominal prince of Transylvania. Elizabeth, though quite old, keeps herself young by bathing in the blood of virgins. She runs afoul of Dracula by competing with him for the beautiful young maidens, and in reprisal, Dracula walls her up inside her castle until the spell of blood wears off and she dies of old age. From here on Dracula spends more and more of his time away from Transylvania, often for decades. It is probalbly during this period that Dracula, for a time, becomes ruler of a province in Spain, which he rules for a time with an iron hand, until he is beset by a demon, who, as he finds out in the 20th Century, is the time-travelling spirit of his last son.

1691

Dracula, in his Borgo Pass castle, establishes a mental rapport with a young girl in Salem, Massachusetts, and an emotional bond is formed between them. Dracula makes his first trip to the New World to meet the girl, but finds when he gets there that she has been

hanged as a witch. Enraged, Dracula turns a West Indian governess into a vampire and bids her turn others into vampires as well, thus precipitationg the Salem witch trials and hangings. 250 years after the death of his beloved Maria, this is the first time, as a vampire, Dracula has felt love for another being. Up until now, most of his encounters with women have been similar to his encounter with the pirate Hellyn DeVill, which probably occurred a few years before the Salem incident: mockery and hatred for women who find him attractive, combined with deep remorse for the death of Maria. But from this point onwards, his relations to women become more sensual, if not less predatory.

1762

It is around this date that Dracula moves his place of residence to France. At this time the Turks nominally controlled Transylvania, and the Russians were amassing their military might under Catherine the Great. Dracula evidently sees the gathering storm clouds and moves to France, which, under Louis XV, is enjoying peace and prosperity. In 1768 the Russo-Turkish war breaks out, and Dracula decides to stay in France on a permanent basis. However, another, more personal war is also transpiring, as Dracula meets and confronts one of his greatest opponents, Count Alessandro di Cagliostro. Cagliostro makes one of his most daring attacks in 1769; using a sculptor named Jacques DuBois who creates a living gargoyle to attack Dracula. Dracula defeats the gargoyle and seeks out DuBois, whom he casts into a vat which turns him into a living gargoyle himself.

DuBois survives into the 20th century, when he is finally shattered by Dracula. Despite this sparring with Cagliostro, Dracula maintains a low profile in France until the year 1785. Louis XVI has been reigning for eleven years, and his court is shaky and scandal-ridden. It is probable that the event which causes Dracula to appear at court at Versailles and become an adviser to the king is the notorious Affair of the Diamond Necklace, in which a member of court, the Comtesse de la Motte, dupes Cardinal Rohan into purchasing a fabulously expensive

diamond necklace for her under the pretense that it is for Marie Antoinette, the queen. When Rohan is unable to meet payments on the necklace, the jewelers from whom it was bought confront the queen directly. Instead of hushing up the scandal, Louis has Rohan imprisoned and tried. Rohan is acquitted on all counts, yet he is deprived of his holdings and exiled, showing the despotic and insecure nature of Louis' rule. Dracula and Cagliostro are both present at Versailles at the same time, and they have their most important battle at that point, where Dracula turns Cagliostro's wife, the lovely Loreza Serafina, into a vampire. Even so, they coexist at court until 1789, when Cagliostro leaves France in a mysterious attempt to cure his wife. (Dracula much later claims to have killed Cagliostro, but this has never been documented, and may be the Count's colossal pride speaking.) Dracula, as one of the King's advisors, is imprisoned in the Bastille to be executed by a devious noble, Montpelier, with democratic sentiments, but is accidentally freed by the storming of the Bastille on July 14th, 1789. Dracula flees France and does not return for many years.

1795

Count Dracula returns to his Borgo Pass castle at the onset of the French Revolution, only to find that a number of nobles have encroached on his lands during his more than 30 year absence. The most powerful of these is a Baron Russoff, who refuses to acknowledge Dracula's primacy. Dracula kills Russoff's wife Louisa, and Russoff retaliates by coming to Castle Dracula in daylight and driving a stake through Dracula's heart. He wreathes the coffin in garlic and casts it into the Bistrita river, but does not decapitate the vampire. Russoff later finds a woman named Lydia imprisoned in the castle, and frees her. She however is a werewolf, and infects Russoff and all his offspring (by a second wife, evidently) with the curse of the werewolf.

1809

Dracula's death does not last long, for by 1809, he is back in Castle Dracula and preying upon the people of Transylvania again. By this time Transylvanians have had long experience in combatting him, but two things work in Dracula's favor: the first, that since 1766, western and southern Transylvania has been part of the Military Frontier against the Turks, and the governors do not believe in vampires. Secondly, since Russoff's attempt on him, the first to succeed inside the castle itself, the Count adopts defenses for Castle Dracula, such as his Pit of Death. As a result, when Dracula kills the blind wife of a peasant named Lupescu, and Lupescu drives a stake through her heart to prevent her from rising as a vampire, the authorities imprison him for murder. Lupescu escapes, but finds a more difficult time in the castle than Baron Russoff did, since Dracula is on his guard and casts him into the abovementioned pit, which contains his vampire brides. Lupescu does die at Dracula's hand, but not before Lupescu has killed all his brides and arranged their bodies in the shape of a cross, preventing Dracula from resurrecting them, since he cannot approach them. Evidently they decompose before Dracula can use the pit again.

1862

Dracula is in Germany. Though seemingly occupied in Transylvania for the first part of the 19th Century, the events of 1848 (the establishment of the Second Republic in France, the revolution establishing the Frankfort National Assembly in

Germany) convince Dracula that a period of turmoil is once again in the offing for Europe, and he feels he can increase his power. Ilsa Strang, the wife of one of Otto von Bismarck's rivals, who is secretly in love with Bismarck, convinces Dracula to murder Strang and so insure Bismarck'a ascention to the post of Minister-President of Germany. Dracula kills Strang, but Ilsa betrays him, slaying him. Dracula is nonetheless revived, and when Bismarck spurns Ilsa's advances, Dracula turns her into a vampire under his rule. However, that same year she is killed by Abraham Van Helsing. This is the first recorded action of Van Helsing against Count Dracula and his servants, but both Dracula and Van Helsing assert that their feud started earlier.

1870

In a culmination of Dracula's political ambitions, he invades Vienna with an army of vampires, intent on usurping the Hapsburg throne. Timing his coup to coincide with the outbreak of the Franco-Prussian War, his accession to the throne of the Austro-Hungarian Empire would give him sufficient leverage to control the destiny of all of Europe. Driving regular troops before them like chaff in the wind, the vampire legions occupy Vienna, and Dracula enters the Imperial Palace, only to be stopped, as he had been in Spain in the 1600's by the time-travelling spirit of his son Janus, born in the 1970's. The attempt fails utterly as Dracula flees in terror and drops out of sight.

1875

Dracula is discovered aboard a small sailing ship in the Mediterranean Sea, heading for England from France with a load of lower-class passengers. Dracula is travelling incognito, dressed as the corpse of an English cavalry officer being sent home for burial. Pirates, also in an out-of-date sailing vessel, board the ship in search of treasure and open his coffin. Dracula kills the pirate captain, turning him into a vampire. However, Dracula apparently changes his course and returns from Transylvania. This uncharacteristic caution can only be explained by the unreasoning terror the spirit Janus instilled in him (although the fact that his current nemesis, Abraham Van Helsing is currently in England may explain Dracula's desire to enter England secretly.)

Within the next decade, Dracula faces what may be his oddest antagonist: an ex-U.S. Marshal. A young American is seduced and murdered by one of Dracula's vampire brides, and his father hires the ex-Marshal to find his son's murderer. Dracula is deluded into thinking the aging gunfighter with the country-bumpkin manners an incompetent, and so lets his guard down long enough for the

man to pump him full of silver buckshot. This sends Dracula once again into a temporary death, but there are so many minute pellets of silver in his body that it is years before his minions can revive him, and even after that, he remains in a debilitated state that resembles premature aging, and makes him the most cautious and careful he has ever been in his long unlife. This is probably the low point in Dracula's vampiric career.

1890

In this year occur the events that, seven years later, are published by Bram Stoker as the novel *Dracula*. Using Jonathan Harker, a young British solicitor, Dracula secures by legal means Carfax Abbey, and surreptitiously enters England and inhabits it. England is a land Dracula had never bothered with, and so he, and vampires in general, are unknown there. He seeks to establish himself in England, but arouses the suspicion of Abraham Van Helsing, evidently before Dracula is quite ready to destroy him. Van Helsing pursues Dracula back to Transylvania where he kills him along a country road. Jonathan Harker is rescued, and marries Mina Murray, and in the same year as Stoker's novel appears, they have a son named Quincy. At an unspecified time in the future, Dracula kills Van Helsing and Harker, leaving Quincy and Van Helsing's granddaughter Rachel to carry on the fight.

1898

After he kills Dracula, Van Helsing decides to settle in Transylvania, where the populace give him the informal title of "Baron." But shortly after he settles down, Dracula, by means of a magic black mirror, returns from the 1970's to attack him. Van Helsing is completely unprepared for this, and even though he is saved from immediate destruction by his granddaughter Rachel and her cohorts who have followed Dracula back in time, Van Helsing sustains injuries which result in his death a year or so later. As for the original Dracula, his body is restored to his coffin somehow and the coffin hidden in a cave, with the cave sealed behind a mammoth stone, that not even a vampire's prodigious strength could move. Evidently this arrangement is the work of some vampire hunter who discovers the bones of Dracula and is insufficiently versed in vampire lore to insure Dracula's eternal death, nor is Abraham Van Helsing alive to correct him. The strength needed to move the rock and open the coffin appears in 1898 in the person of the Frankenstein Monster, who has been frozen in ice for a hundred years and now searches for the descendant of Victor Frankenstein, the man who created him.

The Monster is taken in by a gypsy, Madame Marguerita, who is actually one of Dracula's vampire slaves. She convinces the Monster to open the tomb on the pretense that the last Frankenstein is buried there. The gypsy revives Dracula, only to have the Monster battle him and impale both the gypsy and the Count. This time, however, the crypt remains open, and it is thus not a very long time afterward that another of Dracula's minions removes the stake and the Lord of Vampires walks the earth again.

1903

With both Transylvania and England aroused and alert, Dracula transports himself to Spain, where he once ruled. For a time, he rules night-time Madrid by terror. But in 1903, Dracula encounters the personified entity known as Death. Within the space of a few nights, he has Dracula killed twice, only to have him rise again. Death admits his defeat to Dracula, intimating a truce between the two of them. However, Death admits to himself that he has lied to Dracula, as he still intends to see Dracula dead.

1914

With the Balkan states on the brink of a war which will blossom into World War I, Dracula returns home to Castle Dracula, since the peasantry is more concerned with being turned into soldiers than into vampires. However, a young British nobleman, the brother of Lord Falsworth, otherwise known as the costumed spy-buster Union Jack, invades Castle Dracula and falls prey to the Count. Dracula decides to use John's hatred for his brother and turn him into a weapon against the homeland of the Harkers', England. It is Dracula's only action in a mad war that nearly destroys Europe. Instead, he probably murders Jonathan Harker amid the confusion of war.

1926

Dracula surfaces in Italy. This is only a temporary stopover, since he is at this time preparing for a trip to America. His motivations for this trip are unclear, though Quincy Harker has attained manhood by this point and has organized an extensive task force devoted to tracking down Dracula and destroying him, so it is entirely possible that Dracula is a fugitive, and is seeking some respite from Harker's agents. This is borne out by the fact that Dracula seeks out one of the most desolate places in the United States, Devil's Lake, North Dakota, to stay, even though a rural area makes a steady supply of human blood extremely difficult to come by. From this appearance in 1934, nothing is heard of Dracula during World War II, except for a bizarre incident when a few Nazi soldiers occupy Castle Dracula in early 1944. The spirit of Dracula somehow possesses one Hauptmann Kriss, and he goes on a bloody slaying binge. His victims, however, do not turn into vampires, even though he has powers of man-into-bat transformatiion, so it is difficult to say exactly what that "possession" entailed.

1945

Dracula returns to England after the war is ended, and attacks Quincy Harker and his wife while they are at the opera. Neither of them is fatally wounded, though Elizabeth Harker is almost drained of blood. She is not turned into a vampire, and indeed gives Quincy a daughter, Edith, in 1951. But when Edith is four, in 1955, Elizabeth, beset by nightmares of Dracula's ravaging, commits suicide.

1968

After his revenge on Harker, Dracula once again goes abroad, this time to a region he has not before visited: the Far East. He ravages India and China and Indonesia in 1968, and among his victims are the son of Taj Nital, who later joins Rachel Van Helsing and Quincy Harker, and an unidentified yound Scotsman. While making his home in a Chinese Temple, Dracula is approached by a young Black man named Blade, who offers to bargain with Dracula: his services as an assassin and strategist in return for not being made a vampire. This bargain turns out to be a trap meant to destroy Dracula, but which Blade and his friends only narrowly manage to escape alive. This is to be only the first of Dracula's many encounters with Blade.

1972

Upon his return from the Far East, Dracula finds someone waiting for him at Castle Dracula. It is the father of the young Scotsman that Dracula had murdered in the Orient four years previously. Harker had trained the father in the arts of vampire warfare, and he succeeds in once more driving a stake through the vampire's heart, at the cost of his own life. Dracula tumbles into his own Pit of Death, which he had not used since 1809, and he lays there until a few years later when his descendant Frank Drake together with Clifton Graves visit Castle Dracula and revive him.

It is at this point in Dracula's history that Marvel Comics' continuous treatment of the exploits of Count Vlad Dracula begin in *Tomb of Dracula #1*. If you want to find out more concerning the Impaler of Transylvania, the narrative within those pages is far more complete — and dramatic — than could be told here. However, if you want to see this chronology completed up to the present day, let us know, and we'll see what can be done!

THAT DRACULA MAY LIVE AGAIN!

1459 --32 YEARS BEFORE COLUMBUS MASTERED THREE SHIPS ACROSS THE ATLANTIC IN **SEARCH** OF A NEW TRADE-ROUTE TO INDIA... 3 YEARS **AFTER** GUTENBERG SET TO TYPE THE BIBLE, MAKING IT THE **FIRST** PRINTED BOOK IN MODERN HISTORY..

...AND THREE YEARS **INTO** THE SECOND REIGN OF **DRACULA**-- PRINCE OF **TRANSYLVANIA!!**

ON, MY WARRIORS --ONWARDS! FOR TRANSYLVANIA --FOR **DRACULA** !!!

TWICE BEFORE HAD THE **EASTERN HORDES** BROKEN THROUGH--TWICE BEFORE THERE WAS THE CLASH OF **STEEL** UPON **STEEL**, **BONE** UPON **BONE**, AS SOLDIERS OF THE **TURKISH EMPIRE** FOUGHT TO POSSESS **TRANSYLVANIA** AND ALL LANDS WESTWARD... AND **TWICE** BEFORE HAD THE WARRIORS OF DRACULA RESISTED THEM-- FOUGHT THEM BACK--AND **KEPT** THE LAND AS THEIR OWN!

STORY: **MARV WOLFMAN** | ART: **NEAL ADAMS** | **ARCHIE GOODWIN**: SPIRITUAL ADVISOR

THREE DAYS THEY'VE BATTLED -- DRACULA'S WARRIORS, TURKISH SOLDIERS -- THREE DAYS, AND THEIR FLESH ACHES WITH BLOODIED SCARS AND STILL-GUSHING WOUNDS...
THREE DAYS, AND THE TIDE OF THIS ENDLESS BATTLE SEEMS TO TURN, DESPITE THE STILL-THROBBING ZEAL OF THE TRANSYLVANIAN PRINCES MEN...
THEY FIGHT ON, YET DEEP IN THEIR WARRIOR-SOULS IS THE KNOWLEDGE THE BATTLE IS DONE... THEIR SIDE HAS FALLEN... THEIR LAND IS NO LONGER THEIRS...
BUT THE MEN PANIC NOT, FOR ABOVE ALL THE SEARING PAIN -- THEY CAN STILL HEAR THEIR PRINCE'S VOICE -- THE VOICE OF DRACULA -- THE DEVIL!
AND THE VOICE IS COLD -- HARSH -- AS THE WORDS ARE SPIT OUT --
FIGHT ON, YOU DAMNED DOGS -- FIGHT ON, OR YOU'LL FACE DRACULA HIMSELF!
FIGHT ON! FIGHT ON!
NAY, DEVIL, -- YOU'LL FIGHT NO LONGER!
WHAT? YOU MOVE TOO QUICKLY!
IT SHALL TAKE MORE THAN A TURKISH PIG TO LAY DOWN THE PRINCE OF TRANSYLVANIA, FOOL--
--OR DID YOU REALLY BELIEVE I WOULD LET YOU DEFEAT ME WITH SUCH EASE?

NO, DOG, DRACULA DOES NOT FALL SO EASILY--
--OR DIE BENEATH SOME NAMELESS SCUM'S SWORD!
AGHHHH!!
WHAT--? NO--DRACULA CAN NOT FALL!
BUT HE DOES, DEVIL--HE DOES!
THE BATTLE CONTINUES, YET ITS OUTCOME IS ALREADY CAST--FOR WITH THEIR SUZERAIN DOWNED, DRACULA'S MEN ARE LOST...
...AND THE BATTLE COMES TO A SLOW, BLOODIED HALT...
ACH! WE HAVE WON LORD TORAC --BUT AT WHAT A PRICE! OUR MEN ARE DEAD--THE LAND WE HAVE GAINED RUNS DEEP IN SCARLET!
WAS IT WORTH IT, MY LORD? WAS ALL THIS WORTH IT?
IT WAS AND IS, BARON KORDA--TRANSYLVANIA LIES BETWEEN TURKEY AND ALL WE WISH TO CONQUER...
...FOR OUR EMPIRE TO FLOURISH, TRANSYLVANIA, NO MATTER HOW DISGUSTING IT BE, HAD TO BE OURS--
--WHATEVER THE COST!
BUT WAIT--OVER THERE!
HOLD, MAN--YOU'LL NOT NEED TO BLOODY YOUR MACE ON THAT MAN.
BUT, LORD TURAC--I SAW HIM MOVE.
HE'S ALIVE--I'D STAKE MY HONOR--!
AND IT IS GOOD HE IS, FOOL--DID YOU NOT RECOGNIZE HIM?
THIS MAN YOU WOULD SO SENSELESSLY SMASH--
--IS DRACULA, PRINCE OF THIS OFFENSIVE LITTLE NATION.
DRACULA--THE ONE THEY CALL THE DEVIL--THE IMPALER!
DRACULA--WHO IS FEARED EVEN BY OUR OWN FEARSOME MONARCH!

"AYE, DRACULA,-- LORD AND MASTER OF THIS FOUL-SMELLING LAND. THERE ARE TALES, SOLDIER, THAT AFTER OUR LAST CRUSADE, HE SEARCHED HIS CITIES FOR ANY WHO SYMPATHIZED WITH OUR CAUSE--AND THEN HE BUTCHERED THEM, AND IMPALED THEIR HEADS UPON BLOODSTANED LANCES...
"LANCES WHICH HIS TERRIFIED SOLDIERS HAD TO CARRY THROUGH THE STREETS AND MARKETPLACES --TO SHOW WHAT HAPPENS TO ALL WHO DARE OPPOSE HIS RULE.
"THEY SAY WHEN WE SENT OUR AMBASSADORS TO SPEAK TO HIM, HE DEMANDED THEY REMOVE THEIR FEZZES. WHEN THEY DIDN'T, HE HAD NAILS DRIVEN INTO THEIR HEADS-- THROUGH THEIR FEZZES SO THEY COULD NEVER REMOVE THEM AGAIN.
"DO NOT CRINGE, SOLDIER, --THERE IS MORE-- -MUCH MORE THAT MAKE EVEN THESE DEEDS PALE BY COMPARRISON! ...
...THERE ARE STORIES OF MOTHERS AND CHILDREN MURDERED--AND OF HUSBANDS WHO HAD TO BURY THEIR FAMILIES, ONLY TO BE KILLED THEMSELVES!
AYE, SOLDIER, HE DID NOT EARN THE NAME THE DEVIL FOR NAUGHT BUT A HISTORY OF BLOODTHIRSTY DEEDS!..
"LEGEND SAYS THAT ONCE GYPSIES PLEADED FOR THE LIFE OF A COMRADE --SO HE HAD THEM ALL IMPALED, WHILE HE DUTIFULLY PLAYED WITH HIS YOUNG CHILD AND HIS BEAUTIFUL WIFE.
PERHAPS THESE ARE MERE TALES--UNTRUTHS-- BUT STILL THE MAN REEKS OF AN EVIL STINK...

THEN WHY SAVE HIM, MY LORD? IT WOULD SEEM HE DESERVES DEATH MANY TIMES OVER.
BECAUSE, SOLDIER, THE MAN IS SO FEARED WITH HIM IN OUR HANDS, WE COULD CONTROL HIS WRETCHED NATION WITH NO MORE NEEDLESS DEATHS AMONGST OUR MEN.
AYE, WE REQUIRE HE BE ALIVE--AND BE CONTROLLED BY US!
LORD TURAC, IF I MAY --I'VE HEARD OF A GYPSY WOMAN WHO HAS WROUGHT MANY CURES WHEN HOPE WAS LOST..
PERHAPS SHE CAN AID US!
TALK NO MORE, SOLDIER--LEAD US TO THIS WOMAN.
THE RIDE IS LONG, HARD, AND IT IS INTO THE NEXT NIGHT BEFORE THE SOLDIERS REACH THEIR DESTINATION...
THERE, LORD TURAC--THE GYPSY CAMP--AND THE WOMAN'S WAGON.
IF THIS WITCH IS ALL YOU SAY SHE IS, GORDO, THERE SHALL BE A REWARD FOR YOU WHEN WE RETURN TO ANKARA.
COME.
GET AWAY-- LEAVE ME BE.
I HAVE NO TIME --FOR SOLDIERS.
HOLD, WOMAN! WE HAVE HEARD OF YOUR HEALING POWERS--
--AND WE CAN PAY MUCH FOR YOU TO WORK THEM ON OUR--FALLEN COMRADE.
BAH! YOU LIE THROUGH YOUR ROTTEN TEETH, MAN--BUT IF YOUR MONEY FOLDS WELL--
--PERHAPS LIANDA CAN HELP.
BRING THE MAN INTO MY WAGON.
THIS WILL TAKE THE NIGHT, MAN--NOW LEAVE LIANDA ALONE--COME TOMORROW THIS TIME.

THEY MUST THINK ME A FOOL NOT TO HAVE RECOGNIZED THE MAN HIS SUBJECTS CALL THE DEVIL!
SO, YOUR "FRIENDS" WILL PAY MUCH TO KEEP YOU ALIVE, WILL THEY--DRACULA?
YOU HAVE GIVEN MY PEOPLE MUCH GRIEF, IMPALER --AND NOW I SHALL RETURN THE FAVOR--
--YES, I'LL RETURN LIFE TO YOUR BONES. BUT NOT WITH MY HERBS, FIEND--
--NO, WITH A FAR MORE POTENT MEDICINE--ONE WHICH SHALL LAST FOREVER...
...THE BITE...
...OF THE VAMPIRE!!!
HOW IS MY "FRIEND", WOMAN?
WHAT? I TOLD YOU TO RETURN TOMORROW!
HOW DARE YOU DISOBEY ME, MAN?
GET OUT! GET OUT!
NO, WOMAN--I WISH TO KNOW HIS CONDITION--NOW!
VERY WELL, SOLDIER --HE IS WEAK-- WITH LITTLE BLOOD!
BUT TOMORROW HE SHALL LIVE AGAIN.
WHICH MEANS, SOLDIER, YOU MAY PAY ME, NOW.
PAY YOU, WITCH-- WITHOUT MY SEEING THE RESULTS?
YOU MUST TAKE ME FOR A MINDLESS JACKASS, WOMAN?

BUT YOU PROMISED--
VAARGGHHHH
I PROMISED PAYMENT, WOMAN--
--AND I SHALL PAY YOU --WITH DEATH!
SO, YOU WOULD CHEAT LIANDA-- I THOUGHT AS MUCH OF YOU.
BUT I STILL THIRST, MAN--
AND YOU SHALL SUFFER FOR THAT THIRST.
NO! A VAMPIRE! A VAMPIRE!!
CORRECT, MAN--A VAMPIRE WHO SHALL KI-- ARGHHHHHHH!
NAY, WOMAN, YOU'LL DO NOTHING!
FOR A VAMPIRE DIES AS ANY MAN DIES--WHEN A WOODEN SPEAR IS THRUST THROUGH THE HEART.
--AND YOU, WITCH, ARE NO EXCEPTION.
NOW, AWAY FROM ME, TRASH--!
I HAVE NO NEED FOR YOU NOW--
AYE, RATHER IT IS DRACULA WHO IS NEEDED--
--AND A COUNTRY THAT NEEDS A MASTER...
--EVEN IF THAT MASTER MUST ANSWER TO ANOTHER!
HA! HA! HA! HA! HA!
THE NIGHT'S JOURNEY BACK TO TRANSYLVANIA PASSES QUICKLY, BUT IT IS ANOTHER FULL DAY BEFORE THE SCARLET HAZE WHICH HANGS OVER DRACULA IS RAISED...
WHERE--AM I--? WHERE...?
MY LOVE-- LOOK AT ME-- LOOK!

MARIA-- IS THAT YOU--?
SPEAK WITH ME, MARIA --SPEAK!
DARLING-- PLEASE COME BACK TO ME-- PLEASE...!
ENOUGH, WENCH! THAT WILL BE ALL!
I SAID, THAT IS ENOUGH!
NO, PLEASE --HE NEEDS ME... LET ME GO TO HIM.
MARIA --DON'T STRUGGLE. THE MAN IS MAD.
LET ME DEAL WITH THIS DAMNED TURK!
WHAT?
YOU? DON'T MAKE ME LAUGH, IMPALER. YOU CAN DO NOTHING.
YOU ARE STILL TOO WEAK--BESIDES WHICH --YOU ARE BOUND!
WHILE I AM FREE TO DO ANYTHING I PLEASE-- TO YOU OR TO YOUR MOST BEAUTIFUL WIFE--
--UNLESS YOU COOPERATE WITH ME, THAT IS.
WHAT DO YOU WANT, TURK?
OUR BELOVED MONARCH WANTS CONTROL OF THIS DISGUSTING SWAMP YOU CALL A COUNTRY. YOU HAVE THE CONTROL, BUT WE HAVE YOU.
WE CAN TAKE THIS LAND --BUT THERE WILL BE BLOODSHED! OR, YOU CAN STAY AND RULE FOR US-- IN THE NAME OF THE TURKISH EMPIRE!
NEVER, PIG-- NEVER!
DON'T REFUSE SO HASTILY, DRACULA-
-OR YOUR HANDSOME SON MAY SUFFER FOR YOUR ACTIONS!
VLAD!
PUT HIM DOWN, BUTCHER-- OR YOU'LL ANSWER TO DRACULA!

VERY WELL, THEN, IMPALER-- YOUR ANSWER HAS SEALED YOUR WIFE'S DOOM.
GORDO-- SLAY THE WOMAN-- AND THEN THE INFANT.
YOU WERE A FOOL, DRACULA-- AND THE EMPIRE DOES NOT TOLERATE FOOLS.
TURAC-- WAIT!
YOU WISH ME TO HUMBLE MYSELF! VERY WELL, THEN.
I'LL DO AS YOU SAY, BUT LET MY WIFE AND CHILD BE!
AH, SO THE INFAMOUS DEVIL NOW KNOWS HOW TO BEG FOR MERCY, EH?
AS I SUSPECTED-- DRACULA IS NOTHING BUT A COWARD BENEATH THE FLESH.
HERE, WOMAN, -- YOUR CHILD.
YOU TWO MAY BE TOGETHER FOR THE NEXT FEW MOMENTS, AT LEAST-- I HAVE BUSINESS ELSEWHERE.
BUT WHEN I RETURN, DEVIL, WE SHALL DISCUSS HOW MY MONARCH WISHES THIS PROVINCE GOVERNED.
I AM SORRY, MARIA-- FOR EVERYTHING. I WISH I HAD BEEN SLAIN ON THE BATTLEFIELD THAN HAVE YOU SUBJECTED TO THESE TURKISH PIGS.
MY LOVE, --IT IS NOT FOR YOU TO GIVE YOUR SORROW-- BUT FOR ME...
OH DARLING --WHEN THOSE MEN FIRST CAME HERE, THEY THREATENED TO KILL VLAD --AND YOU-- UNLESS I WENT WITH THEM...
...OH, GOD... THEY BROUGHT ME TO YOUR DUNGEON, AND BEFORE YOUR UNCONSCIOUS BODY, THEY TOOK ME-- ALL OF THEM.
IT WAS HORRIBLE... AND MORE-- I FELT NOT ONLY DISGUST BUT THE SHAME YOU WOULD FEEL WHEN THEY TAUNTED THE FACT BEFORE YOU.
FORGIVE ME, MY LOVE... PLEASE FORGIVE ME.

FOOLISH WENCH-- WE WOULD HAVE SAID NOTHING TO YOUR HUSBAND-- HE MIGHT NEVER HAVE KNOWN--!
BUT NOW THAT HE DOES-- YOU WILL COME WITH ME TONIGHT.
NO!
LEAVE HER ALONE, DAMNED TURK, LEAVE HER--
OR I'LL--
YOU'LL DO NOTHING, IMPALER, BUT SQUIRM IN ANGUISH-- DO YOU UNDERSTAND?
TO MY CHAMBERS, WOMAN.
--NO, --PLEASE --PLEASE DON'T--
WHAT? YOU SCRATCH, YOU FILTHY--
YOU'LL PAY FOR THIS INSULT-- SO HELP ME YOU'LL PAY!
NO WENCH, NO MATTER HOW COMELY SHE MAY BE, MAY REFUSE TURAC-- DO YOU UNDERSTA--
WHAT? SHE FELL INTO THE COLUMN!
MY DARLING....
UUHHHHHHH!
MARIA! NO!
YOU MUSTN'T DIE... YOU MUSTN'T!
NOOOOOOOOOOOOOOOOOO

SNAP
SNAP
NO!-- SHE FELL-- I HAD NOTHING TO DO--
YOU KILLED HER, YOU STINKING SCUM! YOU KILLED HER!
GUARD! STOP HIM-- SLAY HIM..! QUICKLY
YOUR GUARDS WILL NOT STOP ME, DAMNED ONE!
NO-- ALL THEY GIVE ARE MORE TARGETS TO VENT MY RAGE-- TO LET MY HATE FOR YOU GROW--
--STRONGER ...MORE POWERFUL.
--UNTIL I CAN GET TO YOU--
AND THEN NOTHING --NOTHING SHALL STOP ME FROM KILLING YOU--
GET BACK-- YOU'RE MAD --MAD!!

MAD? MORE THAN MAD, DAMNED ONE--
I LIVE TO KILL--TO STRIKE YOU TO THE GROUND--TO TAKE YOUR BLOOD!
WHAT ARE YOU SAYING? WHAT DO YOU MEAN?
YOU DESTROYED YOURSELF, TURK--WHEN YOU FIRST BROUGHT ME TO THAT WITCHES' HOUSE...
FOR I HAVE HER CURSE NOW.--I AM--
--A VAMPIRE!
AND I THIRST FOR MY FIRST KILL.
NO!
--IN THE NAME OF GOD--
AAH
ARGGHHHHHHHHHH
LORD TURAC--THERE WAS A SCREAM--?
YOUR GOD IS NO LONGER MINE, TURK--
--BUT WAIT--
YOUR SOLDIERS, THEY THINK THEY COME TO RESCUE YOU--
BUT THEY ARE FOOLS--FOOLS!
LORD TURAC--LORD TURAC!!
I HAVE NO TIME FOR YOU SCUM--
--SO STARE--QUICKLY--DEEPLY INTO MY EYES...
...STARE--AND PREPARE FOR DEATH!!

UNMOVING THEY STAND, UNTIL THE FINAL MOMENT WHEN TWIN-FANGS DEEP INTO THEIR FLESH--
--THEN, AND ONLY THEN, DO THESE SOLDIERS MOVE-- AND WITH A SILENT, UNSPOKEN GASP, THEY DIE!
FULLY SATIATED, DRACULA STARES INTO THE STAR-FLECKED SKIES TOWARD A SILVERED MOON. STARES--
--AND CHANGES ... ARMS BECOME WINGS ... LEGS ... BECOME TALONED CLAWS...
...AND MAN BECOMES THE HELL BORN VISAGE OF DEATH!
IT RISES UPON LEATHERY WINGS INTO THE CRAWLING BLACKNESS, AND CLUTCHED BETWEEN ITS RAZORED TALONS ARE TWO SMALL FORMS...
...ONE THE CRYING CAST OF A YOUNG, UNTOUCHED CHILD...
... AND THE OTHER, THE LIFELESS FORM OF A WOMAN ONCE DEARLY LOVED...
OUT INTO THE WILDERNESS THE BAT FLIES-- TILL IT COMES TO THE CRAWLING GYPSY CARAVANS WHERE THE CHILD IS DEPOSITED...
...AND ONCE SURE OF ITS SAFETY, THE BAT HURTLES SKYWARD ONCE MORE...
...ONLY TO BECOME A MAN ON A LONELY WINDSWEPT HILL SIDE...
...WHERE A GRAVE IS DUG, AND AN OATH IS PLEDGED...
I SWEAR UPON YOUR GRAVE, DARLING MARIA --THAT NONE WHO WALK THIS WORLD SHALL AGAIN BE SAFE!
THIS WORLD TOOK YOU FROM ME--AND NOW ALL THE WORLD SHALL PAY!
SO SWEARS--
DRACULA
FINIS

LORD OF DEATH... LORD OF HELL!
THE GRAVE TURNED GREY IN THE COLDNESS OF THE NIGHT... GREY FROM THE HELLBORN CURSES WHICH ECHOED PAST ITS EARTHEN EARS...GREY FROM THE ANGRY, TREMBLING LIPS OF THE MAN MEN CALLED THE DEVIL...THE IMPALER...
...THE MAN WE CALL--
--DRACULA!
THEY TOOK YOU FROM ME, THOSE MORTALS WHO DARED CALL ME EVIL--THEY SUCKED AWAY THE LIFE FROM YOUR VERY MARROW.
BUT THEY'LL PAY, MARIA... OH, SHALL THEY PAY.
FOR, ON THIS NIGHT UPON YOUR GRAVE I VOW-- MANKIND SHALL FEEL MY WRATH...
MARIA, DARLING MARIA-- AS WE HAVE BEEN CURSED...AS WE HAVE SUFFERED, SO SHALL OTHERS SUFFER!
...SO SWEARS DRACULA!
STORY: MARV WOLFMAN
ART: JOHN BUSCEMA & SYD SHORES

SO WORRY NOT ABOUT THAT, MY LOVE. THEY SHALL SUFFER--TENFOLD FOR EVERY MOMENT YOU AGONIZED.
"FIRST THEY ASSAULTED YOU, THOSE TURKISH SWINE WHO DARED BELIEVE THEY COULD DEFEAT MY TRANSYLVANIA--
"--AND, WHEN YOU REFUSED THEIR LUSTFUL EYES--THEY MURDERED YOU!
"BUT, TO BE SURE, I SLEW THEM IN TURN, THEN BROUGHT OUR CHILD, VLAD, TO THE WAGONS OF SOME ROVING GYPSIES...
...FOR, HIS PLACE COULD NO LONGER BE WITH ME--WITH A FATHER NOW AS ONE WITH THE UNDEAD.
YOU NEVER KNEW, MARIA--WHAT I HAD BECOME--WHAT HAD CHANGED ME INTO THAT THING WHICH NOW I AM.*
AND, FOR YOUR SANITY, IT IS WELL YOU DID NOT LEARN.
*ALL RECOUNTED LAST ISSUE. IF YOU MISSED IT, SEE OUR BACK ISSUE COUPON ELSEWHERE. -- RT.
BUT NOW--ALL HUMANITY SHALL PAY FOR WHAT THEY DID TO YOU--
HOLD! BATS--ARCING TOWARDS ME--?
NO, NOT BATS--
--MEN--VAMPIRES LIKE MYSELF!
BUT WHAT DO THEY WANT OF--DRACULA?

WRONG, DEVIL--FOR SOON YOU'LL LEARN TO SCRAPE THE FLOOR WITH DELIGHT...

...ONCE YOU'VE BEEN HUMBLED BY NIMROD-- LORD OF THE UNDEAD!

AGGHHH!

LIKE SILENT SHADOWS, THE RAVEN-WINGED FORMS SLITHER UP INTO THE EBONY SKIES, WHILE, ON THE SWAMPY PLAINS BENEATH, FARMERS AND THEIR HURDLED FLOCKS BEND THEIR HEADS LOW--NOT DARING TO GAZE TO THE STARLESS SKIES--

--FOR THEY KNOW IF THEY DID, THEY WOULD ALSO SEE THEIR DEATHS!

HALF THE NIGHT IS SPENT IN TRAVEL AS THE BATS CONTINUE, NEVER RESTING, NEVER PAUSING. AND THEN, HOURS LATER...

UHHHHHH... WHERE--?

YOU ARE IN THE SHADOW OF LORD NIMROD, DRACULA. STAND AND SEE YOUR MASTER!

WHAT?

NO REASON TO ACT SO ASTONISHED, NEW ONE. I AM NOW YOUR MASTER, NIMROD THE FIRST.
WHEN LIFE FLOWED THROUGH YOUR VEINS, YOU POSSESSED YOUR OWN WILL-- YOUR OWN DESTINY.
BUT NOW THE FLUIDS OF DESTINY HAVE BEEN DRAINED-- NOW YOU MUST BOW TO ANOTHER--
--TO NIMROD, KING OF VAMPIRES!
BOW TO NIMROD, NEW ONE--PLEDGE YOUR BLOOD TO ME.
I PLEDGE MYSELF TO YOUR DEATH, NIMROD! NOTHING LESS SHALL PLEASE ME.
I AM DRACULA-- NOT SOME ROTTING CORPSE NOW BECOME AN UNDEAD SLAVE!
VERY WELL THEN, IMPALER-- THOUGH IT HAS BEEN YEARS SINCE I'VE FOUND NEED TO BATTLE, I SHALL MAKE AN EXAMPLE OF YOU.
TOMORROW AT THIS TIME, THERE SHALL BE THE TOURNAMENT OF STAKES.
A BATTLE WHICH SHALL SURELY LEAD-- TO YOUR DEATH!

DRACULA TURNS THEN, AND IS LED TO A CHAMBER SET FOR HIM...
PLEASE DO NOT BROOD, HANDSOME ONE.
...A CHAMBER THAT IS DARK, CRUEL, AND REMINDS HIM MORE OF A DUNGEON THAN A HOME.
YOU? YOU WERE THE WENCH WITH NIMROD.
LALA IS HIS WOMAN, HANDSOME ONE.
BUT HE MERELY POSSESSES MY BODY--NOT MY SOUL.
HE IS CRUEL TO LALA. HE BEATS ME... HE HUMILIATES ME.
BUT IN YOU I SENSE SOMETHING GENTLE. YOU LIKE LALA?
I--
THERE IS A WARMTH FLUSHING THROUGH DRACULA NOW-- A BURNING DESIRE THAT HE CAN NOT PLACE...
...UNTIL, THAT IS, HE THINKS OF A MERE FEW HOURS BEFORE...AND OF A WOMAN HE LOVED BUT DARED NOT MOURN...
...FOR, THE MAN THEY CALLED THE DEVIL WAS A HARD MAN, SOMETIMES A CRUEL MAN... AND TO SHED EVEN THE SMALLEST OF TEARS IS A WEAKNESS HE COULD NOT AFFORD.
NO! BACK, WOMAN-- I MUST NOT BE DISTURBED-- MY THOUGHTS MUST NOT BE INTERRUPTED.
EVEN FOR ONE SUCH AS LALA, LORD DRACULA? EVEN FOR ONE WHO OFFERS YOU HER LOVE?

LALA HAS SO MUCH TO OFFER YOU... SO MUCH JOY--
PLEASE LET LALA TAKE THE SORROW FROM YOUR BROW.
LALA OFFERS YOU HAPPINESS...
LALA OFFERS YOU THE WORLD.
YOU DO WANT LALA, DO YOU NOT, HANDSOME ONE?
FOR A MOMENT, DRACULA FEELS THERE SHOULD BE PASSION BREWING WITHIN HIS UNDEAD FLESH...
...BUT, SADLY, NOTHING STIRS...
...NOTHING BUT THE PERSISTENT COOING FROM A MOST BEAUTIFUL...
...WOMAN--?
WHAT?
NO--GET BACK, DAMNED WENCH-- YOU'VE NOTHING TO GIVE ME--
YOUR FLESH IS AS COLD AS MINE--AS LIFELESS AS MINE--
YOUR PASSIONS ARE FEIGNED, FALSE ONE.
GET OUT-- GET OUT!

I TRIED TO SAVE YOU FROM NIMROD'S WRATH, DRACULA--BUT NOW YOU'VE ONLY INCURRED MINE!
NIMROD SHALL SLAY YOU AGAIN, MY 'LORD' -- BUT THIS TIME YOU SHALL NEVER AWAKEN!
I SAID GET OUT-WOMAN--BEFORE IT IS YOU WHO MEETS YOUR FINAL MAKER.
THE WITCH CALLED LALA LEAVES, BUT THE AFTERGLOW OF HER HATEFUL EYES LINGERS...
...SENDING DRACULA TO SEEK THE COOL FRESHNESS OF THE NIGHT...
...AS THE DREADFUL VAMPIRE BAT.
FOR MINUTES HE SOARS FREELY THROUGH THE SKIES... BUT SOON FINDS HIMSELF OVER A GYPSY CAMP...
...WHERE HE WATCHES A YOUNG FAMILIAR CHILD LAUGHING TENDERLY AT HIS NEW MOTHER'S SIDE.
HIS CHILD IS SAFE...HE HAS ALREADY IN THESE PAST HOURS FORGOTTEN THE HORROR OF THE NIGHT...
...AND FOR THAT, DRACULA IS THANKFUL.
THUS, FOR THE MOMENT, HIS INWARD DESIRES ARE SATISFIED...
NOW ONLY OTHER PASSIONS REMAIN--
--A DRY RASPING THIRST...
...A BLOODLUST.
HIS ATTACK IS QUICK, ALMOST CAT-LIKE, AND BEFORE THE STARTLED LOVERS CAN REACT, THE MALE IS DEAD, FRESH BLOOD ALREADY DRIPPING FROM HIS NECK...

BUT STILL THERE IS HUNGER BUILDING WITHIN DRACULA'S THROAT... STILL THERE IS THE LUST FOR HIS LIFE-ELIXIR...
...BLOOD... BLOOD WHICH ONLY THE FEMALE CAN GIVE...!
THE GIRL STRUGGLES VAINLY AGAINST THE STEEL-LIKE ARMS OF DRACULA, BUT IN THE END, SHE KNOWS ALL IS LOST...
SHE CRUMBLES BENEATH RAZOR-SHARP FANGS... AND SHE DIES WITH AN ALMOST SATISFIED SMILE TATTOOED ACROSS HER LIPS.
FOR, AS SHE DIES, SHE ALREADY KNOWS--SOON SHE SHALL RISE AGAIN.
BUT FOR THE NONCE, IT IS A SATIATED DRACULA WHO RISES TOWARDS THE HEAVENS, DISCARDS HIS HUMAN SHAPE...
...AND TAKES TO THE MIDNIGHT SKIES. DAWN IS COMING... AND DAWN MEANS IT IS TIME FOR SLEEP.
DAYLIGHT SWIMS ACROSS THE BALKAN STATES WITH CARESSING WAVES OF WARMTH...
...AND ALL THE WHILE DRACULA SLEEPS, WAITING FOR THE BITTERNESS OF NIGHT... A NIGHT WHICH SHALL BEGIN WITH TWO LIVES, BUT SHALL END ONLY WITH ONE...
...A NIGHT WHICH SWIFTLY, SURELY COMES.
IT IS TIME FOR YOU TO ACKNOWLEDGE YOUR MASTER, DRACULA BOW TO ME AND YOUR LIFE WILL BE SPARED.
REBUKE ME, AND YOUR FLUIDS SHALL SOAK INTO THE THIRSTING EARTH.
NEVER, DEMON DRACULA'S LIFE AND SOUL ARE HIS OWN, AND NO AGED SCUM SHALL SAY OTHERWISE.
LET THE DUEL BEGIN!

HAH! YOUR BODY STILL MOVES LIKE A HUMAN'S--SLOWLY--PONDEROUSLY...

BUT STILL FAST ENOUGH TO REND YOU THROUGH!

IT IS NOT FOR NOTHING THAT DRACULA IS CALLED--THE IMPALER!

WAS CALLED, FOOL. YOUR HUMAN LIFE MEANS NOTHING HERE.

TO BE REBORN AS A VAMPIRE MEANS A NEW BEGINNING... NEW TRAINING... TRAINING YOU'VE YET TO RECEIVE.

UNNHH!

NOW DO YOU UNDERSTAND, FOOL--?

NOW DO YOU SEE WHY NIMROD IS CALLED "LORD"?

EVEN NOW, DRACULA, DO YOUR LIFE FLUIDS FLOW.
EVEN NOW YOU BECOME WEAKER... WEAKER...!

NO!! NEVER SHALL DRACULA LET HIMSELF DIE AGAIN... NEVER!
BUT-- WHAT--?
I'VE BECOME AS THE VAPORS, IMPALER-- A MIST YOUR PITIABLE STAKE CAN NOT TOUCH.

YOU SEE, THERE STILL IS MUCH YOU NEEDED TO LEARN BEFORE YOU COULD EVEN DREAM OF DETHRONING NIMROD.

BUT, ALAS--YOU'LL NOT HAVE THE TIME TO LEARN ALL YOU NEEDED.
NOW DIE, DEVIL!
NO-- YOU MOVED! I THOUGHT YOU TOO WEAK.

YOU THINK TOO MUCH, NIMROD-- WHEN ONLY ACTION SHOULD BE YOUR STAY.

AND THAT, "LORD FOOL," IS WHY DRACULA SHALL TEAR YOUR MISERABLE LIFE FROM YOU-- NOW!
NIMROD IS WEAK-- I CAN SENSE THE SIGNS. MAYBE NOW LALA CAN GAIN HER REVENGE.

YOU SPURNED ME... YOU HUMILIATED ME, AND NOW YOU SEEK TO STEAL OUR MASTER'S LIFE--
--BUT I WON'T ALLOW IT-- I CAN'T!
YOU SPEAK A GOOD BATTLE, IMPALER, BUT IT'S FROM YOUR FACE THAT THE BLOOD FLOWS, NOT MINE.
NIMROD, YOU ARE MORE A FOOL THAN I THOUGHT. I SAW YOUR WOMAN SNEAK BEHIND ME--
I KNEW YOUR WORDS WERE MEANT MERELY TO RILE ME-- TO DISTRACT ME WHILE THIS TREACHEROUS WITCH SHOVED THE STAKE THROUGH MY BACK.
NOOO!
I THOUGHT YOU POSSESSED HONOR, BUT I SEE THERE IS NAUGHT BUT EVIL REEKING FROM YOUR FLESH.
SO NOW THERE IS NO REASON TO HOLD BACK. HERE'S YOUR WOMAN, NIMROD-- IMPALE HER ON YOUR OWN STAKE.
NO, NIMROD-- DON'T!!!
LALA-- IT IS TOO LATE-- I CAN'T MOVE--!
ARGHHH

MY STAKE MAY HAVE TAKEN HER LIFE, IMPALER-- BUT YOU ARE HER DESTROYER!
NOW IT IS ONLY 'TWEEN THE TWO OF US...

...WHILE ONLY ONE SHALL SURVIVE.
AND I... I HAVE THE ONLY STAKE--THE ONE WHICH SHALL MAKE ME THE VICTOR..

OH, I'LL SAVOR THIS MOMENT, DRACULA--AND AS YOU SCREAM FOR MERCY.
WHAT?
YOU'LL DO NOTHING, NIMROD--

NOTHING BUT DIE UPON MY STAKE --THE ONE YOU LODGED SO TIGHTLY INTO THAT ROCK.
FAREWELL, NIMROD-- FAREWELL, ONCE-LORD!

DRACULA DIPS DEEP INTO NIMROD'S ASHES, AND, IN A SINGLE FURY OF MOTION, SCATTERS THEM INTO THE COLD NIGHT WINDS.
THEN, AS THE OTHERS OF NIMROD'S TRIBE WATCH ON IN CONFUSED HORROR, DRACULA LIFTS THE STAKE AND SHOUTS AN OATH THAT ROCKS THE COSMOS FOR ALL TIME TO COME:

LET ALL THE WORLD TREMBLE BY THESE WORDS... LET ALL THE WORLD FALL AND QUAKE--
--FOR ON THIS NIGHT-- THERE IS A NEW LORD OF THE UNDEAD--
DRACULA! DRACULA!! DRACULA!!
THUS IT BEGAN-- AND THUS SHALL IT EVER BE!
FINIS

FEUDAL SOCIETY IS VERY MUCH ALIVE IN TRANSYLVANIA OF 1459, FLOURISHING AS A CULTURE OF LORD AND SLAVE, KING AND VASSAL... IN WHICH A NOBLE MUST PROVE HIMSELF WORTHY OF RULE, WHETHER HE BE PRINCE OF THE LIVING...

...OR LORD OF THE UNDEAD!

LOOK HOMEWARD, VAMPIRE!

HE SITS IN THERE MY SILENT SLAVES... THE MAN WHO HAS DARED USURP MY CASTLE AND MY HOLDINGS...

...THE MAN WHO WILL DIE THIS NIGHT AT THE HANDS OF HE WHO WAS CALLED THE IMPALER...

...BUT NOW IS KNOWN ONLY AS DRACULA, PRINCE OF DARKNESS!

GERRY CONWAY Script

Vicente ALCÁZAR Art

MEANWHILE, IN THE DARK AND MUSKY TAVERN, THE MAN IN QUESTION IS UNAWARE OF THE MENACE APPROACHING HIM, AND PERHAPS UNCARING AS WELL ...
FREEMEN, A TOAST IF YOU WILL, TO THE FORMER LORD OF THIS DOMAIN --DRACULA, THE MONGREL!
WATCH YOUR TONGUE, MAN... THERE'S SOME WHO SAY THE MASTER ISN'T DEAD, AS YOU TURKS WOULD HAVE US BELIEVE!
SOME THERE ARE WHO SAY HE LIVES ON...
...UNDER THE CURSE OF THE UNDEAD... THE VAMPIRE.
MEN ALSO PRAY TO THE MOON, FOOL. 'TIS ALL SUPERSTITION, AND ANTON LEVKA FOR ONE WILL HEAR NO MORE OF IT!
NOW THEN... THE TOAST. TO DRACULA...
...MAY HIS SOUL BURN HAPPILY IN HELL--EH?
YOU ARE THE ONE CALLED COUNT LEVKA, ARE YOU NOT?
I BELIEVE I HAVE BUSINESS WITH YOU... BUSINESS OF A MOST PERSONAL NATURE.
IS THAT SO? WELL THEN, MAN-- SPEAK UP. THE LORDS OF TURKEY HAVE MADE ME YOUR LEIGE--
IF YOU CANNOT SPEAK TO ME--WHO CAN YOU SPEAK TO?
IT SEEMS YOU DO NOT RECOGNIZE ME, ANTON LEVKA... PERHAPS I SHOULD INTRODUCE MYSELF.
I AM DRACULA...
...AND THESE ARE MY SLAVES.
SAINTED MOTHER IN HEAVEN!
VAMPIRI!

HE'S NOT REALLY A BRAVE MAN, THIS ANTON LEVKA; THE SON OF A NOBLEMAN, HE HAS ALWAYS RIDDEN ONTO THE BATTLEFIELD AFTER VICTORY HAS BEEN WON--
--AND HE'S NOT QUITE SURE HOW TO HANDLE THE UNPLEASANTRIES OF AN ENRAGED GHOST--
--THOUGH HE'S CERTAIN HE NEVER WANTS TO LEARN!
HOWEVER, HE NO LONGER HAS THE POWER TO MAKE DECISIONS CONCERNING HIS LIFE... THAT PRIVILEGE HAS PASSED TO OTHER, MORE RUTHLESS MEN...
IN THE NAME OF ALL THAT'S HOLY, PLEASE DON'T DO THIS THING--I BEG YOU, DON'T KILL ME--
I'LL GIVE YOU ANYTHING-- GOLD, POWER-- NOBILITY--
BUT DON'T KILL ME!
GOLD, ANTON LEVKA? WHAT USE IS GOLD TO A VAMPIRE? WHAT SHALL I PURCHASE WITH IT THAT IS NOT ALREADY MINE TO TAKE?
AND NOBILITY-- HOW MAY YOU OFFER THE LORD OF THE UNDEAD NOBILITY? YOU MOCK ME, ANTON LEVKA!
EVEN THIS TALK OF POWER... IT ILL BEFITS YOU. YOU HAVE NO POWER TO OFFER ME THAT I DO NOT ALREADY POSSESS.
NO, ANTON LEVKA...
YOU POSSESS ONLY ONE THING WHICH IS OF INTEREST OR USE TO ME... THAT LIFE-GIVING EXLIXER--
--YOUR BLOOD!
IIIIIIEEEE!!
THEN IT'S TRUE... THE IMPALER LIVES, IN A FORM MORE HIDEOUS THAN THAT WHICH HE INHABITED BEFORE!
FATHER BORDIA MUST BE TOLD AT ONCE. HE WILL KNOW WHAT TO DO!
HE WILL TELL US WHAT MUST BE DONE!

MOMENTS LATER, NEAR THE OUTSKIRTS OF THE SMALL TOWN WHICH IS DOMINATED BY THE PRESENCE OF CASTLE DRACULA...
PRAY, BE PATIENT. I'M COMING... I'M COMING.

YES? WHO IS IT WHO CALLS FOR ME AT SUCH AN UN-SAINTLY HOUR?
JOSEF--IS THAT YOU, MY SON? JOSEF YURAC?
IT IS, FATHER. MAY I COME IN? THERE IS MUCH WHICH I MUST TELL YOU... FOR THE SAKE OF OUR IMMORTAL SOULS!

THE TALE IS QUICKLY TOLD, AND WHEN THE TELLING IS FINISHED...
YOU DID WELL TO COME TO ME, JOSEF. SOMETHING MUST INDEED BE DONE... BUT MUCH THOUGHT IS REQUIRED BEFORE WE CAN DECIDE WHAT.
LEAVE ME, JOSEF. IT'S TIME FOR MY MEDITATION.
PERHAPS GOD WILL REVEAL TO ME OUR PROPER PATH.

FATHER, IS THIS A NEW CURSE...FURTHER PUNISHMENT FOR OUR SINS?
PERHAPS IT IS, MY SON. ONLY OUR HEAVENLY FATHER KNOWS. TRUST HIM, AS YOU TRUST ME... AS YOU TRUST YOURSELF.
THANK YOU, FATHER. I WILL PRAY FOR YOU.
AND I FOR YOU, JOSEF--

--THOUGH MY PRAYERS WILL FLY TO A DIFFERENT GOD THAN YOURS, MY PEASANT FRIEND--
WE SHALL SEE WHO WORSHIPS THE GREATER POWER--YOU, WITH YOUR CHRIST--

--OR I WITH SATAN--
--HE WHO IS CALLED LUCIFER--
--TO WHOM I HAVE COMMENDED MY EVERLASTING SOUL!

IF JOSEF'S STORY IS TRUE, THEN IT APPEARS I HAVE A RIVAL FOR THE BLOOD OF OUR COUNTRYMEN. IT WAS ONE MATTER WHEN DRACULA WAS MERELY A MAD TYRANT...
...BUT NOW HE SEEKS TO INVADE MY EXCLUSIVE PROVINCE...AND AS EVEN AN IGNORANT SQUIRE COULD SEE...
...THERE CAN BE NO ROOM IN THIS PITIABLE PARISH... FOR BOTH OF US.
DRACULA OR I MUST DIE...AND BORDIA FALLS TO NO ONE!
NO ONE!
BUT AT THIS VERY MOMENT, IN THE ANTECHAMBER OF COUNT DRACULA'S MONOLITHIC CASTLE, A SHOUT RINGS LIKE A DISTANT ECHO, AND--
COUNT LEVKA LEFT SPECIFIC INSTRUCTIONS FOR THE HANDLING OF SUCH TRASH AS THESE TRANSYLVANIANS. AT A TOUCH OF OUR SPEARS, THESE NATIONALS WILL RETREAT, THEN--
INTRUDERS!
GODS! THE SPEARS PASS THROUGH THEM--AS THOUGH NOT TOUCHING THEM! HOW--
NAUGHT CAN PIERCE A VAMPIRE BUT ONE THING, TURK--THE PIERCING EDGE OF A WOODEN STAKE THRUST DEEP THROUGH THE UNDEAD HEART.
YOUR EFFORTS ARE FOLLY--
--AND THEY BORE ME!
THOUGH ONLY A FEW DAYS HAVE PASSED SINCE LAST HE WALKED THESE SHADOWED HALLS, FOR DRACULA, ONCE LORD OF TRANSYLVANIA, IT SEEMS AS THOUGH AN ETERNITY HAS COME BETWEEN HIM--AND THE MAN HE WAS!
HIS BOOTSTEPS SOUND UNFAMILIAR--HIS BREATHING, UNNATURAL--HIS EVERY PERCEPTION IS MUTED BY THE KNOWLEDGE OF WHAT HE HAS BECOME--
--A VAMPIRE--AN UNLIVING CREATURE--ONE OF THE UNDEAD.

AND WITHIN HIS OH-SO-CORPORATE FORM, A RAGING ANGER BUILDS, AND AT LAST--BURSTS OUT!
JACKALS!
THIS DAY, YOU SHALL PAY FOR YOUR DEEDS--
--WITH YOUR SOULS!
OFF ME, WENCH-- IT SEEMS WE'VE ANOTHER OF YOUR MAD COUNTRYMEN TO DISPATCH!
AND FROM THE LOOK OF HIM HE'LL PROVIDE BETTER SPORT THAN SOME OF THE HALF-MEN WE'VE--
GOD IN HEAVEN!
YAGHHHH!
...HE'S A VAMPIRE!
ANTON LEVKA HAS SEEN NIGHTMARES THIS EVE: HE'S HEARD THE VERY RANTINGS OF THE DEVIL HIMSELF, IT SEEMS...
BUT UNTIL THIS MOMENT, THE SOUNDS HE HAS HEARD HAVE BEEN WEAK, UNIMAGINATIVE...
AAARRGHH!!
...PITIABLE NOISES BESIDE THESE GROANS AND CRIES OF UTTER TERROR!

THEN, LIKE SOME GRIM SPECTRE FROM ANTON LEVKA'S ALMOST FORGOTTEN PAST...
ANTON... LORD ABOVE, HELP ME...
IT'S A MONSTER... A CREATURE OF SATAN...
IN THE NAME OF THE HOLY MOTHER.. HELP ME...
WHAT IS IT, ANTON? WHY DON'T YOU SPEAK? ARE YOU MUTE?
IT'S YOUR COUSIN, ANTON... I'M YOUR COUSIN, DON'T YOU RECOGNIZE ME...
FOR GOD'S SAKE, MAN, WHAT--
YAHHAHHHH!
AFTER A TIME, THE SCREAMING STOPS. SILENCE DESCENDS UPON THE CASTLE, A BROODING QUIET LIKE THE HUSH WHICH FALLS BEFORE A STORM. FINALLY, THE SILENCE IS BROKEN, AS...
CASTLE DRACULA IS OURS... AND THAT IS AS IT SHOULD BE.
NOW WE MUST TURN OUR ATTENTION TO OTHER MATTERS. THE QUESTION OF TRAITORS, AND WHAT SHOULD BE DONE WITH THEM.
YOU WOMEN... WERE YOU NOT GAMING WITH THE TURK SWINE? DID I NOT SEE EACH OF YOU... SITTING WITH A TURK, AS THOUGH WITH A LOVER?
WHAT IF WE WERE, MILORD? WE HAD LITTLE CHOICE, WITH OUR MEN ALL DEAD--WITH NO ONE TO PROTECT US FROM THE CONQUERORS' SWORD.
PERHAPS IF THE SONS OF TRANSYLVANIA HAD BEEN BRAVER, MORE BOLD IN BATTLE-- THEIR WOMEN MIGHT NOT HAVE BEEN BARTERED LIKE CHEAP SLAVES!
OURS IS NOT THE FAULT, COUNT. 'TIS YOURS.

IF WE HAD SOLDIERS WITH YOUR BOLDNESS, WOMAN, WE MIGHT NOT HAVE LOST.
TELL ME YOUR NAME.
ZAVERIA, MILORD. MY FATHER WAS BARON JERNAY.
THE TURK SCUM HUNG HIM BEFORE THE CHURCH DOOR.
JERNAY WAS A FOOL...AND A COWARD. BUT YOU...I LIKE YOU, WOMAN.
PERHAPS LATER, WHEN MY AFFAIRS HAVE BEEN PUT TO ORDER, WE MAY--
DEMON FROM HELL! WHAT RIGHT HAVE THEE TO RETURN TO THIS MORTAL SPHERE--AND PLAGUE THY PEOPLE ANEW?
AND WHAT RIGHT HAVE YOU TO ENTER THE CASTLE OF DRACULA?
I AM BORDIA, CONFESSOR OF THIS PARISH. I GO WHERE I WILL, TO DO THE LORD'S WORK.
I ADVISE YOU TO LEAVE AT ONCE, OR FACE THE WRATH OF THE IMPALER.
YOUR THREATS MEAN NOTHING TO ME, COUNT!
I HAVE THE PROTECTION OF THE LORD--HE WHO HAS NEVER FAILED ME!
IT APPEARS I HAVE NO CHOICE, THEN--
--BUT TO REMOVE YOUR PRESENCE MYSELF--
--AS ONLY DRACULA CAN!
BUT, EVEN AS THE LORD OF THE UNDEAD DIVES TOWARD HIS APPARENTLY PARALYZED VICTIM--A STRANGE METAMORPHOSIS OCCURS--
WHAT--?
--A TRANSFORMATION GRANTED TO SOME SPECIES OF THE UNDEAD, BUT NOT TO ALL--
--THE SHIFT--TO THE WOLF!

SCASSH!
WITH A SNARL, THE VAMPIRE-WOLF LUNGES-- ITS MOMENTUM CARRYING IT PAST ITS QUARRY, SMASHING IT AGAINST THE CLUTTERED TABLE.
CATCHING ITS BALANCE, THE CREATURE WHICH WAS ONCE FATHER BORDIA WHIRLS, BLOOD-SHOT EYES SEARCHING THE SMOKY AIR OF THE HALL, FINDING THE DIPPING SHAPE OF THE BAT, AND GUIDING THE WOLF AS--
--IT LEAPS TO THE KILL!
YET, BEFORE THE LUPINE JAWS CAN CLOSE, AND MASH THE BAT'S HOLLOW BONES INTO PULP--
ARRRNNN!
DO YOU THINK ME A FOOL, BORDIA? PERHAPS DRACULA HAS NOT THE ABILITY TO BECOME A WOLF--
--FOR DRACULA IS THE STRONGEST VAMPIRE OF ALL!
--BUT HE HAS OTHER TALENTS WHICH MORE THAN COMPENSATE FOR THAT LACK--
SCUNCH!

HOW LONG HAVE YOU BEEN ONE OF US, PRIEST? HOW LONG HAVE YOU FED ON THE BLOOD OF MY PEOPLE--WHILE PRETENDING TO PROVIDE THEIR SOULS WITH SUCCOR?
A YEAR, FATHER BORDIA? A DECADE?
OR A LIFETIME?
MOCK ME IF YOU WILL, COUNT. IT MEANS NAUGHT--
--FOR THE LAST WORD SHALL BELONG TO BORDIA!
YOU SHAME ME, PRIEST. I THOUGHT NOT TO PREPARE MYSELF SO.
STILL... A WEAPON IS ONLY AS USEFUL AS HE WHO WIELDS IT, AND DESPITE YOUR VAMPIRIC STRENGTH... YOU ARE OLD, BORDIA.
YOU ARE OLD!
DEMON! MONSTER!
I AM OUR LORD'S CONSECRATED PRIEST-- HIS HAND ON EARTH, THE AGENT OF HIS WILL!
WHO ARE YOU TO DEFY HIM? WHO ARE YOU TO CLAIM WHAT IS RIGHTFULLY MINE?
YOU ARE CONFUSED, OLD MAN...
...AND GIVE NAUGHT BUT WHINING IN RETURN!
...YOU WERE ONCE A PRIEST OF GOD, PERHAPS, BUT YOU ARE A PRIEST NO LONGER!
THE LORD OF HELL NEEDS NO SERVANTS OF YOUR KIND--NO PRIESTS TO SING HIM SONGS, NO PRIESTS TO LEAD HIS WORSHIPPERS--
--NO PRIESTS WHO SEEK ONLY HIS PROTECTION--
YOUR TIME ON THIS SPHERE IS LIMITED, BORDIA. YOU'VE LIED TO YOURSELF LONG ENOUGH!
AT LAST-- 'TIS TIME FOR TRUTH!
I'LL DESTROY YOU! DESTROY YOU!

YOU'LL DESTROY NOTHING BUT YOURSELF, OLD MAN. THE ONLY THING WHICH WILL DIE THIS EVE... IS YOUR POMPOSITY.
YOU ARE NOTHING, BORDIA--A PITIABLE VAMPIRE, PERHAPS ONE CREATED BY ACCIDENT, SURELY NOT BY DESIGN!
LIKE ALL YOUR KIND, YOU HAVE CONVINCED YOURSELF OF YOUR OWN IMPORTANCE--
--WHEN THE TRUTH OF THE MATTER IS, YOU ARE NOTHING BUT A TRAITOR TO THE FAITH YOU ONCE SERVED--
--A BETRAYER WHO MERELY TRANSFERRED HIS BELIEF FROM ONE GOD--TO ANOTHER, AND STILL CONSIDERS HIMSELF A PRIEST.
LIES...ALL LIES! YOU'LL PAY FOR YOUR LIES, DEMON--
YOU'LL PAY MOST DEAR!
SWISH!
CHINK!
YAAAGH
IT WAS HE WHO ALLOWED MY FATHER TO BE KILLED... HE DID NOTHING TO STOP THE HANGING, HE MERELY WATCHED.
THE PRIEST IS WELL DEAD, THEN.
BUT WHAT OF YOU, WOMAN? YOU STILL HOLD THE CANDLESTICKS.. YOU MAY STILL USE THEM, IF YOU WISH.
CLATTER!
FINIS

Script: MARV WOLFMAN Art: FRANK ROBBINS, JOHN ROMITA & JOHN TARTAGLIONE

MY LORD, HE APPROACHES THE *CASTLE*.

I KNOW.

HE IS ACCOMPANIED BY THREE ARMED *ADJUTANTS*.

THIS *TOO*, I KNOW.

BID THEM *ENTER* THE THRONE ROOM.

YES, MY LORD.

THERE IS A LONG, OPPRESSIVE SILENCE, DURING WHICH THE GAUNT MAN OF ARISTOCRATIC MIEN PENSIVELY REFLECTS UPON THE PAST. THEN THE PAD OF SOFTLY MUTED FOOTSTEPS... AND THE MAN EMERGES FROM HIS REVERIE, HIS EYES BURNING WITH ALERT FIRE...

WELL? WHAT IS IT YOU WISH TO *DISCUSS*, PRINCE OF WALLACHIA?

...*AND* PRINCE OF *TRANSYLVANIA*-- AS WELL AS *OTHER* THINGS. YOU SEE, MY POWER HAS *SPREAD* SINCE LAST WE *MET*, SULTAN MURAD...

AND YET...I NOTICE YOU FAIL TO *BOW* BEFORE MY *THRONE*.

I COMMEND YOUR *DINING BOARD*, DRACULA...

ITS *LENGTH* PLACES OUR RELATIONSHIP IN PROPER *PERSPECTIVE*.

THE SULTAN'S HOST DOES NOT *REPLY*... BUT MERELY WAITS UNTIL THE HAUNTINGLY BEAUTIFUL HANDMAIDENS HAVE SERVED HIS *GUEST*...

YOU MAY *GO*. THE SULTAN HAS BEEN ADEQUATELY *ATTENDED*.

BUT THEY HAVE YET TO SERVE *YOU*.

I PREFER *NOT*--

--TO *EAT*.

YOU *DON'T*.

THEN... HOW DO I KNOW YOU HAVE NOT LACED THIS MEAL WITH *POISON*?!

BUT THEN, NO ONE IS *FORCING* YOU TO *EAT* IT... MY DEAR, *OBESE* SULTAN.

WE HAVE TRADED *INSULTS* LONG *ENOUGH!*

--AND GET ON WITH THE BUSINESS OF THIS *COURT!*

YOU MAY *KEEP* YOUR PLATES OF *SLOP..*

VERY WELL, MURAD. I SHALL BEGIN BY RELATING A *STORY...*

...A STORY WHICH *BURNS* FROM MY *EYES...*

...AND WHICH SHALL HOLD YOU *SPELLBOUND.*

YOU HAVE *BEWITCHED* OUR SULTAN--!

SOLDIERS. DEAR... SWEET... SOLDIERS...

RELEASE HIM FROM YOUR *ENTRANCE-MENT* OR SUFFER--

WHAT--?!

IT SEEMS YOUR MEN PREFER THE PLEASURES OF THE NIGHT TO THE RIGORS OF STRIFE, MURAD. BUT THEN, THEY HAVE NO CHOICE...
JUST AS YOU HAVE NO CHOICE BUT TO LISTEN TO ME... NOW THAT WE ARE ALONE.
AND NOW MY STORY, MURAD-- A STORY SPUN IN HELL. I AM CERTAIN YOU WILL ENJOY IT... FOR A TIME...
IT BEGINS SOME FIFTEEN YEARS AGO. I WAS BUT A YOUTH, NAIVE AND UNVERSED IN THE WILES OF DIPLOMACY AND TREACHERY. BUT MY FATHER, VLAD THE ELDER, HAD NO SUCH EXCUSE. HE WAS NOBLE, AND TRUSTING...
"...AND MY OLDER BROTHER, POOR RADU, WAS SIMPLY STUPID.
"BY INVITATION, THE THREE OF US JOURNEYED TO TURKEY; THERE TO DISCUSS POLICIES OF PEACE BETWEEN THE MAGYARS AND THE OTTOMAN EMPIRE...
"BUT AS SOON AS WE CROSSED THE TURKISH BORDER--
"--WE WERE AMBUSHED...
"...AND WE WERE BOUND...
"...AND WE WERE DRAGGED THROUGH THE DIRT...

"...DRAGGED LIKE ANIMALS ALL THE WAY TO THE SULTAN'S COURT.
"...EYES OF HATE.
WELCOME, VOIVODE OF WALLACHIA! I SEE YOU HAVE BROUGHT YOUR TWO SONS. HANDSOME YOUTHS INDEED. BUT YOU WILL FORGIVE ME IF I SUSPEND THE AMENITIES...AND ADOPT THE BUSINESS OF THIS AUDIENCE...
"IT WAS THEN THAT I FIRST LAID EYES ON YOU, MURAD...
AS YOU KNOW, OUR RESPECTIVE PRINCIPALITIES ARE BITTER ENEMIES. BUT I HAVE BECOME BORED WITH CONSTANT WAR.

...AND THAT IS WHY I INVITED YOU HERE. IT IS MY EXTREME DISPLEASURE TO INFORM YOU THAT SHOULD YOU FAIL TO IMMEDIATELY ENACT POLOCIES WHICH FAVOR MY COUNTRY... YOUR TWO SONS WILL--

--DIE!!
"I LOOKED AT MY FATHER THEN...
"IT WAS THE FIRST-- AND LAST--TIME I SAW TEARS IN HIS EYES.

THAT IS ALL, VLAD THE ELDER. YOU MAY RETURN TO YOUR KINGDOM NOW...
BUT PLEASE--BEAR IN MIND THAT YOUR SONS ARE NOW MY HOSTAGES.

"YOU KEPT US IN YOUR DUNGEON, MURAD-- AND FORCED US TO FIGHT WITH THE VERMIN FOR WHAT LITTLE BILIOUS GRUEL WE WERE SERVED...
YEEK!
KRANG!

"BUT OCCASIONALLY WE WERE TREATED TO SCRAPS FROM YOUR ROYAL TABLE... IF WE COULD BUT CRANE OUR NECKS TO REACH THEM.

WAHHEE

HYAH

EEHAH

HOHO

SPLAT

HA HA HA

YAAAAHHHGH

PHWAAP

KRAK

HOO! HYAH!

"DO YOU REMEMBER THE TIME YOU CRAVED AMUSEMENT--

"--AND HAD ME TORTURED TO SATIATE YOUR DEPRAVED APPETITE--?

"YOU TORTURED MY BROTHER RADU AS WELL... BUT HE WAS TOO FEEBLE-MINDED TO NURSE MY CAPACITY FOR HATRED. AND IT WAS HATRED, MURAD, WHICH GAVE ME STRENGTH...

AS VOIVODE OF THIS PRINCIPALITY, MY DECISION STANDS!

I WILL NOT JEOPARDIZE THE LIVES OF MY SONS BY INCURRING THE WRATH OF THE TURKS!!

"BUT THE DUKES AND BOYARS OF WALLACHIA HAD GROWN DISGRUNTLED WITH POLICIES WHICH INCREASINGLY FAVORED TURKISH INTERESTS...
"...AND THEY BEGAN PLOTTING BEHIND MY FATHER'S BACK.

"THUS, VLAD THE ELDER DIED IN HIS SLEEP-- A DAGGER REPEATEDLY PLUNGED INTO HIS BREAST BY A MAN WHO HAD ONCE BEEN HIS MOST LOYAL ADHERENT.

"I DID NOT LEARN OF MY FATHER'S DEATH UNTIL MY NINETEENTH YEAR... FOR IT WAS THEN, AFTER FIVE YEARS' IMPRISONMENT, THAT I STRANGLED MY GUARD--
YAHGG

"--USED HIS KEYS TO ESCAPE THAT FOUL DUNGEON--

"AND MY SECOND ACT WAS A MASSED ASSAULT ON THE HORDES OF TURKEY.

"BOTH ACTS WERE BATHED IN THE BLOODY FERVOR OF VENGEANCE.

"YOU SEE, MURAD, THOSE FIVE LONG YEARS SPENT IN THE SQUALOR OF YOUR DUNGEON TAUGHT ME OF HATRED AND CRUELTY, OF DEBAUCHERY AND THE PERVERTED CHEAPNESS OF HUMAN LIFE. THEY WERE LESSONS I LEARNED WELL--

"--AND TO THIS VERY DAY I CONTINUE TO IMPLEMENT THE KNOWLEDGE GAINED FROM THEM. BUT IT IS ONLY NOW THAT I EXERCISE THE POWER TO FULLY EXPLOIT YOUR LESSONS OF BLOOD AND DEATH..."

NO!!
YOU ARE WRONG, YOU DISGUSTING PIG--!!
PHWHAAAK
THIS IS NOT WHO I AM!!
AWAKEN, MURAD-- AWAKEN AND MEET ME FOR THE FIRST TIME--!
WH-WHAT...?
I AM NO LONGER THE ENEMY OF YOUR COUNTRY, BLOATED MAGGOT! I AM NOW THE SCOURGE OF ALL WHO LIVE-- ESPECIALLY YOU!!
MEET DRACULA-- LORD OF THE UNDEAD!
MEET THE FIEND WHO SHALL SLAY YOU IN AN ORGY OF BLOOD-SPLATTERED HORROR!!
N-NO! HELP!! HELP ME!!
YOUR ADJUTANTS CAN NO LONGER NEAR YOU, MURAD--
--FOR THEY ARE FAR TOO PREOCCUPIED WITH THE COMPANY OF MY ALLURING BRIDES...
...MY BRIDES OF BLOOD... AND DEATH.

N-NO--!
AND NOW YOU WILL SHARE THEIR FATE, MURAD...
SKRRP!

MY SCIMITAR--
MY SCIMITAR WILL SAVE ME!!
SSWOOFF

FOOL!!
SWAP!
PHTHUD!
NO MAN'S BLADE CAN HARM DRACULA!

SHRIPPP!
CHOOK!
IT'S...NOT POSSIBLE...
NO...

DRACULA'S LIPS CURL INTO A SMIRK OF DEMENTED GLEE. HE PAUSES, SAVORING HIS VICTIM'S PANIC... AND WAITS UNTIL THE SULTAN'S ADJUTANTS ENTER THE DINING HALL...

THEN, LIKE MIDNIGHT QUICKSILVER, THE LORD OF THE UNDEAD LUNGES FOR HIS GROVELING VICTIM...
YYAAAAAAAAAAAA
A SWIRL OF FRENZY AND CLOAK... WET SUCKING SOUNDS OF OBSCENE GREED...
...AND DRACULA HAS FEASTED.
BEGONE, HARLOTS OF DEATH! JUST AS BARSAC SUCKED ME DRY,* THERE IS NONE LEFT IN THIS PIG FOR YOU!
* SEE DRACULA LIVES #2. --EDITOR.
I SAID FLEE-- SPREAD MY PESTILENCE ACROSS THE LAND! BUT LEAVE ME, AND THIS CASTLE-- NOW!
IT IS NO LONGER SAFE HERE...
...AND THERE IS ONE FINAL ITEM OF BUSINESS I MUST ATTEND.
THEN, AS HE HAD ONCE BEEN DRAGGED, DRACULA DRAGS THE SULTAN... TOWARD A STAIRWAY--

--LEADING TO THE CASTLE ROOF.
TREACHERY RULES US ALL, MURAD. IT WAS DECEIT WHICH MADE HOSTAGES OF MY BROTHER AND I...
...AND IT WAS THROUGH THE SAME FORM OF DECEIT THAT I HAVE SLAIN YOU TONIGHT.
BUT YOUR LOVE OF TREACHERY EXTENDS BEYOND THE BOUNDS OF SANITY--

--AND IS BACKED BY ALL THE MASSED HORDES OF TURKEY!
YOU WERE A FOOL TO THINK YOU COULD TRAP THE PRINCE OF WALLACHIA IN THIS MANNER--FOR DRACULA IS NOW MORE THAN A MERE PRINCE. HE IS ALL.
BUT STILL, YOUR ARMY HUNGERS FOR DEATH-- AND THEY SHALL HAVE THAT DEATH LAID AT THEIR FEET! THE DEATH OF A--

--FOOL!!
AND SOON, MURAD:... SOON YOU WILL RISE FROM THE DEAD TO HAVE THEIR DEATHS!
FIRE!
WHUMP!
INSTANTLY, THE AIR SIZZLES WITH THE SOUND OF SPENT ARROWS--
FFTTT!
FFTT!
TWUNG!
--SLASHING HARMLESSLY THROUGH LANGUIDLY CURLING MIST...
THE MIST COALESCES INTO THE FORM OF A HELLISH BAT WHICH SWOOPS ABOVE THE HEADS OF THE APPALL-ED TURKS...
...LAUGHING DEMONIACALLY IN A VOICE WHICH HAD ONCE BE-LONGED TO THE PRINCE OF TRANSYLVANIA--
--AND WHICH NOW BELONGS TO THE LORD OF THE UNDEAD.
HA HA HA HA HAHA

~Fin~

Writer: GERRY CONWAY Artist: TOM SUTTON

DON'T YOU THINK THAT'S TRUE, LORD VARGAS?
SI. TRULY WE HAVE NEVER SEEN THEIR LIKE IN SPAIN...
PRAY GOD WE NEVER WILL!
DO I DETECT A NOTE OF DISAPPROVAL IN YOUR VOICE, SENOR VARGAS?
NEED I REMIND YOU -- YOUR FRIENDS AND YOU ARE HERE ON YOUR OWN INVITATION.
IF YOU DO NOT LIKE WHAT YOU SEE, THAT IS YOUR MISFORTUNE, GENTLEMEN -- NOT MINE.
PLEASE, COUNT -- DON'T MISUNDERSTAND.
WE'RE ALL MATURE MEN. SURELY, WE CAN DEAL WITH EACH OTHER -- AH -- DESPITE DIFFERENCES IN -- AH -- TASTE?
CAN WE? I WONDER.
WHAT PRECISELY IS IT YOU WISH OF ME, LORD... WHAT IS IT, LORD BENITO?
BENITIO, COUNT. WE ARE EMISSARIES OF OUR RESPECTIVE LORDS ... VARGAS, FROM SPAIN, VON ROON FROM PRUSSIA, AND I FROM BOLOGNA...
YES? AM I SUPPOSED TO BE IMPRESSED?
AH -- MY DEAR COUNT, WHAT WE HAVE COME FOR -- WHAT WE WOULD LIKE -- IS YOUR ASSURANCE -- THAT IS --
SPEAK YOUR MIND, BENITIO. I GROW IMPATIENT.
COUNT DRACULA, WE DO NOT WANT YOU -- OR YOUR FOLLOWERS -- IN OUR COUNTRIES. WE HAVE COME TO GAIN YOUR PROMISE ON THIS. IF WE DO NOT RETURN WITH YOUR PROMISE, THEN -- AH --

YOU WHAT--?
SNIVELING FOOLS, YOU DARE THREATEN ME? DO YOU REALIZE WHO I AM?
HAVE YOU ANY CONCEPTION, ANY INKLING OF THE DOOM YOU'VE CALLED UPON YOURSELVES WITH YOUR ARROGANCE?
I AM DRACULA, YOU CRAVEN CURS--
DRACULA, PRINCE OF VAMPIRES!
FOR AN INSTANT, THEIR MINDS BLANK OUT, AND THEY WONDER WHY THE ROOM HAS GROWN SO SUDDENLY DARK AND OPPRESSIVE...
"A DREAM, SURELY IT'S A DREAM." THEY ALMOST CONVINCE THEMSELVES OF THIS; FOR AN INSTANT, THEY HAVE FORGOTTEN THE REASON FOR THEIR VISIT, THE RUMORS ABOUT THIS MAN, THE DOCUMENTED EVIDENCE...
AND THEN, THEY REMEMBER...
...AND THEY SCREAM...
AAAAAHHHHHHHH
...AND LIKE LOCUSTS ON A FIELD OF WHEAT, THE VAMPIRI DESCEND.

GOD IN HEAVEN, MAN -- HAVE MERCY!
I NEVER INTENDED -- NEVER PLANNED -- YOU MUST UNDERSTAND, THERE WERE ORDERS -- I HAD TO -- WAS FORCED-!
A KING, BENITIO? YOU NEEDN'T WORRY ABOUT HIM NOW...
FORCED? WHO FORCED YOU, BENITIO? WHO MADE YOU COME TO ME?
...FOR YOU'LL SOON HAVE A NEW KING...
THE KING OF THE UNDEAD!
EEEEEEEEEE
AT LENGTH, COUNT DRACULA GROWS WEARY OF REVEL, AND SO TAKES HIS LEAVE OF HIS SUBJECTS, WANDERING THROUGH THE DANK HALLS OF CASTLE DRACULA, FINDING HIMSELF DRAWN AT LAST TO...
...THE TOWER, MILORD? WHY DO YOU COME HERE?
THE OTHERS WILL WONDER--
LET THEM WONDER. DRACULA ANSWERS TO NO ONE.
WHAT DO YOU THINK OF, MILORD? OF ME, PERHAPS...?
YOU FLATTER YOURSELF, WENCH. DRACULA HAS MORE IMPORTANT MATTERS TO CONSIDER THAN WOMEN...
PERHAPS IT'S TIME I LEFT THIS ISOLATED NATION... AND LOOKED ELSEWHERE FOR BLOOD...!

LEAVE, MILORD? OH, NO-- YOU MUSTN'T! WE WOULD BE LOST WITH-OUT YOU--!
BE LOST, THEN.
THESE FOOLS HAVE SPARKED DESIRE IN MY BREAST, A LONGING TO SEE THESE DISTANT LANDS--
--TO TASTE THIS FOREIGN BLOOD.
LET IT BE DONE. DRACULA COMMANDS IT.
AND WHAT IS DRACULA'S WILL--
--MUST BE DONE.
HE FLIES NORTH AT FIRST, TOWARD THE DISTANT PRUSSIAN LANDS...AND BE-YOND. FASTER THAN ANY NATURAL BEAST, HE COVERS DISTANCE WITH A SENSE OF JOYOUS FREEDOM...
...AND WHEN HIS HUNGER GROWS, AND BECOMES TOO GREAT FOR HIS WILL TO BEAR...
...HE SATES IT... AS AN UNHOLY VAMPIRE BAT!
IIEEEEEE

LIKE ANY LIVING CREATIVE, HE THRIVES ON EXPERIENCE; ON THE THRILL OF SOMETHING NEW, OF SOMETHING VARIED... AND FOR A TIME, EXISTANCE SEEMS TO REGAIN ITS JOYS FOR HIM...
...FOR A TIME, HE ALMOST FEELS ALIVE...
...BUT ONLY FOR A TIME.
FOR DRACULA, VARIATION IS AN ILLUSION, SOMETHING HE DISCOVERS AS THE DAYS BECOME WEEKS, AND THE WEEKS MONTHS...
IN THE END, EACH DEATH IS THE SAME...
...AND NONE CAN TRULY GIVE ...SATISFACTION.
THIS PLACE BORES ME, SLAVE. LET US RETURN TO TRANSYLVANIA...
...USING THE ROUTE YOU TOOK TO BRING ME MY COFFIN...
...THOSE MANY WEARYING NIGHTS AGO.

IF NOT BY GOD, THEN ONE OF US MUST DO IT!
THAT FIEND FROM HELL MUST BE DESTROYED!
THAT'S FINE FOR YOU TO SAY, LAD-- BUT WHO DO YOU HAVE IN MIND?

WE'RE NOT ALL AS BRAVE AS YOU, HANS. SOME OF US HAVE WIVES, CHILDREN...
AND NONE OF YOU HAS A SOUL.
MY SISTER WAS SLAIN BY THAT BEAST; NOW I'LL SLAY HIM WITH THIS!

WITH AN ARROW, HANS? YOU'RE INSANE.
NOT JUST AN ARROW... A VERY SPECIAL ARROW. IT'S MADE OF SILVER, AND THE PRIEST IN THE VILLAGE TOLD ME...
...ONLY SILVER CAN DESTROY ...A VAMPIRE.*
*ALSO WOOD.--ENCYCLOPEDIC ROY.

A VAMPIRE, YOU SAY?
WHAT ELSE? THE WAY HE TEARS OUT THEIR THROATS--DRAINS THE BLOOD OF HIS VICTIMS--
A VAMPIRE. THERE CAN BE NO DOUBT.

BUT HANS--IT'S BEEN WEEKS SINCE HE STRUCK. PERHAPS HE'S DECIDED TO LEAVE US--
HE HAS. HE'S RETURNED TO HIS HOME, IN TRANSYLVANIA.
FRIENDS HAVE TOLD ME WHERE TO FIND HIM... THEY'VE GIVEN ME HIS NAME...

...COUNT DRACULA.
IS IT WORTH TAKING THE RISK, HANS? FOR REVENGE?
YOUR SISTER'S DEAD, BURIED THESE SIX WEEKS. FORGET HER, SON. IT ISN'T WORTH YOUR OWN DEATH...

ON THE CONTRARY, OLD MAN...
IT IS.

HIS NAME IS HANS, AND HE IS POSSESSED --NOT BY A DEVIL, NOT DIRECTLY; HIS DEMON IS A SUBTLE ONE, THE SORT OF SPIRIT WHICH LEADS ONE TO SUPER-NORMAL EXPENDITURES OF ENERGY--
--AND THEN ABANDONS ONE, WHEN THE GOAL IS NEAR--ONLY A HEARTBEAT AWAY--A HEARTBEAT THAT SEEMS TO STRETCH ON FOREVER, UNTIL--
--YOU WERE HALF FROZEN. ARE YOU ALL RIGHT NOW? DO YOU WANT SOMETHING TO EAT?
THIS SOUNDS FOOLISH... BUT WHERE AM I... WHO...?
MY NAME IS RACHEL. I'M THE TAVERN MASTER'S DAUGHTER; YOU'RE SLEEPING IN HIS BED.
I'M FLATTERED. WHY DO I DESERVE SUCH TREATMENT?
WHEN WE WERE HELPING YOU TO A BENCH, AFTER YOU FELL THROUGH OUR DOOR--
--WE FOUND THIS. A SILVER ARROW.
WE'VE LIVED IN TERROR UNDER VLAD FOR ALMOST AS LONG AS I'VE BEEN ALIVE. IF YOU INTEND TO SLAY HIM--THEN YOU'RE A FRIEND.
MY THANKS, RACHEL.
I NEED AS MANY FRIENDS AS I CAN FIND...

UNDER STRESS, STRANGE THINGS CAN HAPPEN. A MAN'S EMOTIONS MAY WEAKEN, BECOME VULNERABLE...
...HIS SOUL MAY SOFTEN; HE MAY WELCOME AFFECTION, MAY SEE IT AS LOVE...
...MAY TREAT IT AS LOVE, WHERE BEFORE HE MIGHT HAVE SCOFFED...
...BECAUSE BEFORE, HE DID NOT LIVE IN FEAR.
UNTIL...
RACHEL, I PRAY I'LL RETURN TO YOU BY MORNING... BUT FOR NOW, I MUST LEAVE YOU...
...FOR THERE'S SOMETHING I MUST DO... TO MEET MY DESTINY!
HAAAAN NNNSSS!!

PREMONITION: SHE KNOWS SOMETHING IS WRONG, KNOWS IN HER HEART THAT DEATH HAS STRUCK, THIS MORNING...
HANS! OH GOD IN HEAVEN, HANS!
FATHER, WHERE IS HE? HAVE YOU SEEN HANS? WHERE IS HE?
HE COMES NOW, DAUGHTER...
...THE COUNT HAS SEEN FIT TO RETURN HIM TO US...
... NOW THAT HE'S DONE WITH HIM.
OH, NO... NO!
BREATH ESCAPES HER IN A SIGH; AT THE SAME INSTANT, LIFE ESCAPES HER AS WELL, LEAVING HER WITH A BITTER GRIEF...
...A SLOW BURNING DETERMINATION...
...AND THE STIRRINGS OF THE MEANS OF REVENGE IN HER WOMB.
I CAN FEEL HIM ALIVE WITHIN ME, HANS... YOUR SON, CONCEIVED THE NIGHT OF YOUR DEATH.
HE WILL LEARN OF WHAT HAPPENED HERE... AND ONE DAY, HE OR HIS CHILDREN WILL FACE THAT MONSTER ...AND DESTROY HIM...
SO I SWEAR... RACHE VAN HELSING.
AND SO IT BEGAN, IN THE SIXTH YEAR OF THE DEVIL'S REIGN...
... AND WHERE IT WILL END, ONLY GOD AND SATAN KNOW!

PROLOGUE:

Writer: GERRY CONWAY Artist: STEVE GAN

AND AS FOR "FORGIVING..."
...THOUGH HE IS MANY THINGS, THE MAN CALLED COUNT DRACULA HAS NEVER BEEN THAT.
MAGYAR SWINE!
MOTHER OF GOD! A VAMPIRE!
BLOOD OF MY BLOOD!

Once, a long time ago, Stephan Volpa was a child -- a very superstitious child.
Then he became a man--or thought he did--and put his childish superstitions aside.
Now those superstitions return--and in the last few seconds of his life, Stephan Volpa realizes--
...Please, in the name of mercy...
--He'd never really put them aside after all.!
YAAAHH!
Filthy scum. I've tasted wine that had more flavor than his thin blood.
These raiders are all alike-- spineless worms, without a true man among them.
Yet--for what they've dared do to me and my land, I'll slay them all--and damn their Magyar souls to hell.!
All her life, Giorgia Bathory has been terrified of this man, Count Dracula.
But now, as she watches him stalk to the scene of battle like some great cat, she feels a new emotion replace the old...

SHE FEELS... PROTECTED.
IT'S NOT A FEELING SHE COMPREHENDS AT FIRST, IN FACT SHE'S FRIGHTENED.
THEN THE FEAR FADES, THE FEELING OF PROTECTION PERSISTS, AND ACCOMPANYING THIS NEW EMOTION IS ANOTHER--
THE MATE-INSTINCT: LUST.
HE SAVED ME... THAT MEANS HE WANTS ME FOR HIS OWN..!
AND I WANT HIM-- BLESSED MOTHER, FORGIVE ME! HE'S SO STRONG, SO POWERFUL--!
VLAD DRACUL--TAKE ME! TAKE ME FOR YOUR OWN!
DRACULA DOESN'T HEAR GIORGIA BATHORY'S SILENT PLEA --AND EVEN IF HE COULD, HE'D PAY NO HEED. HIS MIND IS ON OTHER MATTERS...
...AND WHEN HE IS CONCERNED, LIKE ALL MEN OF ACTION--
--HE ACTS!
BARBARIAN SLIME! MY PEOPLE ARE MINE ALONE! TO ATTACK THEM, IS TO ATTACK ME--
AND TO ATTACK DRACULA THE DEVIL--IS TO DIE!

HOW LONG HIS RAGE LASTS, EVEN DRACULA CANNOT SAY, FOR IT CONSUMES HIM TOTALLY, WIPING OUT ALL SENSE OF TIME AND PLACE...
...FADING ONLY WHEN THE LAST RAIDER IS DEAD... AND DRACULA IS VICTORIOUS.

MASTER, I AM YOURS... TAKE ME, DO WHAT YOU WILL WITH ME... I WANT NO OTHER LIFE, SAVE AS YOUR SLAVE!

HE TAKES NO NOTICE AT FIRST; THEN, AS THOUGH DRAWING HIMSELF DOWN FROM SOME GREAT HEIGHT, HE SEES THE GIRL CALLED GIORGIA BATHORY...
WHAT'S THAT? MY SLAVE?

"NO OTHER LIFE," DID YOU SAY?
STUPID GIRL... YOU HAVE NO OTHER LIFE. YOU ARE ALREADY MY SLAVE.

JUST BE THANKFUL I LET YOU LIVE--AND DO NOT PRESUME TO OFFER ME WHAT I ALREADY POSSESS.
EEEEEE!

AND WITHOUT A FURTHER WORD, HE TURNS TO LEAVE... UNAWARE OF WHAT HE LEAVES BEHIND...
HE-HE COULD HAVE HAD ME--TAKEN ME--I WOULD HAVE GIVEN HIM EVERYTHING!
HUSH, CHILD. HE'LL HEAR YOU!

THE NIGHT PASSES SLOWLY, AND DRACULA SPENDS THE NIGHT IN DEEP AND PAINFUL CONTEMPLATION OF WHAT HAS HAPPENED THIS PAST DAY...

...AND WHAT HAS HAPPENED IN RECENT DAYS, ALL OF IT PART OF A PATTERN...

THEY--THE OTHER NOBLES--HAVE CONSPIRED AGAINST HIM: THAT MUCH IS PLAIN TO SEE.

TRANSYLVANIA, AFTER ALL, IS A FEUDAL STATE, ONE COMPOSED OF MANY BARONS AND PRINCES, ALL CONTRIVING TO GAIN ULTIMATE POWER... AND GAIN IT ANYWAY THEY CAN.

TO THIS END, THESE NOBLES WISH TO DESTROY ALL OPPOSITION...

AND WHAT BETTER WAY TO DESTROY A COUNT'S OPPOSITION THAN BY DESTROYING THE MEANS OF HIS WEALTH --HIS SERFS--HIS SLAVES?

YES, THE PLAN IS CLEAR NOW. WHAT ISN'T CLEAR IS THE SOLUTION HE KNOWS HE MUST FIND...

...AND MUST FIND QUICKLY IF HE IS TO SURVIVE AS A POWER IN TRANSYLVANIA... AND NOT AS A MERE... VAMPIRE.
NO, NEVER "MERE"--!
IF ALL FAILS, I MAY ALWAYS FALL ON THAT--
--FOR, REGARDLESS OF WHAT DISASTER OVERTAKES ME, STILL AM I DRACULA-- LORD OF THE UNDEAD--
PRINCE OF THE ETERNAL DARKNESS!
BRIEFLY, HIS TRANSFORMED FIGURE IS FRAMED AGAINST A NIGHT SKY HEAVY WITH VIOLET AND PURPLE...
...AND THEN IT PASSES FROM VIEW... BUT NOT BEFORE IT IS SEEN, RECOGNIZED... AND CURSED, BY ONE WHO BELIEVES SHE HAS REASON TO HATE...
HER REASONS: WHAT SHE CALLS A BROKEN HEART.
BUT AGAIN, DRACULA IS UNAWARE OF WHAT HE LEAVES BEHIND.
HIS THOUGHTS REMAIN RIVETED ON THE FUTURE, AND IN THIS, AT LEAST, HE IS LIKE MANY MEN...
...THOUGH NOT LIKE ALL. SOME MEN PREFER THE PAST, FOR THE COMFORT IT GIVES THEM... THE COMFORT OF THEIR OWN PATHETIC DELUSIONS...
SAINTED FATHER! A BAT!
ONE SUCH MAN IS BARON HUNYADI, A MAN WHO WALLOWS IN THE PAST...

...WHO IS ABOUT TO BE CONFRONTED WITH HIS FUTURE.
NOT JUST A BAT, HUNYADI--A VAMPIRE BAT. IT IS I, DRACULA--HE WHOM YOU SEEK TO DESTROY!
DR-DRACULA--? YOU--HERE--?
I DON'T KNOW HOW YOU MANAGED THAT BIT OF TRICKERY, DRACULA--B-BUT I ASSURE YOU, I AND MY GUESTS WERE NOT IMPRESSED!
YOU SEEM TO HAVE YOUR SERFS FRIGHTENED WITH THESE LEGENDS--BUT YOU HAVEN'T FRIGHTENED US--NO, I SAY--!
MY SERFS. I'M GLAD YOU MENTIONED THEM, BARON...
...IT MAKES MY TASK SIMPLER.
STAY AWAY FROM THEM IF YOU VALUE YOUR STINKING CARCASS, DO YOU UNDERSTAND?
YOU'RE NOT WORTH THE EFFORT IT WOULD TAKE TO KILL YOU NOW... BUT I WARN YOU, TROUBLE MY SERFS AGAIN, AND YOU'LL SUFFER.
THEY ARE MINE, HUNYADI. MINE.
AND MINE THEY WILL REMAIN, TILL I FREE THEM--OR TILL THE END OF TIME!
MEN WHISPER AMONG THEMSELVES--FEARFUL MEN WHO DOUBT THE EVIDENCE OF THEIR EYES, WHO DOUBT, INDEED, THEIR OWN SANITY...
THEN, WHEN ONLY A FEW MINUTES HAVE ELAPSED SINCE DRACULA'S DEPARTURE...

MY LORD BARON... WE HAVE A VISITOR.
NOW THE NIGHT NEARS ITS END, AND FOR THE THOUSANDTH, THOUSANDTH TIME SINCE HE ASSUMED CONTROL OF THIS FIEF, DRACULA PONDERS THE LANDS WHICH ARE HIS OWN...
WHAT HE HAS DONE THIS EVE IS LESS THAN A VICTORY; IT SOLVED NOTHING...
INDEED, IT MAY HAVE CREATED ITS OWN PROBLEMS.
HE MUST FIND A MORE PERMANEN SOLUTION... ONE WHICH WILL SOLVE, FOR ALL TIME, THE DIFFICULTY PRESENTED BY HIS SLAVES...
PERHAPS TOMORROW WILL PROVIDE AN ANSWER.
HE'LL SLEEP ON IT.
THE HOURS CREEP BY: SEVEN OF THEM, IN THEIR TURN; AND AS THE SHADOWS OF AFTERNOON LENGTHEN...
...A NEW SHADOW JOINS THOSE CAST BY THE GUARDS WHO PROTECT THEIR COUNT DURING HIS SLEEP...
THEY DON'T STOP THE GIRL THEY KNOW AS GIORGIA BATHORY; AFTER ALL SHE IS A SERF, ONE OF THE COUNT'S SLAVES, EVEN AS THEY ARE...
AND BECAUSE THEY DON'T STOP HER, THEY DON'T SEE WHAT SHE CARRIES...

SHE HAS BEEN HURT, GIORGIA HAS; NOW, SHE WILL PAY BACK THAT HURT, WITH THE TOOLS GIVEN HER BY HER LORD'S ENEMIES...
BUT, BECAUSE HE IS HER LORD, SHE HESITATES... FOR SECONDS THAT BECOME MINUTES, PRECIOUS MINUTES WHICH LEAVE HER FOREVER...
...UNTIL, WHEN SHE FINALLY BRINGS HERSELF TO ACT...
...SHE ACTS...
...TOO LATE.
YOU WANTED ME TO TAKE YOU, WITCH? THEN TAKE YOU I SHALL--AND LET THIS BE FITTING PAYMENT FOR YOUR ATTEMPTED TREACHERY!
SADLY, THE COUNT DOES NOT UNDERSTAND, AND WOULD NOT UNDERSTAND, IF HE WERE TOLD...
UNTIL THE PURPOSE WAS FULFILLED...
...THAT GIORGIA HAS ACCOMPLISHED HER ONLY PURPOSE IN COMING HERE THIS EVE, A PURPOSE EVEN SHE DIDN'T REALIZE...
...AND GIORGIA BATHORY'S LOVE... IS SATISFIED.

STILL AND ALL, A DEATH MAY SERVE MANY PURPOSES... INCLUDING A PURPOSE NEITHER PARTY INTENDED...
SLAVES OF MY LAND, MEN OF MY FLESH, BLOOD OF MY BLOOD...
A DEATH CAN BE MORE THAN AN ENDING...IT CAN BE A CATALYST FOR A NEW BEGINNING, AS WELL.

...THIS IS WHAT YOUR SERFDOM HAS GIVEN ME...

...ANNOYANCE UPON ANNOYANCE, PROBLEM UPON PROBLEM... A CONTINUING MADNESS I NO LONGER CARE TO ATTEND!
AS MY PEOPLE, AS MY SERFS, YOU ARE RESPONSIBLE TO ME--AND I TO YOU. THUS, MY ENEMIES MAY STRIKE AT ME THROUGH YOU--

--AND I SAY TO YOU NOW, I WILL SUFFER THIS NO MORE!
AS OF THIS MOMENT, YOU ARE FREE MEN--YOUR LIVES ARE YOUR OWN CONCERN, NOT MINE!
DEFEND YOURSELVES, PROTECT YOURSELVES--BUT LEAVE ME. I WANT NO FURTHER PART OF YOU--

--NOW--
--UNTIL THE END OF TIME!
FOR JUST A MOMENT, OTHER WORDS SPOKEN IN ANGER MOCK HIM. THEN THEY FADE, AND HE TURNS AWAY.
SOME SAY THAT ELSEWHERE IN EUROPE, SERFDOM STILL EXISTS... THAT MEN ARE BOUGHT AND SOLD, AND STOLEN. PERHAPS THAT IS SO... ELSEWHERE IN EUROPE. AS OF TONIGHT, IT ISN'T SO HERE... IN TRANSYLVANIA.
FINIS

Writer: DOUG MOENCH Artist: SONNY TRINIDAD

"BUT MY EXISTENCE IS A LONELY ONE. RESTRICTED TO ACTS OF HORROR CULMINATING IN THE DEATHS OF ALL INVOLVED.

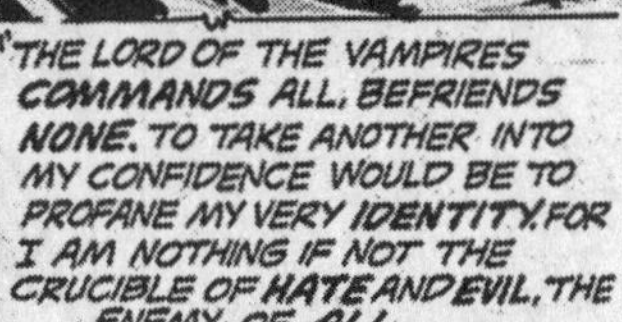

"THE LORD OF THE VAMPIRES COMMANDS ALL. BEFRIENDS NONE. TO TAKE ANOTHER INTO MY CONFIDENCE WOULD BE TO PROFANE MY VERY IDENTITY. FOR I AM NOTHING IF NOT THE CRUCIBLE OF HATE AND EVIL. THE ENEMY OF ALL.

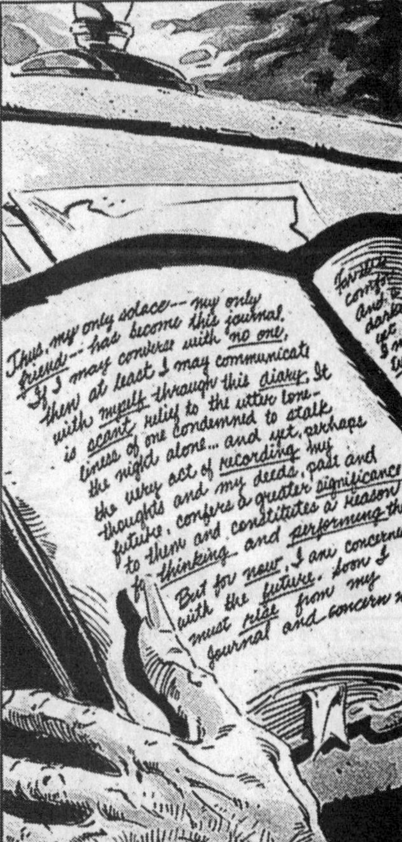
Thus, my only solace -- my only friend -- has become this journal.
If I may converse with no one, then at least I may communicate with myself through this diary. It is scant relief to the utter loneliness of one condemned to stalk the night alone... and yet, perhaps the very act of recording my thoughts and my deeds, past and future, confers a greater significance to them and constitutes a reason for thinking and performing them.
But for now, I am concerned with the future. Soon I must rise from my journal and concern

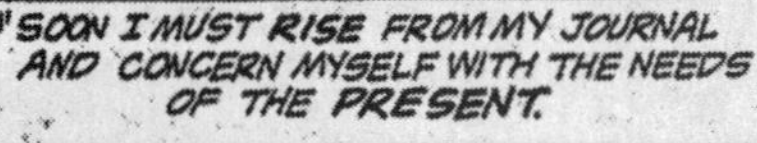
"SOON I MUST RISE FROM MY JOURNAL AND CONCERN MYSELF WITH THE NEEDS OF THE PRESENT.

"FOR IT IS NIGHT, AND THE DAY EVER FOLLOWS ITS COMFORTING SHADOWS.

"AND I MUST USE THE NIGHT WHILE ITS DARKNESS YET HOLDS SWAY.
"I MUST USE IT -- AND MY SUPERNATURAL POWERS OF TRANSFIGURATION -- TO LEAVE CASTLE DRACULA --

"-- AND TO SEEK SUSTENANCE FROM THE LIVING.
"I MUST GO TO THE VILLAGE IN THE VALLEY, AND I MUST STALK THE MORTALS WHO DWELL THERE...

"...FOR IN THEIR FLESH PULSES THE BLOOD WHICH IS THE LIFE...

"...AND I WOULD DRINK OF THEIR BLOOD TO SUSTAIN MY OWN PERVERTED LIFE...

"...FOR I AM DRACULA--

"-- AND I THIRST.

"BUT I FEAR THAT MY TASK THIS NIGHT SHALL BE A FORMIDABLE ONE. I FEAR THAT SLAKING MY THIRST SHALL BE EVEN MORE DIFFICULT THAN IT HAS EVERY NIGHT FOR THE LAST MONTH...
...I FEAR THAT THE VILLAGE, WHICH HAS GROWN INCREASINGLY MORE DESERTED, WILL TONIGHT FINALLY PROVE...DESOLATE.

"I HAVE SLAIN MANY OF THEM IN MY LUST FOR BLOOD, AND EACH KILL HAS INSTILLED GREATER FEAR IN THE HEARTS OF THE SURVIVORS.
"IT IS THIS FEAR WHICH LOCKS THEIR DOORS AT SUNSET... AND IT IS MY CURSE WHICH PREVENTS ME FROM OPENING THOSE DOORS WITHOUT INVITATION.
LOOK AT HIM OUT THERE -- THE VERY SPECTER OF DEATH -- STANDING IN OUR STREETS AS THOUGH HE OWNS THE ENTIRE VILLAGE.

AYE--HE'S THE BLOODY DEVIL HIMSELF!
FORCING US TO HUDDLE INDOORS LIKE FRIGHTENED CHILDREN AT THE FIRST HINT OF DARKNESS! IT'S DISGRACEFUL--!
THEN WHY DON'T YOU DO SOMETHING ABOUT IT?

DO SOMETHING, DURENYI? WHAT WOULD YOU HAVE US DO--STRIDE OUT INTO THE STREET AND OFFER HIM OUR BLOOD?
BETTER THAT THAN TO COWER INSIDE IN DISGRACE...
BUT THERE IS A MORE CONSTRUCTIVE COURSE OF ACTION...

AND WHAT COURSE MIGHT THAT BE?
THE ONE WHICH LEADS TO THE COUNT'S CASTLE...AND POSSIBLY TO HIS DEATH.

YOU'RE MAD, DURENYI! NO MAN WOULD DARE ENTER THAT DEVIL'S LAIR--NO MAN WHO FEARS LIVING HELL, THAT IS.
YOU ACT AS THOUGH THE FIEND WERE INVINCIBLE... AND THEREBY DEFEAT YOURSELF WITHOUT TRYING.
BUT IS IT NOT POSSIBLE THAT COUNT DRACULA HAS A WEAKNESS, SOMETHING WE ARE AS YET UNAWARE OF...?

AND IS IT NOT LOGICAL THAT THE SECRET OF HIS WEAKNESS MIGHT BE FOUND SOMEWHERE IN HIS CASTLE...?
AND WOULD IT NOT BE MOST PRUDENT TO SEEK OUT THAT SECRET NOW-- WHEN WE KNOW HE IS NOT IN HIS CASTLE...WHEN HE IS OUT SEARCHING FOR A VICTIM HE WILL BE A LONG TIME IN FINDING...?

PERHAPS, DURENYI, PERHAPS...
AND YET...WHO WOULD BE WILLING TO RISK HIS SOUL ON SUCH A MEAGER VENTURE?
I WOULD... FOR A PRICE.

A PRICE...?
YES, A PRICE--OR ISN'T IT WORTH A THOUSAND COINS...
...TO BE FREE OF DRACULA'S VILE DEPREDATIONS?

YES, DURENYI, I SUPPOSE IT IS WORTH THE PRICE... WORTH ANY PRICE.
GOOD. THEN I SHALL EXPECT PAYMENT IN THE MORNING... SHOULD I SUCCEED...

AND I SHALL LEAVE NOW... OUT THE BACK DOOR--
--WHILE DRACULA STILL PROWLS AT THE FRONT.

"YES, I FEAR THAT THE VILLAGE SHALL PROVE BARREN THIS NIGHT... BEREFT OF ANY LIFE...
"BUT I VOW THAT I SHALL CONTROL MY INSATIABLE LUST FOR HUMAN BLOOD... AND I SHALL NOT LINGER IN THE VILLAGE AS I HAVE UPON OTHER OCCASSIONS...
"...SHALL NOT FLIRT WITH THE DAWNING OF THE SUN, HOPING BEYOND HOPE THAT SOME MORTAL FOOL WILL BRAVE THE DARKENED STREETS...

"NO, THIS NIGHT I SHALL SWIFTLY LEAVE THE VILLAGE AND ITS BLEAKNESS--

"--TO CONTINUE MY HUNT IN THE FOREST.

"THE FOREST, WHERE THE BLOOD IS NOT HUMAN...
"...WHERE IT IS FOUL WITH BITTERNESS...

"...BUT IS, NEVERTHELESS, BLOOD...THE BLOOD OF LIFE.
"AND BY LOWERING MYSELF IN THIS MANNER, I SHALL AVOID THE DANGER OF THE COMING SUN--

"--AND RETURN AT MY LEISURE TO THIS CASTLE.

"THIS CASTLE AND ITS COMFORTS...

"...CHIEF AMONG THEM MY DIARY.

...comforts, chief among them my diary.
It is later, and I begin this new entry with the disconsoling news that my suspicions were well-founded. The mortals in the village have become too cautious, and I have been forced to feast upon blood of an animal. But it is the last time I shall degrade myself with such a substitution for human blood.

PLENTY OF TIME...WHILE DRACULA SEARCHES IN VAIN FOR HIS PRECIOUS BLOOD.

"FOR TOMORROW NIGHT I SHALL BEGIN TO PREY UPON THE VILLAGE OF BIASTRITZ... WHERE THE NAME OF DRACULA IS UNKNOWN...

"...AND WHERE NEITHER CAUTION NOR DANGER EXISTS.

"AND NOW, DAWN APPROACHES. I MUST CONCLUDE THIS ENTRY IN MY JOURNAL...

"...AND GO TO MY CRYPT, THERE TO REST FOR MY IMPENDING ACTIVITIES IN THE TOWN OF BIASTRITZ.

NOW... MUST BEGIN SEARCHING... BEFORE DRACULA RETURNS.

KRASH!

CLUMSY FOOL THAT I AM--
AND DAWN APPROACHES-- BEST TO LEAVE NOW, BEFORE DRACULA ARRIVES...

SOMEONE DARES TO INVADE MY CASTLE--?!
THE FOOL SHALL PAY FOR HIS FOLLY-IN BLOOD!

PERHAPS THAT STAIRWAY AHEAD LEADS TO THE DOOR...

OH MY GOD--!
YOU WILL NOT FIND YOUR GOD HERE, FOOL!

YOU WILL FIND NOTHING BUT YOUR HELL!

AAAAAHHHH!!?!

MY FACE-- GOD, MY FACE--!
YOU CANNOT RUN, MORTAL FOOL!

YOU ARE LOST, MORTAL--LOST!
THE CORRIDOR LEADS NOWHERE.

YOU ARE TRAPPED!

THERE IS NOWHERE YOU--
NO--!
SHRIPPP

THE SUN--!

AHRRR
THE CROSS--THE DAMNED CROSS!

THEN YOU DO HAVE A WEAKNESS, COUNT DRACULA...
SUNLIGHT WAS EASY TO GUESS--FOR NEVER ONCE HAVE YOU BEEN SEEN BEFORE DARK...

...BUT I NEVER WOULD HAVE GUESSED THE CROSS WOULD AFFECT YOU IN SUCH A MANNER.
AND YET, IT IS A PERFECTLY--PERFECTLY--LOGICAL DEFENSE AGAINST FILTH SUCH AS YOU...

BREESH
IT IS ALSO A DEFENSE DEAR COUNT, I SHALL NOT SOON--

--FORGET.
FLEE, MORTAL--FLEE INTO YOUR CURSED SUNLIGHT...

...BUT KNOW THAT DRACULA WILL STALK YOU IN THE DARKNESS--STALK YOU THROUGH A THOUSAND NIGHTS OF HORROR, IF NEED BE--

--AND HE SHALL KNOW YOU BY THE FACE HE HAS SCARRED THIS FOUL MORNING...

...AND THAT FACE IS SOMETHING HE WILL NOT SOON FORGET!
END PART ONE

Parchments of the DAMNED

PART TWO of a TRILOGY

The Stealer of DRACULA'S Soul

I HAVE BEEN PROMISED A ***THOUSAND GOLD-PIECES*** IN RETURN FOR THE SECRET OF ***DRACULA'S WEAKNESS***

I AM HERE TO TELL YOU THAT I HAVE ***ENTERED*** THE VAMPIRE'S CASTLE--AND I HAVE ***DISCOVERED*** HIS SECRET!

BUT ***MORE*** THAN THAT--I AM HERE TO TELL YOU THAT THIS VILLAGE OF SNAGOV IS NOW AND FOREVER AFTER ***FREE*** OF THE FIEND'S DREAD SPECTER... FREE TO WALK THE NIGHT STREETS WITHOUT ***FEAR***--!

FOR I, DURENYI, HAVE ***SLAIN COUNT DRACULA!***

Writer: DOUG MOENCH Artist: YONG MONTANO

IMPOSSIBLE -- THE CREATURE WHO IS DRACULA IS INVINCIBLE! NO MAN CAN FACE HIM AND LIVE-- MUCH LESS SLAY HIM--!
AND YET THAT IS PRECISELY WHAT I HAVE DONE...

THESE SCARS WHICH NOW RUIN MY FACE ATTEST TO MY ENCOUNTER WITH DRACULA... FOR THEY WERE MADE BY THE VAMPIRE'S TALONS...
AND AS FOR MY CLAIM TO DRACULA'S DEATH--

--THAT SHALL BE PROVED BY THE VAMPIRE'S ABSENCE IN YOUR STREETS THIS NIGHT AND EVERY NIGHT HEREAFTER!

THEN, DURENYI, WOULD YOU NOT AGREE THAT WE WOULD BE FOOLS IF WE DID NOT OBSERVE AT LEAST ONE NIGHT OF OUR NEW FREEDOM FROM VAMPIRISM...
...BEFORE PAYING YOU THE AGREED SUM...?

I HAVE EXPERIENCED THE FAMINE OF TRUST BEFORE, CITIZEN OF SNAGOV...
...AND I AM THEREFORE ABLE TO UNDERSTAND YOUR MISAPPREHENSIONS --YOUR RELUCTANCE TO PAY ME IN GOOD FAITH...

SO OBSERVE YOUR FIRST NIGHT OF SAFETY, AND THROUGH IT BECOME CONVINCED OF MY SUCCESS... FOR I SHALL RETURN ON THE MORROW TO COLLECT MY DUE PAYMENT.
BUT FOR NOW, I MUST LEAVE YOU-- TO DEVOTE MYSELF TO MATTERS OF MORE IMMEDIATE CONCERN.
FAREWELL... UNTIL TOMORROW.

HE TAKES THE ROAD TO BIASTRITZ... TO ESCAPE US, DO YOU THINK?
AYE, IF HE LIED ABOUT DRACULA'S DEATH. BUT WE SHALL KNOW SOON ENOUGH. WE SHALL KNOW WHEN--

"--THE DAY TURNS TO NIGHT."
THE SONGBIRDS ARE SILENT, HAVING LONG SINCE FLED THE ADVANCE OF DARKLING RAVENS... AND DARKNESS SHROUDS THE CRUEL MAJESTY OF CASTLE DRACULA.

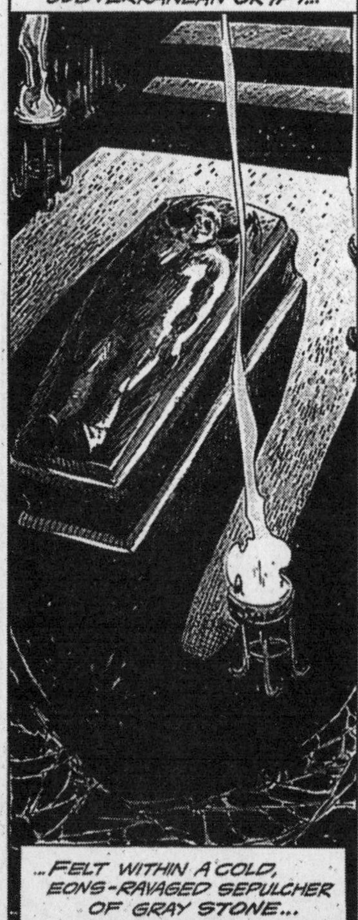
A DARKNESS WHICH IS FELT EVEN HERE, IN THE CASTLE'S SUBTERRANEAN CRYPT...
...FELT WITHIN A COLD, EONS-RAVAGED SEPULCHER OF GRAY STONE...

...A SEPULCHER WHOSE PONDEROUS LID BEGINS TO MOVE WITH THE HARSH GRATE OF STONE AGAINST STONE... UNTIL THE SEPULCHER IS OPENED--

KRUMPP
--FROM WITHIN.

IT IS NIGHT--

--AND DRACULA THIRSTS!

BUT TONIGHT I SHALL NOT DEBASE MY LUSTS ON THE FOUL BLOOD OF FOREST ANIMALS-

TONIGHT I SHALL EXULT IN THE FULL GLORY OF HUMAN BLOOD... FOR NO LONGER SHALL I HARRY THE VILLAGE OF SNAGOV, WHOSE CITIZENS HAVE BECOME AWARE OF MY PRESENCE AND MY NEEDS...
...AND WHO HIDE THEMSELVES BEHIND LOCKED DOORS!

TONIGHT I SHALL PREY UPON A NEW COMMUNITY OF MORTALS--A VILLAGE IGNORANT TO THE EXISTENCE OF COUNT DRACULA.

TONIGHT I GO TO--

"--BIASTRITZ!"
THE NIGHT IS SHREDDED BY THE ERRATIC ASCENT OF A HUGE, GLISTENING BAT... AND NOW, EVEN THE RAVENS FLEE IN TERROR...

...FOR DRACULA HAS ENTERED THE NIGHT, AND HIS PRESENCE IS FELT EVERYWHERE--
--IN WHATEVER FORM HE CHOOSES TO PLY HIS UNSPEAKABLE ATROCITIES...

...AND WHEREVER HE CHOOSES TO COMMIT THEM.
AS, FOR EXAMPLE, THIS VILLAGE OF BIASTRITZ... WHOSE VARIOUS LIGHTS CAUSE IT TO GLITTER LIKE A SEDUCTIVE JEWEL IN THE VAMPIRE-LORD'S GREEDY EYES...

...DRAWING HIM GROUNDWARD LIKE A MOTH TO FLAME.

THE STREETS OF THIS VILLAGE TOO ARE DESERTED... DESOLATE!

BUT THEY CANNOT KNOW OF ME HERE... THEY MUST WALK THE NIGHT... SOMEWHERE...

AND DRACULA SHALL FIND THEM--WHEREVER THEY ARE!
MOVING WITH THE FLUID GRACE OF MIDNIGHT, DRACULA GLIDES DOWN THE SQUALID ALLEY... STALKING DEEPER IN FILTH UNTIL HE REACHES...

--A DEAD-END.
THE STREET HAS NO OUTLET, AND STILL I HAVE NOT FOUND WHAT I SEEK...
KLEK!

A SOUND-- FROM BEHIND ME--!

NO!
THE CROSS--!

HE IS AFRAID OF THE CROSS --AS THE STRANGER CLAIMED!
CLOSE IN ON HIM--!
KLAK!

NO-- EVERYWHERE--!
THE CROSS IS EVERYWHERE--!

HOW COULD THEY KNOW--?!!
WE HAVE HIM TRAPPED--HE CAN'T ESCAPE!

BUT THE LORD OF THE VAMPIRES IS NOT WITHOUT POWER OF HIS OWN--
LOOK--!

--AND IS NOT ABOUT TO BE TRAPPED BY MERE MORTALS.
HE CHANGED... INTO MIST--!
HE'S THE DEVIL HIMSELF!

DID I NOT WARN YOU HE WAS...
AYE, DURENYI... YOU DID INDEED WARN US.

AND DID I NOT PROVIDE YOU WITH THE SECRET OF HIS ONE WEAKNESS ... AND THEREBY SAVE BIASTRITZ FROM HIS EVIL LUST?
YOU DID.
THEN I BELIEVE WE HAVE A SLIGHT BUSINESS-MATTER TO DISCUSS...

...THE MATTER OF THREE-THOUSAND GOLD-PIECES-- FOR SERVICES FULLY RENDERED.

YOU DESERVE THE PRICE, DURENYI...
...FOR AS LONG AS WE WIELD THE POWER OF THE CRUCIFIX, THE BEAST CALLED DRACULA IS HELPLESS...
YOU LEARN QUICKLY, CITIZEN OF BIASTRITZ...

AND NOW, I SHALL SPEND THE NIGHT IN YOUR INN.
THE JOURNEY BACK TO SNAGOV IS A LONG ONE--AND ONE I MUST UNDERTAKE IN THE MORNING.
IT HAS BEEN A PLEASURE, MY FRIENDS, TO DO BUSINESS WITH YOU.

RAGE FILLS COUNT DRACULA NOW, AS HE CUTS THE NIGHT FROM FOREST TO CASTLE...
...FOR IT IS NOW THE SECOND NIGHT HE HAS BEEN FORCED TO SATIATE HIS OBSCENE LUST ON THE BLOOD OF AN ANIMAL--

--AND HE WOULD KNOW WHY.

HOW COULD THEY KNOW--?
HOW COULD THEY EXPECT MY ARRIVAL IN A VILLAGE I HAVE NEVER BEFORE PREYED UPON--?!

I MUST THINK...
...AND PLACE MY THOUGHTS IN MY--

--JOURNAL.
IT IS GONE... MY DIARY IS GONE--!

THE RECORD OF OF MY EVERY THOUGHT -- MY EVERY PLAN--
STOLEN!

AND THE THIEF MUST HAVE BEEN THE MORTAL WHO DARED ENTER MY CASTLE LAST NIGHT--
--THE MORTAL WHO NOW BEARS THE SCARS OF MY RAGE...

...AND WHO WILL SOON BEAR THE MARK OF VENGEANCE--
--AND DEATH!

I DON'T CARE WHAT YOU SAY, DRUSILLA-- I'M STILL AFRAID TO BE OUT AT NIGHT.
FORGET YOUR FEARS, ZINA. IT'S PAST MIDNIGHT-- AND DRACULA HAS BEEN NOWHERE SINCE SUNSET. IT MUST BE AS DURENYI CLAIMED--

--DRACULA IS DEAD.
BUT STILL, THE SHADOWS...

YOU WOULD LET THE SHADOWS PREVENT YOU FROM GOING HOME ?
REALLY, ZINA, I SHOULD THINK YOU WOULD BE GLAD TO GO HOME--AFTER MONTHS OF BEING FORCED TO SLEEP IN THE BACK ROOM OF THE INN, THE SMELL OF THE SOUR ALE WE SERVE ALL NIGHT STILL CLINGING TO OUR DRESSES...

YOU MUST WELCOME THE OPPORTUNITY OF A HOT BATH FOR A CHANGE.
YES, BUT--

THE NIGHT SPOKE THE TRUTH TO ME...

...WHEN IT WHISPERED THAT YOU WALK IN ITS EMBRACE.
IT HAS BEEN TOO LONG SINCE DRACULA LAST MET MORTALS IN THE STREETS OF SNAGOV...

...AND IT IS NOW TIME THAT I REACQUAINT MYSELF WITH THE PLEASURES YOU HAVE TO OFFER.

COME TO ME.
BOTH OF YOU...

...FOR I WOULD SPEAK TO YOU, OF A MAN WHOSE FACE HAS BEEN SCARRED...
...AND OF OTHER MATTERS OF THE NIGHT.
YES, MASTER...
WE WILL... SPEAK...
END PART TWO

Writer: DOUG MOENCH Artist: STEVE GAN

SHE MOVES THROUGH A MIRROR OF LIQUID DARKNESS, KNOWING NOTHING BUT REFLECTIONS OF LANGUOR AND CHILLING WARMTH. HER SOUL IS NUMB.
SOON IT WILL BE STOLEN.
YOU ARE PRIVILEGED, DRUSILLA...AND YOU ARE DAMNED.
PRIVILEGED TO DRACULA'S LUST--
AND DAMNED TO A LIFE OF ETERNAL DEATH.
SHE FEELS IT THEN, THE WITHERING VAPORS OF HIS HOT BREATH, THE SLIGHT CARESS OF HIS COLD LIPS.
...AND THE HELLISHLY ABRUPT PENETRATION OF HIS DISTENDED FANGS.
LIKE THE FANGS OF A VIPER, THEY PUNCTURE THE SMOOTH CONTOURS OF HER PULSING THROAT TO RELEASE A FLOOD OF DEATH-VENOM INTO HER RUPTURED VEINS...
BUT UNLIKE THE VIPER, DRACULA IS NOT CONTENT TO MERELY BESTOW DEATH UPON HIS VICTIMS...
...BUT MUST ALSO STEAL THE BLOOD OF THEIR LIVES...
...AS WELL AS THE DIGNITY FROM THEIR SOULS.
YOU HAVE WATCHED ME TAKE HER, ZINA. WHAT HAVE YOU WITNESSED?
ECSTASY. I HAVE WITNESSED ECSTASY.

AND WHAT WAS THIS ECSTASY LIKE, ZINA?
IT WAS... BEAUTIFUL...
AND WHAT DID YOU FEEL AS YOU WITNESSED THIS BEAUTIFUL ECSTASY?
I FELT... ENVY... AND I FELT DESIRE...
THEN YOU WISH TO PARTAKE ON THIS BEAUTIFUL ECSTASY YOURSELF, ZINA?
YES... YESSSS...
BUT IT IS IMPOSSIBLE, ZINA. I MUST DENY YOU THIS PLEASURE... FOR YOU HAVE NOT EARNED IT.
HOW MAY I EARN IT? WHAT MUST I DO? NAME IT, DRACULA AND IT IS DONE...
YOU MUST SPEAK TO ME OF THE MAN WITH A FACE OF SCARS. YOU MUST TELL ME EVERYTHING YOU KNOW OF HIM. DOES HE LIVE HERE IN SNAGOV...?
NO, DRACULA... HE IS A STRANGER...
THEN I MAY FIND HIM IN BIASTRITZ?
I DO NOT KNOW. BUT TOMORROW HE RETURNS HERE... FOR HIS REWARD...
YES...? AND HIS NAME?
DURENYI.
VERY GOOD, ZINA. YOU HAVE EARNED YOUR ECSTASY.

THE SHADOWS TREMBLE AT WHAT HAPPENS NEXT... AND WHEN IT IS DONE...
SLEEP THE PEACE OF DEATH WHILE YOU MAY... FOR IT SHALL NOT LAST LONG... AND DRACULA WILL RETURN FOR YOU BEFORE DAWN.
BUT UNTIL THEN I MUST OCCUPY MYSELF WITH OTHER MATTERS IN THESE NEWLY-PEOPLED NIGHT STREETS OF SNAGOV...
...FOR I WOULD PREPARE A WELCOME FOR THIS...DURENYI.
BIASTRITZ AT DAWN IS NOT AN UNPLEASANT PLACE FOR THE MAN CALLED DURENYI... DESPITE THE SCARS WHICH NOW MAR HIS FACE.
NOW, ONE LAST ITEM OF BUSINESS HERE BEFORE I JOURNEY TO SNAGOV...
AND I SHALL OBTAIN THREE PAYMENTS FOR THAT SINGLE NIGHT'S WORK.
INDEED, THOSE SCARS ARE INDIRECTLY RESPONSIBLE FOR HIS NEWLY GAINED WEALTH OF THREE-THOUSAND GOLD-PIECES... AND WILL SOON SECURE HIM ANOTHER THOUSAND UPON HIS RETURN TO THE VILLAGE OF SNAGOV.
YES? MAY I HELP YOU?
I'M NOT SURE, OLD MAN. I WAS LED TO BELIEVE THIS WAS A BOOK SHOP...

IT IS.
BUT I SEE NO BOOKS ON DISPLAY. WHERE ARE THEY?

IN THE CRATES, READY TO BE SHIPPED TO ENGLAND.
YOU SEE, MY SHOP CLOSES TODAY... AND I RETIRE TOMORROW.

THEN YOU WOULD NOT BE INTERESTED IN THE RARE BOOK I WISH TO SELL...
ON THE CONTRARY-- I SHOULD BE EXTREMELY INTEREST ED. IT MIGHT VERY WELL BE MY FINAL OPPORTUNITY TO MAK A PROFIT.

YOU SEE, I HAVE BEEN SUCCESSFUL IN CLOSING A MOST SHREWD DEAL WITH THE BOOK AGENCY IN LONDON...
THEY ARE PAYING ME BY THE ITEM, RATHER THAN BY LOT. A SINGLE VALUABLE BOOK COULD MAKE A CONSIDERABLE DIFFERENCE IN THE FINAL SUM OF MY RETIRE-MENT FUNDS.

THEN I ASSURE YOU THAT THE BOOK I WISH TO SELL IS WORTHY OF YOUR EXAMINATION.

HERE IT IS-- DRACULA'S DIARY.
DIARY of COUNT DRACULA

AH YES, DRACULA. THEN YOU MUST BE THIS DURENYI WHO ROBBED OUR TREASURY OF THREE-THOUSAND GOLD-PIECES LAST NIGHT.
ROBBED--?! MY GOD, MAN, I SAVED YOUR VILLAGE FROM HELL!
ARE YOU NOT AWARE OF WHO DRACULA IS?

AS FAR AS I'M CONCERNED, HE'S JUST ANOTHER COMMON CUTTHROAT.
I'LL GIVE YOU FORTY PIECES FOR THIS BOOK--AND THAT MUCH ONLY BECAUSE IT APPEARS TO BE EXTREMELY OLD.
BUT IT'S WORTH TEN TIMES THAT AMOUNT--!

YOU'LL NOT CONVINCE A SINGLE BUSINESSMAN OF THAT CLAIM. YOU'LL CONVINCED NOBODY BUT FRIGHTENED OLD MAIDS AND IGNORANT PEASANTS--AND THEY'D BE AFRAID TO BUY DRACULA'S DIARY, EVEN IF THEY COULD AFFORD IT.

AND I'D CERTAINLY BE UNABLE TO CONVINCE THE LONDON AGENCY TO BELIEVE IN SOMETHING AS FOOLISH AS VAMPIRES...

SO YOU SEE, IF I CAN GET ONLY SIXTY FOR THE BOOK... I'LL PAY YOU ONLY FORTY. WILL YOU TAKE IT OR NOT?

I'LL TAKE IT... BUT IF YOU ASK ME, OLD MAN--
--YOU'RE THE COMMON CUTTHROAT AROUND HERE.

AND WHEN DURENYI HAS BEEN PAID...

HMPH--!

DRACULA'S DIARY--

--INDEED!

DIARY of COUNT DRACULA

TAKE HIM TO THE INN--!
WE'LL MAKE HIM PAY WELL FOR HIS CRIME!
BUT DRACULA COULD NOT HAVE COME HERE LAST NIGHT--IT'S IMPOSSIBLE--!
IMPOSSIBLE DURENYI, BECAUSE YOU MURDERED DRACULA...? WE SHALL SEE HOW IMPOSSIBLE IT IS!... ONCE IT HAS GROWN--
"--DARK."
UNTIE HIM--!
AND THROW HIM OUT IN THE STREETS--THE STREETS HE HAS CLAIMED ARE NOW SAFE!
OUT IN THE STREETS --WHERE HE MAY SUFFER THE SAME FATE MY DAUGHTER DRUSILLA HAS SUFFERED... A FATE WOVEN FROM HIS BASE LIES!
CAN IT BE THAT DRACULA DID RETURN TO SNAGOV LAST NIGHT--AFTER BEING DRIVEN FROM BIASTRITZ...?
AND YET... WHAT IF HE HAS? I NEED NO LONGER FEAR HIM--
--NOW THAT I KNOW THE SECRET OF HIS WEAKNESS...

GRRR...
WHAT'S THAT--?!
A WOLF--!!
IT SNATCHED THE CROSS FROM MY HAND... AS THOUGH WITH A MAN'S INTELLIGENCE...
...AND IT WAS WRITTEN IN DRACULA'S DIARY THAT HE MAY COMMAND WOLVES, AS WELL AS OTHER CREATURES OF THE NIGHT..
I'M DEFENSELESS.--
--AND THEY WON'T LET ME BACK INSIDE--!
THEY EMERGE FROM THE SHADOWS THEN, SILENT WOMEN GLIDING THROUGH DARKNESS, THEIR EYES BURNING WITH INNER FIRES OF LUST...
THERE ARE BUT A FEW AT FIRST..
NO--WHO ARE YOU? WHAT DO YOU WANT?!
...BUT SOON JOINED BY MORE... AND STILL MORE
...ALL OF THEM SILENT, WRAITHLIKE, MOVING LIKE ETHEREAL SPECTERS OF DEATH...
ANSWER ME-- WHAT DO YOU WANT OF ME?

THEY WERE ONCE THE DAUGHTERS OF THIS BEREAVED VILLAGE OF SNAGOV...
...BUT NOW ARE THE DAUGHTERS OF THE NIGHT.
WHO ARE YOU--?
AND WHEN THEY FINALLY REPLY TO DURENYI'S ANGUISHED PLEAS... IT IS IN SILENCE--
--AND WITH A SMILE OF WICKED GLEE WHICH RIPPLES THROUGH THEIR SLOWLY ADVANCING RANKS.
MY GOD-- NOOOOO!!
AND THEN A TERRIBLE VOICE SPAWNED IN HELL SPLITS THE GLOOM...
HALT!
...AND ALL IS STILL.
I WOULD SPEAK TO THIS... DURENYI.
I WOULD ASK HIM IF HE REMEMBERS OUR PREVIOUS MEETING... IF HE REMEMBERS THE ONE WHO INFLICTED THE SCARS WHICH SLASH HIS FACE...
...AND IF HE REMEMBERS STEALING MY DIARY.
WHERE IS IT... DURENYI?
PLEASE... PLEASE --I BEG OF YOU--DO NOT HARM ME!! I... I'LL DO ANYTHING -- ANYTHING YOU WANT... BUT PLEASE DO NOT--
WHERE IS THE DIARY?
I... I SOLD IT... IT HAS BEEN SHIPPED... TO LONDON... BUT YOU MUST UNDERSTAND THAT I--

LONDON, 1896... THREE CENTURIES LATER.

THIS BLOOD IS MINE!
IN THE EARLY YEARS OF THE SEVENTEENTH CENTURY-- 1606, TO BE EXACT-- A GIRL FLEES FOR HER LIFE IN THE DARK, DISMAL FORESTS OF TRANSYLVANIA!
BEHIND HER, THE HUNTING HOUNDS OF THE COUNTESS ELIZABETH BATHORY COME BAYING ALONG HER TRAIL, URGED ON BY THE CRIES OF THEIR KEEPERS...
ABOVE HER, A GIGANTIC BAT FLAPS HIS LEATHERY WINGS, ITS FLARING NOSTRILS SCENTING THE YOUTHFUL BLOOD POUNDING IN HER TERRORIZED BODY...
SOBBING, IN DREAD OF SOMETHING EVEN WORSE THEN DEATH, SHE RUNS ON... AND ON ... AND ON ...
MERCIFUL MOTHER IN HEAVEN-- PROTECT ME!
DON'T LET THE COUNTESS GET ME!
GARDNER F. FOX -- WRITER
DICK AYERS -- ILLUSTRATOR

EVEN AS THE DOGS NARROW THE GAP BETWEEN THEM AND THEIR QUIVERING VICTIM...

A GREAT BAT SWOOPS LOW ABOVE THE GROUND-- ITS BLACK OUTLINE BLURRING -- CHANGING ITS SHAPE WITH EVERY STROKE OF ITS WINGS...

AT THIS MOMENT IN A LONELY NOOK OF CASTLE CSEJTHE THE COUNTESS ELIZABETH BATHORY LEANS TO STUDY HER WRINKLES WHICH SHOW THE TOUCH OF AGING...
I GROW-- OLD!
WRINKLES MAR MY FACE-- WHICH ONCE WAS THE FAIREST IN THE LAND.

SIGH
IF ONLY THERE WERE SOME WAY-- TO GROW YOUNG AGAIN...
I WOULD DO ANYTHING-- ANYTHING--TO HAVE MY YOUTH BACK!

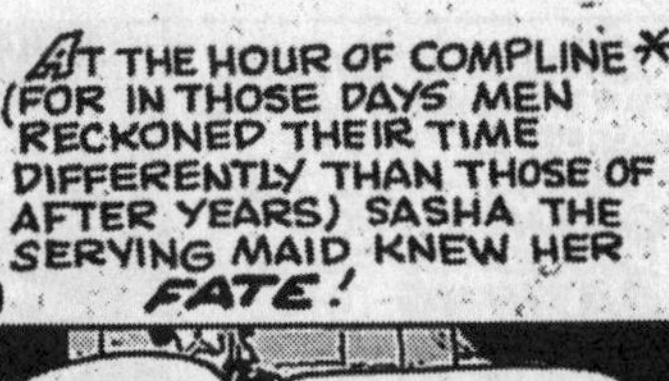
AT THE HOUR OF COMPLINE* (FOR IN THOSE DAYS MEN RECKONED THEIR TIME DIFFERENTLY THAN THOSE OF AFTER YEARS) SASHA THE SERVING MAID KNEW HER FATE!

STRIP HER!
WITH MY OWN HANDS I'LL FLOG HER!
DEAR LORD-- NO!
* 8 P.M.

I'LL TEACH HER TO BREAK MY DISHES!
I WANT TO SEE BLOOD FLOW THIS NIGHT.

NEITHER THE COUNTESS NOR ANYONE ELSE NOTICES THE HUGE BAT THAT FLUTTERS AT THE BARRED WINDOW, PEERING INWARD....

NOR DOES ANYONE HEAR THE BAT-LIKE SQUEAK IT GIVES AS THE COUNTESS BATHORY LASHES THE BARED BACK OF THE SCREAMING GIRL!....

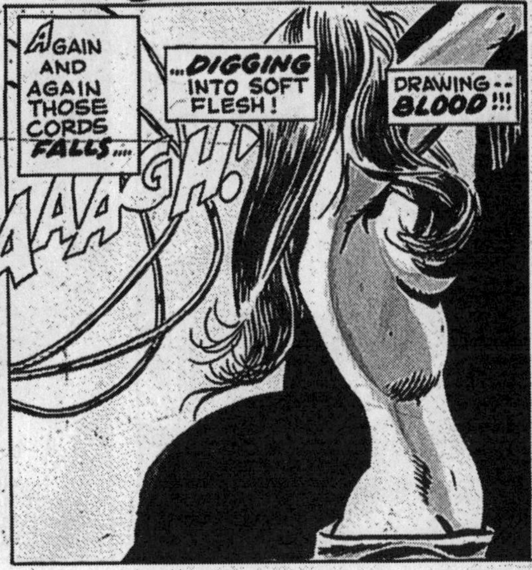
AGAIN AND AGAIN THOSE CORDS FALLS....
...DIGGING INTO SOFT FLESH!
DRAWING.. BLOOD!!!
AAAAGH!

UNTIL -- AFTER ONE PARTICULARLY VICIOUS SWIPE OF THOSE THONGS -- BLOOD GUSHES FROM LACERATED FLESH -- BATHING THE FACE OF THE COUNTESS! ....
INSOLENT WRETCH!
YOU DARE TO SPATTER ME WITH YOUR PEASANT BLOOD?

WHIP HER, FICZKO -- UNTIL SHE DIES.
THEN THROW HER CARCASS ON THE DUNG-HEAP.

AS SHE WALKS FROM THE DUNGEON, THE SHADOW OF A MONSTROUS BAT TOUCHES THE WALL BESIDE HER, BRANDED BY THE MOON ON THE COLD STONE...
I AM TIRED.
I MUST REFRESH MYSELF BEFORE BED.

AND THEN -- AS SHE BATHES AWAY THE BLOOD THAT MARS HER FLESH ...
WHY -- WHAT'S THIS?
MY SKIN, WHERE THE BLOOD TOUCHED IT --
-- SEEMS ALMOST YOUTHFUL!

IT IS!
THERE ARE NO WRINKLES -- NO SAGGING SKIN!
THIS, THEN MUST BE THE SECRET OF ETERNAL YOUTH FOR WHICH I'VE SEARCHED -- THE TOUCH OF HUMAN BLOOD!

I SHALL NEVER GROW OLD NOW.
I HAVE DISCOVERED THE WAY TO STAY YOUNG -- FOREVER!

MOMENTS AFTERWARD, A BAT FLITS THROUGH THE TRANSYLVANIAN NIGHT, WINGING ITS WAY TOWARD CASTLE DRACULA

UNFED -- ITS LONG JOURNEY GONE FOR NAUGHT -- IT SETTLES GROUNDWARD...

UNTIL THE APPROACH OF DAWN DRIVES HIM INTO HIS COFFIN, COUNT DRACULA PACES RESTLESSLY...
THIS COUNTESS BATHORY THREATENS MY VERY LIFE.
ALREADY I HAVE HAD TO RANGE FAR AFIELD FOR THE BLOOD I MUST DRINK TO STAY ALIVE.
SOMEHOW, IN SOME MANNER, I MUST FIND A WAY TO STOP HER!

NOW BEGINS, IN THOSE LANDS ADJACENT TO CASTLE CSEJTHE -- A REIGN OF HORROR AND OF BLOOD-LETTING! FOR GIRLS ARE KIDNAPPED OR HIRED AS SERVANTS...
...ONLY TO GIVE THEIR LIFE'S BLOOD TO MAKE THE COUNTESS YOUNG!

ALWAYS, THERE IS AN OBSERVER AT THESE EVIL RITES WHICH DRAIN THE BLOOD FROM LIVING VIRGINS!
TAKE THAT ONE -- AND THAT!
FATTEN THE OTHERS UP THAT THEY MAY PROVIDE ME WITH THEIR BLOOD NEXT WEEK.

NIGHTLY SHE BATHES IN THAT SCARLET FLUID...
I GROW YOUNGER BY THE HOUR.
AND THE BLOOD DID IT!

IT IS EVEN AS ANCIENT LEGENDS SAY!
WHOEVER SHALL BATHE IN VIRGINS' BLOOD SHALL KNOW THE SECRET OF ETERNAL LIFE!
I SHALL BE IMMORTAL-- AND EVEN MORE BEAUTIFUL!

THEN ONE MOONLIT NIGHT, AS THE COUNTESS HERSELF DIRECTS THE SEARCH FOR MORE VICTIMS TO FEED HER BLOOD-BATH...
I HEARD A CRY, FICZKO!
AYE, YOUR GRACE-- IT CAME FROM UP AHEAD!

A GIRL-- TIED TO A TREE.
PROBABLY HER LOVER DID IT, TO PUNISH HER.
BUT NO MATTER FOR THAT.

THE GIRL IS OURS.
HER BLOOD IS-- MINE!
I THINK NOT, COUNTESS.

AND WHO ARE YOU?
MY NAME IS COUNT DRACULA.
I PUT THAT GIRL HERE-- TO LURE YOU TO ME!

TOO LONG HAVE I WATCHED YOU BATHE IN BLOOD-- IN BLOOD THAT MEANS MY VERY LIFE.
IT IS TIME NOW-- TO STRIKE BACK AT YOU.
FIZCKO! CARLOS! STEFAN!
SLAY THAT MAN!
RASH MORTALS!
NONE MAY STAND BEFORE DRACULA!
NOTHING MUST STOP ME IN MY QUEST FOR YOUTH!
I AM -- THE UNDEAD!
MY MUSCLES ARE NOT AS THOSE OF OTHER MEN.
TO ME-- YOU ARE WEAKER THAN NEWLY BORN BABES!
ZONK!
MY CONCERN IS WITH YOUR MISTRESS-- NOT WITH YOU!
SHE ALONE SHALL FACE MY FANGS.
NO! OHHH-- NO!

AIEEE!
SCREAM OUT YOUR LUNGS IF YOU WILL, COUNTESS-- SO LONG AS YOU DON'T SHED A DROP OF YOUR PRECIOUS BLOOD!
FOR THIS BLOOD IN YOUR VEINS IS-- MINE!

STOP! YOU DON'T KNOW WHAT YOU'LL DO TO ME.
I'LL GROW OLD-- OLD!
WHAT CARE I FOR THAT, DEAR COUNTESS--
--SO LONG AS I LIVE?

THOSE GLITTERING FANGS SINK DEEP! BLOOD FLOWS! DRACULA DRINKS--
--DRINKS DEEP!

AS SHE HAS REVELED IN BLOOD, SO NOW HER TORMENTOR REVELS IN ITS TASTE!....
HAVING TAKEN YOUR BLOOD, I AM NOW YOUR MASTER!
I COMMAND YOU THEREFORE, THAT THESE GIRLS YOU CAPTURE FOR YOURSELF-- YOU BRING TO ME!
AND WHAT MAKES YOU THINK-- I'LL OBEY YOU?

YOU MUST! FOR WHOSOEVER A VAMPIRE BITES-- BECOMES THAT VAMPIRE'S SLAVE!
NOT I!
PERHAPS THE BLOOD IN WHICH I HAVE BATHED PROTECTS ME.
AND YET-- I WOULD MAKE AN ALLIANCE WITH YOU.

MUCH LATER, AS THE TRANSYLVANIAN MOON RISES IN THE NIGHT SKY....

AND YET--THERE MAY BE A WAY!
FOR THIS SARCOPHAGUS THAT HOLDS ME IS OLD-- ROTTED IN MANY PLACES.
AND THE FLOOR BELOW IS CRACKED!

SOMEWHAT PROTECTED FROM THE GARLIC BECAUSE THE COFFIN LID IS CLOSED, THE GREAT VAMPIRE SUMMONS UP HIS POWERS. SLOWLY HIS BODY BEGINS TO CHANGE...
THIS TAKES ALL MY STRENGTH!
BUT ONCE I CHANGE MY BODY SHAPE INTO THAT OF AN EBON FOG...

AND HE EMERGES FROM THE ROTTED COFFIN ALONG THAT VERY CRACK IN THE FLOOR WHICH PERMITS HIS MISTLIKE PROGRESS!
I CAN ESCAPE THE TRAP THE COUNTESS SET FOR ME!

I OFFERED THAT WOMAN MY FRIENDSHIP.
SHE HAS REJECTED ME-- THOUGHT TO TRICK ME.
NOW, BY THE BLOOD THAT FLOWS IN HER VEINS--SHE SHALL PAY THE PENALTY!

I COULD DRINK HER BLOOD-- BUT NOT YET!
FIRST, I MUST SEE HER DISGRACED! HER NAME MADE A BYWORD OF HORROR!

EVEN NOW SHE'S BELOW IN THE DUNGEONS TORTURING THOSE GIRLS.
SO WHILE SHE'S BUSY I'LL HUNT ABOUT FOR WHAT I SEEK.

AHHH-- AND HERE IT IS!
THE COUNTESS' OWN JOURNAL-- DETAILING HER KILLS, THE GIRLS FROM WHOM SHE HAS TAKEN BLOOD!
FASCINATING-- WHO WOULD HAVE DREAMED HER DEPRAVITY EXTENDED BEYOND PEASANT GIRLS--
--TO NOBLEWOMEN!

THESE PAGES SHALL MAKE EVEN MORE FASCINATING READING TO THOSE WHO SERVE KING MATHIAS OF HUNGARY!
AND THESE I SHALL SEND TO COUNT GYORGY THURZO, THE GOVERNOR OF THIS PROVINCE!

UNFORTUNATELY, I CANNOT TAKE THEM TO HIM MYSELF, SO AS TO URGE THE MERITS OF HER INSTANT IMPRISONMENT.
FOR COURT-ROOM TRIALS ARE CONDUCTED IN THE DAYTIME-- WHEN I MUST BE ASLEEP IN MY COFFIN.
BUT JUSTICE SHALL BE DONE!

IN THE COURSE OF TIME, THEN, COUNTESS ELIZABETH BATHORY WAS BROUGHT TO TRIAL...
IT IS THE SENTENCE OF THIS COURT THAT YOU BE WALLED UP ALIVE IN YOUR OWN CASTLE, THERE TO BE FED AND CARED FOR BY THE SERVANTS OF THE KING...
...UNTIL GOD, IN HIS INFINITE WISDOM, SUMMONS YOU TO A HIGHER JUDGMENT THAN OURS!

HER PRIDE AND ARROGANCE BROKEN AT LAST, THE COUNTESS CRUMPLES TO HER KNEES...
MERCY!
I BEG YOU-- LET THE KING HAVE PITY ON ME!
WHAT MERCY DID YOU SHOW THOSE GIRLS YOU TORTURED?
WHAT PITY HAD YOU FOR THEIR SCREAMS OF AGONY?
LET THE SENTENCE OF THIS COURT BE CARRIED OUT!

BRICK BY BRICK, WITH MORTAR AND STONE, A DOORWAY IN CASTLE CSEJTHE IS WALLED UP, LEAVING ONLY A SMALL SPACE THROUGH WHICH TO PASS FOOD...
I'LL GROW OLD IN HERE!
OLD! OLD! OLD!

THERE WAS ALSO A SMALL WINDOW THAT LET IN AIR...
ONCE I OWNED ALL THAT LAND I SEE-- AND THE PEOPLE LIVING THERE.
NOW I OWN NO MORE THAN THIS ROOM!

NOW, ON THIS MOON-DRENCHED NIGHT, THE WINDOW LETS IN ONE MORE THING!

COUNTESS ELIZABETH BATHORY WAKES TO SEE, IN THAT MOON-LIGHT...
YOU!
I HAVE COME FOR THAT BLOOD WHICH IS MINE, COUNTESS!
TOO LONG HAVE YOU DENIED IT TO ME!
NO!
PLEASE LET ME GO...

FANGS SINK DEEP INTO SOFT FLESH!
AND THE BLOOD THAT KEPT HER YOUNG IS NOW DRAINED FROM HER BODY!

THEN-- IN THE MORNING LIGHT...
...THE JAILERS LEARN THE TERRIFYING SECRET OF ELIZABETH BATHORY...
...AND KNOW SHE WILL PREY ON INNOCENTS NO MORE.
FINIS

BEYOND THESE WALLS, THE YEAR IS 1691. YET, WITHIN, TIME IS FORBIDDEN TO TREAD ...SAVE IN THE TORTURED MIND OF THE LORD OF CASTLE DRACULA...
LOOK, SISTERS! SEE HOW OUR MASTER BROODS!
HE'S NOT HIMSELF TONIGHT... NOR STIRS HE ABROAD!
YOU'VE FEASTED WELL ENOUGH THIS FORTNIGHT PAST, BETTINA.
AYE. DON'T THINK TO BREAK HIS MOOD WITH YOUR SIMPERING WAYS.
WE'RE ELDER THAN YOU... AND MUCH YOUR BETTERS IN THAT REGARD!
ROY THOMAS STORY
ALAN WEISS and DICK GIORDANO ART
"SUFFER NOT A WITCH..."

YOU ARE INSOLENT, SISTERS... BUT I'LL BE THE ONE TO SHARE HIS COLD CARESSES TILL THE MORN.
A WAGER, THEN?
DONE!
THERE ARE NAMELESS WORDS AND WHISPERS BEST UNHEARD BY HUMAN EARS...
...THOUGH, TRUTH TO TELL, NO OTHERS SEEM TO HEAR THEM THIS NIGHT...
TILL, SUDDENLY--
AWAY FROM ME, YOU DAMNABLE WRETCHES!
MASTER! HOW HAVE WE OFFENDED YOU?
WE MEANT TO PLEASE, MERELY...!
THEN PLEASE AND PLEASE WELL--
--BY KEEPING CLEAR OF MY SIGHT TILL THE SWEET REST OF DAWN!!
THE SOUND OF SCAMPERING FORMS WHICH CAST NO SHADOW IN MURKY, UNMIRRORED HALLS...THEN, SILENCE...
TILL, AT LENGTH...
HOW COULD THEY EVER HOPE TO PLEASE ME?
WANTONS THEY WERE WHEN I TOOK THEM, IN THE ALLEY-WAYS OF BISTRITZ...
...AND WANTONS THEY SHALL EVER REMAIN.
IT'S A PURER BRIDE I WANT...
...A DEARER BRIDE OF DEATH, AFTER TWO HUNDRED YEARS OF UNLIVING HELL.
A WOMAN WHO'LL COME TO ME WILLINGLY...NOT LIKE THE CHATTEL OF CONQUEST.
BUT WHERE IS SUCH A ONE? WHERE??
WOULD THAT MY ONCE-SOUL COULD SEEK HER OUT...!

Not long ago, America was a VIRGIN LAND. Now, hard stern men have made her their own.
And now, she breeds a softer, GENTLER kind of woman ...girls such as young CHARITY BROWN...

Now, of a sudden, she knows without thinking that she has MORE...
...MUCH more!

MASTER! At last--I see your FACE!
Even more forceful, more GODLIKE than in the DREAMS which came to me, amid last night's troubled SLEEP!
Then, the VOICE whispers again:

"Call me not MASTER, Charity Brown... for I am master of many men, countless women...
"...And my sovereignty has brought me nothing but EMPTINESS and unending PAIN.
"Call me rather your SLAVE... for such I AM!
"A slave to the untouched, untrammeled DELIGHT of you... the VIRTUE I have sensed across a world, and which has summoned me HITHER.
"Will you be MINE, Charity Brown?
"Mine to share ETERNITY with... of your own FREE WILL?"

YES! Oh, in the name of all that's HOLY...
...And by all UNholy things, too...
YES!
Then I will COME to you, girl... as swiftly as I MAY!
And TILL that night, as TOKEN of my troth...
"THIS SIGN...
"...UPON YOUR PURE WHITE BOSOM...!"

THEN, THE VISION VANISHES... THE NIGHT IS STILL ONCE MORE.
AND NOW THE GIRL DANCES AGAIN... EACH MOVEMENT AN ORCHESTRATION OF SHEER SENSUAL DELIGHT, A SYMPHONY OF ECSTASY WHICH WOULD BE OBSCENE IF DANCED BY MANY WOMEN...
...YET WHICH HERE WOULD SEEM STRANGELY, BEAUTIFULLY INNOCENT TO MOST EYES...

...IF NOT TO ALL!

GOODMAN ALDEN, THEY CALL HIM IN THE NEARBY VILLAGE.
HE TOOK LITTLE CHARITY BROWN IN, WHEN HER PARENTS DIED IN THAT HARD COLD WINTER NOW TEN YEARS AGONE.
SHE HAS CHANGED, SINCE THEN...

...AND SO, PERHAPS, HAS HE!
WHY--GOODMAN ALDEN! HOW CAME YOU HERE? I--
DID YE THINK TO STIR FROM MY HOUSE, GIRL--AND I NOT SEE YE?

WAIT--PLEASE! Y-YOU'RE HURTING ME...!
SO YE'VE NO KIND WORDS FOR HIM THAT'S RAISED YE, eh?
YE SAVED THEM FOR THE EMPTY NIGHT--
--OR MAYBE FOR THE DEVIL'S EARS ALONE, IS THAT THE WAY OF IT?

WELL, HE CAN HAVE YOUR WORDS--AND WELCOME TO THEM!
IT'S YOUR KISSES I BE WANTING--AND THEM I'LL HAVE--OR NO ONE SHALL!
NO--PLEASE--

NO!!
STRICKEN, MILES ALDEN FALLS.

CHARITY BROWN FLEES TOWARD THE VILLAGE, AND DOES NOT SCREAM...
...FOR WHO WOULD BELIEVE HER TALE?
WHO... WOULD BE-LIEVE EVIL OF GOODMAN ALDEN?

RUN AS YE WILL, WENCH! DO YE THINK I'LL STOOP TO CHASE THE BEDEVILED LIKES OF YE?
THERE BE OTHER WAYS, GIRL!
OTHER WAYS, DO YE HEAR?
BUT CHARITY BROWN IS TOO FAR AWAY TO HEAR...

...OR CARE.
FOR HER DEMON LOVER IS EVEN NOW ON HIS WAY TO HER, AND EVERY PASSING HOUR BRINGS HER CLOSER TO HIM... AND TO SWEET MYSTERIES OF LIFE-IN-DEATH...
AND SO, SHE WALKS THE STREETS OF THE VILLAGE UNBOWED AND UNASHAMED, NOT THINKING AT ALL OF THE AROUSED WRATH OF GOODMAN ALDEN...

...TILL FAR, FAR TOO LATE!
LOOK AT HER-- THE BRAZEN STRUMPET!
WALKING THE STREET-- AMID GOD-FEARING FOLK!
HOLD HER! SEE IF SHE HAS THE MARK!
WAIT! YOU DON'T KNOW WHAT--

OHHH--!
THERE IT BE!
THE WITCH'S MARK--
--JUST WHERE GOODMAN ALDEN SAID 'TWOULD BE!

THEY ARE GOOD MEN, THE ELDERS OF THE TOWN. THEY WOULD NOT HAVE CONDEMNED CHARITY BROWN, IF THEY HAD A CHOICE...
BUT THE EVIDENCE OF THEIR EYES IS TOO MUCH FOR THESE GOOD MEN. SURELY, THE GIRL IS THE WITCH THAT MILES ALDEN SAYS SHE IS.

AND SO, YOUNG CHARITY LANGUISHES IN JAIL, AFTER A BRIEF AND NIGHTTIME TRIAL...
...A TRIAL SO SHAMEFUL TO THE TOWNSPEOPLE THAT NONE WILL EVER SPEAK OF IT AGAIN...

NONE, THAT IS, SAVE ONE.
DO YE SEE THEM WORKING, GIRL? DO YE HEAR THEM POUND THE HAMMER?
WOULD THE KISSES OF MILES ALDEN HAVE BEEN MORE BITTER THAN THE EMBRACE OF MASTER HEMP?
THE GIRL DOES NOT ANSWER.
HER THOUGHTS ARE BAT-WINGED LEAGUES AWAY...

...In TRANSYLVANIA, which means "The Land beyond the Forest"...

...WHERE THE LORD OF CASTLE DRACULA HARSHLY FLAILS HIS FIERY, NIGHT-BORN STEEDS...

...AND DREAMS OF THAT WHICH IS TO BE!

IT IS SAID THAT THE VAMPIRE CAN CONTROL THE WEATHER, THE VERY ELEMENTS... AND SO IT WOULD TRULY SEEM...
FOR, THE WINDS BLOW WEST-WARD ALL, THIS SPRING OF '91...
...AND A SHIP'S CREW TALKS OF GOOD LUCK ONE DAY, AND WIZARDRY THE NEXT...

...THOUGH HE WHO HAS HIRED THE SHIP SEEMS SCARCELY TO NOTE THEIR CHANGELING MOODS AS HE WALKS THE MID-NIGHT DECKS!

THE PURCHASED COACH, TOO, MAKES BETTER TIME THAN SUCH ARE WONT TO DO... ...TILL, OUTSIDE A VILLAGE FAR FROM BOSTON PORT, IT STOPS IN DEAD OF NIGHT...
AND A SINISTER SHAPE FLITS FORTH!

HIGH ABOVE SPIRES AND ROOFS IT SOARS, AS IF SEARCHING... SEARCHING FOR SOMETHING...
SOMETHING WHICH, AT LAST...
...IT SEES!

THE LIMP, LIFELESS BODY STILL IS FAINTLY WARM.
HE CAME SO CLOSE...SO CLOSE...
BUT NOW, WORDS SPIRAL UPWARD...
SPURN ME, WOULD YE, WENCH?

YE SAVED YOUR SWEET YOUNG KISSES FOR BEELZEBUB; AND NOW HE ALONE WILL HAVE OR WANT 'EM.
I SWORE I'D HAVE YE --OR ELSE NO MAN WOULD!
WELL, I MADE GOOD MY VOW!

--AND WHO'LL RAISE A HAND FOR YE NOW, 'LESS IT BE THE DEVIL

HIMSELLL!
FAITH! WHO BE YOU, SIR-- THAT YOU'VE SO STRONG AN ARM? I--
YOU ASKED FOR THE DEVIL. HE WAS TOO BUSY STOKING HIS FIRES IN EUROPE--

--BUT HE SENT ME IN HIS STEAD!!

TWO SOUNDS, AMID THE STILLNESS OF NIGHT :
THE FAINT FLAPPING OF A DRESS IN THE BREEZE...
THE CRACKING OF BONES THAT CANNOT STAND INHUMAN STRESS.

AND THEN, OF A SUDDEN...

...THERE'S BUT ONE SOUND AGAIN.

OH, CHARITY BROWN-- DEAR MAIDEN--I'D HAVE MADE YOU MINE, A QUEEN OF DARK ETERNITY!
BUT NOW YOU ARE LOST TO ME--LOST, LOST FOREVER!

THEN, WHILE THIS VILLAGE ABIDES...

...WHILE THOSE WHO CONDEMNED YOU YET SLEEP IN FEATHERY BEDS...

...A DEBT IS STILL TO PAY!

THEY'LL FIND MILES ALDEN THERE, COME MORNING, WHEN THEY RISE TO HAUL DOWN THE SWAYING FORM OF CHARITY BROWN.
AND THEY'LL ASK QUESTIONS IN PLENTY, AND PRAY TO A GOD WHO HAS TURNED HIS BACK...
BUT, IN THE END, THEY'LL BURY HIM IN HALLOWED CHURCH-GROUND...

...WHICH IS MORE THAN THEY'LL EVER DO FOR CHARITY BROWN.
AND THRU IT ALL, ONE DARK-SKINNED FIGURE WATCHES, SILENT...

...WATCHES TILL SHADES OF NIGHT FALL ONCE MORE OVER GABLE AND SPIRE.

AT LAST, TOWARD MIDNIGHT, SHE TURNS AND WALKS, EMPTY-EYED, TOWARD THE BECKONING FOREST...
SHE NEVER HEARS THE FOOTSTEPS WHICH PAD SOFTLY, SURELY, BEHIND HER...

...TILL SUDDENLY, TALON HANDS REACH OUT...!
YOU, WOMAN!
I KNOW YOU--FOR YOUR DREAMS HAVE TOUCHED ON MINE, AS WELL!

THEY CALL YOU TITUBA... THEY WHO STOLE YOU AS A YOUNG GIRL FROM ISLANDS FAR TO THE SOUTH...
THEY THINK YOU A BARGAIN, FOR YOU MAKE THEIR MEALS AND TEND THEIR BRATS...

BUT NOW--

AH YES, BUT NOW--YOU'VE THINGS TO DO, TITUBA.
YOU'LL WAIT A TWELVEMONTH, TILL THE HORRIBLE THING THEY'VE DONE THIS NIGHT PAST HAS VANISHED FROM THE MIND AND MEMORY OF THIS SALEM VILLAGE--
AND THEN--YOU KNOW WHAT YOU MUST DO!
YES... MASTER...
I KNOW...

THE FUTURE IS AS DARK AND UNKNOWN TO DRACULA AS TO ANY ROGUE OR FETTERED SLAVE.
AND YET, IT SEEMS FOR A MOMENT AS IF THE BLACK GATES OF TIME STAND OPEN--AND HE CAN GAZE CLEARLY UPON THE EVENTS OF THE YEAR TO COME--
...THE MAD SPECTRE OF A PEOPLE MORE AT WAR WITH EACH OTHER, THAN WITH THE SPIRITS OF NIGHT.
HE SEES IT ALL, OR SO IT SEEMS..
AND HE LAUGHS.
BUT IT IS HOLLOW LAUGHTER, EVEN FOR ONE WHOSE MIRTH IS TINGED WITH THE PALLOR OF THE GRAVE.
AND AT LENGTH, DRACULA THINKS GRIMMER THOUGHTS ONCE MORE.
HE THINKS OF THE GIRL...
...OF CHARITY.
AND HE TURNS, TO STRIDE SADLY BACK TOWARD COACH AND SNORTING STEEDS.
FOR, DAWN IS NEAR...
DAWN, THAT WILL BRING LOVE AND LIFE AND RICHER, FULLER LAUGHTER TO SOME.
AYE... TO SOME.
FINIS

GERRY CONWAY ~ SCRIPT • FRANK SPRINGER ~ ART

HOW SHALL WE TAKE HIM, PIERRE? YOUR KNIFE... OR MY NOOSE?

WE'LL DECIDE THAT WHEN THE MOMENT COMES, MY FRIEND. FOR NOW, WE MUST WAIT. LET MONSIEUR COUNT DRACULA HAVE HIS DINNER.

LATER, WHEN HE SLEEPS...THEN SHALL WE FULFILL OUR LITTLE CONTRACT.

MINUTES MOVE SLOWLY BY, WASHED DOWN WITH SEVERAL MUGS OF FINE WINE... AND WHEN AT LAST THE COUNT HAS RETIRED, HIS WOULD-BE ASSASSINS MAKE THEIR FIRST TENTATIVE MOVE...

...FIRST FLOOR, THIRD ROOM TO THE RIGHT. HE INSISTED ON THE BEST, THE ARISTOCRATIC PIG.

I HAD TO GIVE HIM MY OWN ROOM... MINE!

HE IS INDEED AN ANIMAL, MY FAT FRIEND. IF YOU WOULD HAVE HIM RECEIVE HIS DUE...

...SEE THAT WE'RE NOT DISTURBED

YOU UNDERSTAND?

OUI, MONSIEUR... I UNDERSTAND.

THAT NOOSE WAS FOR *ME*, WAS IT NOT? HOW FORTUNATE THAT I AM A MOST *FORGIVING* MAN.

ANY *OTHER* MIGHT SEEK *RETRIBUTION!*

PIERRE, IN THE NAME OF *GOD*--

HELP ME! HELP MEEEEEGHH!

YAAAAAAAAAAAAAHH!

MON DIEU! YOU TORE HIS *THROAT* OUT, LIKE SOME SORT OF WILD *ANIMAL!*

NOT *TRUE*, MY NIGHT-STALKING ENEMY... NOT AS A WILD ANIMAL AT *ALL*.

PERHAPS IN FRANCE YOU ARE *UNFAMILIAR* WITH BEINGS OF THE *SUPERNATURAL...*

...IN WHICH CASE, I MUST *COMPLETE* YOUR EDUCATION. FOR YOU SEE, MY FRIEND...I COME FROM *TRANSYLVANIA*...AND THERE I AM CALLED BY QUITE *ANOTHER* NAME--

--I AM CALLED *VAMPIRE!*

IEEEEEEEEEE

IS IT DONE? IS THE NOBLEMAN DEA-- URLP.
NO, OBESE ONE. I AM NOT DEAD. AT LEAST...NOT IN A MANNER YOU WOULD COMPREHEND.
KARLOS, READY THE COACH, AND TRANSFER MY...LUGGAGE. WE SHALL NOT STAY THE NIGHT HERE AFTER ALL.
...AND I WISH TO REACH PARIS BEFORE THE DAWN!
AT THAT MOMENT IN A PLUSH, DARKENED ROOM IN THE PALACE OF LOUIS XVI, THE KING OF FRANCE, A MUTTERED CURSE CUTS THROUGH A HEAVY SILENCE...
DAMN HIS NOBLEMAN'S EYES!
ALESANDRO...WHAT WILL YOU DO NOW? THIS COUNT DRACULA IS NOT AS EASY TO DISPOSE OF AS YOU THOUGHT.
...FOR AM I NOT ALESANDRO DI CAGLIOSTRO, THE GREATEST MASTER OF MAGIC SINCE THE DAWN OF MODERN MAN?
WHAT IS THIS DRACULA TO ME? I, WHO HAVE LIVED TWO THOUSAND YEARS...
...I, WHO KNOW THE SECRETS OF ALCHEMY THE MASTERS THEMSELVES COULD NEVER DEFINE. HE IS NOTHING TO ME.
NOTHING!
...YET STILL... HE MUST BE DESTROYED!
SO IT APPEARS, LORENZA, MY DARLING WIFE.
STILL... THOSE TWO MERCENARIES WERE BUT PAWNS IN THIS GAME. I HAVE OTHER, FAR MORE POTENT PIECES TO PLAY...
THIS I SWEAR! LET IT FALL ON MY IMMORTAL SOUL!

A DAY PASSES, AND EARLY THE NEXT EVENING, IN THE COURT OF THE KING OF FRANCE...
...FURTHER BUSINESS, OR ANY NEW VISITORS TO OUR COURT? THE HOUR GROWS LATE AND WE WOULD HAVE OUR SUPPER.
SIRE, I BELIEVE THERE IS YET ANOTHER GUEST TO OUR LAND.. ..A COUNT FROM DISTANT TRANSYLVANIA.
HE SENT A MESSAGE BEGGING AN AUDIENCE WITH THE KING!
A COUNT, YOU SAY? FROM TRANSYLVANIA? HOW UNUSUAL.
BY ALL MEANS... SHOW THE COUNT INTO OUR PRESENCE. WE WILL BE MOST PLEASED TO MEET HIM.
SIRES, THE LORD COUNT... DRACULA.
YOUR MAJESTIES, I AM INDEED HONORED.
EVEN IN MY DISTANT COUNTRY...THE GOODNESS AND NOBILITY OF LOUIS THE SIXTEENTH AND OF HIS QUEEN, MARIE ANTOINETTE...IS LEGEND.
I HAVE COME TO PRESENT A HUMBLE GIFT...
...AND TO BEG A SMALL BUT MEANINGFUL FAVOR.
WHY... THESE JEWELS ARE MOST DELIGHTFUL, COUNT DRACULA. NEVER HAVE I SEEN SUCH GEMS...OR SUCH SETTINGS.
YOU DO FLATTER US WITH YOUR GIFTS ...DOES HE NOT, LOUIS?
MOST ASSUREDLY. THESE BAUBLES ARE QUITE...PLEASANT.
WHAT MAY WE DO FOR YOU IN TURN, COUNT?
AT THE MOMENT, MY COUNTRY IS IN TURMOIL...AND FOR THE PRESENT-- I PREFER TO AVOID THAT TURMOIL.
IF YOUR MAJESTY DOES NOT OBJECT... I WOULD LIKE TO REQUEST A PLACE AT YOUR COURT...
AS ONE OF YOUR ADVISORS, PERHAPS.

BUT OF COURSE, COUNT DRACULA! A SUITE WILL BE FOUND FOR YOU AT ONCE!
IN THE MEANTIME, YOU MUST MEET OUR OTHER ADVISOR, THE COUNT ALESSANDRO DI CAGLIOSTRO!
I AM PLEASED TO BE AT YOUR SERVICE, COUNT DRACULA.
AND I, AT YOURS, COUNT CAGLIOSTRO!
AT YOUR SERVICE, THAT IS, UNTIL YOU MOVE AGAINST ME ONCE MORE...
THEN SHALL WE SEE WHO IS THE MORE POWERFUL FORCE...CAGLIOSTRO OR DRACULA!
BUT, A VAMPIRE DOES NOT LIVE BY HATRED ALONE: THERE MUST ALSO BE SUSTENANCE OF A SORT...AND SO, THAT EVENING, AFTER ALL OTHERS IN THE PALACE HAVE GONE TO THEIR REST...
THE YOUNG WOMAN HURRIES. HER MISTRESS MUST HAVE GIVEN HER AN IMPORTANT ERRAND TO RUN...ELSE SHE WOULD NOT BE OUT ON SUCH A BITTER EVENING...
WHAT A PITY FOR HER SHE WAS NOT MORE INDEPENDENT.
HER OBEDIENCE HAS COST HER--HER LIFE!
EEEEEEEEEEE
EEEEEEEE
THE MASTER HAS FOUND HIS NIGHT'S REPAST. HE WILL WISH HIS COFFIN READY, THAT HE MAY REPOSE IN THE EARTH OF HIS HOMELAND.
IT IS KARLOS' PLACE TO SERVE...AND SO HE SHALL...
...FOR THE MASTER TREATS ME WELL...
...AND MORE THAN THIS, NO SERVANT MAY RIGHTFULLY BEG...

A SERVANT MAY RIGHTFULLY EXPECT LIFE...AND WHEN HIS LIFE IS THREATENED BY HIS VERY PROXIMITY TO HIS MASTER, THEN A SERVANT MAY LEAVE...
...IF OF COURSE...HE EVER GETS THE CHANCE.
YOU SEE, LORENZA MY MAGICKS PERFORM PERFECTLY.
THE COUNT'S SERVANT DIES QUICKLY--ALMOST WITHOUT RESISTANCE. THE TENDRILS OF DEATH --AS ALWAYS--WORK THEIR POWERS WELL.
YOU ARE INDEED A MASTER, HUSBAND.
NONE CAN SURPASS YOU.
SOON, DRACULA, TOO, WILL FALL BEFORE MY SORCERY...AND NO ONE WILL RIVAL MY INFLUENCE IN LOUIS' COURT.
DRACULA WAS A FOOL TO ATTEMPT TO USURP MY POSITION AS THE KING'S EXCLUSIVE ADVISOR...I SAW HIS INTENTIONS AT ONCE, IN MY CRYSTAL.
NOW, IN A MATTER OF HOURS...
...THE LORD OF DARKNESS... WILL BE ONE WITH DEATH.
JUST THEN, IN THE SUITE, ASSIGNED TO THE COUNT FROM TRANSYLVANIA...
KARLOS!
CAGLIOSTRO DARES TOUCH ME HERE -- AND IN SUCH A MANNER?
THE MAN HAS THE ARROGANCE OF A JACKAL. HE SHALL PAY FOR THIS HUMILIATION.
HE SHALL PAY A PRICE MOST DEAR!

YOU!
I WOULD HAVE WORDS WITH YOU, IMPOSTER.
THEN ENTER, DEVIL PRINCE. AS I TOLD YOU BEFORE...
...I AM YOURS TO COMMAND.
IN THAT CASE, I COMMAND YOU--DIE!
YOUR CONTINUED EXISTENCE ANNOYS M--EH?
SORCERY!
WHAT ELSE DID YOU EXPECT, COUNT? AM I NOT THE MASTER OF THE BLACK ARTS?
IS NOT THE VERY NAME OF CAGLIOSTRO A BYWORD FOR MYSTIC CONTROL?
STRUGGLE, DARK PRINCE-- FEEL THE VAPOR CLAWS TIGHTEN ABOUT YOU, CHOKING YOU--REACHING WITHIN YOUR VERY SPIRIT.
YOU HAVE MERE SECONDS OF LIFE REMAINING, DEAR COUNT. USE THEM WISELY.
THEY ARE THE LAST YOU SHALL EVER KNOW.
BY SATAN'S SEVEN SINS-- NO!
DRACULA IS NO MAN'S SLAVE...NOT NOW... NEVER!
YOUR STRENGTH SURPRISES ME, VAMPIRE. I'D LIKE TO TEST IT IN A MORE MORTAL FORM--
--AGAINST THAT PHYSICAL POWER GIVEN ME BY MY SPELLS--
--A MIGHT WHICH WILL STILL DESTROY YOU--FOR ALL TIME!

I FEAR YOU WILL BE DISAPPOINTED IN THAT GOAL, COUNT CAGLIOSTRO. YOURS IS THE PHYSICAL STRENGTH OF MORTAL MAN--
--MINE IS THE POWER OF THE UNDEAD!
YOUR EYES--SO COMPELLING--!
RELEASE YOURSELF, CAGLIOSTRO. RELEASE YOURSELF WILLINGLY TO MY FANGS--
--FOR WILLING OR NO, YOUR THROAT--AND SOON YOUR SOUL--IS MINE! MINE!
LORENZA! IN THE NAME OF PITY, WIFE--HELP ME!
KRAK!
THANK YOU, MY DEAR. I WAS ABOUT TO COMMIT AN ERROR MOST GRAVE.
I MEANT TO REPAY YOUR HUSBAND IN KIND FOR THE OFFENSE HE COMMITTED WHEN HE KILLED MY MAN-SERVANT... AND ALMOST, I FORGOT THIS INTENTION...
...BUT YOU HAVE BEEN A RATHER EFFICIENT REMINDER!
IIEEEEEEEEEEEEEEE

THE NEXT NIGHT, AS THE COURT RECONVENES AFTER A LENGTHY SUPPER...
AHHH... COUNT DRACULA. I SEE YOU ARE STILL AMONG US.
THAT IS A SITUATION I STILL HOPE TO RECTIFY, I ASSURE YOU.
SO? ARE YOU WELL, COUNT CAGLIOSTRO?
YOUR WIFE LOOKS... ILL.
SHE ALMOST DIED, DRACULA...AS YOU WELL KNOW. BUT FOR MY DOCTORING, SHE WOULD NOW BE A CORPSE...
...BECAUSE OF YOUR INSANE APPETITE FOR BLOOD.
I SEE. NOW I AM THE VILLAIN, IS THAT IT?
OR, DO YOU FORGET, COUNT, YOU WERE THE MAN WHO FIRST ATTACKED ME?
I ADMIT NOTHING OF THE KIND.
THE FAULT IS YOURS, BECAUSE YOU DARE ATTEMPT TO WEAKEN MY INFLUENCE ON THE COURT.
YOU ARE A PETTY FOOL, CAGLIOSTRO... BUT A DANGEROUS ONE.
I, TOO, CAN BE DANGEROUS, HOWEVER, AS YOU WILL SHORTLY LEARN, BUT NOW, PLEASE FORGIVE ME...
I HAVE BUSINESS ELSEWHERE...AND HAVE NO TIME FOR DEALING WITH A FOOL AND HIS PITIFULLY DECEASED WIFE.
YOU HAVE BUSINESS ALL RIGHT, MY FRIEND--WITH A STONECUTTER OF MY ACQUAINTANCE. BUT THAT YOU WILL DISCOVER FOR YOURSELF. FOR NOW...
WHAT DID YOU MEAN ABOUT MY WIFE?
SPEAK CLEARLY, OR NOT AT ALL.
THEN YOU TRULY DON'T KNOW? MY POOR, IGNORANT ENEMY!
HUMANS DIE FROM A VAMPIRE'S BITE... A TRUE DEATH WHICH LASTS ONE FULL DAY.
AT THE END OF THAT TIME, THEY RISE AGAIN, SEEMINGLY ALIVE...
...AND YET AS DEAD AS THE DEAD ONE WHO KISSED THEM.
FOR YOU SEE, THEY ARE DEAD...YET UNDEAD... FOR THOSE BITTEN TAKE ON THE CURSE...
...AND JUST AS YOUR WIFE, THEY GAIN THE NAME... AND THE ATTENDANT NEED OF A NIGHTMARE-BORN...
VAMPIRE!
YAAAAAAAAH!
FIN

SHADOW OVER VERSAILLES
STORY: TONY ISABELLA
ART: JOHN BUSCEMA & PABLO MARCOS
IT IS SUMMER IN FRANCE, A TIME OF WARM EVENING BREEZES THAT CARESS THE SOUL... A TIME OF YOUNG THINGS BURSTING INTO VIBRANT LIFE. THE YEAR IS 1789.
PLANCHET HAD PRETENDED NOT TO NOTICE HENRI'S FURTIVE EXIT FROM THE TAVERN WHERE HE EMPLOYED THE LAD. HE'D SEEN HENRI TALKING TO THAT RADIANT YOUNG WOMAN EARLIER AND HE KNEW...
...KNEW, AS ONLY AN OLD MAN COULD, THE WAYS OF THE YOUNG.
A MOON-LIT MEETING, WHISPERED WORDS, AND WARM KISSES UNDER THE STARS... THESE WERE THE THINGS PLANCHET KNEW HENRI WOULD FIND THIS NIGHT.
HE WAS WRONG. HENRI HAD FOUND SOMETHING ELSE.
HENRI HAD FOUND DEATH.

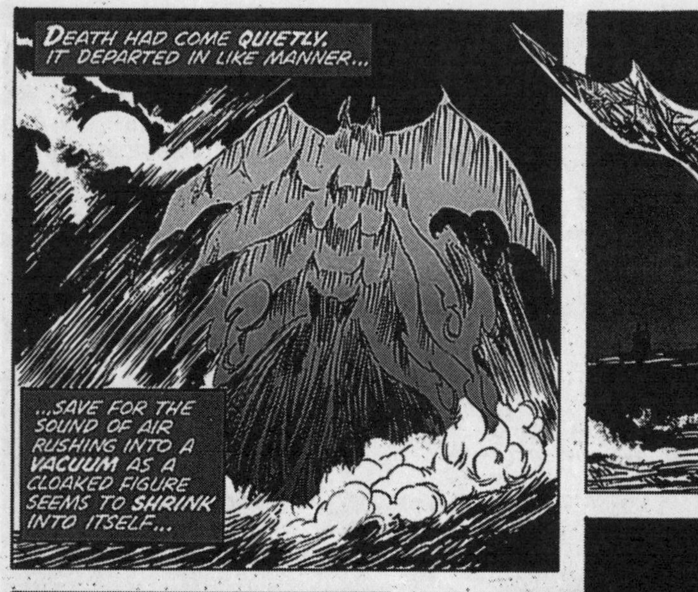
DEATH HAD COME QUIETLY. IT DEPARTED IN LIKE MANNER...
...SAVE FOR THE SOUND OF AIR RUSHING INTO A VACUUM AS A CLOAKED FIGURE SEEMS TO SHRINK INTO ITSELF...

...AND THE RUSTLE OF LEATHERY WINGS HEADING TOWARD THE GAUDY BRIGHT LIGHTS OF THE PALACE OF VERSAILLES.

FROM A TOWER WINDOW, A MAN WATCHES THE FLIGHT OF THAT DARK SHADOW.
HE IS NOT LIKE OTHER MEN.

HE IS CALLED DRACULA...
...LATE A TRANSYLVANIAN COUNT...
...CURRENTLY SERVING AS AN ADVISOR TO THE COURT OF LOUIS XVI AND MARIE ANTOINETTE...
...BUT NOW AND FOR-EVER...
...PRINCE OF EVIL, LORD OF VAMPIRES!
SOME SAY THERE IS NOT A BEING ON EARTH WHO DOES NOT SHUDDER AT HIS PENETRATING GAZE...
...EVEN AMONG HIS OWN UNDEAD LEGIONS.
THEY EXAGGERATE, OF COURSE. THERE ARE THOSE WHO DO NOT FEAR DRACULA...
MERELY HATE HIM.
SOME, LIKE THE TWO MEN WHO STAND BY A WAITING CARRIAGE IN THE COURTYARD BELOW, FOR REASONS...
...THAT SPRING FROM THE MOST ALL-CONSUMING DIRECTIVES OF THEIR IMMORTAL SOULS!

GOOD LORD! IS THIS THEN WHY YOU ORDERED SUCH ODD PREPARATIONS IN THE VILLAGE? WHY YOU EVEN NOW PREPARE TO ABAN-DON FRANCE AT SUCH A CRUCIAL MOMENT IN HER HISTORY?

WOULD YOU HAVE ME ABANDON INSTEAD THE WOMAN WHO IS LIFE ITSELF TO ME? NO! I WILL FIND A CURE FOR THIS CURSE DRACULA HAS PLACED UPON HER*--

--AND I WILL ALSO HAVE MY VENGEANCE ON THE TRANSYLVANIAN--IF YOU AND OTHERS CARRY OUT THE PLAN I HAVE OUTLINED FOR HIM!

*LAST ISSUE. --R.T.

"THE SIGNS ARE THERE-- FOR THE ALERT.
"LOUIS' LACK OF INITIATIVE... THE UNPOPULARITY OF HIS FOREIGN-BORN QUEEN...MARIE'S FILLING THE COURT WITH FRIENDS AND MERCENARIES FROM OTHER SHORES.
"NO WONDER THE CLERGY AND MY FELLOW NOBLES WERE ABLE TO PRESSURE THE CROWN INTO SUMMONING THE ESTATES-GENERAL.
"THE AMERICAN REVOLUTION HAS STIRRED THE HEARTS OF THE LOWER CLASSES. THEY WANT EQUALITY.
"TODAY, THEY ARE SATISFIED WITH REPRESENTATION IN THE ESTATES-GENERAL.
"BUT WHAT OF TOMORROW?
"THE SAD STATE OF THE ROYAL TREASURY LEAVES THE KING WITHOUT SUFFICIENT RESOURCES TO REGAIN HIS DWINDLING POWER.

"THE TENSION BETWEEN THE KING AND THE ESTATES-GENERAL GROWS DAILY. LOUIS IGNORES THEIR DEMANDS TO BE FREE OF THE ROYAL VETO IN MAKING THEIR DECISIONS.
"THE PEOPLE ARE DISGRUNTLED.

"AND THE LESSON OF HISTORY IS THAT DISSATISFIED PEOPLE CAN BE USED...
"...BE THEY NOBLES SEEKING THE 'ADVICE' OF THE COURT'S LEADING ADVISOR WHOM THEY 'KNOW' TO BE SYMPATHETIC TO THE CAUSE THEY ESPOUSE...

"...OR BE THEY COMMONERS BELIEVING IN GOOD LORD MONTPLIER, THE KINDLY OLD NOBLE WHO TREATS THEM AS EQUALS...
"...AND FOR WHOM THEY WOULD DARE ANYTHING!

"WE WERE MOVING THE COURSE OF THE FUTURE IN OUR FAVOR, CAGLIOSTRO AND I, UNTIL THE DAY DRACULA CAME TO COURT.*
"AND, INSTEAD OF SEEING THE FOREIGN COUNT AS AN ALLY, CAGLIOSTRO DEEMED HIM AN ENEMY! THE FOOL OF AN ALCHEMIST!"
*ALSO LAST ISSUE. --R.T.

BUT THIS FEUD BETWEEN THE COUNTS IS NOT UNWELCOME. IT HAS ALREADY DRIVEN CAGLIOSTRO FROM FRANCE...

...AND NOW PROMISES TO DESTROY THIS SELF-STYLED LORD OF VAMPIRES. WHO KNOWS BUT THAT WHEN THIS LITTLE SEGMENT OF HISTORY HAS COME TO A CLOSE...

...EVEN ONE SUCH AS I MIGHT CONCEIVABLY RULE IN FRANCE? EVEN ONE SUCH AS I...

OUTSIDE VERSAILLES LIES THE VILLAGE. IT HAS HAD MANY NAMES, EACH DETERMINED BY A WHIM OF WHOEVER HAPPENED TO BE WARMING THE ROYAL THRONE AT THE TIME.
IT HAS OUT-LIVED ALL ITS PREVIOUS NAMES, EN-DURING WITH A KIND OF IM-MORTALITY KINGS CAN ONLY DREAM ABOUT.
DANIELLE ROBINET HAS LIVED HERE ALL OF HER EIGHTEEN YEARS. SHE HAS LOOKED AT THE LIGHTS OF THE VERSAILLES PALACE AND WONDERED WHAT GRANDEUR LAY BEYOND THAT ILLUMINATION.

SOMEDAY, SHE THINKS, SHE WILL FIND OUT.
BUT NOT TONIGHT.
FOR DRACULA HAS LOOKED UPON DANIELLE ROBINET AND FOUND HER FAIR.

SHE SEES THE BAT-FORM HOVERING ABOVE HER, BUT REVEALS NO FEAR. SHE MERELY WALKS INTO THIS DEAD END ALLEY AS THE LORD MONTPLIER HAD ASKED.
SHE DOES NOT QUES-TION THE WHY OF THIS.
SHE ONLY REMEMBERS THAT ONCE THE KINDLY LORD SENT HIS PERSONAL PHYSICIAN TO CARE FOR HER SICK MOTHER.

AND THAT IS ALL SHE NEEDS TO KNOW.

FOR DRACULA, LIFE IS NOT QUITE SO SIMPLE. HE HAS TO BE CAREFUL IN THIS FOREIGN LAND.

ANY MYSTERIOUS DEATHS AMONG THE NOBLES COULD AROUSE THEIR SUSPICIONS ABOUT THE FOREIGNER A-MONG THEM. TOO MANY DEATHS AMONG THE COM-MONERS COULD EMPTY THE STREETS AT NIGHT.
AND THAT WOULD NEVER DO.
STILL, EVEN THE CAUTIOUS MAKE MISTAKES...

...AS WHEN DRACULA FAILS TO NOTICE THAT DANIELLE WAS THE ONLY PERSON WHO WALKED THE VILLAGE STREETS THIS EVE...

...BAIT FOR A TRAP...

...WHICH HAS NOW BEEN SPRUNG!

GO NO FURTHER, VAMPIRE!

AYE! OR WE'LL BURN THE VERY LIFE OUT OF YOU WITH THESE CROSSES!

WHAT--A MOB? AN ACCURSED MOB!

MOB WE BE, DEMON--BUT STILL MASTERS OF YOUR FATE!

NO MAN IS MY MASTER!

I SAY WE KILL HIM NOW!

NO! HE'LL BE TURNED OVER TO LORD MONTPLIER--AS WE PROMISED!

HE NEVER SUSPECTED WE WAITED FOR HIM ABOVE AS WELL AS BELOW!
HA! I STRUCK HIM!

THIS GARLAND OF GARLIC WILL STILL HIS FLIGHT!
SEE? HE FALLS!

SAINTS! HE'S CHANGED BACK TO HIS HUMAN FORM BEFORE OUR VERY EYES!

HE'S DOWN!
AT HIM! LET'S SHOW MARIE WHAT WE THINK OF HER FOREIGN MERCENARIES!

BACK, YOU MURDEROUS RABBLE!

LORD! HE CURSED AND FOUGHT TILL THE END!
NO MATTER! IT WILL BE MANY HOURS AFORE HIS EYES OPEN AGAIN!
JUST THE SAME--
--LET'S HAVE HIM OFF TO MONTPLIER LONG BEFORE THEY DO!

IT IS AN HOUR BEFORE DAWN WHEN BLOOD-RED EYES GROGGILY OPEN TO STARE DOWN AT MOSS-WET STONES...
...AND PUNGENT GARLIC BALLS THAT RELEASE AN OFFENSIVE FRAGRANCE INTO THE VAMPIRE-LORD'S FACE.
THE STIFLING SCENT CAUSES TEARS TO FORM IN HIS EYES. BUT WHEN HE TRIES TO WIPE THEM DRY...
...HE FINDS HIS ARMS SECURELY BOUND TO CROSSES THAT BURN HIM AT THE SLIGHTEST TOUCH.
AT LAST YOU AWAKE, MY DEAR COUNT DRACULA. I FEARED MY FRIENDS HAD BEEN OVERLY ENTHUSIASTIC IN DELIVERING MY INVITATION.
THOUGH HIS MIND SEETHES AT THE THOUGHT, DRACULA KNOWS WHAT HAS BEFALLEN HIM...
HE IS A PRISONER!

MONTPLIER! YOU SHALL PAY FOR THIS IGNOMINIOUS SCHEME OF YOURS--
--PAY WITH YOUR LIFE!

OH REALLY, COUNT?
REALLY?
GAGGHHH!

SAVE YOUR THREATS, DRACULA! YOU HAVE BEEN BROUGHT TO THIS LITTLE-USED PARISIAN PRISON FOR ONE PURPOSE ONLY--
--TO HERALD THE COMING OF A NEW FRANCE!

YOUR EXECUTION WILL BE THE FIRST REAL ACTION TAKEN AGAINST THE CROWN. IT WILL INSPIRE THE PEASANTS TO REVOLT!
FOOL! YOU CANNOT KILL A VAMPIRE!
AU CONTRAIRE, COUNT--

"THE GUILLOTINE WILL SERVE ADMIRABLY IN THAT RESPECT. BEHEADING HAS BEEN KNOWN TO DESTROY YOUR KIND.
"AND WHEN THE REVOLUTION YOU WILL AID IS FINISHED, WHO ELSE WILL THE RABBLE TURN TO FOR LEADERSHIP THAN THEIR LOYAL FRIEND--
"--THE GOOD LORD MONTPLIER!"

LORD MONTPLIER! THERE'S SOME SORT OF DISTURBANCE WITHOUT! PEASANTS ARE CHARGING THE GATES-- TRYING TO RAM DOWN THE DOORS!
WHY?
AH, MONTPLIER, STUDENT OF HISTORY, HOW COULD EVEN YOU KNOW THAT WHOLE FUTURE TEXTS WOULD BE DEVOTED TO EXPLAINING JUST WHY--
--ON JULY 14, 1789, THE LOWER CLASSES OF PARIS CHOSE--
PEASANTS ATTACKING THIS FORTRESS? BUT WHY? FOR HEAVEN'S SAKE, MAN--
--TO STORM THE BASTILLE!

IT'S MONTPLIER!
HE PRETENDED TO BE OUR FRIEND--BUT KEEPS THE KING'S POLITICAL ENEMIES PRISONERS HERE!
SOMEBODY FREE THAT POOR MAN!

PATIENCE, MON AMI! ANDRÉ THE LOCKSMITH WILL SOON RELEASE YOU FROM THESE ROYAL CHAINS!

DRACULA THANKS YOU, GOOD LOCKSMITH!
DRACULA?
ANDRÉ! HE'S ONE OF THE FOREIGN KILLERS WHO SERVES MARIE AND LOUIS!

SEIZE THE-- UHN!
ARE ALL FRENCH-MEN INSANE?
DRACULA SERVES NO ONE'S INTERESTS--
SAVE HIS OWN!
AND WITH THAT, HE IS GONE...
...UNTIL THE FOLLOWING EVENING...

I DEEPLY REGRET THIS INCIDENT, COUNT DRACULA, BUT PERHAPS WE CAN TURN IT TO OUR...ADVANTAGE?
AND HOW WOULD WE DO THAT, YOUR HIGHNESS?
YOU COULD USE YOUR VAMPIRIC POWERS TO...KEEP SOME ORDER IN FRANCE. NO ONE WOULD QUESTION OUR REIGN WITH YOU SERVING AS OUR...ADVISOR.

SO...YOU WHO HAVE FAILED TO KEEP A STRONG REIN ON YOUR KINGDOM WOULD NOW RULE BY TERROR. I FEAR I CANNOT AID YOU, YOUR MAJESTIES...
...FOR, I FIND THE PRESENCE OF FOOLS EVEN MORE ODIOUS THAN THE MOST FOUL GARLIC!

HAVE A CARE, COUNT, WE CAN--
NO, MY KING. WE CANNOT THREATEN SUCH AS HE WITH DEATH...

"...FOR HE WALKS EVER IN ITS SHADOW...

"...WHILE MORTALS MUST TREMBLE IN FEAR AND SADNESS...
"...AT ITS INEVITABLE APPROACH."
FINIS

ASSAULT OF THE SHE-PIRATE!

--A WOMAN WHOSE NOTORIETY STRETCHES FROM TRIPOLI TO CONSTANTINOPLE...
...A WOMAN NAMED... HELLYN de VILL!
...WHOSE CUT-THROAT CREW FOLLOWS HER LEAD LIKE DROOLING DOGS...
LOWER THE BOATS, YE LOUSY SCUM!
WE LEAVE THIS BLACK SEA FOR OUR GREATEST PLUNDER!
SOMEWHAT LATER...
...AND NOW TO RIVERBANK! WE TAKE TO THE LAND!
'TWILL BE NONE THE SOONER--
--WE'VE ROWED A MONTH UP THIS DAMNED DANUBE!
HUSH YE-- HELLYN'LL HAVE YOUR HEAD IF SHE HEARS YE!
HUSTLE YER BLASTED BUTTS, MAGGOTS--OR I'LL BE ROASTIN' 'EM ON TONIGHT'S FIRE!
TWO WEEKS HENCE...
WE T'AINT SEEN EVEN A RIVER IN A FORT-NIGHT, CAPTAIN!
AND YOU'VE A FEW MORE NIGHTS AWAY, CURS--
--BUT OUR TREASURE'LL BE ALL THE FINER FOR IT!
THEN FINALLY...
THERE IT IS!
CASTLE DRACULA-- THE RICHEST MANOR IN TEN THOUSAND LEAGUES!
YE'LL SOON BE BATHIN' IN BOOTY, MATIES--
--WHILE THE DRACULA PENDANT SHALL BE MINE FOR THE WEARIN'!
BUT FIRST-- THERE LIES A VILLAGE 'TWEEN US-- AND WE'VE BEEN LONG FROM SOME HEARTY PLEASURES!
THE CREW NEEDS NO FURTHER INVITATION-- AND THE QUIET WALLACHIAN VILLAGE SCARCELY EXPECTS AN ONSLAUGHT OF A PIRATE'S LUSTS--
--FOR INSANE PLUNDER--
KRASH!
--INSENSITIVE RAPE--
BAM!
--AND YES, FOR BLOOD!
THERE ARE THOSE WITH SLEEP-FILLED EYES WHO RESIST--

--BUT THEY ARE CUT DOWN LIKE HARVEST WHEAT!
DIE, PEASANT--YE'LL NOT STOP OUR RAID ON THE CASTLE!
CASTLE... DRACULA?...
THEN... MY DEATH IS NOTHING TO WHAT... YOU FACE... ARRRRRGGG
DAWN BREAKS--AND THE CASTLE IS OURS!
TO THE CASTLE!
TO THE CASTLE!
AND SO, AS DRACULA SLEEPS THIS DAY, THE MARAUDERS ENTER...
AIIEE? WHAT DEMONS HAUNT THIS PLACE? 'TIS COMPLETE-LY DESERTED.
THE SUN SHINES FULL OUTSIDE--BUT NO LIGHT ENTERS 'ERE!
AYE'VE 'EARD STORIES ABOUT THIS DRACULA! COULD IT BE--?
DAMN YE FOR SWINE!
ARE YE LIKE COWERING SCULLERY-MAIDS?
FIND ME THE PENDANT! AND HE WHO DOES, SHALL WARM HELLYN'S BED TONIGHT.
AS FOR THE REST OF YE--
--THERE'S TREASURE A-PLENTY FOR YE ALL!
BY ME MOTHER'S LOVER--HELLYN'S RIGHT, ME MATES!
'ERE'S LIQUID GOLD--THE FINEST BREWS IN ALL 'O EUROPE!
DRINK T'YER DEATH, YE DAFT LUSH!
THE REST OF US ARE SEEKIN' THE PENDANT--
--AN' HELLYN'S WARM REWARD!
CAP'N--CAP'N--LOOK! THE PENDANT YE'RE WISHIN'--
--AYE'VE FOUND IT!

TIS ENOUGH TO WARM A QUEEN'S HEART--
--AND NOW, TO WARM MINE!
'AT AIN'T ALL YE'LL HAVE TA GET YE HOT, HELLYN--
--BACK 'N ROME THEY CALL BLACKIE, 'ERE, A REG'LAR STOVE! HAR! HAR!
HMMM... WE'LL SEE WHO WARMS WHO, BLACKIE AN' I -- BUT YE'LL NOT BE WATCHIN', ABDUL!
WHERE'D YE FIND IT, BLACKIE?
IN 'ERE, CAP'N-- NEXT TA THIS 'ERE COFFIN!
TOO BAD THE COUNT ISN'T HERE--HE MUST BE A MADMAN!
COME, NOW--YE'VE HAD TIME ENOUGH FOR GRABBIN' YER BOOTY! LET'S BE OFF--BACK TO TH' SHIP!
BOOMP!
LOOK 'ERE-- PATCH'S DRUNK AGAIN!
DROOLIN' PIG!
LET'S LEAVE TH' SLOB-- DESERVES 'IM RIGHT! AFTER WE DID ALL THE WORK.
HIC HIC
DEE-VINE... DEE-VINE... HIC
SO THE PIRATES' LONG RETURN JOURNEY IS MADE--ALL THE SWIFTER FOR THEIR DESIRE TO LEAVE THE LAND AND REACH THE SEA!
THEN ABOARD...
...YE'VE BEEN PUTTIN' MY RE-WARD OFF LONG ENOUGH, CAP'N--YOU SAID--
DID YE THINK HELLYN DIDN'T WISH TO MAKE HERSELF SOFT FOR YE, BLACKIE?
OR THAT HELLYN DIDN'T DESIRE YE...
NOW...
...I AM READY.
THE MOIST BLACK SEA AIR GLISTENS ON HER PASSIONATE, PERSPIRING SKIN--
--AND BLACKIE THEN TAKES HELLYN'S OFFER WITH AN ANIMAL'S GROWL--

--BUT IT'S NOT HALF AS LOUD AS THE HOWL OF OUTRAGE HEARD WHEN--
--DRACULA WOKE!
WHAT--? MY CASTLE-- RANSACKED WHILE I SLEPT!
AND THE PENDANT-- MARIA'S PENDANT IS GONE!
WHAT'S THIS-- A VOICE?
YO-HO! BLOW TH' MAN DOWN BA-DA DUM-BE-DE-DUM
DRUNKEN SINGING?
IF THIS SOUND BE THE ROOT-- OR EVEN THE REMAINS-- OF THIS TRAVESTY--
--THEN DRACULA'S VENGEANCE WILL BE SWIFT-- AND MERCILESS!
A PIRATE-- A HUNDRED MILES FROM THE SEA-- SHAMELESSLY GUZZLING MY FINEST BRANDIES AND LIQUEURS-- SWILLING WHISKY LIKE A SWINE!
HICE YE... THE GUV'NOR... 'ERE? ...FINE... BREWS!... 'AVE A... DRINK!
WHCK UP
I THINK I SHALL--!
HICE ...OH, 'ELL!...
YES, MY FRIEND... HELL!
THEN, AS THE WIND RISES INTO A SATANIC SCREAM-- AND THE OTHER ELEMENTS SHRIEK IN SYMPATHETIC FURY...
YOUR KEEPSAKE WILL BE RETURNED, MY MARIA--
--SO SWEARS DRACULA!

THAT DULLARD COULD NEVER HAVE OPERATED ALONE--
--THE OTHERS OF HIS CREW--AND THEIR CAPTAIN--MUST HAVE PORTAGED ACROSS TRANSYLVANIA--TO THE DANUBE--
--THENCE DOWN TO THE SEA!
THEY HAVE A DAY'S DISTANCE ON ME--BUT I SHALL STILL FOLLOW THEM--
--IF NOT IN A MAN'S FORM--THEN AS THE BAT!
THE VAMPIRE KING MAKES HIS JOURNEY--UNTIL, NEAR THE MOUTH OF THE DANUBE...
...WE RETURN TO THE FORTUNES OF THE PENDANT-FINDER BLACKIE...
HIS THOUGHTS ARE OF HIS EVENING'S EARLIER SENSUAL ESCAPADE-- OF THE FIRE-FILLED FORM OF HELLYN deVILL...
...THOUGHTS WHICH MAKE THE SOLITARY CROW'S-NEST WATCH MOST BEARABLE...
UNTIL, THAT IS, A SHADOW FLITS ACROSS THE MOON...;
...BECOMES LARGER, THE SHAPE OF A BAT...
...AND THEN... THE BAT BECOMES... MAN!
ALL HIS MEMORIES OF HIS PREVIOUS PLEASURE ARE LOST--
--AS THE DARK-SHADOWED FORM LOWERS...
...AND KILLS!
VAAMPIRE

ALERTED BY THE SHRIEK...
A STOWAWAY--COMIN' DOWN FROM CROW'S NEST!
'E'S KILLED BLACKIE!
RUN 'IM THROUGH, LADDIES!
I'M TH' NEAREST--'E TASTES MY STEEL FIRST! URGG
KLOP!
SLOVENLY FOOL. YOU'VE NOT HARMED ME! ONLY SILVER OR WOOD CAN DO THAT!
QUITE THE CONTRARY, RED-BEARD--
--YOU'VE PROVIDED ME WITH A WEAPON--
--WITH WHICH I MAY HAVE SPORT!
SPORT, 'TIS IT? YE CALL LOSIN' YER HEAD "SPORT"?
IGNORANT ROGUE--
--ONCE I WAS SWORDSMAN, A PRINCE--
--AND A SLAYER OF FAR SUPERIOR MEN THAN YOU. THEN I WAS CALLED VLAD THE IMPALER--
--BUT NOW I AM ONLY--DRACULA!
AGGH!
A PRINCE ARE YOU, STOWAWAY?
TURN THEN AND FACE THE CAPTAIN!
YOU COMMAND THIS SHIP--A WOMAN?
WAIT!
YOU WEAR THE PENDANT OF DRACULA!

ONLY ONE OF YOUR CREW BARS MY WAY!
NAY, WOMAN-- VLAD THE PRINCE DIED LONG AGO--
--AND IN HIS STEAD WAS BORN A KING!
DRACULA-- LORD OF THE VAMPIRES!
ARRRR
SO THE LEGENDS I'VE HEARD OF YE ARE TRUE, DRACULA!
BUT HELLYN deVILL FEARS NOT EVEN A VAMPIRE! IF YOU WISH YOUR PRECIOUS PENDANT BACK, DRACULA--
--YE SHALL HAVE TO COME GET IT!
SLAM!
TRANSFORMING FROM MAN... TO BAT... TO MAN AGAIN... TO REACH THE UPPER DECK...
KRUMP!
I KNOW NOT HOW THIS WOMAN FORCES HER WILL UPON HER CREWMEN--
--BUT NO MATTER HOW STRONG IT BE--
--DRACULA'S IS ALWAYS GREATER!

NO NEED FOR ANGER, MY LORD-- HELLYN WELCOMES YOU!
ACTUALLY, I AM WILLING TO SHARE EVERYTHING WITH YE!
SEE-- HOW MY FEATURES BECOME ROUND AND SOFT FOR YE?...
... HOW MY LIPS BECOME FULL, WET AND WIDE?...
... HOW MY HANDS BECOME WARM WITH DESIRE--
--ENOUGH TO HEAT EVEN THE ICY SKIN OF A VAMPIRE?...
AWAY WITH YOU! IF DRACULA DESIRED A WOMAN, HE COULD CHOOSE ONE--FROM A WORLD OF THEM--
--AND NOT SELECT A DECEPTIVE WENCH!
I SEE NOW SUCH DECEIT-- ARTFULLY MIXED WITH YOUR POWER-- IS WHAT GIVES YOU YOUR AUTHORITY--
--AND DRACULA WILL HAVE NONE OF IT!
THUMP
YE FATHERLESS DOG!
YOU AMUSE ME, WOMAN--! I SEE RIGHT THROUGH YOU--AND YOU ARE POWERLESS AGAINST ME!
NO ONE HAS EVER DARED REFUSE HELLYN'S CHARMS!
YE WILL DIE A SECOND TIME FOR THIS, VAMPIRE--
--AND A THIRD OR FOURTH TIME, IF NECESSARY!
WE SHALL SEE ABOUT THAT, DRACULA--
VAMPIRES CAN BE STOPPED-- AND I'VE STILL SOME CREW LEFT ALIVE--

--ALL WILLING TO FOLLOW MY EVERY COMMAND!
HELLYN'S REWARD WILL BE GIVEN TO ALL WHO SCORE WITH A THRUST!
SKEWER HIM WITH YOUR WOODEN STAKES!
ARMS AKIMBO, DRACULA STANDS FEARLESSLY BEFORE THEM!
HE HAS A GREATER POWER THAN THE MERELY HUMAN MUSCLES ARRAYED AGAINST HIM--
--SOUL-DEEP HYPNOSIS, SUFFICIENT TO TURN FLESH TO QUIVERING JELLY!
AND THROUGH IT ALL... DRACULA LAUGHS!
HA HA HA HA
THOSE EYES--!
CAN'T... MOVE...!
CAN'T... TH-THINK...!
THEN THE LAUGHING LIPS TURN INTO A SNEERING SNARL...
BAH! YOU ARE LOWER THAN THE SLIME ON THE BELLIES OF SNAKES--
--AWAY WITH YOU!
PLAP!
AND NOW, WOMAN--
--NOW I WILL TAKE YOU!
THEN PERHAPS I HAVE YET A CHANCE--!

YE MEAN... YE ARE NOT GOING TO KILL ME?
OH, NO, NO, DEAR LADY--YOU DO NOT DESERVE SUCH A FATE!
THEN YE'LL HAVE MY KISSES?
AH-HA! I'VE GOT HIM!
NO, YOU DESERVE NOT THAT, EITHER!
NO, I HAVE A MORE SUITABLE FATE!
HO! YOU WHO CALL YOUR-SELVES MEN--
--WATCH--AND LISTEN WELL!
MINE HAS NOT BEEN THE ONLY HYPNOSIS ON THIS SHIP!
YOU, CUT-THROATS, HAVE SUFFERED UNDER ANOTHER'S DELUSION--
"--THAT OF HELLYN!
"HER MAGIC HAS BLANKETED HER TRUE BEING FOR YEARS!
"SEE--SHE TRIES TO HIDE AS I STRIP AWAY THE ILLUSION!
"SHE FIGHTS MY POWER--BUT DRACULA, AS ALWAYS, PREVAILS!"
LOOK! THIS IS YOUR PRECIOUS "QUEEN OF THE SEA"!
WOULD YOU BE SUBJECT TO... THIS?
OUR CAPTAIN--?
SHE'S A WITCH!

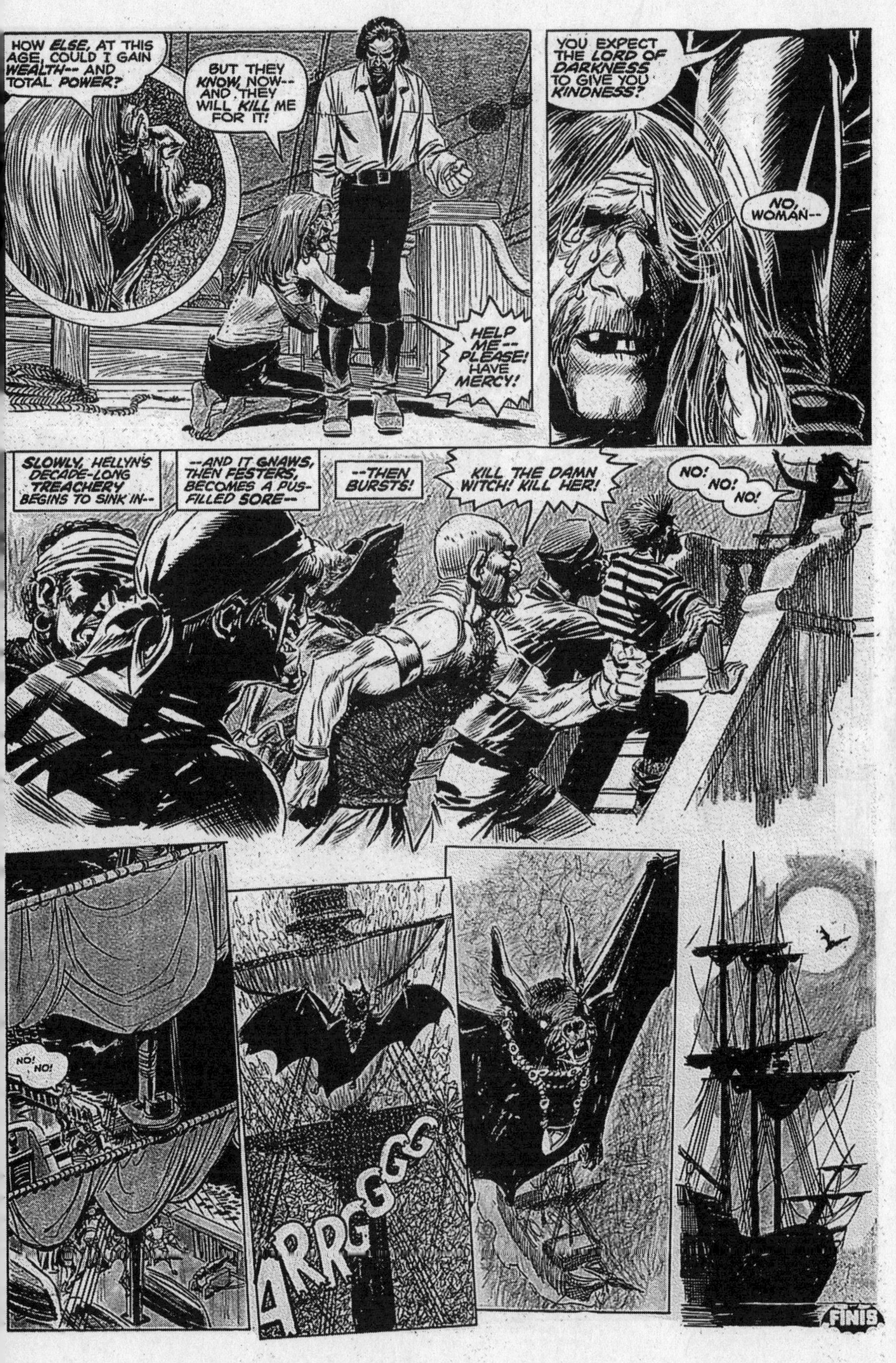
HOW ELSE, AT THIS AGE, COULD I GAIN WEALTH-- AND TOTAL POWER?
BUT THEY KNOW, NOW-- AND THEY WILL KILL ME FOR IT!
HELP ME-- PLEASE! HAVE MERCY!
YOU EXPECT THE LORD OF DARKNESS TO GIVE YOU KINDNESS?
NO, WOMAN--
SLOWLY, HELLYN'S DECADE-LONG TREACHERY BEGINS TO SINK IN--
--AND IT GNAWS, THEN FESTERS, BECOMES A PUS-FILLED SORE--
--THEN BURSTS!
KILL THE DAMN WITCH! KILL HER!
NO! NO! NO!
NO! NO!
ARRGGGG
FINIS

THE PIT OF DEATH
TRANSYLVANIA, OCTOBER 12, 1809: CASTLE DRACULA JUTS STARKLY AGAINST BLEAK, STORM-SWEPT SKIES... A BROODING MONUMENT TO DEATH AND DEPRAVITY.
ABRUPTLY, AN OBSCENE BAT BURSTS FROM THE DECADENT CASTLE'S UPPERMOST WINDOW... CHURNS THE NIGHT AIR WITH POWERFULLY WHIPPING WINGS...
IT WHEELS ALOFT IN JERKILY SPORADIC SPURTS OF MOTION... THEN DIPS INTO A SOARING GLIDE...
...AND SWOOPS DOWN TOWARD THE VILLAGE BELOW...
...CARRYING WITH IT THE MOST VIRULENT DISEASE KNOWN TO MAN.
VAMPIRISM!
THAT'S WHAT I'M TALKING ABOUT! THE COUNT IN THE CASTLE ABOVE OUR VILLAGE IS A VAMPIRE--!
VAMPIRE?! YOU CALLED US OUT OF OUR HOMES IN THE MIDDLE OF THE NIGHT TO RAVE ABOUT A VAMPIRE--?

I AM NOT RAVING!
AND I DID NOT ASK YOU, MAYOR, TO COME TO THIS MEETING. YOU CAME OF YOUR OWN FREE WILL. AND I WISH YOU HADN'T--
-FOR IT IS TIME THE CITIZENS OF THIS VILLAGE TOOK MATTERS INTO THEIR HANDS... INSTEAD OF WAITING FOR YOU AND YOUR LAZY POLICE CHIEF TO ACT!
BRIDLE YOUR TONGUE... LEST YOU FORCE ME TO PROVE THE POLICE CHIEF CAN ACT IN A MANNER WHICH IS ANYTHING BUT LAZY!
I WILL NOT BRIDLE MY TONGUE--NOT WHILE ONE OF OUR WOMEN WAITS EVEN NOW TO BE BURIED... DRAINED OF EVERY DROP OF BLOOD!
I TELL YOU, COUNT DRACULA IS A VAMPIRE--AND HE MURDERED THAT GIRL LAST NIGHT.
AND I TELL YOU--YOU'RE MAD!
AM I MAD TO PROMOTE THE DESTRUCTION OF AN INHUMAN FIEND--
"--WHEN ANY ONE OF OUR WIVES MAY BE HIS NEXT VICTIM?!"
"--MEN CAN TRANSFORM INTO BATS... AND BATS INTO MEN--?"
YES--YOU ARE MAD.
WHO ELSE BUT A MADMAN WOULD SERIOUSLY BELIEVE IN VAMPIRES--WHO ELSE WOULD BELIEVE THAT--

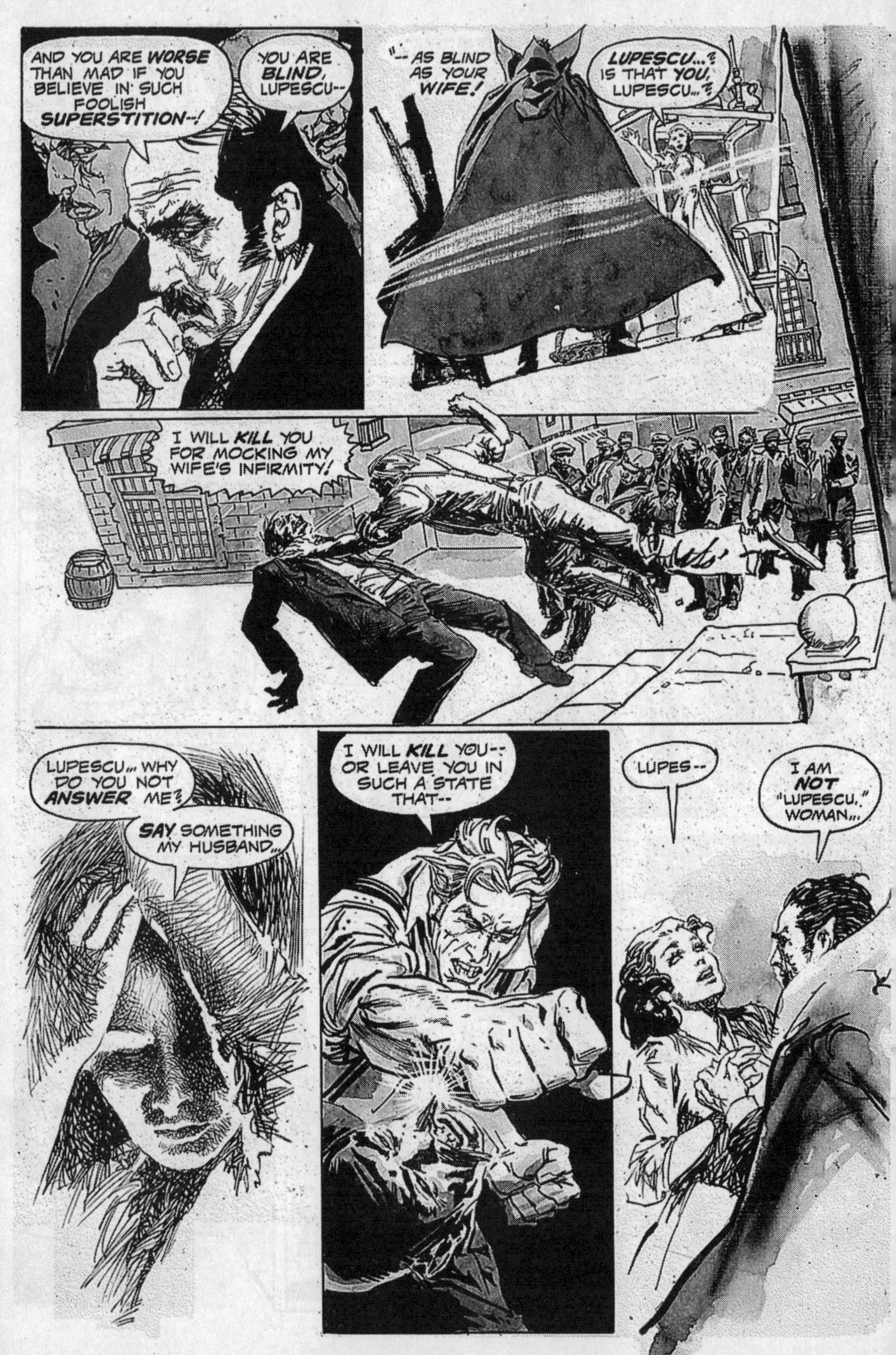

AND YOU ARE WORSE THAN MAD IF YOU BELIEVE IN SUCH FOOLISH SUPERSTITION--!
YOU ARE BLIND, LUPESCU--
"--AS BLIND AS YOUR WIFE!
LUPESCU...? IS THAT YOU, LUPESCU...?
I WILL KILL YOU FOR MOCKING MY WIFE'S INFIRMITY!
LUPESCU... WHY DO YOU NOT ANSWER ME?
SAY SOMETHING MY HUSBAND...
I WILL KILL YOU-- OR LEAVE YOU IN SUCH A STATE THAT--
LUPES--
I AM NOT "LUPESCU," WOMAN...

WOULD THAT IT WERE YOUR BLOOD DRAINED BY THE FIEND...RATHER THAN THAT OF INNOCENT WOMEN!
FOR IT IS YOU-- AND YOUR POMPOUS INACTION-- WHICH HAS--

"--ALLOWED THE VAMPIRE TO CONTINUE HIS FOUL DEPREDATIONS!"
I AM DRACULA.

I WILL WASTE NO MORE TIME ON YOU MAYOR...
...FOR I HAVE MORE IMPORTANT MATTERS TO ATTEND.

MATTERS SUCH AS--

"--PROTECTING MY WIFE."

IF ONLY THE FOOLS WOULD LISTEN TO ME... IF ONLY THEY WOULD JOIN ME.
TOGETHER WE COULD STORM DRACULA'S CASTLE AND--

"--DESTROY HIM FOREVER."

NO..!

MY GOD--

NOOO..!

DON'T JUST STAND THERE, YOU SPINELESS FOOLS!
FETCH THE POLICE CHIEF-- LUPESCU WILL PAY FOR THIS!

VELANNA... MY WIFE... THAT THIS SHOULD HAPPEN TO YOU!
IT IS MORE THAN I CAN BEAR...

...BUT I SWEAR TO YOU, VELANNA-- BY ALL THAT'S HOLY TO ME...
...I SHALL NOT ALLOW YOU TO BECOME THE SAME MANNER OF FIEND AS YOUR MURDERER ... NO MATTER WHO--

"--TRIES TO STOP ME."
ARREST LUPESCU WITHIN THE QUARTER-HOUR... IF YOU DO NOT WISH TO SPEND THE REST OF YOUR LIFE CLEANING STABLES!
YOU SHALL NOT RISE AS A VAMPIRE, VELANNA...
...THE LEAST YOU DESERVE IS--
"--ETERNAL PEACE..."
GOOD LORD--!
BRASH!
HE'S MURDERED HIS OWN WIFE--!
KRAK
NO--YOU'RE WRONG--
I DIDN'T KILL HER--I LOVED HER, FOR GOD'S SAKE! THE VAMPIRE KILLED HER--DRACULA KILLED HER!
TAKE HIM AWAY.

BUT THEN, ON THE THIRD NIGHT, HIS MIND FILLED WITH GHASTLY VISIONS OF HIS WIFE. HE PICTURED HER AGAIN AND AGAIN, SPRAWLED THERE ON THE FLOOR, HER THROAT SMEARED WITH LIVID BLOOD...

...AND HIS SOUL BEGAN TO NOURISH ITSELF...ON HATE AND OUTRAGE AND A FIERCE DETERMINATION WHICH INFUSED HIM WITH STRENGTH...

HE HAS NOT SLEPT THESE LAST THREE NIGHTS. AND NOW, HE FEIGNS SLEEP...

HE HAS NOT EATEN, ALTHOUGH TRAYS OF FOOD HAVE BEEN BROUGHT TO TO HIM ON THREE OCCASSIONS...

BUT NOW, AS THE JAILER BRINGS A FOURTH TRAY--

REACHING HIS HOME, HE PAUSES ONLY BRIEFLY... TO NOTICE THAT HIS WIFE'S CORPSE HAS BEEN TAKEN AWAY...

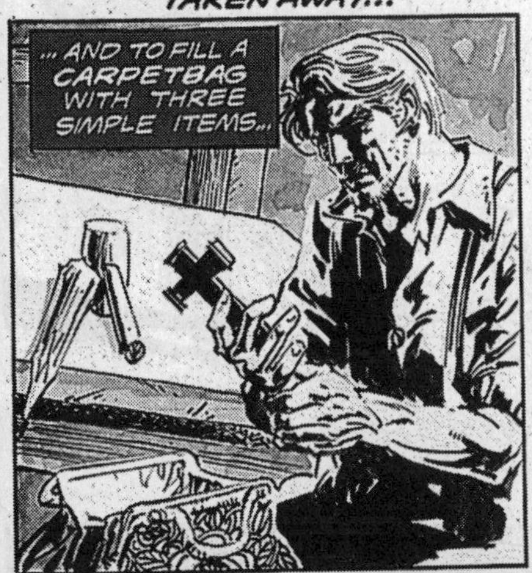

STEALTHILY, HE MOUNTS THE VAST HALL'S SWEEPING STAIRWAY...

...AND WHEN HE REACHES THE TOP--
GOOD EVENING. YOU HAVE ENTERED FREELY...AND OF YOUR OWN WILL.

STAND BACK, HELLFIEND!
THE CROSS WILL NOT HELP YOU HERE...

WITLESS FOOL--
--SEE HOW EASILY DRACULA SENDS YOU TO HIS--

--PIT OF DEATH!

AS THOUGH CAUGHT IN A FUNNEL OF QUEASY VERTIGO, LUPESCU PLUMMETS DOWN THROUGH THE SEEMINGLY BOTTOMLESS PIT--

--FINALLY SPLASHING INTO THE FRIGID WATERS OF A TURBULENT SUBTERRANEAN RIVER--

--WHICH CLUTCHES HIM IN ITS FRENZIED, ROILING GRASP... AND SWEEPS HIM THROUGH A NARROW LABYRINTHINE TUNNEL.

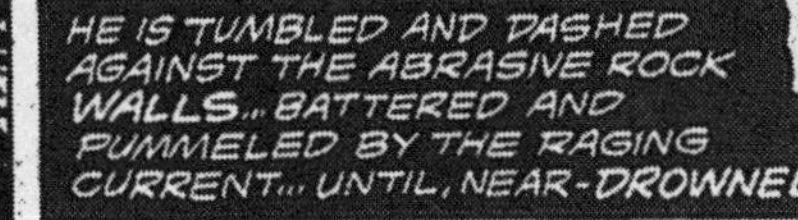
HE IS TUMBLED AND DASHED AGAINST THE ABRASIVE ROCK WALLS... BATTERED AND PUMMELED BY THE RAGING CURRENT... UNTIL, NEAR-DROWNED--

--HE IS SPIT FROM THE TUNNEL INTO A LARGE ROCK CHAMBER...

... AND INTO A POOL IN THE CENTER OF THAT CHAMBER.
THE WATER IS NOT DEEP. HE RISES TO HIS FEET, STILL CLUTCHING HIS PRECIOUS CARPETBAG... AND HE LOOKS ACROSS THE CHAMBER. TORCHES GUTTER IN RECESSED WALL-NICHES, CASTING A LURID GLOW ON A SERIES OF...
...COFFINS.

SPEECHLESS WITH HORROR, LUPESCU WATCHES AS THE COFFIN LIDS BEGIN TO MOVE... IN SLOW UNISON...

...AND HE WATCHES AS THE COFFINS' WICKEDLY BEAUTIFUL OCCUPANTS RISE FROM DEATH...

...LUPESCU'S BLIND WIFE AMONG THEM.
AN EXPRESSION OF UNHOLY GLEE-- AND LUST-- LIGHTS HER FACE... FOR NOW SHE IS A BRIDE OF DRACULA.
TO BE CONTINUED!

Writer: DOUG MOENCH Artist: TONY DeZUNIGA

THEN THERE IS A WHISPERED RUSTLE, AS SHEER GOWNS SLITHER ACROSS SATIN... AND THE WOMEN EMERGE FROM THEIR COFFINS, AS THOUGH PERFORMING SOME PERVERTED RITUAL OF RESURRECTION...
HSSSSSS
...AND AGAIN LUPESCU NOTES THAT THERE ARE SEVEN... SEVEN OF THESE DARKNESS-SPAWNED CREATURES...

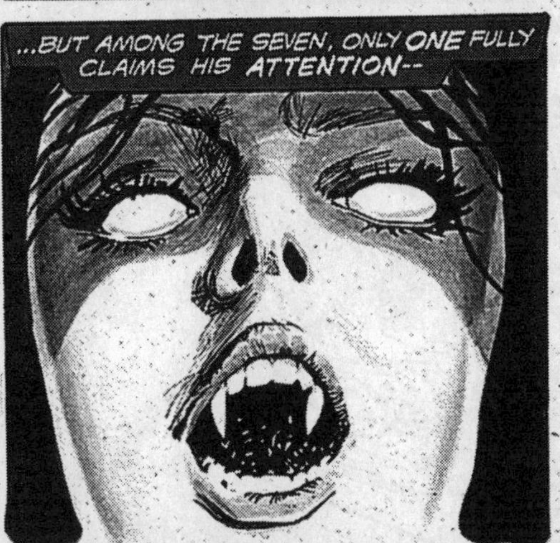
...BUT AMONG THE SEVEN, ONLY ONE FULLY CLAIMS HIS ATTENTION--

VELANNA--!
--HIS BLIND WIFE, RECENTLY SLAIN IN A FILTHY DEBAUCHERY OF BLOOD BY THE MAN WHO HAS CONDEMNED HIM TO THIS STINKING PIT OF DEATH --BY DRACULA, THE UNDEAD AGENT OF HELL.

THEIR FLUID MOVEMENTS ARE ENHANCED BY THE UNDULATING FLOW OF DRAPING GOWNS, THE BRUSHING CARESS OF A COOL WIND...
...AND WERE THEY NOT ADVANCING ON HIM, LUPESCU MIGHT FIND THEM... DESIRABLE.

THEY KNEEL NOW, WITH THE SUPPLE GRACE OF ANIMALS, AND THEY LEAN OVER THE RUNNING WATERS OF THE BRACKISH POOL... THEIR HELLISH EYES CONVERGING ON LUPESCU IN A GAZE OF FOUL LUST--
--LUST THEY WOULD SATIATE IN A FEAST OF BLOOD...
VELLANA... MY WIFE... DON'T YOU RECOGNIZE ME--?!

AND THE LOUDEST OF THESE GROWLS, AS THOUGH TO COMPOUND THE HORROR, ORIGINATES FROM HIS WIFE.

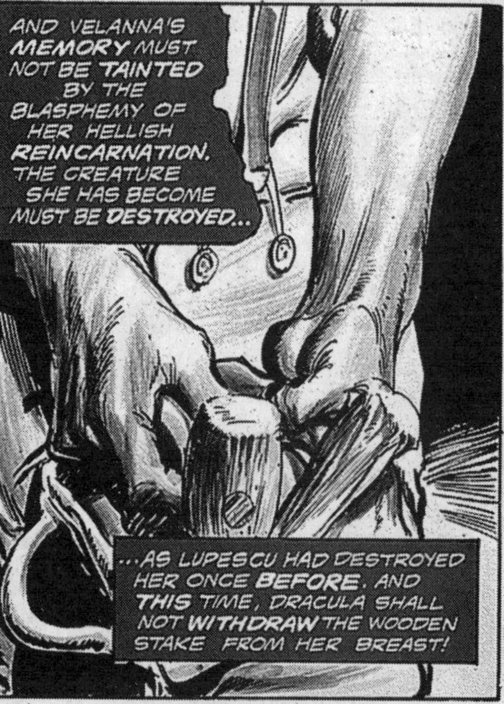

BUT HOW TO GRANT VELANNA HER ETERNAL PEACE WITHOUT FIRST FALLING PREY TO THE FRENZY OF THE OTHER VAMPIRE-WOMEN...?
IF ONLY HE COULD SOMEHOW KEEP THEM AT BAY...

THERE.
THERE, BOBBING IN THE FETID ICHOR OF THE POOL...

THE CRUCIFIX--!
THE CRUCIFIX EARLIER SWATTED FROM HIS GRASP BY A WILDLY SWOOPING BAT IN DRACULA'S THRALL... THE CRUCIFIX WHICH HAD FALLEN DOWN INTO THE PIT OF DEATH EVEN AS HE HAD, AND WHICH HAS NOW BEEN SWEPT INTO THE POOL, AS HE HAS...

HE SNATCHES THE CROSS FROM THE SQUALID MUCK--

--AND WITH A DESPERATE FLOURISH, BRANDISHES IT BEFORE THE VAMPIRE-WOMEN.
THEY BLEAT, AND SQUEAL IN PANIC, AS THEY SHRINK FROM THE UPHELD SYMBOL OF SELF-LESS PURITY...

AND THOUGH IT SEARS HIS SOUL TO PLACE HIS WIFE IN SUCH UNHOLY AGONY, LUPESCU CLIMBS FROM THE POOL AND PRESSES THAT AGONY FORWARD...

A PLAN HAS OCCURED TO LUPESCU, A SCHEME OF BLOOD AND REDEMPTION... AND OF RETRIBUTION. HE WILL MURDER TO ATTAIN THE SALVATION OF HIS WIFE'S IMMORTAL SOUL... AND THEN HE WILL MURDER AGAIN AND AGAIN, TO AVENGE THE RAPE OF HER SOUL BY THE BLOOD-FIEND CALLED DRACULA...

LUPESCU WILL NOT SOON FORGET THE ATROCITIES OF THIS NIGHT... BUT HE IS DETERMINED THAT NEITHER WILL THE LORD OF THE UNDEAD.
HE WEDGES THE CRUCIFIX INTO A CRACK IN THE POROUS SURFACE OF THE GROTTO WALL.

...AND ITS PRESENCE BOTH REPELS THE VAMPIRE-WOMEN--
--AND FREES HIS HANDS TO SEIZE VELANNA.
LET GO OF ME, FILTHY MORTAL!!

SHE SQUIRMS AND HISSES IN AWFUL RAGE AS LUPESCU BEARS HER TO THE GROUND...
...AND WHEN HE STRADDLES HER, ARMED WITH MALLET AND STAKE, HER STRUGGLES TAKE ON THE CAST OF TERROR.

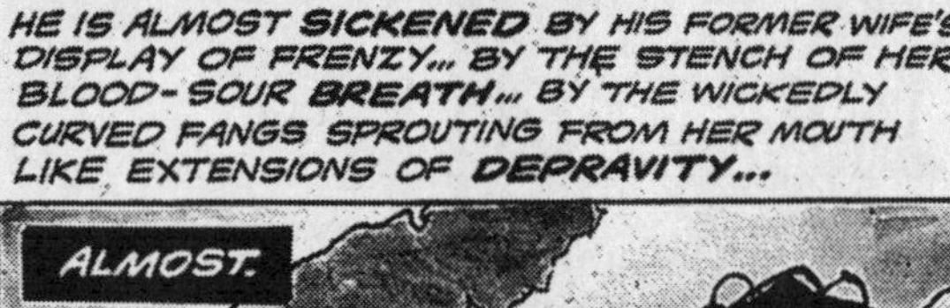
HE IS ALMOST SICKENED BY HIS FORMER WIFE'S DISPLAY OF FRENZY... BY THE STENCH OF HER BLOOD-SOUR BREATH... BY THE WICKEDLY CURVED FANGS SPROUTING FROM HER MOUTH LIKE EXTENSIONS OF DEPRAVITY...

ALMOST.
KRAK!

THE STAKE IS DRIVEN INTO VELANNA'S BREAST, PUNCTURING HER HEART FOR THE SECOND TIME... BUT THIS TIME THE EXPLOSION OF BLOOD WHICH GREETS THE STAKE'S ENTRY IS NOT HER OWN...
...BUT, RATHER, THE STOLEN BLOOD OF OTHERS.
AAIEEEEEE!
KRAK!

LUPESCU RISES FROM HER, WONDERING WITH HORROR WHOM HER VICTIMS HAD BEEN...
...AND THEN THE HIDEOUS VISAGE OF THE BLOOD-BEAST SOFTENS TO A MASK OF SERENITY, AND VELANNA AGAIN KNOWS THE PEACE OF PERPETUAL DARKNESS. AND HER SERENITY SOMEHOW ASSUAGES LUPESCU'S HORROR.

BUT HE KNOWS THAT HIS WORK HAS NOT ENDED. SOLEMNLY, HE CROSSES TO ONE OF THE VACANT COFFINS--
--AND RIPS THE LID FROM ITS HINGES.
SPRAK!

DRACULA'S BRIDES WATCH IN CONFUSED APPREHENSION AS LUPESCU CARRIES THE COFFIN LID ACROSS THE ROCK CHAMBER AND LODGES IT AGAINST FLOOR AND WALL--
--THERE TO STAMP UPON IT...
KRATCH!

...SHATTERING IT INTO A DOZEN SLENDER SHARDS--
--FRAGMENTS OF WOOD NOT UNLIKE SHARPENED STAKES.

THEN, WITH THE PROTECTIVE CRUCIFIX STILL WEDGED IN THE WALL BEHIND HIM, LUPESCU STRIDES INTO THE MIDST OF THE PANICKED VAMPIRE-WOMEN--
--TO SEIZE THEM, ONE BY ONE...

...AND, USING THE SHARPENED PIECES OF THE SPLINTERED **COFFIN LID**, TO **END** THEIR VILE EXISTENCES...

...ONE...

...BY...

EEEE!

EEEE!

...ONE...

...UNTIL ALL **SEVEN** OF THE CREATURES HAVE BEEN SLAIN...

...AND **RELEASED** FROM THE PERVERTED BONDS OF VAMPIRISM.

NOW LUPESCU KNOWS THAT HE MAY BEGIN THE **FINAL STAGE** OF HIS DESPERATE PLAN.

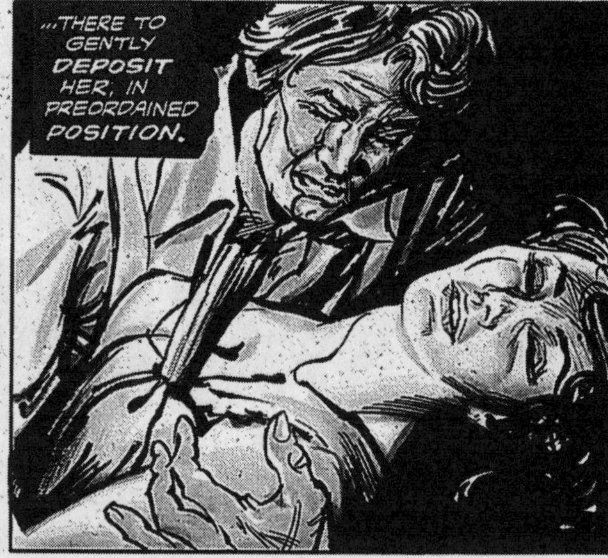

AND WHEN HE HAS MOVED ALL OF THE SLAIN WOMEN, LUPESCU CROSSES TO THE EDGE OF THE POOL--

--AND DIVES INTO SLIME-SWIRLED WATER...
...TOWARD THE TUNNEL THROUGH WHICH THE POOL'S EXCESS WATER DRAINS OFF..

HALF-SWIMMING, HALF BORNE BY THE CURRENT, LUPESCU ENTERS THE GLOOMY TUNNEL...

...AND, STILL CLUTCHING HIS CRUCIFIX, ADVANCES DOWN ITS CLAUSTROPHOBIC LENGTH.

SWEPT THROUGH THE SERPENTINE TUNNEL FOR LONG MINUTES, LUPESCU FINALLY REACHES ANOTHER GROTTO, THIS ONE SMALLER THAN THE FIRST--
--AND HOSTING, INSTEAD OF A NEST OF VAMPIRE-WOMEN, AN ASCENDING STAIRWAY.

LUPESCU HAD HOPED THE TUNNEL-CONTAINED STREAM WOULD CARRY HIM OUT OF THE CASTLE... HAD PLANNED TO JOURNEY BACK TO ITS FRONT ENTRANCE AND THERE CONFRONT HIS WIFE'S MURDERER ANEW.
BUT THIS STAIRWELL CAN ONLY LEAD DIRECTLY TO A DIFFERENT SECTION OF CASTLE DRACULA... AND FOR THAT, LUPESCU IS GRATEFUL. IT MAKES HIS TASK THAT MUCH MORE FACILE.

THE STAIRWELL IS DANK, INFESTED WITH DENSE GLOOM--

--AND WITH OTHER THINGS AS WELL.
SCREECHING, SWOOPING BATS FOR ONE.
LUPESCU SHIELDS HIS FACE FROM THEIR VICIOUS FLURRY OF ATTACK, FLAILS WILDLY AT THEIR BLACKLY GLISTENING FORMS.

AND WHEN THE SPURTING NIGHT-THINGS HAVE PASSED, LUPESCU AGAIN ASCENDS THE STEEP STAIRWELL...
...TOWARD THE MASSIVE DOOR VAGUELY GLIMPSED AT ITS SUMMIT.

IT SWINGS FREELY, THE THICK DOOR...
...AND OPENS UPON A GAUNT SHADOW...

...THE SHADOW OF COUNT DRACULA.
WELCOME, MORTAL. I HAVE BEEN WAITING FOR YOU...
...TO OFFER YOU MY CONGRATULATIONS ON PASSING THROUGH THE PIT OF DEATH... ALIVE. YOU ARE THE FIRST TO DO SO.

AND I SHALL NOT BE THE LAST, HELL-FIEND.
I HAVE COME HERE FOR ONE REASON, DRACULA-- TO TELL YOU THAT I HAVE SEEN YOUR BRIDES...

...AND THAT THEY AWAIT YOUR PRESENCE.
AND THUS, LUPESCU HAS ACHIEVED HIS GOAL. HIS PLAN HAS BEEN ENACTED, AND IT IS ALL HE CAN HOPE FOR AGAINST AN OPPONENT SUCH AS DRACULA...

...AND HE ATTEMPTS NO MORE.
NOW, DRACULA, I HAVE TOLD YOU WHAT I MUST. I WILL OPPOSE YOU NO FURTHER.
YOU ARE WISE, MORTAL, TO SUBMIT WITHOUT STRUGGLE...

FOR THE END MUST ALWAYS REMAIN--

"-- THE SAME."
AND DRACULA GORGES HIMSELF ON THE SWEET BLOOD OF A MAN WHO HAS SACRIFICED HIS SOUL TO REDEEM THE SOUL OF HIS WIFE.

BUT WHEN THE VAMPIRE-LORD RISES FROM HIS FEAST, HE IS TROUBLED BY SOMETHING...
...BY HIS VICTIM'S FINAL, ENIGMATIC WORDS...

WORDS HE MUST INVESTIGATE.
"YOUR BRIDES AWAIT YOU," THE MORTAL HAD SAID...AND THERE HAD BEEN SATISFACTION IN HIS VOICE.

THERE HAD AL-MOST BEEN A TAUNTING RING TO HIS VOICE... AND DRACULA WILL SUFFER NEITHER THE TAUNTS NOR THE SATISFACTION OF MORTALS.
HE DESCENDS A DIFFERENT STAIRWAY, THIS ONE LEADING DOWN TO A WALL OF SHEER ROCK

...BUT A WALL WHICH NEVERTHELESS HAS AN OPENING--A DOORWAY CUT FROM THE VERY ROCK ITSELF...
...A DOORWAY WHOSE ALMOST IMPERCEPTIBLE BORDER HAD RECENTLY HELD A WEDGED CRUCIFIX.
...A DOORWAY WHICH LEADS TO THE VILE PIT OF DEATH...
...AND TO DRACULA'S WAITING BRIDES, THE PURIFIED WOMEN WHOSE VERY POSITIONS NOW PREVENT DRACULA FROM APPROACHING THEM, AND WITHDRAWING THE STAKES FROM THEIR HEARTS.
AND SUDDENLY, THE SWEET BLOOD HE HAS JUST CONSUMED...
...TAKES ON A VERY BITTER TASTE INDEED.
FINIS

EVEN IF TRUTH COUNTERS OTHERWISE... AND RESULTS IN A MODERN GIRL'S IMMEDIATE REGRET.

THE SHADOWS RIP WITH A SHARP HISS, SPITTING FORTH A BLURRED FIGURE OF MENACE. THE GIRL CHOKES ON A WELLING SCREAM... AND THE DARK FIGURE WRAPS HER IN A TATTERED SHROUD OF SWIRLING FRENZY AND BRIGHT HORROR.

THE NIGHT SWELLS WITH BRUTAL MOTION... AND THE AIR TURNS--

SCARLET IN GLORY!

Story: DOUG MOENCH Art: PAUL GULACY & MIKE ESPOSITO

SHE WHIMPERS, A SOFTLY BLEATING TESTAMENT TO PANIC... AND WHIMPERING, GASPING, SHE IS VIOLENTLY DRIVEN TO THE GROUND.
SHE STRUGGLES, WRITHING AND TWISTING AGAINST HER ASSAILANT'S IM LACABLE GRASP. HER SKIN SHREDS AS SHE SQUIRMS AGAINST THE ROUGH COBBLES.

AND WHEN THE FIGURE CLOAKED IN GLOOM RISES...
...IT IS FROM A STILLED--AND LIFELESS--BODY... A BODY WHOSE THROAT IS SMEARED WITH THICK GOUTS OF BLOOD...

...A BODY QUICKLY ABANDONED AS THE FIGURE STEALS AWAY, MERGING ONCE AGAIN WITH SHADOW.

WHILE ELSEWHERE, HIGH ABOVE THE VILLAGE, THE AIR RIFFLES WITH THE JERKING FLAP OF MIDNIGHT-GLISTENING WINGS...

...THE WINGS OF A BAT IN SWIFT DESCENT.
...AND EQUALLY RAPID TRANSFORMATION--

--INTO COUNT DRACULA, LORD OF DEPRAVITY AND PURVEYOR OF VILE ABOMINATIONS.

DRACULA STANDS, SHRINED IN THE MOON'S LAMBENT RADIANCE, AND HE FEELS THE RHYTHM OF THE NIGHT PULSE DEEP WITHIN HIM.
HE SURVEYS THE BLEAK AVENUE SPRAWLING BEFORE HIM, KNOWING WHAT HE NEEDS. HE HAS VISITED THIS VILLAGE ONCE BEFORE, LONG AGO, AND HE HAD RICHLY SATISFIED HIS NEEDS UPON THAT OCCASION...

BUT IT HAD BEEN A DIFFERENT VILLAGE THEN, ONE TEEMING WITH LIFE... WITH UNWARY VICTIMS...
...NOW IT IS DESOLATE, A BARREN FACADE OF LIFE... COMPLETELY DEVOID OF VICTIMS.
THE BLOODLUST SCREAMS WITHIN HIM... OBSESSES HIM, DEMANDING APPEASEMENT.

AND DRACULA KNOWS THAT TO PERPETUATE HIS EXISTENCE, AS PERVERTED AS IT MAY BE, HE MUST PENETRATE THE VILLAGE'S DESOLATE FACADE--

--AND GNAW AT THE LIFE HIDING WITHIN.

BUT NO.
PAINFULLY, NO.

IT IS NOW MOST APPARENT THAT THIS VILLAGE HAS ALTERED FAR MORE DRAMATICALLY THAN FIRST GLANCE HAD INDICATED...

...AND THE CHANGE IS AMPLE CAUSE FOR DRACULA'S SLOW WRATH...
THEY HAVE BECOME WISE...
...MOST EFFECTIVELY BARRING MY ENTRANCE.
EVERY DOOR-- EVERY WINDOW-- SHIELDED BY THE REPULSIVE CROSS!

BUT WHY?
IT HAS BEEN YEARS SINCE I BURDENED THIS VILLAGE WITH MY LUST...

THERE, ON THAT UNTENDED NEWSPAPER DISPLAY, IS THE ANSWER...

...AND IT IS THE ONE I SUSPECTED.

Sixth Victim Of
Vampire" Murders:
ANOTHER VAMPIRE DARES TO HARRY THIS VILLAGE IN THE COUNTRY I CLAIM AS MY OWN.

THE MORTAL WEAKLINGS! THE NEWSPAPER PROCLAIMS THE IDENTITY OF THE VAMPIRE--
--AND YET THEY COWER BEHIND CROSS-ADORNED DOORS, AFRAID TO CONFRONT THE BEING WHO NIGHTLY STEALS THE BLOOD OF THEIR DAUGHTERS!
BUT DRACULA IS NOT AFRAID--
Vampire
Girl Found

"--TO VISIT THIS COUNT VRYSLAW IN HIS CASTLE ON THE MOUNT.'"

BUT WERE DRACULA ABLE TO SEE WITHIN THE CASTLE, HE WOULD DOUBTLESS REVISE HIS CONCLUSIONS. FOR, THE MAN SEATED AT A BROAD TABLE IN THE MAIN HALL IS HARDLY A VAMPIRE...
...BUT RATHER, A MAN EQUIPPED WITH INSTRUMENTS OF PIOUS DEATH... AND PATIENCE:
A CRUCIFIX. MALLET AND STAKE OF WOOD. GARLIC BULBS. A CROSSBOW NOTCHED WITH A WOODEN BOLT. MIRROR. AND A FLASK OF HOLY WATER.

NO, HE IS HARDLY A VAMPIRE...
...BUT HE IS A MAN WHOSE PATIENCE--

--HAS NOW ABRUPTLY PREVAILED.
KRESSH!
YOU!

WELCOME, NIGHTFIEND. I HAVE BEEN WAITING FOR YOU.
GOD, HOW I HAVE BEEN WAITING!

DRACULA CARES LITTLE ABOUT YOUR WAITING.
MY ONLY CONCERN IS YOUR PUNISHMENT-- FOR STRIPPING THIS VILLAGE OF MY POTENTIAL FULFILLMENT!

I WILL NOT BE THE ONE TO TASTE PUNISHMENT THIS NIGHT, DRACULA--

NO, YOU SHALL BE PUNISHED--
--BY THE SIGHT OF YOUR OWN HIDEOUS COUNTENANCE IN THIS MIRROR!

AAARRRH!

FOOL! DRACULA CANNOT BE HARMED BY A MIRROR!
IT IS, AT MOST, A PETTY ANNOYANCE.

THEN PERHAPS YOU WILL BE MORE IMPRESSED BY THIS FLASK OF HOLY WATER.
PERHAPS ...WERE IT NOT FOR DRACULA'S SPEED, MORTAL!

IT IS OBVIOUS THAT YOU ARE NOT THE ONE I SEEK... FOR HE WOULD SCARCELY FLAUNT THE IMPLEMENTS WITH WHICH YOU HAVE CHOSEN TO GREET ME.
BUT NO MATTER. YOU STILL REQUIRE PUNISHMENT... EVEN THOUGH IT IS NOW FOR A DIFFERENT TRANSGRESSION.

NO-- I'VE VOWED TO STOP YOU!
AND I WILL STOP YOU... WITH THE--

--CROSS... AAAGK-K-K!
THE PRINCE OF DARKNESS SLAMS INTO THE OLD MAN, SEIZING HIM BEFORE THE CROSS CAN BE SEIZED...

KLAK!
...AND INITIATING A STRUGGLE WHICH TOPPLES THE CRUCIFIX TO THE FLOOR--

--WITHIN DRACULA'S AGONIZED SIGHT.
AND THE MOMENTARY RESPITE ENABLES THE OLD MAN TO SNATCH--
THIS CROSS-BOW, DRACULA...
IT IS PRIMED WITH A QUARREL OF WOOD--
--AND IT IS AIMED AT YOUR HEART!

SO FOLLOW ME UP THESE STAIRS IF YOU DARE, DRACULA ... I WANT YOU TO.
BUT KNOW THAT YOU WILL NOT TAINT HER AGAIN! I WILL SEE TO IT!

--THIS!

DON'T YOU REMEMBER THE NIGHT, DRACULA, TWENTY YEARS AGO, WHEN YOU GRAPPLED WITH ME... AFTER TURNING MY WIFE INTO A VAMPIRESS...?!

I'VE NEVER FORGOTTEN IT. I'VE BEEN REMINDED OF IT EVERY TIME I'VE LOOKED IN THE MIRROR... EVERY DAY I'VE HAD TO KEEP MY WIFE LOCKED BEHIND BARS FOR FEAR SHE'D ATTACK ME.

REMINDED OF IT EVERY TIME I'VE LOOKED AT HER AND SEEN THE YOUTH AND BEAUTY OF CORRUPTION. SHE HASN'T AGED A MOMENT SINCE THAT NIGHT, DRACULA... WHILE I'VE AGED TO THE BRINK OF DEATH.

AND DO YOU SEE THIS BOWL, DRACULA IT'S FILLED WITH BLOOD-- BLOOD STOLEN FROM A INNOCENT GIRL WHOSE THROAT I RIPPED OUT EARLIER TONIGHT..

...JUST AS I'VE KILLED SIX OTHER GIRLS SINCE MY WIFE BEGAN REFUSING ANIMAL BLOOD!
THAT'S WHY I WANT REVENGE, DRACULA...
...WHY I MUST KILL YOU!

HA HA HA HA HA
CROSS-BOW SHAFTS CANNOT HARM ONE WHO HAS THE ABILITY TO TRANSFORM INTO MIST, OLD MAN...

...AS OTHERS BEFORE YOU HAVE ALREADY LEARNED.*
*RACHEL VAN HELSING FOR ONE, IN MYRIAD ISSUES OF TOMB OF DRACULA. --ROY.

NOW DO YOU SEE THAT NOTHING MAY STOP ME FROM DRINK-ING YOUR BLOOD--
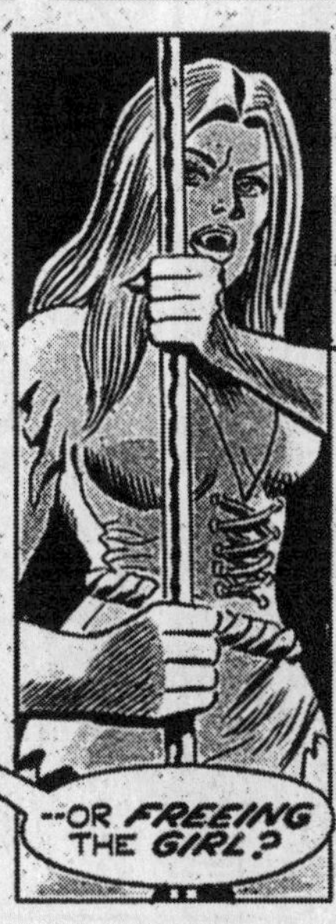
--OR FREEING THE GIRL?

"YOU WANT BLOOD, DEMON?"
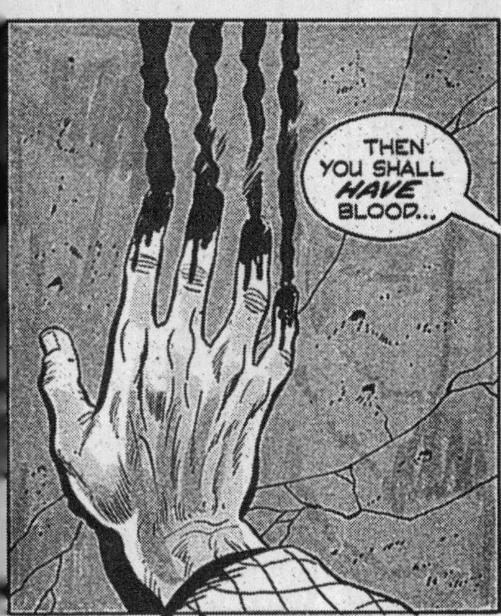
THEN YOU SHALL HAVE BLOOD...

...IF YOU CAN COME NEAR ENOUGH TO LICK IT OFF THE WALL.

AN ADMIRABLE PLOY, OLD MAN. AND NOW IT IS A STANDSTILL-- I CANNOT APPROACH YOUR CROSS OF BLOOD...
...AND YOU CANNOT SLAY ME. BUT I CAN WAIT... AND EVENTUALLY I WILL TAKE YOU BOTH.
YES... I SEE THAT NOW, BLOODFIEND. I AM OLD. MY HEART RAGES EVEN NOW. I WILL DIE SOON...

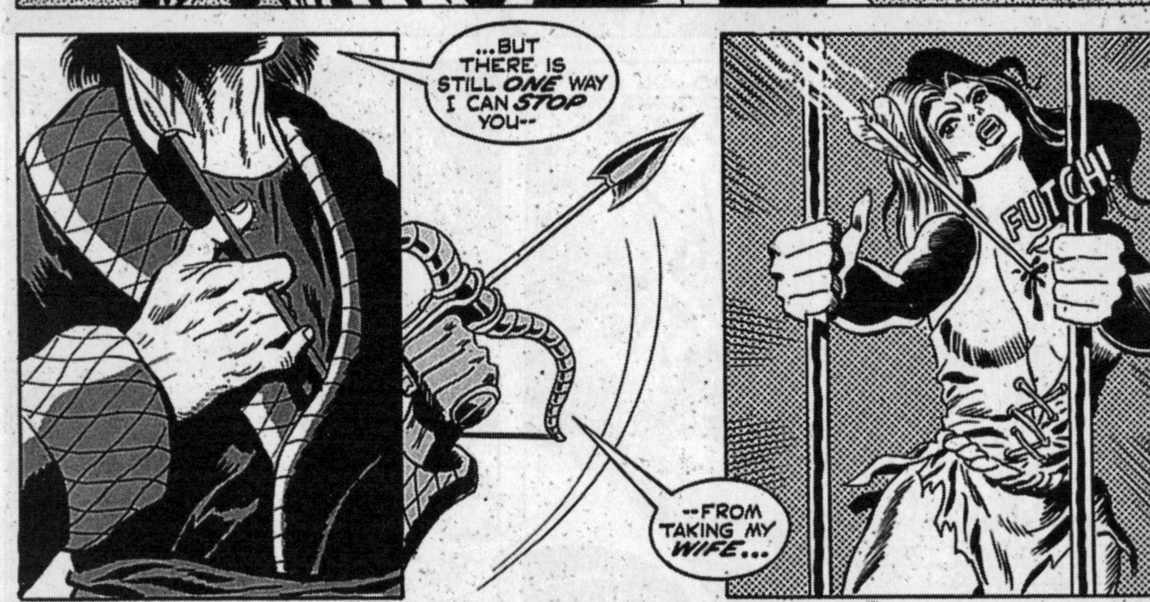
...BUT THERE IS STILL ONE WAY I CAN STOP YOU--
--FROM TAKING MY WIFE...
FUTCH!

...BEFORE I DIE...
UHHHNNN!

YOU HAVE WON, OLD MAN. THE CROSS SMEARED ON THE WALL PREVENTS ME FROM APPROACHING YOUR WIFE, AND EXTRACTING THE ARROW FROM HER HEART.
YES, YOU HAVE WON. AND THERE ARE FEW, INDEED, WHO HAVE BEATEN--

"--COUNT DRACULA!"
FIN

DEATH VOW!
HE-YAAAAAHH!
OUT OF MY WAY, THERE! OUT OF MY WAY!

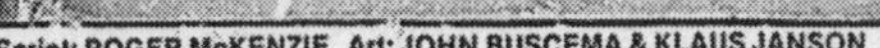
Script: ROGER McKENZIE Art: JOHN BUSCEMA & KLAUS JANSON

BUT THERE IS A PROMISE TO BE KEPT TONIGHT.

A GRIM PROMISE THAT HAS DRAWN--HIM--HERE...

...TO COLOGNE, DEEP WITHIN THE HEART OF THE GERMAN RHINELAND, THIS YEAR OF OUR LORD, 1823.

BUT THE LORD HAS HAD LITTLE TO DO WITH THIS DARK COVENANT...
Reichenbach Clinic
...PLEDGED NEARLY A LIFETIME AGO AND NOT FORGOTTEN.

AFTER ALL, WHAT IS ONE LIFETIME...OR A DOZEN...
...TO SOMEONE, SOME ...THING... THAT HAS ENDURED CENTURIES?

NURSE, WAS A WOMAN JUST BROUGHT HERE BY AMBULANCE?
WHY, YES, THERE WAS. SISTER MARIE EISNER, BLESS HER SOUL.
IT IS MUCH TOO LATE FOR THAT. I HAVE JOURNEYED A GREAT DISTANCE AND WISH TO SEE HER.
I'M AFRAID THAT'S IMPOSSIBLE, SIR. VISITING HOURS ARE OVER.
YOU'LL HAVE TO COME BACK ...IN THE MORNING...

WHERE IS SHE, DAMN YOU?
R-R-ROOM 477... TAKE...TAKE THE ELEVATOR...

GOTT IN HIMMEL...
...H-HIS EYES... HIS EYES...
THE ELEVATOR, WHEN IT COMES, IS CROWDED...

IT IS FILLED WITH THE DEAD...
...THE DYING...

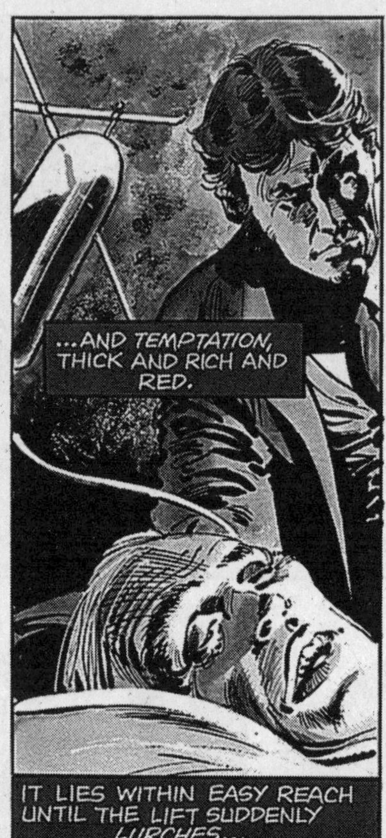
...AND TEMPTATION, THICK AND RICH AND RED.
IT LIES WITHIN EASY REACH UNTIL THE LIFT SUDDENLY LURCHES...

...AND THE FLASK SMASHES AGAINST THE FLOOR LIKE A GUNSHOT.
THE SCENT IS UNMISTAKABLE...BLOOD, PRECIOUS BLOOD.
AND ALL OF IT WASTED...

YOU FOOLS!
FOOLS!

AND WHEN, AT LAST, THE ELEVATOR DOORS BEGIN TO OPEN...
H-HELGA, IS IT JUST MY IMAGINATION...
...OR IS THAT SMOKE?
MORE LIKE FOG, I'D SAY.
AND THAT... KOFF ...SMELL! LIKE SOMETHING...

...SOMETHING...

DEAD.

SHE WAITS, IN DARKNESS AND IN PAIN...
...PRAYING HE WILL FORGET...

...KNOWING HE WILL NOT.
SISTER...
...IT IS TIME.

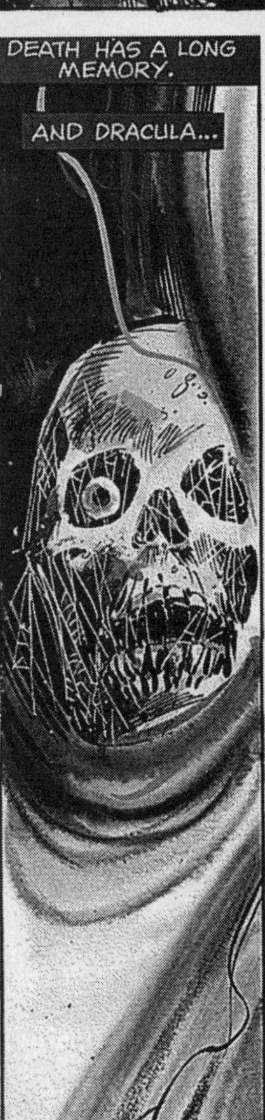
DEATH HAS A LONG MEMORY.
AND DRACULA...

...DRACULA IS DEATH, INCARNATE...
I TOLD YOU THIS WOULD HAPPEN, OLD WOMAN.

I WAS YOUNG, THEN, DEMON. I WAS YOUNG...
...AND FOOLISH.

AND NOW YOU ARE NO LONGER YOUNG.
BUT STILL AS FOOLISH.

THE YEARS HAVE NOT TREATED YOU KINDLY. THEY HAVE CREPT UP ON YOU LIKE THIEVES IN THE NIGHT.
FIRST, THEY STOLE YOUR YOUTH. NOW, UNSATISFIED WITH THAT, THEY STEAL YOUR LIFE.

AND YOU, DEMON. ARE YOU ANY DIFFERENT?
DO YOU NOT CREEP LIKE A THIEF IN THE NIGHT, STEALING LIFE?
YOU MOCK ME, OLD WOMAN!

MORE THAN THAT, DEMON, I REVILE YOU. I DENOUNCE YOU WITH ALL MY HEART AND SOUL.
BE GONE--! LET ME DIE IN PEACE!

OLD WOMAN, IS THAT ANY WAY TO TALK...
...TO YOUR SAVIOR?

"OR HAVE YOU FORGOTTEN WHAT HAPPENED THAT DAY, SEVENTY YEARS AGO?"
DAMN YOU! DAMN YOU ALL TO HELL!
"NO, DEMON, I HAVE NOT. IT WAS, I REMEMBER, THE DAY YOU DIED."
YOU'LL DAMN NO ONE, NOSFERATU! NEVER AGAIN!
SOMEONE GET FATHER EISNER! TELL HIM WE HAVE THE BEAST!

DELIVER US, FATHER! DELIVER US FROM THIS EVIL!
WE HAVE SUFFERED ENOUGH!
YES.

BUT NONE MORE THAN MARIE.
TAKE THIS, CHILD, AND KEEP IT WITH YOU ALWAYS. FIND WHATEVER COMFORT YOU CAN.
AND, ABOVE ALL ELSE, HAVE FAITH.

THIS...DEMON... HAS SLAIN YOUR PARENTS. BUT, AS HEAVEN IS MY WITNESS, IT SHALL NOT SLAY ANOTHER!

MAY GOD GIVE ME THE STRENGTH...
...TO DO WHAT MUST BE DONE!

THIS IS WHAT I THINK OF YOU, OLD MAN! AND YOUR GOD!

THINK WHAT YOU WILL, DEMON.

BUT BE THOU SILENT!
NNOOO--! DAMN YOU, OLD MAN! AND DAMN THAT ACCURSED HOLY WATER!

I AM DRACULA! DO YOU HEAR ME? DRACULA!

AND I AM LIFE, EVER-LASTING!

BUT YOU, OLD MAN, YOU ARE A HYPOCRITE!
DOES NOT YOUR INSIPID GOD PREACH --LET HE WHO IS WITHOUT SIN CAST THE FIRST STONE?
I DO NOT CAST STONES, DEMON.

I CAST WOOD...

...TO STILL YOUR FOUL HEART FOREVER!
CHOK!

NO, NEVER!
I...AND ALL I TOUCH... WILL ENDURE FOREVER!

WE WILL INHERIT THE EARTH!

NO, DEMON, ALL YOU WILL INHERIT IS HELL!
AND MAY YOU ROT THERE NOW AND EVER MORE!

YOU HAVE NOT WON...OLD MAN.
YOU... CAN NOT ...WIN.

DEATH...HOLDS NO TERROR... FOR ME.
I...KNOW IT... FOR WHAT IT IS.

DO YOU... OLD MAN?

I--I KNOW THE LORD IS MY SHEPHERD--
AND THAT...MAKES YOU A LAMB...OLD MAN!
A LAMB... THAT WILL BE SLAUGHTERED!
"YOU WERE DYING, BUT WITH THE LAST OF YOUR STRENGTH YOU PULLED FATHER EISNER EVER CLOSER TO YOUR BLOOD-STAINED LIPS.
"THEN THE STORM ABRUPTLY ENDED."

NNOOOO--! NOT THE SUN! NOT THE DAMNED SUN!
"YOU SCREAMED IN UNHOLY AGONY AS YOUR COLD FLESH WARMED, THEN BURNED, FROM YOUR BONES."

IT'S OVER, DEMON!
OV--
"THEN FATHER EISNER SUDDENLY CLUTCHED HIS CHEST.

"AND FELL.
FATHER!

IT'S HIS HEART!
HE'S HAD ANOTHER ATTACK!
TAKE HIM TO THE RECTORY. AT LEAST HE'LL BE COMFORTABLE THERE!
GET DOCTOR HOLTZ! HURRY! THE FATHER IS DYING!

DYING--?
"THEY CARRIED HIM AWAY, THAT GENTLE MAN, AND I WAS ALONE..."

"SO TERRIBLY, TERRIBLY ALONE.
"EXCEPT FOR...

"...THE DARK *SHADOW* OF DEATH.
"AND THE *WIND*, COLD AND FOUL...

"...MOANING LIKE A *WOLF* AT BAY."

IS THERE NO HOPE, DOCTOR?

NEIN. I HAVE DONE *ALL* I CAN.
BUT THE *END* IS VERY NEAR.
POOR LITTLE MARIE WILL BE HEART-BROKEN.

SHE *LOVES* THE FATHER SO. HE TOOK HER IN, GAVE HER A *HOME* AFTER HER FAMILY WAS KILLED.
NOW SHE WILL BE AN *ORPHAN* ONCE AGAIN.
IT ISN'T *FAIR*, DOCTOR. IT JUST ISN'T FAIR.

AH, AT LEAST SHE IS SLEEPING.
WE WILL *ALL* SLEEP EASIER, THANKS TO FATHER EISNER.
GOD REST HIS SOUL.

"BUT I WAS NOT ASLEEP..
...OR EVEN IN MY ROOM.

"HOW COULD I SLEEP? FATHER EISNER WAS DYING.
"AND HE NEEDED ME.
"SO I HURRIED THROUGH THE NIGHT...

"...RETURNING TO THE TOWN SQUARE...THE CROSS...
"...AND YOU.
"'I AM DRACULA,' YOU HAD SAID. 'LIFE EVERLASTING. I...AND ALL I TOUCH...WILL ENDURE FOREVER!'

"I TREMBLED AS I REACHED UP...

"...AND PULLED FREE THE STAKE!

"AND THEN...
"...THEN..."
DRACULA WAS REBORN!

DEMON! HEAR ME OUT! YOU MUST HELP ME!

HELP YOU?! WHY SHOULD I HELP YOU...
...WHEN IT IS MUCH MORE ENJOYABLE TO HELP MYSELF?
I HUNGER, CHILD! I BURN WITH HUNGER!

NNOOOO--!

BLASPHEMY!?
OUT OF MY SIGHT, SLUT!

DRACULA, WAIT--! ONE FAVOR IS ALL I ASK.
ONE FAVOR...
...THEN...YOU MAY DO WITH ME WHAT YOU WILL...
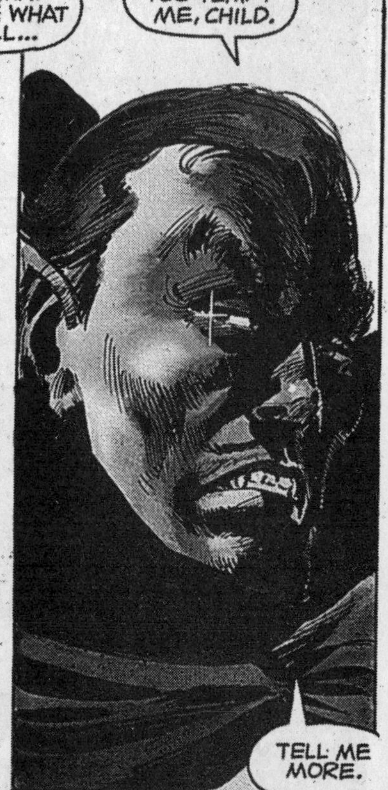
YOU TEMPT ME, CHILD.
TELL ME MORE.

FATHER EISNER IS DYING, BUT YOU HAVE THE POWER TO SAVE HIM!
ETERNAL LIFE, DEMON. GRANT HIM THAT AND I AM YOURS!

AGREED, CHILD!
AND GLADLY!
"WITH THOSE WORDS OUR DARK BARGAIN WAS STRUCK."

"AND YOU WERE GONE.

"AYE, OLD WOMAN. THERE WAS MUCH TO DO.
"AND ALL OF IT...ALL OF IT... BROUGHT ME PLEASURE!"

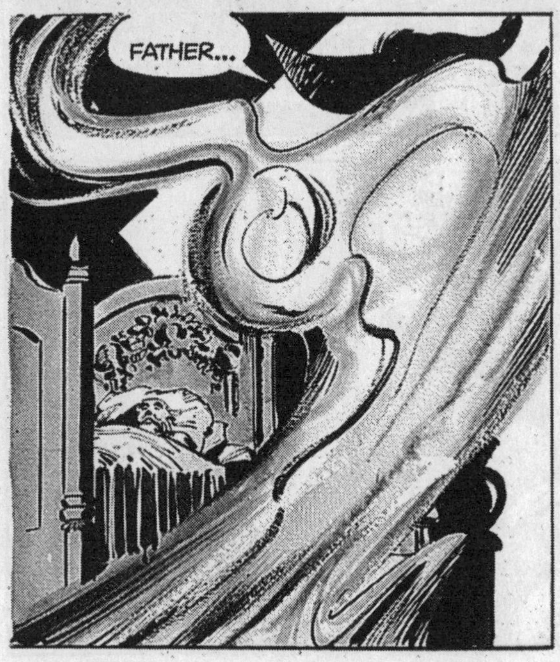
FATHER...

...MARIE SENDS HER BLESSINGS!

NNOOOOO--

"THE NIGHT WAS COLD.
"BITTERLY COLD."

CHILD, THE DEED IS DONE.
THEN FATHER EISNER LIVES?

"BUT THE NIGHT WAS NOT AS COLD AS YOUR VOICE, OR YOUR CARESS...
JOIN ME, CHILD, JOIN ME AND EVER-LASTING LIFE IS YOURS FOR THE TAKING!
...OR YOUR EMPTY, HOLLOW PROMISES. I WAS A FOOL, I KNOW THAT NOW, AND I WAS LOST...

"OR NEARLY SO."

NO! YOU DID NOT ANSWER MY QUESTION, DEMON!
WHAT OF FATHER EISNER?
LOOK CHILD, AND SEE FOR YOURSELF!
I HAVE YOU A MOMENTO! JUST A LITTLE SOMETHING TO REMEMBER HIM BY!

"YOU HELD HIS HEART IN YOUR HAND.

"AND YOU LAUGHED."

DAMN YOU, DEMON! AND DAMN YOUR ETERNAL LIFE!
I DO NOT WANT IT!

BUT YOU WILL, CHILD! YOU WILL!
THE DAY WILL COME WHEN YOU WILL BEG ME FOR LIFE! AND ON THAT DAY, I WILL COME FOR YOU!
I VOW IT, CHILD! DRACULA WILL COME FOR YOU!

SISTER, IS ANYTHING WRONG? I THOUGHT I HEARD--
GET OUT!

WHAT DID YOU SAY?
GET... OUT!

SSSSsss

THIS--
--THIS IS EVERYTHING!

TO DIE, THEN TO RISE, REBORN...
...CAST IN MY IMAGE!

OLD WOMAN, I CAN GIVE YOU POWER! POWER BEYOND YOUR WILDEST DREAMS!

JUST ACKNOWLEDGE ME AS YOUR LORD AND MASTER! ADMIT IT!
DEMON...

...FATHER EISNER SENDS HIS BLES-SINGS!

OH, NO--
NO!

DAMN YOU, OLD WOMAN!

YOU WILL NOT REJECT ME!

I AM YOUR ONLY HOPE! WITHOUT ME, YOU WILL DIE!
ADMIT IT, OLD WOMAN! ADMIT! I AM YOUR SAVIOR! I AM LIFE EVERLASTING!

NO, DEMON, YOU ARE DEATH!
DEATH EVER-LASTING!
AND YOU DECEIVE NO ONE...EXCEPT YOURSELF...

BEG, DAMN YOU, BEG!
I VOWED I WOULD MAKE YOU BEG!

NO--! SHE'S DEAD!

OLD WOMAN, YOU HAVE ESCAPED ME! BUT THERE WILL BE OTHERS!
THERE WILL ALWAYS BE OTHERS!

"And I say unto you, my friends, be not afraid of them that kill the body, and after that have no more that they can do."
"But I will forewarn you whom ye shall fear: Fear him, which after he hath killed hath power to cast into hell--" ST. LUKE, CHAPTER 12, VERSES 4 AND 5...

A HOUSE DIVIDED

SEPTEMBER 13, 1862, EIGHT BELLS. THE FRIGATE RAVEN, FIFTEEN DAYS OUT OF DUBROVNIK, BEARS WESTWARD ACROSS THE STORM-TOSSED ATLANTIC, BOUND FOR SAVANNAH, GEORGIA.

HEEDLESS OF THE SCREECHING GALE AND THE COLD, STINGING SHEETS OF RAIN, THE SHIP'S NEW OWNER AND SOLE PASSENGER STANDS NEAR THE BOW, STARING AHEAD INTO THE FORBIDDING GLOOM AS HE HAS FROM DUSK TO DAWN EVERY NIGHT SINCE THE VOYAGE BEGAN.

BLOODY WEIRD, THAT'S WOT 'E IS!

QUIET, JACOB! 'E'LL 'EAR!

Script: JAMES SHOOTER

Art: GENE COLAN & DAVE SIMONS

I CAN'T UNDERSTAND WHY YOU AND THE OTHERS IS AFEARED OF 'IM, MIKEY BOY! 'E'S A MADMAN, SURE, AND 'E KEEPS UNGODLY HOURS, BUT 'E'S JUST FLESH AND BLOOD!
I TELL YOU, HE'S THE DEVIL 'IMSELF, JACOB! AN' IT AIN'T 'IS 'EATHEN WAYS I FEAR! IT'S--IT'S BECAUSE OF THE RATS!

THE RATS?
I-I SEEN HIM TALKING TO THEM--
--AN' THEY LISTEN! THEY OBEY HIM!

THE STORM PASSES WITH THE NIGHT. DAWN BRINGS A GRIM, OVERCAST SKY.
FROM THE WEST, A CHILL AND STEADY SQUALL DRIVES THE CLOUDS BEFORE IT IN ROILING FURY. LIKEWISE, THE RAVEN, UNBURDENED BY CARGO, SCUDS HELL-BENT BEFORE THE WIND'S WICKED LASH.
THE WINDS DON'T BLOW THIS WAY, I TELL YOU!
ARE YE DAFT, MR. SPENCER? 'TIS BITTER, TRUE, BUT 'TIS DEAD ON COURSE, AND REAL ENOW!

AYE, AN' IT'S FILLIN' ALL THE CANVAS WE CAN HOIST--BUT IT'S SATAN'S OWN BREATH, MATES, MARK THIS!
WE'VE 'AD NAUGHT BUT FAVORABLE WINDS, AN' THAT AIN'T NATURAL IN ANY SEASON!
BLACK POWERS BE AT WORK ON THIS VESSEL! WE'RE ALL DOOMED, I TELL YE--
--AND DAMNED TO BOOT!

AND BELOW DECKS...
MORNIN', LUKE.
THERE'LL BE NO GOOD MORNINGS ON THIS CURSED VOYAGE, MIKEY.
ACH! MURPHY, YOU'RE AS BAD AS SPENCER AND THE REST!
DO YOU FEAR OUR MYSTERIOUS PASSENGER TOO, MURPHY?
AYE, LAD, AN' WITH GOOD REASON!

I WAS THERE AT THE BEGINNINGS O' THIS VOYAGE. IT WERE IN A ROADHOUSE OUTSIDE O' DUBROVNIK.
A STRANGER SUDDENLY APPEARED IN THE DOORWAY. NO COACH ARRIVED, NO HORSE WAS 'EARD, AND YET 'E WAS THERE!
'E STALKED STRAIGHT AWAY TOWARD THE TABLE WHERE THE RAVEN'S FORMER OWNER SAT, DISCUSSING 'ER NEXT VOYAGE WITH CAPTAIN MEADE.

A WORD WITH YOU. ARE YOU THE OWNER OF THE RAVEN?
I AM! AND WHO ARE YE TO BE INTERRUPTING MY BUSINESS WITH MY VESSEL'S CAPTAIN?
YOUR BUSINESS WITH HIM IS ENDED! I AM BUYING THE SHIP!
SHE'S NOT FOR SALE, SIRRAH!

I SAID I AM BUYING THE SHIP. TEN THOUSAND DRACHMAS... IN GOLD.
WHY, THAT'S-- THAT'S THREE TIMES HER WOR-- I- I MEAN, SOLD! BUT, MAY I ASK--
TAKE YOUR MONEY AND BEGONE!
CAPTAIN! WE SAIL FOR AMERICA IN THREE DAYS.

THREE--!? IT CANNOT BE DONE!
WHAT DID YOU SAY?
UH... I... WE'LL BEGIN WORK AT ONCE, MASTER!

"AN' SO WE BEGAN LABORIN' DAY AN' NIGHT, FITTIN' OUT THE RAVEN TO SERVE 'ER NEW LORD'S WHIM. SUPPLIES, WE LOADED, BUT NO CARGO-- INSTEAD, A STATEROOM WAS MADE READY FOR 'IM-- FITTED WITH A STOUT LOCK AND BLACK VELVET CURTAINS OVER THE PORTHOLES, AYE, AND I MYSELF DID PRY A CRUCIFIX FROM A TIMBER IN 'IS LORDSHIP'S CHAMBER-- BY 'IS OWN ORDER.

"ON THE THIRD DAY, A WAGON BEARING 'IS LORDSHIP'S FURNISHINGS ARRIVED, TRAVELLING SOMEHOW THROUGH THE HILLS UNMOLESTED BY ROBBERS. WE BORE TO 'IS CHAMBER A THRONE-LIKE CHAIR--
"--BUT NO BED OF ANY SORT.

"THERE WAS... A BOX--FULL AS LARGE AS A CASKET... AYE, BUT IT WEIGHED ENOW THAT IT TOOK TEN MEN TO CARRY IT ABOARD.

"AS DARKNESS FELL ON EVENING OF THE THIRD DAY WE WERE WELL-NIGH FINISHED. ALL THAT REMAINED WAS A PACKAGE WRAPPED IN FINE VELVET.
ACH! 'TIS A PAINTING OR I'M DAFT!
WHAT 'ARM TO HAVE ME A LOOK--?

LORDY! 'ER DO BE A BEAUTY! AN AMERICAN, BY 'ER LOOK--?
PERHAPS THIS LASSIE BE THE CAUSE FOR OUR LORD'S 'ASTE TO SAIL TO THE NEW WORLD.

"SUDDENLY, 'E APPEARED, AS IF OUT OF THE SHADOWS THEMSELVES, NEARLY IN OUR MIDST! 'E WERE RIGHT FURIOUS!
GI' ME LOOK-SEE, KIRBY!
AH! I'D SWIM TO THE STATES FOR A PIECE O' THAT ARSE!
HO-HO!
YOU DARE--?!

GIVE ME THAT!
GET YOU ABOARD, SCUM, WE SAIL NOW! AND THINK YOU WELL BEFORE YOU AGAIN DEFILE MY POSSESSIONS WITH YOUR TOUCH!
"'IS ANGER... 'IS STRENGTH WEREN'T HUMAN! 'E COULD EASILY 'AVE SLAIN EVERY MAN!

"THUS, THE RAVEN WEIGHED ANCHOR AT MIDNIGHT... AND WE SET SAIL UNDER A WAN AN' BLOODLESS MOON.
"NOW THE SCUTTLE IS THAT THE LADY IN THE PICTURE BE A YOUNG LASS FROM VIRGINIA, SENT BY 'ER LANDED FATHER TO STUDY IN VIENNA.

T'WAS THERE, 'TIS SAID, OUR NEW LORD ESPIED 'ER. I SUSPECT THAT SHE SINCE RETURNED TO HER HOME AND FAMILY, AND THAT NOW, OUR DARKSOME MASTER PURSUES 'ER, OUT OF LOVE!
OR LUST! BUT NO, I CAN'T BUY EVEN THAT!

FAIR OR NO, SHE'S JUST ANOTHER WENCH! NO MAN SAILS ACROSS 'ALF A WORLD FOR A WOMAN!
NO MAN! BUT 'E'S MORE THAN 'UMAN, JACOB-- AND PER'APS LESS, TOO!
BILGE! THERE'S A WAR ON IN AMERICA, MATE! AND WHERE THERE'S WAR, THERE'S PROFIT TO BE MADE!
I THINK I CAN GUESS WHAT MADE 'EAVY THE BOX YOU BORE ABOARD!

HOURS LATER, AS EVENING'S SHROUD CLOAKS THE RAVEN...
THERE 'E IS AGAIN, KEEPING 'IS HEATHEN VIGIL!
AN' PER'APS, I, TOO, WOULD BE RESTLESS AT NIGHT WERE I SMUGGLING GOLD BULLION TO REBELS IN THE STATES!
HMM... 'TWOULD BE EASY ENOUGH TO SLIP BELOW DECKS UNSEEN...

...AN' A CRAFTY FELLOW MIGHT BE 'AVING 'IMSELF A LOOK IN THAT "COFFIN-BOX!"
EH? RATS-- CLUSTERED 'ROUND 'IS DOOR! AN' BOLD ONES, TOO-- THEY DO NOT FLEE AT MY APPROACH!
HMMPH! MUST BE 'E'S MADE PETS O' THEM, TO FRIGHTEN FOOLS LIKE MIKEY. 'E PROBABLY DROPS CRUMBS FOR 'EM!

OUT O' MY WAY, SCURVY VERMIN!

THE DOOR'S LOCKED TIGHT-- BUT A FEW BLOWS WITH THIS KEG O' NAILS WILL SNAP THE BOLT! SO!
NOW WE'LL SEE THIS MYSTERIOUS LORDSHIP'S 'ORDE-- AYE, AND PARE A FEW SLIVERS FROM 'IS GOLD FOR ME OWN POCKETS!

'E'LL DARE NOT EVEN MAKE KNOWN THE LOSS, LEST THE CREW TAKE A NOTION TO SEIZE IT ALL.

MEANWHILE, ON DECK...
A BITTER WIND FOR SEPTEMBER, EH, M'LORD?
M'LORD? I SAY--
I DO NOT PASS IDLE CONVERSATION WITH COMMON SCUM, SAILOR. BE SILENT.
UH... YES, SIR!

SKEEK! SKEE!
WHAT ON GOD'S EARTH--?
EH?

RATS! DOZENS OF THEM-- MAKIN' A RACKET LIKE ALL THE TRUMPETS OF HELL! LIKE THEY WAS CRYIN' OUT A WARNIN'!

I NEVER SEEN ANY-THING TO MATCH--
SIR?
'E'S GONE! BUT-- I JUST TURNED AWAY FOR AN INSTANT! THERE'S NO PLACE 'E COULD'VE GONE SAVE... OVERBOARD!
I'VE GOT TO CRY OUT THE... ALARM...
...OR DO I? LORD 'ELP ME, I HOPE 'E'S FALLEN IN! I PRAY--!

AND IN THE MASTER'S STATEROOM...
THIS MUST BE THE TRUNK OL' MURPHY SPOKE OF.

EH? NO GOLD! JUST... DIRT?!

BUT WHY WOULD--
AHH!

AAARRR
'EAVEN HELP US!

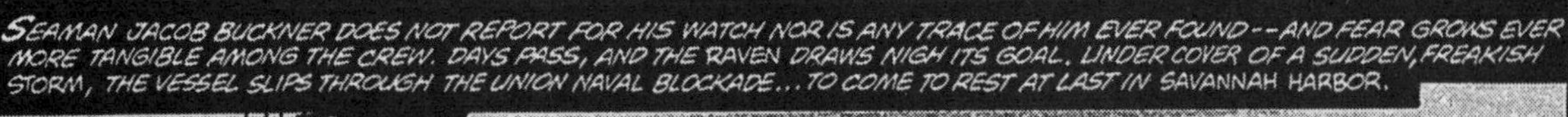
SEAMAN JACOB BUCKNER DOES NOT REPORT FOR HIS WATCH NOR IS ANY TRACE OF HIM EVER FOUND--AND FEAR GROWS EVER MORE TANGIBLE AMONG THE CREW. DAYS PASS, AND THE RAVEN DRAWS NIGH ITS GOAL. UNDER COVER OF A SUDDEN, FREAKISH STORM, THE VESSEL SLIPS THROUGH THE UNION NAVAL BLOCKADE... TO COME TO REST AT LAST IN SAVANNAH HARBOR.

THE VESSEL IS MET BY A WELCOMING COMMITTEE OF UPSTANDING CITIZENS--

--AND SOON, IN THE NEARBY, STATELY HOME OF NATHAN BEAUREGARD, LEADING MERCHANT...
WE ARE DISAPPOINTED, OF COURSE, THAT Y'ALL BROUGHT NO CARGO--UH, FOR TRADE! SEEMS LIKE A FINE VESSEL Y'ALL HAVE THERE--GOOD, UH... BLOCKADE RUNNER EH?
OFFER OUR GUEST SOME WINE, BESSIE.
YASSUH, MASSAH BEAUREGARD.
I DO NOT DRINK...WINE.
AND I DO NOT LIKE THE THIN VENEER OF YOUR "HOSPITALITY." WHAT DO YOU WANT?
WELL, UH... I'LL BE DIRECT. IT WOULD HELP OUR WAR EFFORT RIGHT SMARTLY IF Y'ALL'D SEE FIT TO, UH, DONATE YOUR SHIP TO US!
THE CONFED-ERACY HAS GREAT NEED, SIR. YOU'D BE SERVING A NOBLE CAUSE!
I SERVE NO CAUSE BUT MY OWN.
BUT IT IS CLEAR THAT YOU INTEND TO SEIZE THE SHIP SHOULD I REFUSE.

YOU UNDERSTAND, WE'RE JUST WARNIN' Y'ALL! WE CAN'T BE RESPONSIBLE FOR THE SAFETY OF YOUR CREW!
MY CREW HAS UNDOUBTEDLY ALREADY DESERTED. THEIR FEAR IS AS GREAT AS YOUR IMPUDENCE!
TAKE THE SHIP-- BUT BE WARNED--

--I ALSO SHALL TAKE WHAT I NEED!
THIS MAN NATHAN, I FEAR HIM! WHO--WHO IS HE?
I...DON'T KNOW, SARAH, MY LOVE...BUT SOMEHOW I THINK IT MIGHT BE A GOOD IDEA TO APPEASE HIM.

LATER, IN A SHADOWED HOTEL ROOM...
A LAND OF MADMEN! THEIR NOBLE "CAUSE" SERVES THEM--TO LINE THEIR OWN POCKETS.

EH?

WHAT DO YOU WANT?
M-MY NAME IS BESSIE! I BEEN SENT BY MASSAH BEAUREGARD...
...TO S-SERVE Y'ALL, SIR.

THAT PIG! DOES HE HOPE TO PACIFY ME THIS WAY? IS THERE NO LIMIT TO HIS ARROGANCE?
IF'N I DON'T PLEASE Y'ALL, SIR, I'LL GET SKINNED! PLEASE, I'LL DO WHATEVER Y'ALL WANT!
THIS EFFRONTERY IS INSUFFERABLE! AND YET IT HAS BEEN DAYS! I HUNGER!

BAH! VERY WELL THEN... I ACCEPT YOU AS THE MEREST TOKEN OF THE TRIBUTE I'LL EXACT!
YOU ARE TREMBLING, CHILD. FEAR NOT. LOOK INTO MY EYES.
YOUR EYES... I-I'M NOT SCARED NO MORE.

ENOUGH! I DO NOT WISH FOR MY HUNGER TO BE SATED... JUST YET. I HAVE... BUSINESS WITH YOUR "MASTER" GIRL!
I... AIN'T GOT NO MASSUH... BUT YOU, SIR!
BE GLAD THAT YOU ARE SPARED, GIRL. I DRANK BUT A LITTLE BLOOD.
PLEASE... DON'T GO!
BEFORE HER EYES THE DARKSOME FIGURE DISSOLVES INTO SWIRLING MIST--
--TO AGAIN TAKE TERRIFYING FORM AS A BLACK AND TERRIBLE BAT.
NO FEAR HAS THE SLAVE GIRL--ONLY HELLISH LUST FOR THE CREATURE THAT WINGS AWAY INTO THE NIGHT--

--TO ASSUME HUMAN FORM MOMENTS LATER OUTSIDE THE STATELY HOME OF SQUIRE NATHAN BEAUREGARD...

WHO'S THAT KNOCKING? BESSIE, IF THAT BE YOU BACK THIS EARLY, I SWEAR I'M GOING TO WHUP Y'ALL--
--OH! YOU!? SIR, I--
SHUT UP! LOOK INTO MY EYES!

I WISH TO ENJOY THE HOSPITALITY OF THIS DWELLING ONCE AGAIN!
P-PLEASE, SIR, W-WON'T YOU COME IN?

MY THANKS, SLAVE! A VAMPIRE--EVEN I, DRACULA, LORD OF THE UNDEAD--CANNOT ENTER A HOUSE UNBIDDEN!
NOW I GRANT YOU A BOON IN RETURN! I WILL MERELY RENDER YOU UNCONSCIOUS INSTEAD OF SNAPPING YOUR NECK!
AHHGH!
CRASH

MOMENTS LATER...
WHAT IN HEAVEN'S NAME WAS THAT NOISE? IT SOUNDED LIKE IT CAME FROM THE KITCHEN!
I DECLARE, IF EZRAEL HAS BROKEN ANOTHER PIECE OF MY GOOD CHINA--!

I THOUGHT I HEARD THE DOOR.
NATHAN--? IS THAT YOU?

OH, MY GOD--!
DID I STARTLE YOU? MY APOLOGIES.
WH--WHAT ARE YOU DOING HERE?

H-HOW DID YOU GET IN? I DIDN'T SEE YOU IN THE MIRROR! HOW--?
MY KIND CASTS NO REFLECTION, WOMAN! LOOK INTO MY EYES...
Y-YOUR EYES...
YOU WILL OBEY ME, SARAH... OBEY ME!
Y-YES!

GOOD! UNDRESS FOR ME. SLOWLY.

MEANWHILE, IN THE KITCHEN...
EZRAEL!
SOMEONE MUST'VE BROKEN IN!

THEY'RE AFTER MY MONEY! THEY WANT MY GOLD! WELL, NO ONE ROBS NATHAN BEAUREGARD...NO ONE!

MOMENTS LATER...
MY SAFE WAS UNTOUCHED! THERE'S NO ONE DOWN-STAIRS! COULD THEY BE UPSTAIRS--?
OH,NO.. SARAH!

OH, SWEET LORD!
YOU--YOU'LL PAY FOR THIS! I'LL KILL YOU!
HARDLY, STUPID!

YOU--? SLAY THE LORD OF VAMPIRES? BAH!
DON'T COME ANY CLOSER! I WARN YOU!
BLAM
FALL, DAMN YOU! FALL!

BULLETS CANNOT HARM A VAMPIRE, FOOL!
OH...N-NO! DON'T HURT ME! Y'ALL CAN HAVE HER AGAIN IF YOU LIKE!
DRACULA TAKES WHAT HE PLEASES, LITTLE MAN--

--INCLUDING YOUR WORTHLESS LIFE!
CRASH

YOU ARE A WIDOW, SARAH. DO YOU MOURN?
ONLY THAT I CANNOT SERVE YOU BETTER, MY LORD!

HOURS LATER AS DAWN THREATENS FROM THE EAST...
AS YOU COMMANDED, MY LORD, I HAD YOUR POSSESSIONS LOADED ONTO ONE OF NATHAN'S WAGONS.
HOTEL
GOOD, SARAH. THE NIGHT EBBS. WE MUST BE ON OUR WAY.

AH! MY COFFIN! I MUST REST EACH DAY ON THE SOIL OF MY NATIVE LAND, WITHIN... OR PERISH!
WOULD THAT I COULD LIE WITH YOU ON ANY BED, MY LORD. I CRAVE YOUR TOUCH SO!
YOU MUST DRIVE, SARAH: OUR JOURNEY IS LONG.

AS THE WAGON RUMBLES ON ITS WAY, THERE IS ONLY ONE WITNESS-- A SLAVE GIRL WHO CARESSES TWO SMALL PUNCTURE MARKS ON HER THROAT-AND WISHES THAT SHE HAD BEEN THE ONE TO SERVE DRACULA.

DAYS GATHER INTO WEEKS, AND STILL THE WAGON ROLLS NORTH AND WEST INTO VIRGINIA, DAY... AND NIGHT..
TELL ME AGAIN, MASTER... WHAT WOULD BECOME OF ME IF YOU DRINK ALL OF MY BLOOD?
PLEASE, MY LORD--!

IF I DRAINED YOUR BLOOD, YOU WOULD DIE... TO RISE AGAIN IN THREE DAYS A VAMPIRE, EVEN AS I AM. YOU, TOO, WOULD HAVE TO SEEK HUMAN BLOOD FOR FOOD... AND HAVING NONE OF YOUR OWN, YOU WOULD BE OF NO USE TO ME.
BUT WOULD I NOT THEN BE IMMORTAL? COULD I NOT THEN SPEND ETERNITY SERVING YOU?
I HAVE OTHER PLANS FOR ETERNITY! YOU MUST NOT DWELL UPON--
LORD, DO YOU EVER DESIRE ANY WOMAN... AS A MORTAL MAN DOES?

SOME. FEW!
HO, THERE! PULL UP!
GOT TO INSPECT YORE WAGON!
THE YANKS AIN'T FAR OFF, FOLKS! CAIN'T BE TOO CAREFUL!
EH? SENTRIES! WE MUST BE NEAR THE FRONT!

THE ST. JOHN PLANTATION'S ABOUT SIX MILE THATAWAY. THAR'S A ROADHOUSE Y'ALL CAN FIND ROOMS AT JUST DOWN THE ROAD A PIECE.
NOTHIN' MUCH, IN HERE, ZEKE! JUST A BOX OF... OF DIRT?
HMM... WALL, I RECKON Y'ALL CAN MOVE ON, FOLKS.

DID Y'ALL GET A GANDER AT HIS MISSUS? PALE. MUST BE SICKLY.
MEBBE SHE'S ONE OF THEM THAR EL-BINOS, ZEKE!
I DUNNO... I SEEN WOUNDED WHAT DONE LOST A LOT OF BLOOD WHO LOOKED LIKE THAT... 'CEPT THEIR EYES WAS EMPTY-LOOKING. HERS WAS LIKE BLAZING COALS!

SOON, OUT OF SIGHT OF THE SENTRIES...
STOPPING, MY LORD? PERHAPS, AGAIN, YOU WANT ME?
NO... I HAVE NO DESIRE FOR YOU TONIGHT, SARAH.
BUT... I DESIRE YOU! PLEASE, MASTER, TAKE ME!

YOU DO NOT UNDERSTAND, SARAH. YOU ARE NOT MY LOVER. JUST AS SLAVES ARE PROPERTY TO YOU, YOU ARE MERE PROPERTY TO ME. YOUR BLOOD, IN FACT, IS NO DIFFERENT THAN THE BLACK GIRL'S TO ME. IT IS JUST... FOOD!
SURELY IT IS MORE THAN THAT, MY LORD?!

YOUR SILENCE-- SO ELOQUENT! I SEE NOW... YOUR THOUGHTS, YOUR LOVE, IS WITH ANNABELLE! SHE ALONE AMONG WOMEN STIRS YOUR DESIRE IN THE MANNER THAT MORTAL MEN KNOW IT! AND, NOW THAT YOU ARE NEAR HER... I AM A LIABILITY!
YES. YOU MUST LEAVE ME NOW... RETURN TO YOUR HOME!
I... CANNOT, MY LORD! I WILL FOLLOW YOU TO THE GATES OF HELL... AND BEYOND!

THEN YOU LEAVE ME NO CHOICE! MUST I COMMAND YOU TO SLAY YOURSELF?
NO, MY LORD I'LL DO SO WILLINGLY!
IF YOU WANT ME NOT, IT IS I WHO HAVE NO CHOICE!
THE RIVER SEEMS TO BECKON ME! HOW PLEASANT IT WOULD SEEM... TO DROWN IN ITS DARK GRASP!

--BUT THE NEW DAY COMES, WAXES FULL, AND FINALLY DIES. IN THE COOL OF THE EVENING, THE MANOR HOUSE OF THE ST. JOHN PLANTATION IS AGLOW WITH FESTIVITIES WHICH BELIE THE NEARNESS OF THE SPECTRE OF WAR...

FATHER... WAS IT WISE TO GO ON WITH THE FUND-RAISING BALL WITH THE UNION FORCES JUST ACROSS THE RIVER?

THEY'RE NOT YET READY TO STRIKE, CORNELIUS--

--AND AS YOU WELL KNOW, MONEY AND SUPPLIES ARE A MORE PRESSING PROBLEM THAN THE YANKEES! IS ANNABELLE READY YET?

SHE'LL BE DOWNSTAIRS PRESENTLY, SIR.

AH, GOOD!

CITIZENS OF THE NOBLE CONFEDERACY, YOUR ATTENTION PLEASE! THE TIME HAS COME TO PRESENT TO YOU A CERTAIN YOUNG LADY--
--A LADY WHO BRAVED THE PERILS OF THE UNION BLOCKADE TO RETURN FROM EUROPE TO HER FAMILY AND HER BELOVED VIRGINIA IN THIS TIME OF UNCERTAINTY!

LADIES AND GENTLEMEN. MY DAUGHTER... ANNABELLE ST. JOHN!
FOR THE BENEFIT OF THE CONFEDERACY, I'D LIKE TO AUCTION OFF HER FIRST DANCE.
YOUNG GENTLEMEN, WHAT AM I BID?

ONE HUNDRED DOLLARS, SIR!
ONE-TWENTY-FIVE!
SHE'S PRETTIER THAN *THAT!* ONE-*THIRTY-FIVE!*

ONE THOUSAND DOLLARS... IN GOLD!
WHAT--?
WHO COULD--
MY WORD!

I HEAR NO FURTHER BIDS!
I PRESUME, THEN, THAT I HAVE MADE A *PURCHASE?*

WELL, I BEG YOUR *PARDON,* SIR--
GRANTED! HERE IS YOUR MONEY! AND NOW--
--LET THE MUSIC BEGIN!

THE MUSIC BEGINS... AND THE OTHER GUESTS GAPE IN AWE...
WHO IS HE?
WHO IS HE?
WHO CAYAHS? HE'S GOOD LOOKIN'-- AND RICH!
I DON'T KNOW... BUT I DON'T LIKE HIM!

OUTSIDE...
BAH! THAT POMPOUS, ARROGANT BUFFOON! ONLY FOR ANNABELLE'S SAKE DO I SPARE HIM!
THE SIGHT OF HER--. IT IS ALMOST MORE THAN I CAN BEAR!
ARRRH! I MUST HAVE BLOOD TONIGHT... TO SLAKE MY THIRST... AND TO QUELL THE FIERY RAGE SEETHING IN MY HEART!
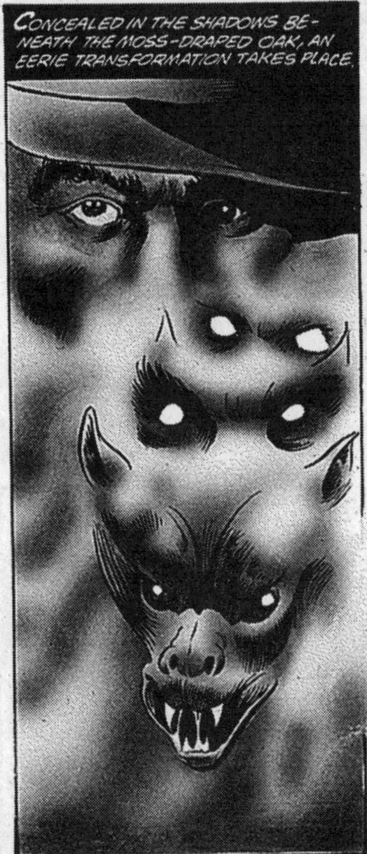
CONCEALED IN THE SHADOWS BENEATH THE MOSS-DRAPED OAK, AN EERIE TRANSFORMATION TAKES PLACE.

--THEN, ONCE AGAIN, A FOREBODING SHAPE WINGS SILENTLY ACROSS THE MOON...
I DO NOT WISH FOR THE LOCALS TO YET BE AWARE OF ME. I WILL FLY NORTH, ACROSS UNION LINES-- THERE TO SATE MY HUNGER.

SOON...
THERE ARE MANY CAMPFIRES... THOUSANDS OF TENTS.
THE UNION FORCES ARE FORMIDABLE THE SOUTHERN ARMY IS OUTMATCHED TEN-TO-ONE.

BUT WHAT GOOD IS ARMED MIGHT AGAINST ONE SUCH AS I?
JOE...D'HEAR SOMETHING?

SUDDENLY, DRACULA IS UPON THE HAPLESS SENTRIES! CLUBLIKE BLOWS FROM HIS MIGHTY FISTS SNAP THEIR NECKS LIKE FRAGILE CRYSTAL.
THEN, SATISFIED THAT HIS VICTIMS ARE DEAD, HE QUENCHES HIS TERRIBLE THIRST WITH THEIR BLOOD... UNAWARE THAT HIS GRUESOME ACT IS OBSERVED.
DRACULA... HERE!? THIS CANNOT BE! WHEN I LEFT MY NATIVE AUSTRIA I THOUGHT THAT, HERE IN THE NEW WORLD, I WOULD BE FREE OF THE HORRORS THAT PLAGUE THE CONTINENT!

SOON, AT THE ST. JOHN PLANTATION...

MOVE OUT! THEM YANKS IS ON THE MARCH!

THE CONFEDERATE TROOPS CAMPED HERE ON THE GROUNDS ARE MOVING TO THE FRONT. AS I SUSPECTED, THE BATTLE DRAWS NIGH.

I AM COUNT VLAD DRACULA.
YASSUH' MISSY'S BEEN EXPECTIN' Y'ALL.
Y'ALL DON'T LOOK WELL, SUH... ARE Y'ALL SURE--
I AM FINE. LET ME IN.
YASSUH.

INSIDE...
OH, VLAD! I'M SO GLAD YOU CAME.
YOUR FATHER--?
HE'S ORGANIZING THE DEFENSES ALONG THE RIVER.
CLARRIE, PLEASE LEAVE US ALONE FOR A WHILE.
BUT YO' FATHER DON'T WANT--
CLARRIE, IF I ALWAYS DID WHAT FATHER WANTED I'D STILL BE IN EUROPE. I WISH TO SPEAK TO THE COUNT PRIVATELY. I CALL... IF EITHER OF US NEEDS HELP.
YES, MISSY.

AS THE POLISHED DOORS CLOSE BEHIND THE FLUSTERED NANNY...
WE MET SO BRIEFLY IN VIENNA, VLAD... AND, YET, I FELT THINGS FOR YOU THAT I DIDN'T KNOW I COULD FEEL.
I-I'M SORRY I LEFT SO SUDDENLY! THE WAR--I WAS AFRAID FOR MY HOME... MY FAMILY.
BUT, SURELY, YOU HAVE A THOUSAND WOMEN. WHY FOLLOW ME SO VERY FAR?
YOU ARE THE ONE I DESIRE. YOU, ALONE, IN ALL THE WORLD!
YOU ARE YOUNG AND BEAUTIFUL, BUT MORE, THERE IS FIRE IN YOUR SOUL... A WILL STRONG ENOUGH TO RESIST EVEN MINE!

YOU ALONE STIR THE... OLD PASSIONS WITHIN ME! I WANT YOU TO RETURN WITH ME.
I...LOVE YOU!
I'M NOT SURE I KNOW WHAT LOVE IS. I KNOW THAT YOU FASCINATE ME. I WANT YOU...
...BUT I-I COULDN'T LEAVE... NOT UNTIL MY BROTHERS AND FATHER COME HOME SAFELY.
BUT I KNOW THEY'LL WIN... THEY MUST WIN!

ANNABELLE, I HAVE SEEN THE UNION FORCES. THEY ARE FAR SUPERIOR. YOUR FATHER'S RAGGED ARMY WILL BE SLAUGHTERED. BY SUNDOWN TOMORROW, THIS LAND WILL BE IN ENEMY HANDS... AND YOUR FAMILY WILL BE DEAD.
YOU MUST COME AWAY WITH ME NOW...LEST YOU BE SLAIN...OR WORSE!
OH, VLAD ...NO.
IF THAT'S TRUE... THEN I CAN'T LEAVE! IF MY FAMILY AND MY HOME SHOULD FALL... I WANT TO DIE!

VERY WELL, THEN! I HAD NOT PLANNED TO INTERFERE IN THIS SENSELESS CONFLICT... HOWEVER... IF I PREVENT THE INVASION AND SAVE YOUR FAMILY, WILL YOU THEN RETURN TO TRANSYLVANIA WITH ME?
GLADLY! BUT--
--BUT... HOW CAN ANY ONE MAN--
ONE MAN CANNOT... BUT I CAN! FAREWELL.

LATER, AS DARKNESS FALLS OVER THE REBEL DEFENSES...
WHAT ARE THEY WAITING FOR? WHY DON'T THEY ATTACK?
THEY GONNA KEEP US UP ALL NIGHT WORRYIN' ABOUT IT, THAT'S WHY.
THEN, IN THE MORNING, THEY'LL COME THROUGH LIKE A TWISTER.
I HEAR THEY GOT BREECH LOADERS AND REPEATERS.
LORD, I DON'T WANT TO DIE.

HEY--! WHAT IN TARNATION--!
FOG... BUT I AIN'T NEVER SEEN IT SPRING UP SO SUDDEN BEFORE--HEY!
THAR'S A MAN IN THAT MIST... BUT HOW'D HE GET THAR?
HALT! WHO GOES THAR?

PUT DOWN YOUR WEAPONS! THEY HAVE NO POWER AGAINST ONE SUCH AS I!
HE'S A GHOST! HE FORMED OUT OF THE MIST, I SWEAR! A GHOST!
SILENCE! YOU HAVE BEEN CHOSEN!

YOU ARE NINETY-NINE MEN! PERFECT!
LOOK INTO MY EYES! ALL OF YOU!

YOU WILL OBEY ME... OBEY ME... OBEY...
YES... SIR!
EXCELLENT! NOW, FETCH ME A MOUNT!

MINUTES LATER...
WE MARCH DOWN-RIVER... TO THE MARSHES!
FORWARD, MY LEGION OF THE DAMNED! TONIGHT WE SHALL CON-QUER!

SOON...
THE UNION COMMANDERS BELIEVE THIS SWAMP TO BE IMPASSIBLE... BUT THERE IS A SAFE PATH! FOLLOW ME!
PLACES OF EVIL, SUCH AS THIS, HAVE NO SECRETS FROM DRACULA! THE VILE CREATURES THAT DWELL HERE GUIDE ME!
BEHOLD! I SUMMON A FOG TO MASK OUR ADVANCE!

THE NINETY-NINE WADE UNHESITATINGLY THROUGH THE DARK, FETID WATER. THEY SHOW NO FEAR, NOR DO THEY HEED THE PIERCING COLD--

--AND ON THE OPPOSITE BANK...
QUIETLY, NOW... ONWARD! SOON THEY WILL BE AT OUR MERCY!
AS THE LAST OF THE ARMY OF NINETY-NINE CLAMBERS OUT OF THE MURKY WATERS--

--AN ARMY OF A DIFFERENT SORT FOLLOWS CLOSE ON THEIR HEELS-- AN ARMY OF VERMIN, COUNTLESS THOUSANDS OF THE FOULEST, BASEST CREATURES OF THE MARSH, UNDER THE SWAY OF THE DARK LORD!
THE NINETY-NINE ARE OBLIVIOUS TO THEIR BIZARRE ALLIES.

EVEN IN THE DEAD OF NIGHT, THE UNION CAMP IS ALIVE, BUSTLING WITH THE PREPARATIONS FOR AN ALL-OUT ASSAULT AT DAWN...

SERGEANT, I WANT THESE MEN DEPLOYED AROUND THE POWDER WAGONS.

YES, SIR.

EEAAAAH!

THE SIGHT OF BLOOD SEEMS TO DRIVE THE ATTACKING REBELS INTO A BERSERKER FURY! THEY FEEL NO PAIN... NO WEARINESS DULLS THEIR BLAZING EYES. THEY ARE AS INHUMANLY VICIOUS AS THEIR BASE ALLIES--

--AND THE SLAUGHTER IS SWIFT!

DAMN THIS FOG! IT'S-IT'S AS IF THE REBS PLANNED IT! THERE MUST BE THOUSANDS OF THEM! THEY'RE OVERRUNNING US!
TURN THE BATTERY ON THE CAMP! PREPARE TO FIRE!
BUT, MAJOR--! OUR OWN MEN ARE DOWN THERE!
I KNOW, DAMMIT... BUT WE'VE GOT TO HOLD 'EM HERE! READY... AIM...

F--AHHHGH!
MAJOR!
JEHOSEPHAT! THAT REB JUST POPPED OUT OF THE CLOUD OF SMOKE!

HOLY--! HE'S LIFTIN' A CANNON! BUT NOBODY CAN--
SHUT UP, YOU FOOL! CUT HIM DOWN! FIRE!

AIEEE!
HE AIN'T HUMAN!

SECONDS LATER, DRACULA'S LEGION OF MEN AND VERMIN SWEEPS OVER THE BATTERY.
AHHGH!

ONWARD! BURN THE REST OF THE CAMP! KILL THEM IN THEIR TENTS! DESTROY ALL IN YOUR PATH!

LEGIONS OF THE DAMNED... ATTACK!

FIRST THE TENTS ARE TORCHED... THEN THE SUPPLIES... AND FINALLY THE POWDER...
KABOOOM

AND, SOON...
IT IS DONE! THE ENEMY HEADQUARTERS HAS BEEN DESTROYED! LEADERLESS AND TERRIFIED, THE UNION SOLDIERS FLEE BY THE THOUSANDS!
VICTORY IS MINE!

SO IT IS, LORD OF FILTH AND DEGRADATION--
--BUT THIS NIGHT SHALL YOUR WRETCHED EXISTENCE BE FORFEIT!
YOUR UNHOLY ALLIANCE WITH THE REBELS HAS WROUGHT DISASTER... BUT ONCE YOU ARE SLAIN, THEN VICTORY TRULY BELONGS TO THE UNION... AND GOD!

"LORD OF FILTH AND DEGRADATION"? SO YET ANOTHER TITLE HAS BEEN BESTOWED UPON ME! BY WHOM, MAY I ASK?
I KNOW BETTER THAN TO TELL YOU MY NAME, EVIL ONE!
NOW TURN... AND DIE!

YOU WOULD END MY "WRETCHED EXISTENCE" WITH A GUN, OLD MAN?
AYE, MONSTER--

--A GUN WITH A BULLET MADE OF SILVER!
WHA--
AARGH!
BAM

SO... I MISSED YOUR BLACK HEART! NO MATTER! YOU ARE WOUNDED... HELPLESS... AND I HAVE OTHER WEAPONS!
IT PAINS YOU, AS DOES THE GARLIC STRUNG AROUND MY NECK!
AHHH! THE CURSED CROSS! TAKE IT AWAY!
I KNOW YOU TOO WELL, DEMON!

NOOOO!
IN SEARING AGONY THE LORD OF VAMPIRES WRITHES, FLAILING BLINDLY AT HIS TOR-MENTOR--

--UNTIL...
UHH! THE CROSS--
WHAK!

YOU SHOULD NOT HAVE WASTED TIME TORTURING ME! NOW, YOU ARE UNDONE!
BAH! AN IDLE THREAT! YOU HAVE GAINED NOTHING! YOU ARE TOO WEAK TO FLEE, AND MY GARLIC WILL PROTECT ME WHILE I DRIVE HOME THIS STAKE!

I THOUGHT YOU KNEW ME WELL, SCUM! YOU ARE A FOOL!
AT MY COMMAND, LET THE ELEMENTS STRIKE--

--AND DESTROY YOU!
KRAKKA
EEYAHH!
BOOOM

DRACULA'S WOUNDS HEAL QUICKLY. DAWN IS NEAR WHEN HE GATHERS THE THIRTEEN WHO REMAIN OF THE NINETY-NINE...
BACK! ACROSS THE SWAMP! HURRY!

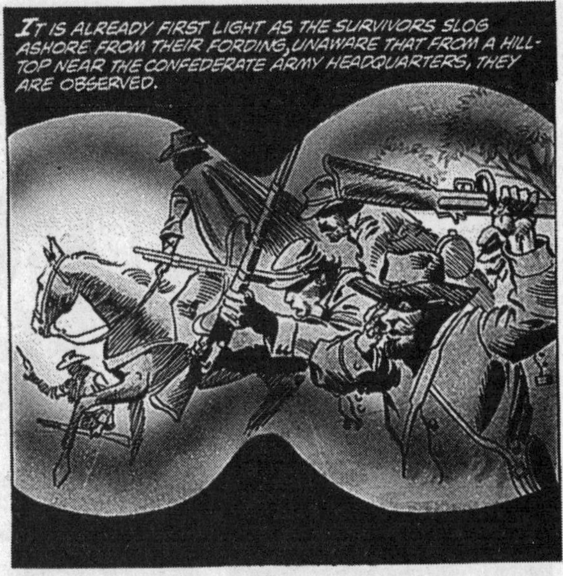
IT IS ALREADY FIRST LIGHT AS THE SURVIVORS SLOG ASHORE FROM THEIR FORDING, UNAWARE THAT FROM A HILL-TOP NEAR THE CONFEDERATE ARMY HEADQUARTERS, THEY ARE OBSERVED.

IF--I CAN'T BELIEVE IT! IT'S THAT COUNT VLAD DRACULA FELLOW LEADIN' A PLATOON OF OUR MEN!
AND LEAVIN' THE UNION ARMY IN RUINS BEHIND HIM!
PERHAPS WE WERE WRONG ABOUT--WAIT! WH--L-LOOK AT HIM!

"LOOK AT WHAT HE'S DOIN'! WHAT HE'S BECOME!"
THE THIRTEEN SURVIVORS OF THE NINETY-NINE STARE BLANKLY AS DRACULA TRANSFORMS BEFORE THEIR EYES, AND TAKES WING. WITH THE SUN'S FIRST RAYS THEY WILL FULLY AWAKEN, REMEMBERING NAUGHT OF THEIR ORDEAL, INCLUDING THIS--

--BUT OTHERS WILL NEVER FORGET THE AWESOME HORROR THEY HAVE JUST WITNESSED...
MY GOD!
FATHER... THAT--THAT THING IS AFTER ANNABELLE!

SOON...
ANNABELLE!
FATHER! THANK GOD YOU'RE SAFE--
--JUST AS VLAD PROMISED! OH, I'M SO HAPPY!

HE...PROMISED?
YES! IN EXCHANGE FOR MY HAND! I... I AM HIS, NOW, FATHER!
MY GOD...NO!
YOU DON'T KNOW WHAT WE SAW-- WHAT HE IS!

HE'S A MONSTER! A CREATURE INHUMAN! WITH MY OWN EYES I SAW HIM CHANGE HIS FORM TO THAT OF A BAT!
IS HE A WITCH, FATHER? IS THAT WHAT YOU'RE SAYING?
I DON'T DOUBT THAT! I KNEW HE WAS NO ORDINARY MAN! HIS EYES TOLD ME THAT!

BUT IF HE'S THE DEVIL HIMSELF, NONETHELESS, I GAVE MY WORD!
WE'LL SEE ABOUT THAT! GO TO YOUR ROOM, YOUNG LADY!
WHEN HE COMES TO CLAIM YOU...HE'LL GET MORE THAN HE BARGAINED FOR!

ANNABELLE PASSES THE DAY IN HER ROOMS, UNDER GUARD, WATCHING THE AFTERNOON SHADOWS GROW LONG AND MELT INTO VELVET NIGHT.
AN HOUR AFTER SUN-DOWN SHE HEARS HIS HORSE'S HOOVES ON THE CARRIAGE WAY.

IT IS ALREADY TOO LATE TO CRY OUT A WARNING.
WHA--?
GET HIM! PULL HIM DOWN!
TAKEN UNAWARES, THE LORD OF DARKNESS FALLS.

DOZENS OF SLAVES WEARING GARLANDS OF GARLIC AND ARMED WITH CROSSES RUSH FORWARD TO PIN DOWN THE VAMPIRE LORD...
ARRHH!
HOLD HIM! HOLD HIM!
KEEP THOSE CROSSES NEAR TO WEAKEN HIM OR ELSE HE'LL TURN INTO MIST AND SLIP AWAY!
I KNEW HE WAS A MONSTER FROM THE MOMENT HE REGISTERED AT MY INN! I WORKED HARD TO LEARN HIS SECRET... HIS POWER...AND HIS PURPOSE--

--AND TO LEARN THE WAYS TO DESTROY A VAMPIRE!
CURSE YOU! I CURSE YOU ALL!
AHHHGH!
THE DARK LORD'S CURSES AND SCREAMS REND THE NIGHT. HIS VOICE IS GUTTERAL AND FIENDISH, STRIPPED OF ITS MASK OF GENTEEL HUMANITY.

IN HER ROOM, ANNABELLE HEARS THE SCREAMS AND TURNS AWAY. SHE SHUDDERS, AND A TEAR STAINS HER CHEEK.

THE SCREAMS END AS THE STAKE PIERCES THE VAMPIRE'S HEART. FLESH MANY HUNDREDS OF YEARS OLD EVAPORATES FROM THE BONES IN A DARK HAZE OF ACRID VAPORS...

THEN ONCE AGAIN STILLNESS REIGNS...
IT'S OVER! MY THANKS FOR YOUR HELP, INNKEEPER!
MY PLEASURE! BUT IT'S NOT OVER YET!

AT THE DAWN WE MUST SEVER THE HEAD AND STUFF IT WITH GARLIC, AND BURN IT SEPARATELY FROM THE BODY! UNTIL THIS IS DONE, HE MIGHT BE REVIVED, MERELY BY PULLIN' THE STAKE!
STATION A GUARD TO WATCH THE CORPSE TILL DAWN! THEN... LET IT BE DONE!

THE WITCHING HOUR COMES AND GOES. IN THE DARK OF THE NIGHT, THE RESIDENTS OF THE MANOR HOUSE ALL REST IN FITFUL SLUMBER--
--ALL BUT ONE.
THE GUARD, EXHAUSTED FROM THE VIGIL OF THE PREVIOUS NIGHT AWAITING THE UNION ATTACK THAT NEVER CAME, SLEEPS.

UNSEEN AND UNHEARD, WITH TREMBLING HANDS, ANNABELLE ST. JOHN GRASPS THE STAKE--
--AND PULLS.

SUDDENLY THERE IS A SWIRL OF MIST, AND THEN...
YOU RESTORED ME! WHY?
I...MADE A VOW!

SO YOU DID... BUT NOW YOU KNOW WHAT I AM... AND THE TERROR IS RIPE IN YOUR EYES! SURELY YOU DO NOT MEAN TO KEEP YOUR PROMISE!
I--I AM AFRAID...BUT I REALIZE NOW THAT YOU MIGHT HAVE EASILY TAKEN ME BEFORE!

PERHAPS, THEN YOU DO...LOVE ME!
PERHAPS LOVE CAN CONQUER EVEN THIS!

DAYS LATER, A WAGON RUMBLES EASTWARD ALONG A SELDOM-USED ROAD.

IN THE BACK RESTS THE COFFIN OF THE VAMPIRE LORD. AT THE REINS IS HIS CHOSEN ONE.

AHEAD LIES A HARBOR TOWN, THE SEA, AND ACROSS IT THE BROODING TURRETS OF CASTLE DRACULA.
FAR BEHIND, LIES A SMALL VIRGINIA TOWN, WHERE SOLEMN MOURNING BELLS STILL RING, THIS EVE... FOR ANNABELLE ST. JOHN.

PROLOGUE: SO THE MARSHAL CAME TO THE CASTLE, BOOTS LEAVING HUGE TRACKS IN DUST THAT HAD BEEN COLLECTING ON THOSE UNYIELDING STONE FLOORS FOR OVER THREE HUNDRED YEARS. HE WONDERED (WITHOUT REALLY THINKING ABOUT IT) HOW LONG IT WOULD TAKE FOR HIS FOOTSTEPS TO BE OBLITERATED BY THE ALL-CONQUERING DUST.
THE MARSHAL DIDN'T LIKE THE FEEL OF THE CASTLE. IT SCALPED HIS SENSES TO THE RAW.
THERE WAS A SMELL OF DECAY THAT HUNG LEECH-LIKE TO HIS NOSTRILS AS HE MOVED THROUGH THE ONCE-COURTROOM. THE HUMID AIR PASSING OVER HIS TONGUE TASTED LIKE THE DUST ON THE FLOOR.
IT WAS DARK THERE-- THE MOON SHINING THROUGH UNSHUTTERED WINDOWS WAS THE ONLY SOURCE OF LIGHT AND EVEN THAT SCANT RELIEF WAS BEING DISPERSED BY THE SMALL CLOUDS OF DUST HIS PASSAGE RAISED.
DUST. THE CASTLE WAS FULL OF IT.
WORSE, THERE WAS NO SIGN OF THOSE CRITTERS OLD MAN BRIDGES HAD SENT HIM HERE TO KILL.
THEN HE HEARD THE CANDLESTICK FALL, ITS UNPOLISHED GOLDEN SURFACE STRIKING THE FLOOR WITH A DULL...
THUD!
FOOL! THE MORTAL HAS HEARD US!
DOES IT MATTER?
DOES IT TRULY MATTER?
HE STILL--
--DIES!
BDOW
BDOW
BDOW!

BOUNTY FOR A VAMPIRE
THE MARSHAL WAS A LONG WAY FROM HIS BELOVED DAKOTAS.
THERE, HE HAD THOUGHT THE SILVER BULLETS A DAMN FOOL WASTE OF MONEY.
HERE, THEY HAD BOUGHT HIM THREE DEAD...
...VAMPIRES.
THE MARSHAL DIDN'T LIKE THIS JOB.
BUT THEN, HE'D LIKED THE ALTERNATIVE THE PEOPLE OF KUTTNERVILLE HAD OFFERED HIM EVEN LESS.
HM...NOT BAD SHOOTIN' FER A WASHED-UP HAS-BEEN.

WISH OLD MAN SHERTON COULD A' BIN HERE TO SEE IT.
COURSE, FROM WHUT BRIDGES TOLD ME BACK IN KUTTNERVILLE THESE POLECATS AIN'T REALLY DEAD.
SOMEBODY KIN BRING 'EM BACK TO LIFE--JEST BY DIGGIN' THE SLUGS OUT OF 'EM!
BRIDGES SAYS THERE AIN'T BUT ONE SURE WAY TO MAKE SURE THET DON'T HAPPEN.
CAN'T SAY THET AH LIKE IT MUCH...
...BUT A JOB'S A JOB.
NNNOOOK
YEAH...A JOB'S A JOB.
HOW MUCH DOES YORE JOB PAY YUH, MARSHAL? DOES IT PAY ENOUGH TO GET YORESELF KILLED TRYIN' TO TAKE ON BILLY WALKER HISSELF?
AH AIN'T DEAD YET, BILLY.
YORE JEST THE PICTURE OF HEALTH, MARSHAL.
'CEPT FER MEBBE THE FOUR PIECES A' LEAD AH PUMPED INTO YUH.

AH NEVER DID MUCH LIKE THE LAW, MARSHAL.
YOU CAN'T GUN DOWN THE LAW, BILLY. YOU KIN GUN DOWN ME--MEBBE A DOZEN LIKE ME--BUT NOT THE LAW. IT'LL BE AROUND A LONG TIME AFTER YORE FINISHED DANCIN' AT THE END OF A ROPE.
THET'S WHY AH MAKE A HABIT A' GUNNIN' IT DOWN IF IT GETS IN MUH WAY.
THE LAW AIN'T GOT A CHANCE 'ROUN BILLY WALKER.
THET'S A RIGHT PRETTY SPEECH, MARSHAL.
TOO BAD IT WON'T FIT ON YORE TOMBSTONE!

B-DOW!

A SCOUT COULDN'T ALWAYS SEE OR HEAR DANGER IN THOSE DAYS. A SCOUT GOT SO HE COULD JUST KIND OF SENSE IT COMING.
THE MARSHAL HAD BEEN A GOOD SCOUT.
HE SURVIVED HIS TOUR OF DUTY.
AWRIGHT! AH KNOW SOMEBODY'S BEHIND THEM FANCY CURTAINS!
DO YOU COME OUT OR DO AH SEND A LOAD OF BUCKSHOT IN TO FETCH YUH?

I'LL COME OUT, MARSHAL.
AFTER ALL, I HAVE NO REASON TO FEAR YOU!
--NOR YOU REASON TO FEAR ME!

RECKON NOT-- SINCE AH'VE GOT--

--THIS!

HOW FOOLISH OF YOU, MARSHAL. LOOK AT ME.
WOULD YOU KEEP ME AT A DISTANCE--
--WHEN I AM YOURS TO CRUSH IN A LOVERS' EMBRACE?

SHE WAS DIFFERENT THAN THE MARSHAL HAD IMAGINED. HERE WAS A WOMAN OF SOPHISTICATED SEDUCTIVENESS SUCH AS HE'D BEEN ASSURED ONLY IN THE WEALTHY CAPITALS OF EUROPE--
--AND NOT THE HOT-BLOODED VILLAGE GIRL BRIDGES' SON HAD WRITTEN HOME ABOUT WITH BARELY-CONCEALED YOUTHFUL EXUBERANCE AND ILL-CONCEALED YOUTHFUL BOASTFULNESS.

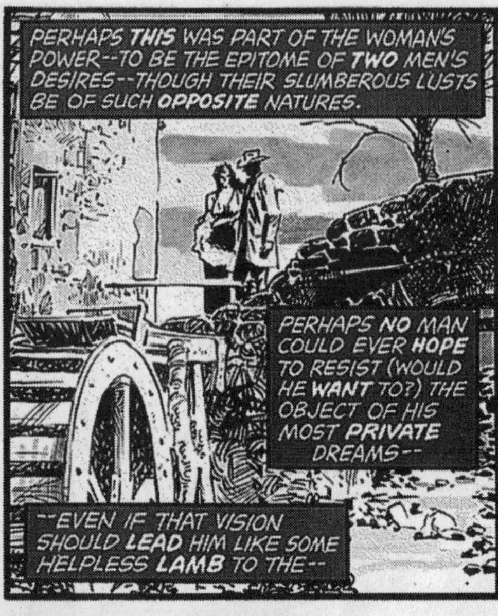
PERHAPS THIS WAS PART OF THE WOMAN'S POWER--TO BE THE EPITOME OF TWO MEN'S DESIRES--THOUGH THEIR SLUMBEROUS LUSTS BE OF SUCH OPPOSITE NATURES.
PERHAPS NO MAN COULD EVER HOPE TO RESIST (WOULD HE WANT TO?) THE OBJECT OF HIS MOST PRIVATE DREAMS--
--EVEN IF THAT VISION SHOULD LEAD HIM LIKE SOME HELPLESS LAMB TO THE--

--SLAUGHTER.

THE YOUTH HAD NOT DIED INSTANTLY. HE DIED KICKING AND SCREAMING AND BLEEDING AND CRYING AND ALL AT LENGTH.

HIS SECOND DEATH, WHEN HE AROSE THREE NIGHTS LATER, HAD NOT BEEN ANY MORE PLEASANT.
OLD MAN BRIDGES WAS A MAN OF SIMPLE PHILOSOPHY.
HE WANTED HIS SON'S MURDERERS ...DEAD.
AND SINCE THE TRANSYLVANIAN AUTHORITIES HAD REFUSED TO COOPERATE, HE WOULD SEND HIS OWN MAN TO BRING DRACULA AND HIS EVIL BROOD TO JUSTICE.
HE WOULD SEND THE MARSHAL.

THE YOUTH WAS JUST THAT, MARSHAL--YOUNG AND INEXPERIENCED. HE MEANT NOTHING TO US.
YOU ARE DIFFERENT. YOU WE WOULD OFFER ETERNAL LIFE AND, SOMEDAY, THE SPOILS OF THIS EARTH.

TOSS AWAY YOUR FOOLISH LITTLE TRINKET, MARSHAL.

JOIN ME IN THE PLEASURES OF THE DAMNED--
--FOREVER!

AAIIEEE!
SORRY, MA'AM. AH GUESS A MAN KINDA LOSES INTEREST IN ETERNAL LIFE--
--WHEN HE'S SEEN AS MUCH UGLINESS AS AH HAVE IN JEST THE ONE LIFETIME THET'S NATURALLY HIS.
THEN I'LL BE DELIGHTED TO PUT AN END TO YOUR DISCOMFORT, FOOL--
--BY ENDING YOUR LIFE!
WHUT THE HELL?!
AH DIDN'T HEAR ANY-BODY COME IN!
PERHAPS YOU RELY OVERMUCH ON AGING SENSES, MARSHAL...
OR PERHAPS I SIMPLY DID NOT WANT YOU TO HEAR ME ENTER? I ASSURE YOU, THE LATTER IS WITHIN THE POWER OF--
--DRACULA!
I ALLOWED YOU THIS FAR BECAUSE THE IDEA OF ONE SUCH AS YOU TRYING TO BRING ME TO "JUSTICE" AMUSED ME GREATLY.
I ALLOWED YOU TO DISPOSE OF THE THREE LACKEYS I SENT TO GREET YOU BECAUSE THEY WERE OF NO REAL VALUE TO ME.
BUT THIS COMELY ONE HAS PROVEN OF GREAT WORTH. I CAN'T HAVE YOU DISPATCH HER AS PERMANENTLY AS YOU HAVE THOSE OTHERS.
PERHAPS I WILL ALLOW HER TO KILL YOU ONCE THAT STAKE HAS BEEN REMOVED FROM HER HEART...
UNLESS YOU'D CARE TO RECONSIDER THE VERY REAL OFFER SHE MADE YOU...
AH DON'T SWITCH SIDES IN THE MIDDLE OF A JOB.

SUCH SURPRISING DEDICATION TO YOUR NEW OCCUPATION, MARSHAL.
OR SHOULD I CALL YOU...

WASHED-UP HAS-BEEN?!
NOW SEE HERE, MAYOR SHERTON. AH BIN DEFENDIN' KUTTNERVILLE 'FER GOIN' ON TWENTY YEARS NOW AND AH AIN'T NEVER ONCE LET HER DOWN.
NOBODY'S DENYIN' THET, MARSHAL.
BUT THE JOB REQUIRES A YOUNGER MAN.
DON'T SEE WHUT YORE GETTIN' ALL RILED UP ABOUT.
WE'RE GIVIN' YUH A PENSION.

AH DON'T WANT A PENSION.
AH JEST WANT TO DO MUH JOB!
AH AIN'T GIVIN' UP MUH BADGE!

ORNERY CUSS!
V-DHUG!

SORRY IT HAD TO COME TO THIS, MARSHAL.
NOW DON'T YOU WORRY NONE ABOUT THE TOWN.

WE GOT US A SHERIFF THET WAS TAUGHT BY THE BEST LAW-MAN IN THE DAKOTAS.
YORE DEPUTY!

YOU JEST PULL UP A ROCKIN' CHAIR, MARSHAL--
--AND ENJOY YORE RETIREMENT.

...BOUNTY-HUNTER.

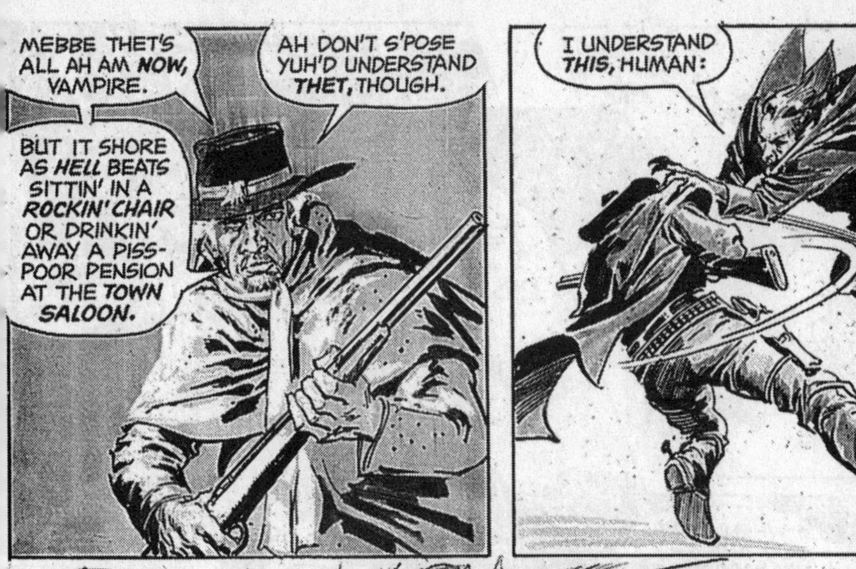

MEBBE THET'S ALL AH AM NOW, VAMPIRE.
AH DON'T S'POSE YUH'D UNDERSTAND THET, THOUGH.
BUT IT SHORE AS HELL BEATS SITTIN' IN A ROCKIN' CHAIR OR DRINKIN' AWAY A PISS-POOR PENSION AT THE TOWN SALOON.
I UNDERSTAND THIS, HUMAN:
ALL WHO OPPOSE DRACULA MUST PERISH!

K-DHOG!
YOU KIN STOP GAWKIN' AT MY RIFLE BUTT, VAMPIRE. IT'S JUST WHUT YUH THINK IT IS--
--PURE SILVER!
DO NOT THINK ME DEFEATED, MARSHAL.

DRACULA HAS POWERS--
--BEYOND MORTAL COMPREHENSION.
AH'LL ADMIT IT'S A MITE UNNERVIN' TO SEE A MAN TURN INTO A BAT--

--BUT AH'VE SEEN STRANGER THINGS WHEN AH WUZ A SCOUT FOR THE 7TH.

INDIAN MAGIC'S PRETTY POWERFUL STUFF--

--BUT *IT* DIDN'T SPOOK ME *NEITHER!*
V-DOOOOM!
SILVER *BUCKSHOT,* VAMPIRE.
YOU *STILL* SO ALL-FIRED *AMUSED* BY THE IDEA A' ME BRINGIN' YUH TO *JUSTICE?*
JUSTICE, MARSHAL--
--WHEN *HERE YOU* ARE THE *TRANSGRESSOR?*

JEST DON'T **STAND** THERE, YUH BLAMED **FOOLS!**
GUN 'EM DOWN!

K-BLAM!
K-DAM!
B-DAM!

AH'M AFRAID WE'RE GONNA HAVE TO HOLD SOME BRAND NEW **ELECTIONS**, FOLKS.

SALOON
MAYOR GREIM JUST **RESIGNED**.

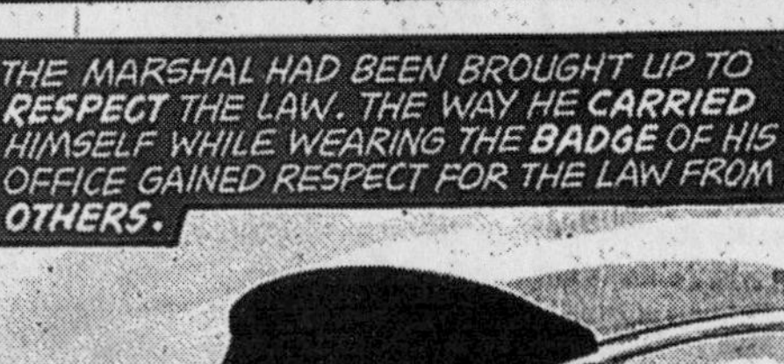
*THE MARSHAL HAD BEEN BROUGHT UP TO **RESPECT** THE LAW. THE WAY HE **CARRIED** HIMSELF WHILE WEARING THE **BADGE** OF HIS OFFICE GAINED RESPECT FOR THE LAW FROM **OTHERS**.*

*THE MARSHAL KNEW THAT SIMPLE BADGE OF **TIN** WAS A HEAVIER **BURDEN**--A HEAVIER **RESPONSIBILITY**--THAN MOST MEN COULD EVER MANAGE.*

*YOU COULD **TAKE OFF** THE BADGE--OR YOU COULD HAVE IT **TAKEN** FROM YOU.*
*YOU COULDN'T TAKE OFF THE **RESPONSIBILITY**.*

YOU PROBABLY DESERVE KILLIN' **MORE** 'AN ANY CRITTER AH **EVER** MET, DRACULA.
AH WISH I COULD GO **THROUGH** WITH IT.

AH GUESS AH BIN FOLLOWIN' THE LAW TOO LONG FER ME TO START GOIN' AGAINST IT NOW.
AH'LL BE BACK, DRACULA--

--WITH A WARRANT FOR YOUR ARREST!
GOD!
IS THE MAN BEREFT OF HIS SENSES?

DOES HE THINK I'LL ACTUALLY ALLOW HIM TO ESCAPE MY CASTLE UNSCATHED?
THE MAN IS A TRUE FOOL--

--AND HE'LL SOON BE A DEAD FOOL AS WELL!

V-VHOOM!

AH COULDN'T BREAK THE LAW, VAMPIRE--
--BUT AH AIN'T GOT NO SCRUPLES AGAINST SELF-DEFENSE!
THE MARSHAL NEVER COLLECTED MORE THAN THIS ONE REWARD IN HIS BRIEF CAREER AS A BOUNTY-HUNTER. HE USED THE MONEY OLD MAN BRIDGES PAID HIM (PLUS HIS SAVINGS) TO BUY A CATTLE RANCH.
HE CALLED IT THE SILVER BUCKSHOT RANCH.
THERE WAS NARY A ROCKING CHAIR TO BE FOUND ANYWHERE ON THE SPREAD.
FINIS

PROLOGUE:

VIENNA-- THE LATE 1800'S.

BY THE LIGHT OF A FLICKERING MIDNIGHT CANDLE, COUNT DRACULA READS OF THE RESEARCHES OF A DOCTOR CALLED DU MONTE.

AND IN THEM... HE FINDS SOMETHING.

FOR TWO CENTURIES, DRACULA HAS MOURNED THE DEATH OF THE WOMAN... THE DOOMED GIRL NAMED CHARITY BROWN...
AND NOW...

HE SEEKS A WAY--
--OUT.

OUT OF THE DARKNESS.
OUT OF THE CURSE WHICH FORCES HIM TO SUSTAIN HIS OWN LIFE BY DRINKING THE BLOOD OF OTHER MEN.

AND SO, HE MUST FIND THIS FRENCHMAN, DU MONTE... THIS SCIENTIST...
FOR IN THAT MAN'S BRAIN RESIDES... THE ANSWER!

A SHADOW ON THE MOON...
A DULL FLAP OF LEATHERY WINGS...
AND THEN-- THE CHANGE!
WINGS BECOME CAPE-- BAT BECOMES... MAN!
CAN YOU DO IT, DU MONTE? YOU, WHO ARE THE MOST FAMED OF ALL RESEARCHERS INTO THE SINISTER SECRETS OF VAMPIRISM?
CAN YOUR SCIENCE SUCCEED WHERE ALL ELSE HAS FAILED?
OF ALL THE MEN ON EARTH, WILL YOU BE THE ONE TO MAKE IT POSSIBLE FOR DRACULA--
HOTEL IMAGE
"TO WALK AGAIN IN DAYLIGHT!"
SCRIPT STEVE GERBER
ART RICH BUCKLER and PABLO MARCOS

WELL, WE SHALL SEE...
M'SIEU LE DOCTEUR...

QUEL...?
BON SOIR...!
...MON DIEU--!

I HAVE COME FOR YOU, DU MONTE.
NO! STAY BACK!! DON'T TOUCH ME!!

FEAR? YOU FEAR ME?
NO, IT RUNS DEEPER THAN THAT, DOESN'T IT?
IT'S REVULSION YOU FEEL-- REVULSION AT MY--

...CONDITION.

FURIOUS, THE PRINCE OF DARKNESS SEIZES THE COWERING DOCTOR, AND--
CHARLATAN! LEECH!
"MEDICAL SCIENCE"-- BAH!

AND TO THINK I CAME SO FAR-- TO SEEK AID FROM SUCH AS YOU!
I-- DRACULA!
YOU WANT...
...HELP?

AT THE THOUGHT, A CHURLISH GRIN TWISTS THE FRENCHMAN'S LIPS--AND HE SOMEHOW OVERCOMES HIS DEEP-ROOTED LOATHING--
--IN TIME TO CALL OUT--

WAIT!
I HAVE A... PROPOSITION.
SPEAK THEN, WRETCH.

FIRST--I MUST KNOW YOU WILL NOT KILL ME--
--EVEN AFTER OUR ENTENTE IS CONCLUDED.

AND SO...
...A BARGAIN IS STRUCK.

AND THE COUNT DEPARTS...

...ON AN ERRAND:

THUNDER ROARS, AND LIGHTNING SHATTERS THE SKY INTO JAGGED FRAGMENTS.
A VAMPIRE STALKS THIS NIGHT--!
AND NATURE HERSELF SHUDDERS AT HIS FOOTFALLS.

I MUST BE MAD TO THINK DU MONTE CAN HELP ME--
--AND MADDER STILL--

--TO BELIEVE THAT THERE IS A CURE...
...FOR THE WALKING DEATH THAT IS MY CURSE!

AND YET--
THIS TASK OF DU MONTE'S IS SIMPLE ENOUGH.
ALL I NEED DO--
--IS RETRIEVE CERTAIN PAPERS FROM THIS HOUSE.

PAPERS--
--ESSENTIAL TO HIS VAMPIRITIC RESEARCH, WHICH HE CLAIMS WERE STOLEN FROM HIM.
I HAVE MY DOUBTS...
...BUT THEY MATTER NOT--IF HE CAN SAVE ME.

BUT FINDING THE PAPERS TAKES TIME--
MY PATIENCE WEARS THIN... BUT I MUST HAVE THOSE FORMULAS!
AND I SHALL TEAR THIS ROOM APART TO--
--EH? THAT SKULL PAPERWEIGHT! BENEATH IT!

STOP!! STOP RIGHT WHERE YOU ARE--
THERE'S YEARS OF WORK ON THOSE PAGES--AND THEY'RE MINE! MINE!!
--OR I'LL HAVE YOUR THIEVING HEAD!
QUITE CORRECT, MON AMI--
Formula
78A-2/10
4/10 / 8¾÷
3⁴×1=18
14
HOWEVER, YOU BELONG TO ME!
NO... NO...!
GAZE INTO MY EYES--DEEPER--DEEPER--
A-AAYIAAAAACH!!
--AND DIE!
FANGS SINK SLOWLY INTO BRITTLE, AGED FLESH...
THE TASTE OF THE BLOOD IS WEAK, UNSATISFYING--
BUT DRACULA SAVORS EVERY DROP--EVERY DROP, SUCKING IT SLOWLY, DELICATELY...
...DRAINING THE CORPSE DRY.

LIPS STILL MOIST FROM ITS FEAST--
ITS LEATHERN WINGS BEATING OBSCENELY--
--THE DEVIL-BAT RETURNS!
ITS TERRIBLE THIRST IS YET UNQUENCHED--
BUT, FOR THE MOMENT, THAT CAN WAIT.
FOR, UPPERMOST IN THIS CREATURE'S MIND IS THE HOPE AGAINST HOPE THAT IT NEED NEVER KNOW SUCH SANGUINARY LUST AGAIN.
AND, SO COMES THE AWESOME TRANSFIGURATION--
--FROM NIGHT-BEAST TO LIVING DEAD MAN!
THE FORMULAE, COUNT--
DID YOU GET THEM?
YES... YES! I HAVE THEM.
WELL, SO YOU DO-- SO YOU DO!
AND THE ONE WHO STOLE THEM FROM ME--?
--IS QUITE DEAD.
EXCELLENT!
THEN LET ME--
NOT YET!
FIRST, DOCTOR--YOUR PROGNOSIS!
CAN DRACULA LIVE AGAIN? TRULY LIVE?
OR AM I FOREVER DAMNED--
--TO BE SLAVE TO THE DEMONIAC DRYNESS WHICH CLAWS AT THE BACK OF MY THROAT?

YOU ARE... DISGUSTED, DU MONTE?
THEN, LET ME DESCRIBE IN DETAIL--
--THE FEAST!
THE THRILL OF THE KILL--
THE FEEL OF SHARP FANGS TEARING INTO SOFT, WARM FLESH...
THE FEEL OF STRENGTH RENEWED-- THE GRITTY TASTE OF THE BLOOD--

BUT THE CURE WILL-- WHAT?!
THAT CROSS! NO! TAKE IT AWAY--!

I AM SORRY, COUNT--BUT I DARE NOT.
YOU SEE, FOR YOUR CURSE, NO CURE EXISTS!
NO! IT CANNOT BE!
YOU LIE!

NO, I DO NOT.
BUT YOUR ARTICLES-- YOUR RESEARCHES--!

DU MONTE'S CROSS LASHES OUT--
--AND DRACULA BURNS!
ALL FICTIONS, I FEAR--
--BASED ON OTHER MEN'S WORK.

AH, BUT NOW--
I NEED ONLY WAIT UNTIL DAWN---!

FOR, THEN--
--WITH YOUR SHRIVELED CORPSE TO STUDY--
AND WITH THE FORMULAE-- PURLOINED FROM THE ONE MAN WHO MIGHT HAVE SAVED YOU--!
WHAT? YOU TRICKED ME-- INTO SLAYING MY ONE REAL HOPE?!
THEN, LOOK AT ME, DU MONTE!!
LOOK--
AT--
ME!
THE CROSS! DISCARD IT-- NOW!!
YES-- YES--
I-- MUST--!

POOR DU MONTE...
FATE HAS AT LAST CAUGHT UP TO YOU.
AH! THIS TIME THE BLOOD RUNS THICK AND HOT--
FATE--
--AND THE INCOMPARABLE HUNGER OF--
DRACULA!
NO-OOOOO!
FOR, THE FEAR IN DU MONTE'S HEART EXTENDS FAR PAST DEATH--

1890

In this year occur the events that, seven years later, are published by Bram Stoker as the novel *Dracula.* Using Jonathan Harker, a young British solicitor, Dracula secures by legal means Carfax Abbey, and surreptitiously enters England and inhabits it. England is a land Dracula had never bothered with, and so he, and vampires in general, are unknown there. He seeks to establish himself in England, but arouses the suspicion of Abraham Van Helsing, evidently before Dracula is quite ready to destroy him. Van Helsing pursues Dracula back to Transylvania where he and others kill him along a country road. Jonathan Harker is rescued, and marries Mina Murray, and in the same year as Stoker's novel appears, they have a son named Quincey.

Editor's Note:

Roy Thomas and Dick Giordano began serializing *Dracula in Dracula Lives! #5* with chapters appearing in *Dracula Lives #6-8 and 10-11,* but the magazine was canceled after they had only finished 76 pages of the adaptation, prompting the last chapter they had completed to be published in *Legion of Monsters #1. Thirty* years after beginning their endeavor, Roy and Dick returned to complete their labor of love in the *Stoker's Dracula* series.

FRANKENSTEIN MARVEL COMICS GROUP™

APPROVED BY THE COMICS CODE AUTHORITY

20¢ 7 NOV 02165

THE FRANKENSTEIN MONSTER™

THE FIEND AND THE FURY!

SMASH THEM! DESTROY THEM ALL!

YOU'LL GASP AT OUR SOUL-SEARING SHOCK ENDING!

Stan Lee PRESENTS: THE MONSTER OF FRANKENSTEIN! TM
A WARM, MOONLIT SUMMER NIGHT --
A BEAUTIFUL, OLIVE-SKINNED GIRL --
A COOL, RIPPLING, MOUNTAIN SPRING-FED STREAM! THESE ARE THE INGREDIENTS IN A REAL-LIFE PAINTING OF BEAUTY AND SERENITY ABOUT TO BE SHATTERED BY--
THE FURY OF A FIEND!
EVER SO SLOWLY HE RISES FROM THE CRYSTAL-CLEAR WATER, THE DROPLETS GLIMMERING IN THE MOONLIGHT LIKE STREAKING FIRE-FLIES AS THEY PLUNGE INTO THE POOL BELOW--
--AND FOR ONE FLEETING MOMENT IN HIS TORTURED LIFE, HE KNOWS THE MEANING OF PEACE AND SERENITY! BUT NOT FOR LONG! IN AN INSTANT, HE SEES HER---AND HE KNOWS IMMEDIATELY SHE CAN MEAN ONLY VIOLENCE AND DEATH TO HIM-- FOR HE IS THE MONSTER OF FRANKENSTEIN!
by GARY FRIEDRICH and JOHN BUSCEMA / INKED BY JOHN VERPOORTEN / COLORING · GLYNIS WEIN LETTERING · CHARLOTTE JETTER
ROY THOMAS · Editor

QUICKLY BUT QUIETLY, HE MAKES HIS WAY TO SHORE, KNOWING THAT SHE OR ANY OTHER WOMAN CAN ONLY BRING HIM FURTHER GRIEF!

STILL, IN MIND IF NOT IN BODY, HE IS A MAN-- AND HE CANNOT HELP BUT PAUSE FOR A MOMENT TO DRINK IN HER BEAUTY!

THEN A MOMENT BECOMES A MINUTE, AND HE LOSES TRACK OF TIME AS HE WATCHES AND WISHES HE COULD HAVE A WOMAN OF HIS OWN--A WOMAN HALF SO LOVELY AS THIS MOONLIGHT BATHER--

BUT HIS FANTASIES ARE SUDDENLY SHATTERED-- FIRST BY THE SOUND OF A TWIG SNAPPING UNDERFOOT, THEN BY HEAVY FOOTSTEPS MAKING THEIR WAY TOWARD THE STREAM!

QUICKLY, HIS KEEN EYES SPOT A MISSHAPEN FORM CROUCHING BEHIND A TREE! AND THOUGH HE HAS NO REASON TO BELIEVE THE GROTESQUE CREATURE IS MORE THAN A LONELY VOYEUR SUCH AS HIMSELF--

--A DREAD FEELING OF APPREHENSION CREEPS THROUGH HIM AS SHE SLOWLY WALKS TO SHORE!

AND, AS SHE TURNS HER BACK AND TOWELS HERSELF DRY, THE HUNCH-BACKED FORM LEAPS FORWARD-- AND THE MONSTER KNOWS HIS WORST FEARS ARE ABOUT TO BE CONFIRMED!

DRAKO! YOU SHOULDN'T BE HERE! YOU SHOULD-- OOHHH!
SO--YE WON'T MARRY ME, EH?!

THEN IF I CAN'T HAVE YE, I'LL MAKE SURE NO OTHER MAN DOES!

I SHOULDN'T GET INVOLVED--
--YET, HOW CAN I HELP IT?! I CAN'T STAND BY AND WATCH HER BE MURDERED!

MOVING WITH THE SPEED OF A NORTHERN-BORN WILL O' THE WISP, HE BREAKS THROUGH THE DENSE FOLIAGE AND GRASPS THE STARTLED WOULD-BE KILLER--
LEAVE HER BE, FIEND---AND VENT YOUR PASSIONS ON ONE WHO IS MORE YOUR EQUAL!

PERHAPS A BATH WILL QUELL THE FIRE THAT RAGES WITHIN YOU!

I DON'T KNOW WHO OR WHAT YE BE-- BUT YOU'LL BE DEAD BEFORE LONG!
NO ONE MEDDLES IN DRAKO'S BUSINESS-- AND LIVES TO BOAST ABOUT IT!

--BUT EVEN THEY ARE NO MATCH FOR THE BRUTE STRENGTH OF THE FRANKENSTEIN MONSTER!

AND AS HE STUMBLES BACKWARD FROM THE FORCE OF HIS OPPONENT'S KICK, AN INTENSE SPECTATOR LOOKS UPON THE DEADLY DUEL--

BRASH!
WHAT?! AFTER SUCH A BLOW--YOU STILL STAND?!

THEN I WILL HAMMER AT YOU AGAIN AND AGAIN--UNTIL AT LAST YOU FALL!

NO! IT IS YOU WHO WILL FALL--

--AND IT WILL BE THE FAULT OF NO ONE SAVE YOURSELF!
AAAGGH!

EVIL RADIATES FROM YOU LIKE WARMTH FROM THE SUN--

--AND THIS WORLD WILL BE A BETTER PLACE WITHOUT YOU!
BUT EVEN IN DEATH YOU HAVE DEFEATED ME--FOR YOU HAVE CAUSED ME TO KILL ONCE MORE!

STAY AWAY FROM ME--PLEASE! HAVE YOU SLAIN DRAKO--ONLY TO TAKE HIS PLACE?!

I DON'T BLAME YOU FOR FEARING ME--HORRIBLE SIGHT THAT I AM!
BUT I WON'T HARM YOU! I ONLY WISH TO BE OF ANY FURTHER SERVICE TO YOU THAT I CAN!
NOOOO! YOU'RE LIKE HIM--ANGRY AT THE WORLD BECAUSE OF YOUR OWN DEFORMITY!
AND NOW YOU WISH TO GET EVEN--BY ATTACKING THOSE WHO ARE NORMAL!

I WARN YOU--LEAVE ME BE! OR MY PEOPLE WILL--
CARMEN! WHERE ARE YOUR MANNERS?
MARGUERITA--YOU--YOU SAW?!

I DID--AND I AM SHOCKED THAT MY GRANDDAUGHTER SHOULD BEHAVE IN SUCH A FASHION!

THIS MAN SAVED YOUR LIFE--AND YOU MUST THANK HIM! COME!

I AM SORRY! I WAS SO FRIGHTENED--I FORGOT MYSELF!
GOOD! NOW, SIR--YOU WILL COME WITH US TO OUR CAMP!
I ACCEPT YOUR APOLOGY--AND I WILL BE HONORED TO COME WITH YOU!

THE INTOXICATING SOUND OF MANDOLINS AND CASTANETS--GUITARS AND TAMBOURINES---WAFTS THROUGH THE STILL NIGHT AIR, PAINTING SOUND IMAGES IN THE SKY AS THE GAY GYPSY BAND ENTERTAINS ITSELF AS ITS PREDECESSORS HAVE FOR HUNDREDS OF YEARS--

BUT EVEN ON THE EDGE OF THIS HAPPY GROUP, HE FEELS AFRAID TO JOIN IN--AFRAID THAT THE CONTENTMENT WHICH IS SEEMINGLY THEIRS CAN NEVER BE HIS--
BROTHERS--SISTERS! BE SILENT--WE HAVE A GUEST!
SHE SEEMS SO WARM--YET, DARE I TRY TO BECOME A PART OF THEIR HAPPINESS?!

FOR THE FIRST TIME IN MONTHS, THE MONSTER SLEEPS SOUNDLY! HE HAS AGREED TO TRAVEL NORTHWARD WITH THE GYPSY CARAVAN--AND TO PERFORM WITH THEM IN DRAKO'S PLACE! ONCE AGAIN HE HAS COMPANIONS--AND FOR THE FIRST TIME, HE HAS EMPLOYMENT!

BUT WHILE HE AND THE REST OF THE CAMP SLEEP, MADAME MARGUERITA, CONFIDENT THAT NO ONE IS WATCHING, HAS OTHER, MORE SINISTER BUSINESS TO WHICH SHE MUST ATTEND--

IN A MATTER OF MOMENTS, WHERE ONCE THE OLD WOMAN STOOD, NOTHING REMAINS--
--AND THE ONLY REMINDER OF HER PRESENCE IS A FAINT FLUTTERING OF WINGS--AND THE SHADOW OF A LONE BAT CIRCLING INTO THE EBONY SKY!

LONG WEEKS OF TRAVEL AND A HUNDRED GYPSY SHOW PERFORMANCES LATER, A GIGANTIC FIGURE SITS ALONE ON A HILL OVERLOOKING A LARGE GERMAN TOWN--

--FILLED WITH ANXIETY AT THE KNOWLEDGE THAT HIS JOURNEY IS NEARING ITS END--AND AT THE SAME TIME WITH SORROW THAT HE SOON MUST LEAVE HIS FRIENDS--

--ESPECIALLY THE BEAUTIFUL CARMEN!
HELLO! I HOPE I DID NOT STARTLE YOU!
I HAVE BEEN WATCHING YOU--AND YOU LOOKED SO LONELY! I THOUGHT PERHAPS--

--WELL, I WANTED YOU TO KNOW HOW GLAD WE ALL ARE THAT YOU ARE WITH US!
YOU ARE SO WARM --SO FILLED WITH GOODNESS! I HAVE NEVER KNOWN A MAN AS KIND AS YOU!

IT'S YOU WHO ARE KIND--AND I THANK YOU FOR BEFRIENDING ONE UNWORTHY OF SUCH KINDNESS!
BUT IT MATTERS LITTLE-- SINCE, AFTER TONIGHT'S PERFORMANCE, I MUST BID YOU FAREWELL!

I KNOW--GRANDMOTHER TOLD ME! WE SHALL ALL MISS YOU--ESPECIALLY ME!

WAIT! DON'T GO! CAN'T WE TALK?! LET ME EXPLAIN--
I AM--SORRY! I MUST GO!

WHAT A FOOL I AM! FOR A MOMENT I THOUGHT PERHAPS--BUT NO--SHE WAS ONLY SHOWING PITY!
NOW I MUST ATTEND TO BUSINESS--AND FORGET CARMEN!

WE HAVE ARRIVED, OLD WOMAN--AND NOW I ASK YOU TO SHOW ME!
SO WE HAVE--AND SO I SHALL, BUT NOT UNTIL AFTER OUR PERFORMANCE!

BUT I HAVE WAITED SO LONG! SURELY YOU CAN TELL ME SOMETHING!
DOES HE LIVE IN THIS TOWN?! WILL HE BE AT THE SHOW?!
HARDLY--SINCE HE HAS BEEN DEAD FOR MANY YEARS! BUT I WILL TAKE YOU TO HIS TOMB!

SO PERFORM WELL--AND SHORTLY AFTER, YOU WILL BE REWARDED!
I AM RELIEVED THAT HE IS NOT ALIVE! NOW I WON'T HAVE TO KILL AGAIN!

BUT I MUST SEE THE TOMB! I MUST BE CERTAIN! I WILL MEET YOU IMMEDIATELY AFTER THE SHOW!
SO BE IT! I WILL BE WAITING FOR YOU!

BUT, NO SOONER HAS THE CREATION OF FRANKENSTEIN DEPARTED THEN--

ROTTEN NIGHT DUTY! NO EXCITEMENT IN TOWN! IT'S ALL AT THE GYPSY SHOW!

GOOD EVENING, CONSTABLE! LOVELY NIGHT FOR A WALK, ISN'T IT?!

SO IT IS, BUT I'D THINK A LOVELY FRÄULEIN LIKE YOURSELF WOULD BE WATCHING THE GYPSIES!

OH, NOT ME, SIR! I'VE SEEN THEM BEFORE --BESIDES, I'M MORE INTERESTED IN HANDSOME, YOUNG CONSTABLES!

AND I'LL BET YOU'RE LONELY, TOO! SO PERHAPS WE CAN HELP EACH OTHER, EH?!
COME HERE-- DON'T BE SHY! KISS ME-- JUST ONCE!

ARRGGHH!

WHAT'S HAPPENED, FRITZ?! HAS THERE BEEN A ROBBERY?
IT'S THE CONSTABLE! WHAT HAPPENED? HAS HE BEEN SHOT?!

HE'S DEAD--BUT IT WASN'T A GUN THAT KILLED HIM!
I THOUGHT WE WERE RID OF THEM HERE IN TRANSYLVANIA--BUT IT LOOKS LIKE THE VAMPIRES ARE BACK!

VAMPIRES?! THEN IT MUST BE THE GYPSIES WHO BROUGHT 'EM HERE!
COME ON! WE GOT RID OF THEM BEFORE-- --AND WE'LL DO IT AGAIN, EVEN IF IT MEANS DRIVING A STAKE THROUGH EVERY GYPSY'S HEART!

A MOB--A MOB! THEY'RE COMING UP THE HILL AFTER US! WE MUST RUN FOR OUR LIVES!

BUT WHY WOULD THEY BE ANGRY WITH YOU?! THEY APPLAUDED THE PERFORMANCE LUSTILY!
WE SHOULDN'T HAVE TO TELL YOU ABOUT MAN'S INSANE HATRED FOR HIS FELLOW MAN!

THEN--IF YOU MUST FLEE--THE TIME HAS COME FOR YOU TO SHOW ME, OLD WOMAN!
AND SO I SHALL! COME WITH ME--TO THE TOP OF THE HILL --AND YOU WILL SEE --IF WE LIVE THAT LONG!

LIKE THIEVES IN THE NIGHT, THE PERSECUTED GYPSIES MAKE THEIR WAY THROUGH THE DENSE FOREST TOWARD THE TOP OF THE MOUNTAIN --THE ANGER-DRIVEN MOB OF TOWNSPEOPLE IN HOT PURSUIT..

BUT NOT EVEN THEIR STEALTH AND KNOWLEDGE OF THE WILDS CAN HELP THEM TO ESCAPE THE TRANSYLVANIANS' WRATH--

HURRY! WE HAVE REACHED THE SUMMIT --AND STILL THEY FOLLOW! ONLY YOU CAN SAVE US!
HELP US ROLL AWAY THIS ROCK-- AND PERHAPS ALL OF US CAN BE SPARED!

DO NOT STAND THERE AND STARE-- MOVE THE BOULDER! BEHIND IT YOU WILL FIND THAT FOR WHICH YOU SEARCH!

FINALLY GRASPING THE MEANING OF THE OLD WOMAN'S WORDS -- HIS BLOOD BOILING WITH THE LUST FOR REVENGE-- HE WRAPS HIS ARMS ABOUT THE HUGE ROCK AND PULLS AT IT WITH ALL HIS STRENGTH--
--KNOWING FULL-WELL THAT IT ALONE MEANS THE DIFFERENCE BETWEEN LIFE AND DEATH FOR ALL OF THEM!

THE TOMB--! THEY'RE TRYING TO GET INSIDE IT!
HURRY! WE MUST STOP THEM--OR IT COULD SPELL THE END OF ALL MANKIND!

KEEP PUSHING, GIANT! THEY'LL BE ON US IN SECONDS!
USE ALL THE STRENGTH YOU HAVE--AS YOU DID AGAINST DRAKO! IT IS OUR ONLY HOPE!

MUSCLES THROBBING--HEAD SPINNING FROM THE STRAIN--BUT I CAN'T--I MUSTN'T GIVE UP!
ALL THAT I'VE LIVED FOR IS BURIED INSIDE--AND I CAN'T DIE UNTIL I'VE SEEN IT!

IT IS DONE, OLD WOMAN! THE VILLAGERS WON'T RECOVER FROM THE BOULDER STRIKE FOR SOME TIME!
NOW YOU MUST KEEP YOUR PROMISE--AND SHOW ME THE TOMB!
AND SO I SHALL! COME THIS WAY--AND AT LAST PEACE WILL BE YOURS!

THE BATS--
SO MANY OF
THEM! WHY?!
THE TOMB
HAS BEEN SEALED
FOR YEARS! NOW ONLY
THE BATS LIVE HERE!

BUT DO NOT BE CONCERNED
WITH THEM--NOT WHEN THAT
YOU SEEK IS JUST BEYOND
THAT ARCHWAY!
WHY DO YOU
HESITATE?! DO
WHAT YOU MUST--WALK
THROUGH AND VIEW THE
COFFIN OF THE LAST
FRANKENSTEIN!

THERE--THERE IT IS! DO
YOU FEEL BETTER NOW?!
IS YOUR LUST FOR
REVENGE CURED?!
NO! NOT YET! I SEE
ONLY A COFFIN! I
MUST HAVE SOME PROOF
AS TO ITS CONTENTS!

THEN OPEN IT! I
ASSURE YOU, YOU WILL
FIND THE PROOF YOU SEEK
INSIDE THE COFFIN!

THAT'S
IT! YOU'RE STRONG
ABLE TO BREAK
THE SEAL!
NOW
RAISE THE LID--
RAISE IT--
RAISE IT!

WHAT IS IT?! WHAT HAPPENED TO HIM?!
WONDERFUL-- AHHH, I KNEW THIS MOMENT WOULD COME!

WHAT ARE YOU TALKING ABOUT, OLD WOMAN?! WHY ARE YOU SO HAPPY--
--AND WHY IS THERE A WOODEN STAKE THROUGH THE HEART?!

OUT OF MY WAY, FOOL! YOU'VE SERVED YOUR PURPOSE! NOW THE REST IS UP TO ME!

I'VE COME, MASTER --AS I PROMISED I WOULD! AND NOW I WILL FREE YOU--
--BY REMOVING THE ACCURSED WOOD FROM YOUR HEART!

THANK YOU, MY DEAR MARGUERITA! THANKS TO YOU, ONCE MORE--
DRACULA LIVES!
NEXT ISH: AS IF YOU COULDN'T GUESS-- DRACULA!!
DRACULA

FRANKENSTEIN MARVEL COMICS GROUP™

APPROVED BY THE COMICS CODE AUTHORITY

20¢ CC

8 JAN 02165

THE FRANKENSTEIN MONSTER™

FRANKENSTEIN MEETS DRACULA!

Stan Lee PRESENTS: THE FRANKENSTEIN MONSTER!™
GARY FRIEDRICH WRITER
JOHN BUSCEMA ARTIST
JOHN VERPOORTEN INKER
JEAN IZZO, LETTERER
LINDA LESSMAN, COLORIST
ROY THOMAS EDITOR
A DARK MISTY CAVE DEEP WITHIN THE BOWELS OF TRANSYLVANIA--
--A DECAYING, COBWEB-COVERED COFFIN--
A GHASTLY-WHITE, HEAVY-SUTURED HAND REACHING FOR THE LID, DARING TO DESECRATE THE GRAVE--
--THE GRAVE OF THE MOST TERRIFYING CREATURE EVER KNOWN TO ROAM THE EARTH!
MY NAME IS... DRACULA--
--AND TONIGHT I THIRST!
I KNOW NOT WHAT YOU ARE, CREATURE --BUT WHETHER YOUR BLOOD BE WARM OR COLD--
--IT SHALL BE MINE!
HE LIVES! THE MASTER LIVES! AND I, MARGUERITA, AM RESPONSIBLE!

HOW LONG HAVE I SLEPT-- A FEW YEARS--A CENTURY?! HOW LONG HAVE I WAITED FOR SOMEONE TO FREE ME FROM THE PRISON OF THE STAKE?!*
*ESMERELDA DID IT LAST ISH!--ROY.

NO MATTER! FOR NOW--ONCE MORE--DRACULA LIVES-- DRACULA STALKS--
I DON'T UNDERSTAND ANY OF THIS--BUT I STAND EVER READY TO DEFEND MYSELF AGAINST ANYONE OR ANYTHING!!

DRACULA SLAYS!
FEED, MASTER-- FEED!

PITIFUL CREATURE --THERE IS NO DEFENCE AGAINST THE LORD OF VAMPIRES!
A VAMPIRE-- YES! I HAVE HEARD OF YOUR KIND!
BUT THOUGH YOUR STRENGTH IS GREAT--

--THAT OF FRANKENSTEIN'S CREATION IS EVEN GREATER!
AND I NOW KNOW I MUST UNDO THE WRONG I'VE COMMITTED BY UNWITTINGLY HELPING TO FREE YOU!

CRASH!!

BY ALL THAT IS EVIL! NEVER HAVE I FACED SUCH A FOE!
BUT EVEN THOUGH YOU HAVE THE STRENGTH OF TEN MEN --

THAT STRENGTH IS NOTHING BESIDE MINE! NOTHING!

NOW FALL, GIANT-- THAT I MIGHT FEAST AND REGAIN THE POWER THAT IS MINE!

AGGHH! THE VAMPIRE IS MIGHTIER THAN I HAD THOUGHT!
HA! AS I SUSPECTED, YOU ARE MORTAL --
--AND THEREFORE VULNERABLE TO MY ONSLAUGHT!

BREATHE YOUR LAST, MY ENEMY-- AND PREPARE TO SURRENDER YOUR VERY LIFE'S BLOOD TO ME!

NOW--WITH ONE MORE BLOW-- YOU WILL BE TOTALLY, COMPLETELY HELPLESS!

NO!! AS LONG AS MY HEART BEATS, I WILL STOP AT NOTHING TO PREVENT YOUR PRAYING ON ALL MANKIND!

THE MASTER HAS NOT FEASTED IN YEARS! HIS POWER IS WEAKENED!
SPAWN OF SATAN, PREPARE TO RETURN TO YOUR ETERNAL GRAVE!

HOLD HIM AT BAY, MASTER! MARGUERITA STANDS EVER AT YOUR SIDE!

DIE, DEMON! YOU HAVE OUTLIVED YOUR USEFULNESS TO ME!
WOK!

STAND ASIDE, OLD WOMAN! THE VAMPIRE MUST DIE!
OOHHHH!

AND, WHILE THE BATTLE OF TITANS RAGES INSIDE, AN INNOCENT YOUNG GIRL ENTERS THE CAVE-- SEARCHING FOR THE GRANDMOTHER SHE NOW KNOWS TO BE A VAMPIRE!

THEN, AS SHE ENTERS THE TOMB, HER HEART IS FROZEN WITH TERROR-- YET SHE INSTINCTIVELY KNOWS WHAT MUST BE DONE!
HE ONCE SAVED MY LIFE-- AND NOW I MUST RETURN THE FAVOR!*
*LAST ISH! -- R.T.

SO, EVEN MY OWN FLESH WOULD TURN AGAINST ME!
I CANNOT LET THAT HAPPEN!
THE WOODEN STAKE, MY FRIEND! IT IS THE ONLY WAY TO DESTROY HIM!

NO, GRANDDAUGHTER! I RAISED YOU TO JOIN US-- NOT FIGHT US!
NEVER! I'D RATHER DIE THAN BECOME ONE OF YOU! LET ME GO!

THE GIRL-- SHE'S IN DANGER! I MUST FORGET THE VAMPIRE AND HELP HER!
SHE'S BEEN GOOD-- KIND TO ME, AND I CAN'T LET HER BE HARMED!

UNHAND HER, WITCH-WOMAN-- AND FACE YOUR FATE!

THE STAKE STRIKES SWIFTLY, POWERED BY THE BRUTE FORCE OF THE STRONGEST BEING EVER KNOWN TO MAN--

THEN, BEFORE CARMEN'S EYES--OPENED WIDE IN SHEER HORROR--THE BODY OF THE VAMPIRE BEGINS TO DIS-INTEGRATE--

UNTIL, IN A MATTER OF SECONDS, NOTHING REMAINS SAVE A SKELETON WITH A WOODEN STAKE IN ITS HEART--

AND, EVEN THOUGH SHE KNEW WHAT TO EXPECT, THE GIRL CAN ONLY SCREAM -- AND SCREAM -- AND SCREAM --

THE OTHER ONE-- THE ONE CALLED DRACULA-- HE'S GONE!
GRANDMOTHER -- I KNEW IT WOULD HAPPEN -- BUT I COULDN'T BELIEVE IT!
I-- STILL DON'T THINK I BELIEVE IT! IT'S TOO HORRIBLE!
NOTHING IS TOO HORRIBLE! YOU NEED ONLY LOOK AT ME TO KNOW THAT!

I'M SORRY. I HAVE NO RIGHT TO BE BITTER IN THE FACE OF YOUR GRIEF.

I WILL TAKE YOU BACK TO YOUR PEOPLE!
THEN I WILL SEARCH OUT THE VAMPIRE AND DESTROY HIM!

NO! YOU MUSTN'T EVEN TRY! THERE IS NO WAY TO DESTROY DRACULA! HE'S TOO POWERFUL!
FOR ANY NORMAL MAN-- PERHAPS! BUT HIS STRENGTH IS NO GREATER THAN MINE!

YOUR CAMP IS OVER THE HILL. BUT BEFORE WE PART, I WANT TO THANK YOU.
FEW PEOPLE ARE CAPABLE OF SHOWING KINDNESS TO ONE SUCH AS I.
IT IS I WHO SHOULD THANK YOU-- FOR SAVING MY LIFE AND--
NOOOO!

BY ALL THAT IS HOLY! HAS MAN NO MERCY LEFT WITHIN HIM?!

THEY STAND IN STUNNED SILENCE, THEIR EYES DRINKING IN A TABLEAU OF TERROR NEARLY BEYOND COMPREHENSION! THE GYPSY CAMP LIES IN SMOULDERING RUINS--
THE GYPSIES SING NO MORE!

RARRRR!

NO--WAIT! REVENGE IS NOT THE ANSWER!

THE TOWNSPEOPLE MUST HAVE DONE THIS--THINKING WE HAD UNLEASHED THE VAMPIRE ON THEM!
BUT I'VE LOST EVERYTHING ELSE-- DO NOT FORCE ME TO LOSE YOU AS WELL!

STAY BACK, WOMAN! SINCE MY CREATION, I'VE SUFFERED ONE INHUMANITY AFTER ANOTHER AT THE HANDS OF MEN!
THIS IS THE FINAL BLOW! I CAN STAND NO MORE! NOW, I MUST STRIKE BACK!

NOW THEY WILL PAY-- PAY FOR ALL THE PAIN THEY'VE INFLICTED ON ME!
AND NOTHING CAN STOP ME! I'LL FIGHT THEM TO THE DEATH!

WAIT! I BEG OF YOU! YOU'LL ONLY DESTROY YOURSELF!

BUT THE GIRL'S PITIFUL CRIES FALL ON DEAF EARS! AND EVENTUALLY SHE FALLS BREATHLESS ON THE SOFT FOREST FLOOR-- SOBBING IN QUIET DESPERATION!

WHILE, ONLY A SHORT DISTANCE AWAY, A TERRORIZED VILLAGE LIES IN MORTAL FEAR BEHIND LOCKED DOORS--

--EVERY MAN, WOMAN AND CHILD AWAITING THE CERTAIN-TO-COME ATTACK OF DRACULA--ALL SAVE ONE, A LOVELY YOUNG GIRL ON THE OUTSKIRTS OF TOWN WHO PREPARES FOR BED UNAWARE OF THE DEADLY DANGER LURKING NEARBY!

THE VILLAGERS HAVE BEEN FOREWARNED! EVERY HOUSE IS GUARDED BY ACCURSED GARLIC--
BUT WHEN DRACULA THIRSTS HE MUST--
--YES! A YOUNG WOMAN-- HER WINDOW OPEN! AT LAST-- I SHALL FEAST!!

HE ENTERS THE DARKENED ROOM EVER SO QUIETLY-- MAKING NO MORE SOUND THAN THE RAYS OF THE MOON THAT REFLECT OFF HIS BARED FANGS--
SLEEP WELL, MY BEAUTY-- SLEEP WELL! FOR SOON, YOU SHALL BE MINE!

AH, THE THROAT-- SO PALE-- SO SMOOTH! HER HUMAN BEAUTY WILL LURE MANY--WHEN SHE HAS JOINED MY LEGIONS OF THE UNDEAD!
BUT I CAN WAIT NO LONGER! IN THIS INSTANT, DRACULA MUST FEAST!!

NOOOOOOO!!

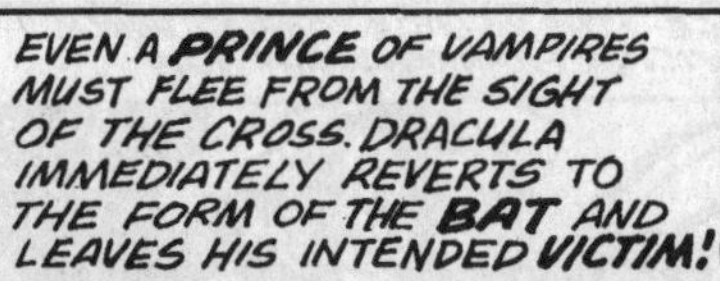
EVEN A PRINCE OF VAMPIRES MUST FLEE FROM THE SIGHT OF THE CROSS. DRACULA IMMEDIATELY REVERTS TO THE FORM OF THE BAT AND LEAVES HIS INTENDED VICTIM!

BUT AS HE SOARS HIGH ABOVE THE MOONLIT FOREST, HIS HUNGER BURNS --AND HE KNOWS HE MUST CONTINUE HIS DESPERATE SEARCH!!

FOR WHAT SEEMS LIKE AGONY-FILLED HOURS HE FLIES THE MIDNIGHT SKIES, UNTIL, FINALLY, HE SPOTS A LIMP, SLEEPING FORM LYING ON THE GROUND BELOW--

DRACULA DOES NOT ASK WHY THE GIRL LIES THUS. HE MERELY STREAKS EARTHWARD--

--CHANGING BACK TO HIS VAMPIRIC FORM AS HE LANDS, AND ATTACKING HIS HELPLESS VICTIM MERCILESSLY!
SHE CRIES OUT FOR HELP-- BUT THERE IS NO ONE TO HEAR! AND IN AN INSTANT, THE RAZOR-SHARP FANGS ARE AT HER THROAT!!

DRACULA DRINKS LONG AND DEEP, THE VICTIM'S LIFE ESSENCE SLOWLY REVITALIZING HIS OWN! AND ONLY WHEN HIS FULL STRENGTH IS RESTORED DOES HE TRULY REALIZE THAT-- HE LIVES ONCE MORE!

HE TAKES TO THE AIR-- THIS LORD OF THE NIGHT--LEAVING BEHIND YET ANOTHER VICTIM--THE LAST OF THE GYPSY BAND!

CUT TO: THE VILLAGE--THE VILLAGE TOWARD WHICH THE CREATION OF VICTOR FRANKENSTEIN NOW STALKS--
THE MONSTER AND THE VAMPIRE STILL WALK OUR FORESTS! I SAY WE MUST FIND THEM -- AND KILL THEM!
THAT IS OUR ONLY COURSE! WE'LL NEVER BE SAFE UNTIL THEY ARE BURIED FOREVER!!

AS YOUR BURGOMEISTER I APPEAL TO YOU! I WANT EVERY ABLE-BODIED MAN TO JOIN THE HUNT!
AND EVEN IF SOME OF US MUST DIE--
--AT LEAST IT WILL BE IN SAFEGUARDING THE FUTURE PEACE AND SAFETY OF THIS ENTIRE VILLAGE!!

BUT HERR BURGOMEISTER-- WHERE WILL WE LOOK FOR THEM?!
WE WON'T HAVE TO LOOK FAR!! DOWN THE STREET THERE-- IT'S THE MONSTER! AND IT'S COMING AFTER US!!

YOU KILLED THOSE WHO BEFRIENDED ME AND NOW--
..I WILL KILL YOU!
LIKE A GIGANTIC WILD BEAST, HIS FACE CONTORTED IN ANGER HIS EYES WILD WITH GRIEF-BORN INSANITY, HIS NOSTRILS FLARING WITH HATRED. THE EIGHT-FOOT MONSTER STALKS STEADILY TOWARD THE STUNNED CROWD OF VIGILANTES!!
YOU MURDERED THEM-- SLAUGHTERED THEM IN COLD BLOOD-- WHEN THEY'D DONE NOTHING TO YOU!
IT'S HIM -- THE FREAK FROM THE GYPSY SHOW!
SLAY HIM!
YES-- THERE ARE MANY OF US! HE HASN'T A CHANCE!

YAAAAAAAA!
HERE'S THE FIRST TO DIE! WHO WILL BE NEXT?!

AS THE VILLAGERS STARE IN DISBELIEF, A HUGE ARM SWINGS BACKWARD AND THEN RAPIDLY FORWARD WITH THE STRENGTH AND SPEED OF A CROSSBOW, HURLING A SINGLE LIMP FORM INTO THE CROWD AS IF IT WERE A MAN-SIZED ARROW!
BONES BREAK IN THAT AWFUL IMPACT!
MEN DIE!

YOU'VE SHOWN ME NOTHING BUT HATRED THROUGHOUT MY LIFE!
WELL--A A MONSTER CAN HATE TOO!

DON'T GIVE UP! HE CAN'T FIGHT THE WHOLE VILLAGE!
KEEP COMING! BRING MORE WEAPONS! ANOTHER FEW MINUTES AND HE'LL BE AT OUR MERCY!!

HE'S TOO STRONG! WE CAN'T HOLD HIM!
AAAAGGHHH!

HOLD HIM A SECOND LONGER -- AND I'LL RUN 'IM OVER WITH MY HORSE AND CARRIAGE!
BE CAREFUL! HE SEES YOU-- I THINK HE HEARD YOU!

FOOLS! DO YOU NOT KNOW HOW STRONG I TRULY AM?
AND NOW YOU WILL PAY FOR YOUR IGNORANCE-- PAY WITH YOUR VERY LIVES!

DON'T RUN, LITTLE MEN! YOU'LL GET THE SAME CHANCE YOU GAVE THE GYPSIES--
--NO CHANCE AT ALL!

AIM CAREFULLY, BOY! THERE'S NO TIME FOR A SECOND SHOT!
I WON'T MISS, ERIC! AND BELIEVE ME, A SHOT FROM THIS WILL STOP HIM!

ZAT!

HE'S DOWN! THE SHOT DROPPED HIM!
GET THE HEAVY ROPE-- WE CAN TIE HIM WITH IT!

I GOT IT! HE'LL BE NO TROUBLE ONCE HE'S BOUND WITH THIS!

HE'S ONLY STUNNED! TAKE HIM TO THE STAKE QUICKLY!
HE'S AS GOOD AS BURNED! HE'LL BE DEAD BEFORE HE RECOVERS!

WITHIN MERE MINUTES, THE GARGANTUAN FIGURE IS BOUND TO A LAMPPOST AND WOOD PILED ABOUT HIM! THEN, AS HIS MIND BEGINS TO CLEAR--
WE'RE READY! LIGHT THE FIRE!

SO--NOW YOU TRY TO DESTROY ME AS YOU MURDERED THE GYPSIES! BUT NOTHING CAN KILL ME! NOTHING! I'LL BREAK FREE AND-- UNGGGH!
YOU'RE HELPLESS, MONSTER! YOU'LL NOT DO A SINGLE THING--
EXCEPT DIE!
NEXT ISSUE: DRACULA UNLEASHED! BUT WHAT ABOUT THE FRANKENSTEIN MONSTER?

FRANKENSTEIN MARVEL COMICS GROUP™

APPROVED BY THE COMICS CODE AUTHORITY

20¢ 9 MAR 02165

THE FRANKENSTEIN MONSTER™

YES, MONSTER! IT WAS DRACULA WHO HAS SLAIN THE GIRL WHO BEFRIENDED YOU--

--AND SO, THIS NIGHT--

..ONE MUST DIE!

Stan Lee PRESENTS: THE FRANKENSTEIN MONSTER!™

GARY FRIEDRICH, WRITER | JOHN BUSCEMA, ARTIST | JOHN VERPOORTEN, INKER | J. COSTANZA, letterer / GLYNIS WEIN, colorist | ROY THOMAS, EDITOR

DRACULA-- A NAME WHICH STRIKES TERROR IN THE HEARTS OF ALL WHO HEAR IT!

DRACULA-- PRINCE OF DARKNESS-- UNCHALLENGED RULER OF THE REALM OF THE UNDEAD!

DRACULA-- SWOOPING THROUGH THE MIDNIGHT SKIES IN THE FORM OF A VAMPIRE BAT-- EVER SEARCHING FOR YET ANOTHER VICTIM TO QUENCH HIS INSATIABLE APPETITE FOR HUMAN BLOOD!

AND WHEN A VICTIM IS FOUND, SHE HAS NO WARNING-- FOR HE MOVES WITH THE SILENCE OF AN INAUDIBLE WHISPER, AND HIS FORM SHOWS NO REFLECTION IN A MIRROR!

THEN, BEFORE SAID VICTIM HAS TIME TO FLEE-- OR EVEN TO SCREAM FOR HELP--

--HE STRIKES!

FINALLY, AS THE LAST DROP OF LIFE'S BLOOD IS DRAINED FROM HER, SHE MANAGES ONE HORRIBLE, DEATH-WRACKED SCREAM--
AIEEEEEE

--A SCREAM WHICH CHILLS HER FELLOW CITIZENS TO THE VERY MARROW!!

IT'S HIM! IT'S DRACULA!
WE'RE FOOLS! WE LEFT OUR WOMEN UNPROTECTED WHILE WE SOUGHT OUR VENGEANCE!
IT'S TOO LATE TO PONDER OUR MISTAKE-- BUT IT'S NOT TOO LATE TO GET HIM!
GRAB A STAKE AND HAMMER! WE CAN'T LET HIM ESCAPE!

BUT THE TERROR-STRICKEN VILLAGERS' EARS ARE NOT THE ONLY ONES ON WHICH THE SCREAM HAS FALLEN! THOUGH IN TERRIBLE PAIN AND ON THE THRESHOLD OF DEATH-- THE MONSTER HAS ALSO HEARD!

AND THOUGH DETERMINED TO LET THEM END HIS WRETCHED LIFE ONLY A SECOND BEFORE, THE SOUND OF ANOTHER'S SUFFERING STIRS HIS WILL TO LIVE-- HIS DESIRE TO PREVENT SOMEONE ELSE FROM SUFFERING AS HE HAS SUFFERED!

THEN, SUMMONING ALL THE STRENGTH WHICH REMAINS IN HIS GARGANTUAN FRAME--THE MONSTER BREAKS FREE!!

ONCE AGAIN, DRACULA IS AT THE HEIGHT OF HIS POWERS--
--REPLENISHED BY THE SWEET TASTE OF RICH, WARM BLOOD!
BUT HOLD.. WHAT DO I HEAR?

THE SOUND OF ANGRY VOICES.. A MOB!
THEY DESTROYED ME ONCE BEFORE, BUT IT WAS A TEMPORARY VICTORY!

FOR I AM DRACULA--
--AND MORE THAN A MATCH FOR ANY MOB!
THERE HE IS!
WHO HAS THE CROSSBOW?

HURRY! FIRE THE WOODEN SHAFT BEFORE HE CAN ESCAPE!
I AM THE BEST MARKSMAN IN THE LAND! TONIGHT, BY MY HAND--
--DRACULA DIES AGAIN!

FOOL! CAN ONE BREATH PUT OUT THE SUN?

CAN ONE MAN SNUFF OUT THE LIFE OF A LEGEND?

THOK!

NOW NO ONE WILL BE SAFE!
HE MISSED!
GOOD LORD! LOOK!

"THE MONSTER HAS ESCAPED!"
"DRACULA IS BEYOND OUR VENGEANCE RIGHT NOW-- BUT WE CAN YET SEND THIS ABOMINATION TO HIS JUST PUNISHMENT!"

FOOLS! WHO ARE YOU TO JUDGE ME--
--WHEN I'VE ALREADY BEEN CONDEMNED?

AWAY WITH YOU ALL! I WILL FIND DRACULA--
--AND I WILL DESTROY HIM!
THEN I WILL LEAVE YOUR LITTLE TOWN TO YOUR LITTLE FEARS AND HATREDS!

THERE'S NO TIME FOR FURTHER ARGUING! DRACULA MUST DIE-- AS SOON AS POSSIBLE!
AND I WILL BE THE INSTRUMENT OF HIS DEATH! IF YOU WANT TO TRY TO STOP ME--
--DO WHAT YOU MUST! OTHERWISE, I'M GOING TO HIS TOMB-- TO LIE IN WAIT UNTIL HE RETURNS!

IF YOU WANT TO FELL ME WITH YOUR WEAPONS WHILE MY BACK IS TURNED-- SO BE IT!

I WANT NOTHING MORE THAN TO END MY WRETCHED EXISTENCE--BUT IF YOU ALLOW ME--
--I WILL DO ONE GOOD TURN FOR MAN-KIND BEFORE MY DEATH --THOUGH I AM NOT AT ALL CERTAIN YOU DESERVE IT!

"PERHAPS WE WERE WRONG ABOUT HIM!"

"ONLY TIME WILL TELL! FOR NOW, LET US PRAY HE SUCCEEDS IN HIS MISSION!"

"FOR IF HE FAILS, GOD HELP US ALL!!"

BUT WHILE THE MONSTER STALKS HIS PREY, THAT PREY'S WORK FOR THE NIGHT IS NOT YET FINISHED--

UNDERTAKER
EST -1796

SO, THE VAMPIRE HAS RETURNED-- AND ALREADY CLAIMED HIS FIRST VICTIM
OH, WELL-- AT LEAST IT WILL BE GOOD FOR THE BUSINESS!
MORNING DRAWS EVER NEARER--BUT I MUST HAVE A RESTING PLACE BEFORE THE SUN RISES!
AND I BELIEVE THAT I HAVE FOUND IT!

SMASH!

PLEASE-- NOOO! I AM OLD-- FEEBLE!
FOOL! I HAVE NO NEED FOR YOUR TIRED BLOOD!
I SEEK ONLY THE HANDIWORK OF YOUR CRAFT--A COFFIN!

THEN TAKE WHICHEVER ONE PLEASES YOU! IT IS YOURS WITH MY COMPLIMENTS!

COWARD! DO YOU THINK IT MATTERS TO ME WHETHER IT IS A GIFT OR SOMETHING I MERELY TAKE?!
THIS ONE WILL BE PERFECT! HOWEVER, BEFORE I TAKE IT--

NOOOOOO!

AS I UNDERSTAND IT, THE VAMPIRE MUST REST IN HIS NATIVE SOIL FROM SUNRISE TO SUNSET!
IT IS NEARLY DAYBREAK NOW! SO IF HE IS NOT HERE-- HE SHOULD RETURN SHORTLY!

AND WHEN HE DOES-- I WILL BE READY FOR HIM!
IT'S HARD FOR ME TO JUSTIFY MY HATRED OF HIM-- EXCEPT FOR THE AURA OF EVIL WHICH SURROUNDS HIM!
BUT THAT IN ITSELF SHOULD BE ENOUGH TO JUSTIFY MY DESTROYING HIM!

I SHOULD HAVE REMEMBERED! HIS COFFIN WAS SHATTERED WHEN WE FIRST CLASHED!*
WILL HE RETURN?
*LAST ISSUE. --R.T.

WHY ARE YOU HERE?! I'VE BEEN SEARCHING FOR YOU EVERYWHERE!
WHA--? I--I DIDN'T THINK YOU WOULD FOLLOW ME!
AND YOU MUST LEAVE! YOU'RE IN GRAVE DANGER HERE!

HOW COULD I BE IN DANGER WITH YOU BY MY SIDE?!
THIS IS WHERE I BELONG-- BY YOUR SIDE FOREVER! I'VE KNOWN IT SINCE I FIRST MET YOU!*
THIS CAN'T BE! I'M NOT A MAN-- I'M A MONSTER!
* ALSO SEEN LAST ISH.-- ON-TOP-OF-IT- ROY.

BUT YOUR BLOOD IS AS WARM AS ANY MAN'S!

RRAAAGHHH

HER RIPPINGS AT MY THROAT-- HER VAMPIRE BLOOD MINGLING WITH MINE-- IT SEEMS TO HAVE DONE SOMETHING TO ME!

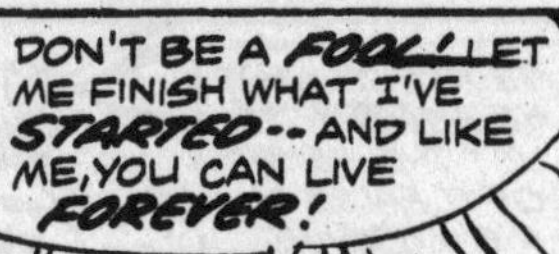
DON'T BE A FOOL! LET ME FINISH WHAT I'VE STARTED-- AND LIKE ME, YOU CAN LIVE FOREVER!

WOULD YOU RATHER BE THE HUNTED-- INSTEAD OF THE HUNTER?

I CAN'T ANSWER-- MY VOCAL CORDS HAVE BEEN PARALYZED SOMEHOW!
BUT THAT MATTERS LITTLE NOW. I MUST FREE CARMEN FROM THIS CURSE!
AND IF TEARS FILL THE MONSTER'S EYES--

--IT IS BECAUSE HE REMEMBERS THE CARMEN WHO DANCED IN FRONT OF GYPSY FIRES AND MADE MEN'S HEARTS GLAD--

--AND HIS TEARS ARE BECAUSE THAT CARMEN IS ONLY A MEMORY, FOR SHE IS NOW A CRUEL HUNT-RESS!

HE KNOWS WHAT HE MUST DO, YET THE WEIGHT OF IT FALLS ON HIS MASSIVE SHOULDERS LIKE THAT OF THE WORLD UPON ATLAS!

BUT HE ACTS--
--THOUGH HE CAN NOT BEAR TO WATCH THE DEED.

OOOOHHHHHH!

AND WHEN THE DEATH-SCREAMS HAVE CEASED--
--HE SEES A LOOK OF UTTER PEACE AND CONTENTMENT ON CARMEN'S FACE.

THERE ARE THOSE WHO SAY THIS MONSTER KNOWS NOT THE MEANING OF LOVE.
THEY ARE WRONG.

BUT HE ALSO KNOWS THE MEANING OF HATE!
WHAT? YOU DARE KILL A BRIDE OF DRACULA?
FOR THAT--YOUR LIFE--YOUR VERY SOUL--IS FORFEIT!

THE MONSTER TURNS TO FACE HIS IMMORTAL FOE AND, THOUGH HE CAN NOT SPEAK...
...HIS EXPRESSION CARRIES HIS PURPOSE QUITE ADEQUATELY.

WHAT, NO CHALLENGE, MONSTER? NO BOISTEROUS VOW TO DESTROY THE LORD OF THE UNDEAD?
OH, I SEE--SOMEHOW DEAR CARMEN MANAGED TO INJURE YOUR VOCAL CORDS BEFORE SHE DIED. NO MATTER...

YOU DO NOT NEED YOUR VOICE--

--TO DIE!

YES, MONSTER--I SEE THE APPROACHING DAWN, TOO--BUT IT WILL NOT ARRIVE IN TIME TO SAVE YOU!
WHEN THE MOON RISES IN THREE NIGHTS, IT WILL FIND YOU, NOT MY ENEMY--

--BUT MY SLAVE!

SLAMMM
THE MONSTER'S INDOMITABLE SPIRIT PUSHES HIM ON. HE WILL NOT SURRENDER --NOT TO DRACULA --NOT TO ANYONE!
NO MATTER WHAT THE ODDS!

FOOL!
DID YOU NOT KNOW DRACULA COULD BECOME AS THE EVENING MIST ITSELF?

NEVER HAVE I FACED A FOE AS MIGHTY AS YOU-- BUT YOUR STRENGTH IS STILL NOTHING BESIDES MY OWN!
AND FOR THAT REASON, THE OUTCOME OF THIS MATCH IS INEVITABLE!

MONSTER, THIS IS YOUR END!
YOU WILL FALL BEFORE THE POWER OF THE MIGHTIEST BEING OF ALL!

THE MONSTER'S KNEES BUCKLE BEFORE DRACULA'S UNYIELDING STRENGTH, BUT HATRED SURGES UP WITH-IN HIS BRAIN...
...HATRED SUCH AS HE HAS KNOWN...

...FOR ONLY ONE OTHER MAN...
...HIS CREATOR!

AND SOMEHOW, THE MONSTER SUMMONS UP THE COURAGE FOR ONE LAST ATTEMPT TO LIVE, TO WIN!

AAGGGHHHH!

AARHHH-- THE SUN!

MORNING LIGHT: AND THE VAMPIRE SCREAMS IN ANGUISH. HE HAS RACED AGAINST TIME AND LOST.

THE MONSTER REACHES FOR TWO PIECES OF WOOD, REMEMBERING A BIT OF VAMPIRE LORE..

--REMEMBERING THAT A CRUCIFIX WILL RENDER ANY VAMPIRE HELPLESS!

THE MONSTER SMILES IN VENGEFUL SATISFACTION...

...AS DRACULA BEGINS TO CRUMBLE BEFORE HIS VERY EYES...

...A VICTIM OF HIS OWN CARELESSNESS AND THE ELEMENTS OF NATURE!

AND, AS DRACULA WRITHES IN AGONY...

...THE MONSTER DELIVERS THE FINAL BLOW!

DRACULA IS NO MORE. YET THERE IS NO TRIUMPH-- ONLY THE BITTER BILE OF REVENGE--
--AND THE MEMORY OF A GIRL NAMED CARMEN.

GOOD MORNING! I UNDERSTAND YOU'VE BEEN COOKING FOR ME...

...MY NAME IS VINCENT FRANKENSTEIN!
NEXT:
MAKE ME A MONSTER!

Story: GERRY CONWAY Art: SONNY TRINIDAD

HE MUST HAVE SENSED MY PRESENCE AT JUST THAT INSTANT, FOR HIS HEAD LIFTED...
BUT, OF COURSE, BY THE TIME HE GLANCED AROUND...
I WAS GONE.
IT TOOK ME ONLY A MOMENT TO REACH A NEARBY TAVERN, A FOUL-SMELLING PLACE NOTABLE MORE FOR THE VIOLENCE IT GAVE NEST TO, THAN FOR THE QUALITY OF ITS WINE...
MEN LOOKED UP AS I PUSHED OPEN THE TAVERN DOOR...
...AND THEY LISTENED AS I SAID...
THERE IS A WOMAN ON THE NEXT STREET OVER... I BELIEVE SHE'S BEING ATTACKED.
SHE WAS SCREAMING... I DIDN'T KNOW WHAT TO DO...
CAN ANYONE HELP?
SPANISH MEN ARE PARTICULARLY PROUD; AND THESE MEN WERE NO EXCEPTION TO THAT SOMEWHAT-SIMPLIFIED RULE...
WE'LL SEE ABOUT THIS! ATTACK A WOMAN, WILL HE?
THE PIG! I'LL STRANGLE HIM WITH MY BARE HANDS!
THAT THEY WERE ALL QUITE DRUNK WAS NATURALLY MOST CONVENIENT...

THERE HE IS!
HEY YOU! WHAT ARE YOU DOING WITH THAT GIRL, HEY?
I SAID WHAT ARE YOU DOING WITH--
HOLY MOTHER OF GOD! A VAMPIRE!
I KNEW THAT THE MEN WOULD BE CONFUSED, FRIGHTENED. IF ALLOWED, THEY WOULD PANIC AND RUN...
...BUT THEY WOULD NOT BE ALLOWED.
DO YOU REMEMBER THE LEGENDS? A VAMPIRE CAN BE KILLED BY A STAKE--
A SHARPENED STAKE OF WOOD, PLUNGED THROUGH HIS HEART!
A-A STAKE?
A FEW MORE URGENT WORDS, A SHOVE--AND LIKE A STAMPEDE OF ENRAGED ANIMALS, THE DRUNKEN MEN CHARGED FORWARD--
--AND DRACULA, DISBELIEVING THAT THEY COULD DO HIM HARM, MERELY ROSE AND SNARLED AT THEM DISDAINFULLY--
--REALIZING TOO LATE THAT THESE MEN MOVED TO A DEADLY PURPOSE--!
BEFORE HE COULD ACT TO FREE HIMSELF, THE SEED WHICH I HAD PLANTED--

--BORE BLOODY, MOST BLOODY FRUIT.
THANK!
AAAAAAAHHHHHHHHHHH
THEN, COMPREHENDING THE HORROR OF WHAT THEY'D DONE, THE MEN DREW BACK, TAKING UP THE BURDEN OF THE YOUNG GIRL SLAIN BY DRACULA...
...AS THOUGH, BY CARRYING HER BODY OFF FOR BURIAL, THEY WERE ATONING FOR WHAT SIN THEY'D COMMITTED...
...IF SIN IT WERE.
I, AT LEAST, THOUGHT NOT... BUT THEN, FEW THINGS ARE SINFUL TO ME.
TWO MONTHS PASSED, AND I THOUGHT MYSELF RID OF COUNT DRACULA... BUT I RECKONED NOT WITH THE GREED OF CERTAIN MEN.
BECAUSE HE APPARENTLY HAD NO KITH OR KIN, DRACULA'S BODY WAS DEPOSITED IN A COMMON TOMB IN MADRID...
...AND ON A NIGHT SEVENTY-SEVEN NIGHTS AFTER A STAKE TORE THROUGH HIS HEART...

...DRACULA RETURNED TO THE WORLD... OF THE UNDEAD.
ARE YOU CERTAIN HE'S A RICH MAN? IF HE'S RICH, WHY IS HE HERE?
BECAUSE HE HAS NO RELATIVES, YOU FOOL. I TELL YOU, HE'S WEALTHY...
MY SISTER'S BROTHER KNEW A MAN WHO WAS PRESENT WHEN HE DIED.
"HE WORE CLOTHES LIKE A NOBLE," THE MAN SAID. "HE MUST HAVE HAD A FAT PURSE... IF THE POLICE DIDN'T FIND IT FIRST."
WHAT IF THEY HAVE?
THEN WE'VE WASTED A FEW HOURS, NO MORE.
WE HAVE WASTED THEM. THIS CAN'T BE THE MAN WHO DIED TWO MONTHS AGO-- IT'S A SKELETON!
AND LOOK, SOMEONE'S LEFT A STICK OF WOOD IN ITS RIBS...
--JUST AS THOUGH HE WERE SOME SORT OF-- SORT OF--
THERE WAS NOTHING MORE TO SAY.
THEY SAID NO MORE.

AAAAAAAAHHHH!
AND ALSO NATURALLY, HIS FIRST THOUGHTS, AFTER HIS FEASTING, WERE OF ME...
SOMEONE BETRAYED ME TO THAT MOB -- TOLD THEM WHAT TO DO, AND HOW TO DO IT.
WHOEVER HE IS, I WILL HUNT HIM DOWN!
NATURALLY, I GREW AWARE OF HIM AGAIN AT ONCE.
--AND HE WILL SUFFER!
HIS DECISION SUITED MY OWN PLANS PERFECTLY.
AT LAST, THE HUNTED WOULD BECOME THE HUNTER... AND I SWORE I'D LEAD THIS VLAD A MERRY CHASE, INDEED...
AFTER A FEW DISCREET INQUIRIES, HE LEARNED WHICH TAVERN IT WAS HIS KILLERS HAD COME FROM...
...AND HE ACTED EXACTLY AS I KNEW HE WOULD.
I AM DRACULA.
AND YOU... ARE MY SLAVES.
DRACULA'S HYPNOTIC POWERS WERE AWESOME; WITH SURPRISE ON HIS SIDE, HE COULD MESMERIZE AN ENTIRE ROOM OF MEN AND WOMEN...
THIS HE DID. THEN...
YOU--

YOU WERE THERE WHEN YOUR SQUALID FRIENDS SLEW ME, WHO WAS IT WHO GAVE THEM THE KNOWLEDGE THEY NEEDED?
WHO WAS IT WHO BETRAYED ME? ANSWER, YOU SLIME!
I'D ALREADY MADE ARRANGEMENTS...
...AND THE POOR MAN KNEW PRECISELY WHAT TO SAY...
HIS NAME... CARLOS MUERTO FROM SAN CRISTO... A COUSIN...
SAN CRISTO?
Y-YES... SAN CRISTO...
THEN I WILL GO TO SAN CRISTO, AND THIS CARLOS MUERTO WILL DIE... MOST UNPLEASANTLY. AS FOR YOU...
SWAK!
AND SO HE CAME, AS I PLANNED THAT HE WOULD. HE ARRIVED THE FOLLOWING NIGHT, AFTER COLLECTING THE TWO MEN WHO'D SUFFER HIS BITE THE EVENING BEFORE...
...AND WHO NOW HAD JOINED HIM IN THAT STATE OF UNDEATH KNOWN ONLY TO A VAMPIRE.
I WAS WAITING FOR HIM WHEN HE ARRIVED...
AT FIRST, HE DIDN'T SEE ME...
...SO I CALLED TO HIM.
SEÑOR... OVER HERE... I AM THE ONE YOU SEEK.
YOU HAVE ONLY TO REACH ME, AND I AM YOURS.
AS I HOPED, THIS ENRAGED HIM.

WITHOUT THOUGHT, HE CHASED ME, SO FILLED WITH FURY THAT ALL REASON WAS GONE FROM HIS MIND.
I REMAINED ELUSIVE..
...AND THE CHASE WENT ON FOR WHAT SEEMED LIKE HOURS...
...BUT IT WAS, IN FACT, ONLY THIRTY-FOUR MINUTES.
A SHORT TIME, IT'S TRUE, BUT LONG ENOUGH FOR MY PURPOSE...
...AND MORE THAN LONG ENOUGH FOR... THE SUN.
IN HELL'S NAME...NO!
IT CAN'T BE DAWN. IT ISN'T TIME YET--IT ISN'T TIME--!
OF COURSE, HE'D FORGOTTEN ONE SMALL THING--SOMETHING WHICH UNDER OTHER CIRCUMSTANCES, HE WOULD NEVER HAVE MISSED.
PERHAPS IT ISN'T TIME YET IN MADRID, SENOR DRACULA...
...BUT IN SAN CRISTO, THE SUN RISES AN HOUR EARLIER!
DAMN YOU! DAMN YOUR EYES!
IN MY CASE, VLAD TEPES, THAT IS A SINGULARLY INEFFECTIVE CURSE.
HE DIDN'T HEAR ME...
HE WAS ALREADY COMPLETELY GONE.

So it would have ended, but I'd not truly understood Dracula's almost **unbelievable** power...

For, at that instant in Transylvania, an unspoken message was received by an **inhabitant** of Castle Dracula...

I hear you, my master... and I will **come!**

I, of course, was **ignorant** of such a message; was not the female also one of the **undead**?

She came quickly, this slave of Dracula, bringing with her a coffin that was her **own** resting place during the daylight hours...

...and **another** box, that would serve her **master.**

I BREATHE... I LIVED...
YOU HAVE DONE WHAT I ASKED OF YOU, AND I AM GRATEFUL.
COME...
...YOU SHALL HAVE YOUR REWARD.
IT WAS THEN THAT I BEGAN TO REALIZE HOW HOPELESS MY PLAN HAD BEEN; NO MATTER HOW OFTEN I WOULD BRING AN END TO THIS "MAN"!, STILL, HE WOULD RETURN...
SHOW YOURSELF, CARLOS MUERTO... I KNOW YOU ARE HERE, AND I KNOW YOU ARE WATCHING...
YOU'VE BEEN WATCHING SINCE THIS FARCE BEGAN!
YOU SEEK ME, SEÑOR DRACULA?
YES, I SEEK YOU, SEÑOR... BUT YOUR NAME ISN'T TRULY CARLOS MUERTO, IS IT?
NO, SEÑOR. AS YOU HAVE ALREADY SURMISED...
...I AM DEATH.
FOR YEARS, YOUR ACTIVITIES HAVE CHEATED ME OF MY VICTIMS. OF ALL THE VAMPIRES WHO LIVE, YOU ARE THE MOST DANGEROUS.
YOU ARE MY GREATEST RIVAL.
YOU ARE ALSO MY ONLY FAILURE. I ADMIT DEFEAT, COUNT DRACULA... IT SEEMS I CANNOT TAKE YOU...
...WHICH DOES NOT MEAN YOU CANNOT DIE.
WE'LL HAVE A TRUCE, THEN?
OF SORTS. I WILL NO LONGER TROUBLE YOU, THOUGH OTHERS WILL.
PERHAPS ONE OF THEM WILL SUCCEED WHERE DEATH HAS NOT.
I LEFT HIM, THEN, TO BE ALONE WITH HIS THOUGHTS, AND ALREADY, I WAS PLANNING FOR THE MORROW.
I LIED, OF COURSE. AFTER ALL... DEATH IS NEVER PROUD...
FINIS

BLACK HAND...BLACK DEATH!
ROME: THE ETERNAL CITY. SINCE 1871, THE CAPITAL OF ALL ITALY, QUITE POSSIBLY THE GREATEST EXISTING MONUMENT TO WESTERN CIVILIZATION.
IN THE YEAR 1926, ROME PLAYS HOST TO PEOPLE OF ALL MANNER AND SORT; THE TOURISTS, STANDING IN QUIET AWE OF THE VIEW FROM ST. PETER'S BASILICA; THE NATIVES, LIVING OUT THEIR OFTIMES HOLLOW LIVES AMIDST THE DECADENT SPLENDOR OF HER BENIGHTED CAFES AND GALLERIES...
THE POOR AND MIS-BEGOTTEN... THE RICH AND PROFANE... ROME HAS SEEN THE LIKE OF ALL OF THEM BEFORE...
WELL, PERHAPS NOT ALL--
--FOR THERE IS ONE WHO WALKS HER SHADOWED STREETS THIS NIGHT-- ONE WHO IS QUITE UNLIKE ANY BEING BEFORE OR BEYOND HIM!
THIS ONE IS-- COUNT DRACULA, LORD OF THE UNDEAD!
BONA SERRE, SIGNORINA. IS THIS SEAT BESIDE YOU OCCUPIED?
NO--ER-- NOT AT THE MOMENT, BUT I...
THEN I WILL JOIN YOU.

AT FIRST, SHE INTENDS TO SCORNFULLY DISMISS THIS BOLD STRANGER-- BUT SOMETHING ABOUT HIS DEMEANOR IS SO CONFIDENT, SO COMPELLING, THAT INSTEAD LUISA MORELLI ONLY SMILES DEMURELY AND INVITES HIM TO SIT.
SHE IS NOT DISAPPOINTED THAT SHE HAS.

HE IS, SHE LEARNS, A COUNT OF TRANSYLVANIAN DESCENT, A SOPHISTICATED, WELL-BRED, WELL-SPOKEN MAN, A WORLD TRAVELLER--
--WHO REGALES HER WITH TALES OF THOSE DISTANT, EXOTIC PLACES SHE'D ONLY HEARD ABOUT IN THE PICTURE BOOKS OF HER CHILDHOOD.

HE IS CHARMING, ENCHANTING, VASTLY MORE ENTERTAINING THAN THE MAN SHE'D COME HERE TO MEET--
--A MAN ONLY NOW ARRIVING.
OKAY, FANCY-PANTS-- OUTTA THE SEAT!

WHERE YOU ADDRESSING ME, SIGNOR?
YEAH-- YOU!
YOU'RE SITTING IN MY SEAT, FANCY-PANTS!
YOUR SEAT, SIGNOR? I'M SURE YOU'RE MISTAKEN.
I SAW NO PLACARD HERE, RESERVING IT IN YOUR BEHALF.

NOW IF YOU'LL EXCUSE US--THE SIGNORINA AND I ARE OTHERWISE INVOLVED AT THE MOMENT.
GUESS YOU DIDN'T UNDERSTAND ME, MR. FANCY-PANTS. THAT'S BIG NICK DIABLO'S SEAT YOU'RE SQUATING IN-- BIG NICK'S LADY YOU'RE FLIRTING WITH--

--AND SINCE I'M BIG NICK DIABLO, I WANT YOU OUTTA MY SEAT--AWAY FROM MY LADY-- AND FAST!
OR MY BOYS HERE WILL HAVE TO HELP YOU OUT-- THE HARD WAY!

REMARKABLY, THE MAN CLAD IN MOURNING BLACK IGNORES THE ANGRY WARNING, TURNING INSTEAD TO HIS LOVELY COMPANION ONCE MORE--
--UNTIL A ROUGH HAND IS LAID HEAVILY UPON HIS SHOULDER--

--AND ONLY THEN DOES THE LORD COUNT DRACULA RESPOND TO THE THREAT-- IN A MOST FLAMBOYANT FASHION!
AWAY FROM ME, YOU WORTHLESS SCUM!
WHAK!
BECAUSE MY MOOD WAS GENER-OUS THIS NIGHT, I TOLERATED YOUR FOUL PRESENCE FOR A TIME--
-BUT, OBVIOUSLY, THAT WAS A MISTAKE!

THERE IS ONLY ONE WAY TO DEAL WITH SUCH AS YOU...
THRASH YOU LIKE THE MONGREL DOGS YOU ARE!
MAMA MIA! HE'S TOSSING MY BOYS AROUND LIKE THEY WERE GARBAGE!
I'LL HAVE TO HANDLE THIS MYSELF

YES-- SIGNOR DIABLO! THIS IS ALL YOUR DOING, ISN'T IT?
WELL--IF YOU CHOOSE TO ACT LIKE A CUR, PERHAPS YOU SHOULD MORE CLOSELY RESEMBLE ONE.
LOOK AT ME, DIABLO! LOOK DEEP INTO MY EYES--

"--AND KNOW YOURSELF FOR WHAT YOU TRULY ARE!"
WH--WHAT DID YOU DO TO POOR NICKY?
NOTHING NOT ALREADY LONG OVERDUE, MY DEAR.
OOOOOWW
NOW COME. THERE ARE OTHER PLACES FOR US TO VISIT BEFORE THIS NIGHT IS THROUGH!

EVEN IN SPRING, THE ROMAN AIR IS MUSTY WITH THE SCENT OF BY-GONE AGES--
--BUT THE TWO WHO STRIDE AMIDST THE QUIET SPLENDOR OF THOSE PROUD OLD PLAZAS AND PALACES SEEM HARDLY TO NOTICE ROME'S TIME-LESS BEAUTY--
--FOR THEY SPEAK SOFTLY, EARN-ESTLY, OF MATTERS FAR OLDER, FAR MORE TIMELESS, THAN EVEN THIS "ETERNAL" CITY.

UNTIL, AT LENGTH, IN THE SHADOWS OF A NEAR-DESERTED AVENUE...
AT LAST, MY DEAR LUISA... WE ARE ALONE.
WHY, SIGNOR COUNT, HOW BOLD OF YOU. HERE?
WHY DON'T WE GO TO MY APART-MENT, SILLY. WE'D BE MUCH MORE-- EH--COMFORTABLE THERE.
GRAZIE, LUISA-- BUT I REQUIRE MORE THAN MERE ANIMAL COMFORT THIS NIGHT--

--MUCH MUCH MORE!

LUISA MORELLI DOES NOT SCREAM AS THE VAMPIRE-LORD BRUSHES HER SOFT NECK WITH HIS COFFIN-COLD LIPS, HIS FANGS REACHING HUNGRILY FOR HER PULSING JUGULAR VEIN-- FOR HIS WINE-DARK EYES HAVE IMPRI-SONED HERS--
--AND THE ONLY SOUND THAT ESCAPES HER PARTED LIPS IS A SIGH OF COM-PLETE FULFILLMENT--

BUT THOUGH LUISA MORELLI'S LIFE HAS ENDED, OUR STORY HAS NOT--FOR AT THE CAFE WHERE DRACULA HAD LEFT A HOWLING NICK DIABLO...
YOU'RE COMING OUT OF IT NOW, BOSS. WE ALL ARE.
TH-THAT GUY WASN'T... HUMAN!
I DON'T CARE WHAT HE WAS, GUISIPPI. NOBODY DOES WHAT HE DID TO NICK DIABLO AND LIVES TO BRAG ABOUT IT!
I WANT YOU BOYS TO FIND OUT WHO HE IS--AND THEN I WANT A CONTRACT PUT OUT ON HIM.
50 MILLION LIRA TO THE MAN WHO BRINGS ME HIS HEAD!!

UNAWARE OF DIABLO'S GRIM RESOLUTION, DRACULA SPENDS THE FOLLOWING NIGHT IN HIS USUAL PURSUITS.
HE'D FOUND THE GIRL ON THE PIAZZA DEL POPOLO. HE HAS ALREADY FORGOTTEN HER NAME--
--BUT THAT IS A TRIVIAL MATTER AT BEST.

SOON HE WILL HAVE WHAT HE REQUIRES OF HER-- SO HE NEED NOT MAINTAIN THE DISTASTEFUL CHARADE FOR VERY LONG.
HE WHISPERS SOMETHING MILDLY AMUSING --AND HER SHATTERED CRYSTAL LAUGHTER RINGS LOUDLY DOWN THE AVENUE, DROWNING OUT THE ROAR OF A SLEEK, BLACK LIMOUSINE AS IT SKIDS AROUND THE CORNER--

--AND A FINGER OF GLEAMING METAL IS THRUST OUT AN OPEN WINDOW--
BHUD-UD-UD-AH!
--TO TATTOO A WILD PATTERN OF DEATH ALONG THE STREET--

--LEADEN DEATH THAT PASSES HARMLESSLY THROUGH A BLACK-GARBED DRACULA...
...BUT TAKES ITS BRUTAL TOLL OF THE VAMPIRE-LORD'S ALL-TOO-HUMAN COMPANION.
THAK-AK-AK-AK-AK-AK-AK!

FOR AN INSTANT, A DOUR-FACED DRACULA CROUCHES AT THE CORPSE'S SIDE--
SHE'S DEAD, HER BODY RIDDLED--
--AND I STILL CANNOT REMEMBER HER NAME!

--THEN THE PRINCE OF EVIL TURNS HIS SATURNINE HEAD TOWARDS THE FLEEING LIMOUSINE--
--AND THE VILE OATHS HE HURLS INTO THE ALL-EMBRACING FOG ARE FAR TOO TERRIBLE TO RETELL HERE.

HE KNOWS ONLY THAT SOMEONE--SOME UNTHINKING MORTAL FOOL--HAS ATTEMPTED TO KILL HIM--
--AND, IN SO DOING, HAS DENIED HIM HIS DINNER FOR TONIGHT!
THUS, AS HIS VELVET CLOAK BECOMES LEATHERN WINGS--
--HIS POWERFUL FIGURE BECOMES THE BLACK-FURRED FORM OF A BAT--
--AND HE SWOOPS SILENTLY OFF INTO THE DARKNESS IN SEARCH OF NEW PREY--
--THE VAMPIRE-LORD VOWS THAT HE WILL FIND THOSE RESPONSIBLE--
--AND MAKE THEM PAY--
--AS ONLY COUNT DRACULA CAN!
BUT THAT MAY PROVE QUITE DIFFICULT--FOR THE NIGHTS THAT FOLLOW ARE NO QUIETER FOR THE MASTER OF THE UNDEAD.
THEY ARE FILLED INSTEAD WITH THE MANIACAL CHATTER OF SMOKING MACHINE-GUNS--
--THE SIBILANT HISSING OF SWIFTLY-HURLED KNIVES--
--THE DEAFENING THUNDER OF HIDDEN EXPLOSIVES!
THEY ARE OBVIOUSLY ASSASSINATION ATTEMPTS, PERFECTLY-PLANNED AND EXECUTED--BUT STILL THE CROWN-LORD OF DARKNESS WALKS AWAY FROM EACH ONE UNHARMED.
UNFORTUNATELY, THE SAME CANNOT BE SAID FOR HIS WOULD-BE ASSASSINS.

BOSS, IT'S FOUR A.M. AND UMBERTO'S NOT BACK YET--
-AND PERSONALLY, I DON'T THINK HE'S COMING!
THAT MAKES FIVE HIT-MEN YOU'VE SENT AFTER THAT DRACULA GUY IN AS MANY DAYS, BOSS--
--AND AIN'T ONE OF THEM COME BACK YET!
YOU THINK I HAVEN'T NOTICED THAT, ALONZO?

OKAY-- SO MUSCLE DOESN'T SEEM TO WORK AGAINST MR. FANCY-PANTS! SO BIG NICK DIABLO IS ALWAYS PERFECT!
BUT THERE ARE OTHER WAYS TO HANDLE DIRT LIKE HIM, ALONZO!
BELIEVE ME... THERE ARE OTHER WAYS!

ANOTHER DAY PASSES--AND WHEN DARKNESS DESCENDS ONCE MORE, THE LORD OF DARKNESS DESCENDS AS WELL--
--UPON THE UNSUSPECTING INNOCENT!
YOU WISH TO ESCORT ME, SIGNOR?
INDEED, SIGNORINA.

MARIA PETRELLA SEEMS RELUCTANT TO COME ALONG AT FIRST-- BUT THE PROPER WORDS AND THOSE ULTIMATELY-ENTICING CRIMSON EYES SOON CHANGE HER MIND.
THEY WALK TOGETHER THRU THE SHADOWED STREETS, THE SLAYER AND THE SOON-TO-BE SLAIN--

--BUT WHEN THE TWO STEP AT LAST INTO THE INEVITABLE CLUSTER OF SHADOWS--

--IT QUICKLY BECOMES DIFFICULT TO TELL WHICH ONE IS WHICH!
THWUCK
DIE, YOU POMPOUS FOOL!

NEED WE DESCRIBE THE AWESOME CHILL THAT RIPPLES UP MARIA'S SUPPLE BACK WHEN THE VAMPIRE-LORD CALMLY PLUCKS THE DAGGER OUT!
DIO MIO-- IT ISN'T POSSIBLE--! THE KNIFE--!
--DID LITTLE MORE THAN ANNOY ME, MY DEAR MARIA!
AS YOU HAVE ANNOYED ME--BY BETRAYING COUNT DRACULA'S TRUST!

BUT YOU SEEM NOT THE TYPE TO HAVE DEVISED SUCH A PLAN YOURSELF! THERE IS SOME-ONE BEHIND YOUR ATTEMPT ON ME THIS NIGHT, WOMAN--
--AND I WANT TO KNOW WHO IT IS!
NO! LET ME GO! HE'LL KILL ME IF I TELL!

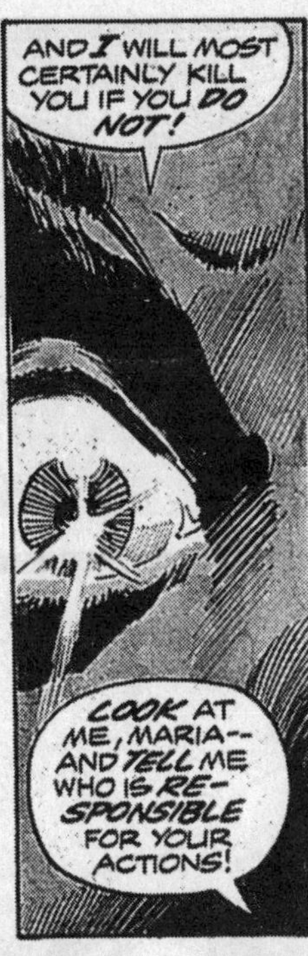
AND I WILL MOST CERTAINLY KILL YOU IF YOU DO NOT!
LOOK AT ME, MARIA-- AND TELL ME WHO IS RE-SPONSIBLE FOR YOUR ACTIONS!

IT... IT WAS DIABLO.. SIGNOR DIABLO! I... I DIDN'T WANT TO DO IT...
...BUT HE MADE ME... HE FORCED ME...!

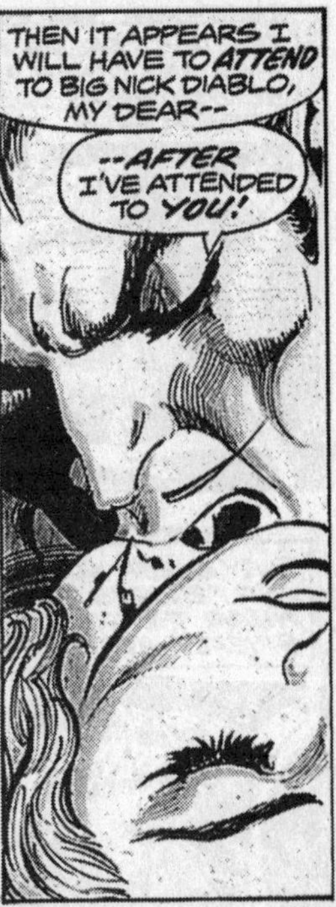
THEN IT APPEARS I WILL HAVE TO ATTEND TO BIG NICK DIABLO, MY DEAR--
--AFTER I'VE ATTENDED TO YOU!

THE TELEPHONE RINGS SCARCELY FIFTEEN MINUTES LATER...
YEAH? WHO IS... YOU!?!
YOU'VE GOT GUTS CALLING ME HERE LIKE THIS, MR. FANCY-PANTS.
YOU WANT TO DO WHAT? SETTLE OUR DIFFERENCES? I'VE BEEN TRYING TO DO THAT ALL WEEK!
YEAH--SURE I'LL SEE YOU. YEAH-- TILL THEN. CIAO.

THAT, MY BOYS, WAS MR. FANCY-PANTS DRACULA! SAYS HE'S COMING TO SEE ME HERE FRIDAY NIGHT--
--TO, QUOTE: "PUT AN END TO OUR VENDETTA ONCE AND FOR ALL"!

WELL, LET MR. FANCY-PANTS COME! I'LL PUT AN END TO OUR VENDETTA, ALL RIGHT!
A .45 CALIBER END TO IT!

THE NIGHT SEEMS NO LONGER THAN ANY OTHER AS NICK DIABLO'S BODYGUARDS SLEEP SOUNDLY IN THEIR BEDS.
THEY KNOW FULL WELL WHAT MUST BE DONE IN THREE DAYS TIME AND ARE NOT BOTHERED BY THE KNOWLEDGE IN THE LEAST.
MURDER IS NOT A CRIME TO THEM. IT IS A WAY OF LIFE!

THEY SLEEP SOUNDLY, TOO SOUNDLY-- AND PERHAPS THAT IS WHY THEY DO NOT HEAR THE SOUND OF WINGS BEATING BRIEFLY AT THEIR WINDOWS--
--OR THE FAINT HISS OF AN ALL-PERVADING MIST THAT SEEPS INTO THEIR BED-CHAMBERS--

--TO BECOME THE LORD OF VAMPIRES--
--WHOSE WORK THIS NOT IS NOT YET OVER!

YES, SIGNOR COUNT. MY MASTER IS EXPECTING YOU.
THE HOURS WHIRL OFF INTO ETERNITY... THREE DAYS DAWN AND DIE.... AND THE NIGHTTIDE BRINGS COUNT DRACULA TO BIG NICK DIABLO'S FRONT DOOR...

NICOLA DIABLO, I HAVE COME TO DEAL WITH YOU.
IS THAT SO? MR. FANCY-PANTS, YOU'RE IN NO POSITION TO DEAL ANYTHING--
--SEEING AS HOW YOU'RE OUT-NUMBERED FIVE-TO-ONE.

THE FIRST THING YOU LEARN IN MY BUSINESS, MR. FANCY-PANTS, IS TO NEVER GO NOWHERE-- ALONE!
TOO BAD YOU WON'T LIVE LONG ENOUGH TO PUT THAT LITTLE LESSON TO USE!

HAHAHAHAHA
BLAM! BLAM! BLAM!
MAMMA MIA! THE BULLETS-- THEY'RE GOING RIGHT THRU HIM--!

DIABLO, YOU TOO HAVE MADE A FATAL MISTAKE--
--IN ASSUMING I CAME TO YOU THIS EVENING UNATTENDED.
IN POINT OF FACT--

"--I BROUGHT ALONG SOME FRIENDS OF YOURS!"

DIO MIO! THEY'RE ALL-- VAMPIRES!

AND THEY'RE NOT THE ONLY ONES, BOSS!
ALONZO! GUISIPPI! NOT YOU TOO!?!

WELL, YOU'RE NOT GETTING BIG NICK DIABLO!
I WARN YOU-- KEEP AWAY FROM ME-- STAY BACK-- STAY BACK!
NOT A CHANCE, DIABLO! WE'RE PROFESSIONAL HIT-MEN!
WE ALWAYS MAKE GOOD ON A CONTRACT--

"--AND OUR NEW BOSS HAS PUT OUT A CONTRACT ON YOU!"
NICK DIABLO'S FINAL SOUND IS A SCREAM OF GIBBERING MADNESS THAT CURLS HYSTERICALLY INTO THE DARKNESS, SPILLING PAST THE BENIGHTED FORM OF A GREAT SOARING BAT--
--AND IF ONE WAS TO LISTEN CLOSELY, ONE MIGHT ALMOST HEAR THAT GRIM NIGHT-FLYER LAUGH-- --A LAUGH OF OUTRAGEOUS TRIUMPH!
FINIS

THE CASTLE.

RETRACE THE PATH OF THE LIFE-GIVING RIVER *ARGES* TO THE SNOW-CAPPED PEAKS OF *TRANSYLVANIA* THAT GIVE IT LIFE, AND THERE YOU WILL FIND... THE *CASTLE.*

HOME ONCE, PERHAPS *STILL*, TO ONE OF THE MOST MALIGNANT EVILS OF ALL HISTORY.

VLAD THE IMPALER...

VLAD THE DEVIL...

DRACULA!

THE CASTLE: *HEADQUARTERS* NOW -- IN *1944* -- OF A *NEWER* EVIL--

--AN EVIL WHOSE BANNERS *TAINT* THE BREEZES THAT PASS THROUGH THEM--

--AN EVIL IN NO WAY LESSER THAN --

THE TERROR THAT STALKED CASTLE DRACULA!

STEVE GERBER, *PLOT* | TONY ISABELLA, *SCRIPT* | JIM STARLIN, *LAYOUT* | SYD SHORES, *ART*

DID I NOT TELL YOU, LEUTNANT HANSON, THAT OUR LOYAL SERVICE WOULD SOMEDAY REAP US GREAT REWARDS?
LOOK AROUND YOU, MY YOUNG FRIEND! SEE THE SPLENDOR WE HAVE BEEN GIVEN AS OFFICERS OF THE THIRD REICH!
I DO NOT LIKE IT, HAUPTMAN KRISS. THIS CRUMBLING CASTLE MAKES ME FEEL... UNEASY.

THERE IS AN AURA OF EVIL IN THIS PLACE. THIS I FEEL VERY STRONGLY.
IT'S AS IF THE SPIRIT OF VLAD THE IMPALER LURKED IN EVERY CREVICE OF THE CASTLE
THE IMPALER? YOU MEAN THE MAN IN THE PICTURE--?
--THE MAN CALLED DRACULA?

*YOU HAVE BEEN LISTENING TO THE STORIES THE GYPSIES TELL THEIR CHILDREN TO FRIGHTEN THEM! VAMPIRES? HAH! THE MAN IN THAT PICTURE WAS JUST THAT... A MAN!
"NOTHING MORE."
YOU ARE DOUBTLESS RIGHT, MEIN HAUPTMAN. YET THERE'S SOMETHING IN HIS BURNING EYES, HIS MIEN, THAT MAKES ME--
--UNEASY.
*HAUPTMAN= CAPTAIN.--RT.

WE WILL TALK OF THIS LATER. WHERE ARE THE PRISONERS?
HERE THEY COME, SIR. GYPSIES--BAH! THEIR DAMNABLE WANDERLUST MAKES THEM ALMOST AS GREAT A PROBLEM AS THE ACCUSED JEWS!
HEIL, MEIN HAUPTMAN!

LOOK AT THEM, LT. HANSON! TATTERED... FILTHY... MEEK... FIT ONLY TO INHERIT WORMS! WHY DO WE WASTE OUR TIME WITH THEM?

YES, BOCHE, WE ARE POOR. BUT WE ARE NOT SOULLESS MONSTERS WHO MURDER MILLIONS TO INFLATE THEIR OWN PITIFUL EXISTENCES! WE GYPSIES LOVE LIFE! YOU RAPE IT!
RESISTANCE? REMARKABLE! NORMALLY, I WOULD FIND THAT HIGHLY COMMENDABLE, EVEN ADMIRABLE, IN A MAN--

BUT YOU ARE NOT A MAN--YOU ARE A GYPSY!
WHAP!
UHNN!

TAKE HIM AND PUT HIM WITH THE BEASTS OF BURDEN IN THE CASTLE STABLES! HE IS TO BE TREATED EXACTLY LIKE THEM AND DO TWICE THEIR WORK!

WITH YOUR PERMISSION, SIR, I WILL SUPERVISE HIS WORKING CONDITIONS... PERSONALLY!

AND WHAT SHALL I DO WITH YOU, MY DEAR? HMM.... YOU DO NOT FALL TO THE FLOOR AT MY TOUCH AS THE OLD MAN DID. PERHAPS YOU WILL BE TREATED MORE KINDLY THAN HE.

GUARDS! TAKE THE YOUNG LADY TO MY ROOM AND SEE THAT SHE IS COMFORTABLE...

...PERHAPS SHE CAN HELP ALLEVIATE THE CHILL OF THESE HARSH TRANSYLVANIAN NIGHTS.

YOU, BOY, HAVE A FAINT SPARK OF INTELLIGENCE IN YOUR EYES. YOU WILL BE MY PERSONAL MESSENGER! WHEN I CALL, RUN TO MY SIDE. IF YOU ARE TOO SLOW--

--I'LL FEED YOU TO THE VAMPIRES!

YES, SIR!

BAH! THESE GYPSY PEASANTS ARE ALL COWARDS OR FOOLS! PERHAPS I SHOULD SHORTEN THEIR AGONY AND BE RID OF THEM AT ONCE! AND YET--

AND WHAT IS A KING WITHOUT SUBJECTS?

--I FIND MYSELF BECOMING VERY FOND OF THIS SITUATION.

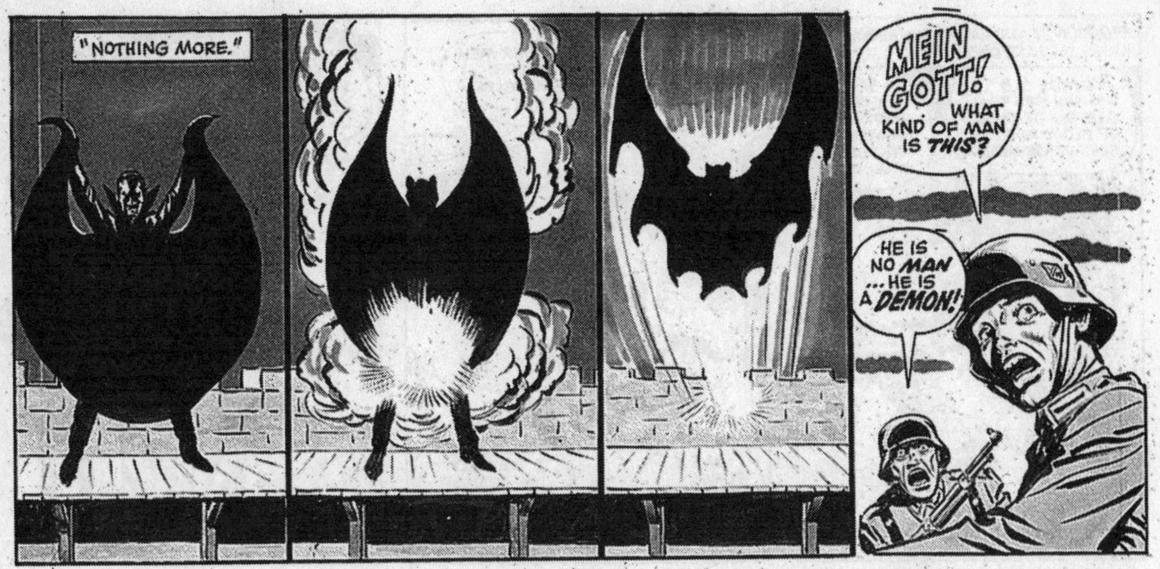
"NOTHING MORE."
MEIN GOTT! WHAT KIND OF MAN IS THIS?
HE IS NO MAN ...HE IS A DEMON!

THE PAWNS OF A MODERN EVIL FLEE BEFORE THE KNIGHT OF A MORE ANCIENT ONE.

AND THEY PRAY, THESE DOOMED CHESSMEN, TO A GOD THEY HAVE LONG SINCE FORSAKEN FOR A MAD AUSTRIAN DIETY.

THEIR PRAYERS GO UNANSWERED--
--SAVE FOR THE RUSTLE OF DEATH SPLITTING THE DANK CASTLE AIR BEFORE THEM--!

--OF DEATH REACHING OUT FOR THEM!
MY SHOULDER! IT'S LIKE BEING CAUGHT IN A VICE!

ARRGGGH! HE HAS THE STRENGTH OF A HUNDRED MEN!
CORRECTION: TWENTY... BUT 'TIS ENOUGH, 'TWILL SERVE--

--SERVE TO HOLD TWO GUARDS MOTIONLESS WHILE A SOMBRE FIGURE PRONOUNCES SLOWLY... COLDLY... THE CHARGE AGAINST THEM.
YOU HAVE INVADED THE CASTLE OF DRACULA!

THAT DONE, THE CREATURE OF THE NIGHT PREPARES TO CARRY OUT ITS MULTIPLE FUNCTIONS--
--AS JUDGE--
--AS JURY--

--AS EXECUTIONER!

NOOOOOOOO

MORNING: AND HAUPTMAN RUDOLPH KRISS IS DISTURBED.
NO! YOU OLD WOMEN SEE TWO CORPSES DRAINED OF BLOOD AND YOU SCREAM "VAMPIRE!"
I SAY THERE IS ANOTHER ANSWER TO THESE KILLINGS!
FETCH THE OLD GYPSY FROM THE STABLES!

I DON'T KNOW HOW YOUR MEN ACCOMPLISHED THE MURDERS, GYPSY, NOR HOW YOU SMUGGLED THE ORDER TO THEM, BUT...
ME? SURELY YOU DO NOT BELIEVE I...
SILENCE! I WAS NOT IMPRESSED BY YOUR PARLOR TRICK, OLD MAN.

BUT I PERCEIVE A NEED TO TEACH YOU MISERABLE PEASANTS RESPECT FOR THE POWER OF THE THIRD REICH--
KA-POW!
--AND TEACH I SHALL!

NIGHT: AND IF THE ENSLAVED GYPSIES HAVE LEARNED RESPECT FOR THEIR ENSLAVERS, THERE IS ANOTHER WHO HAS NOT!

FOR, HE HAS HIS OWN LESSON TO TEACH--
--A LESSON IN TERROR!

ONCE MORE, MORNING: AND HAUPTMAN RUDOLPH KRISS HAS REALIZED HIS MISTAKE.
HE DOES NOT LIKE MAKING MISTAKES.
THERE IS A VAMPIRE AT LARGE IN THIS CASTLE. THIS I MUST ACCEPT IN VIEW OF THE OVERWHELMING EVIDENCE.
LT. HANSON'S SEARCH FOR A COFFIN WILL DOUBTLESS FIND NOTHING. I KNOW FROM MY BOYHOOD READING THAT SUCH CREATURES CAN SOMETIMES WALK BY DAY.

BUT WHO IS THE VAMPIRE? CERTAINLY NOT DRACULA. HE WAS KILLED BY ABRAHAM VAN HELSING DECADES AGO.
IT MUST BE ONE OF THE GYPSIES. THEY WERE KNOWN TO HAVE SERVED DRACULA BEFORE HIS DEATH. PERHAPS THEY SERVE HIM AFTER IT, AS WELL.

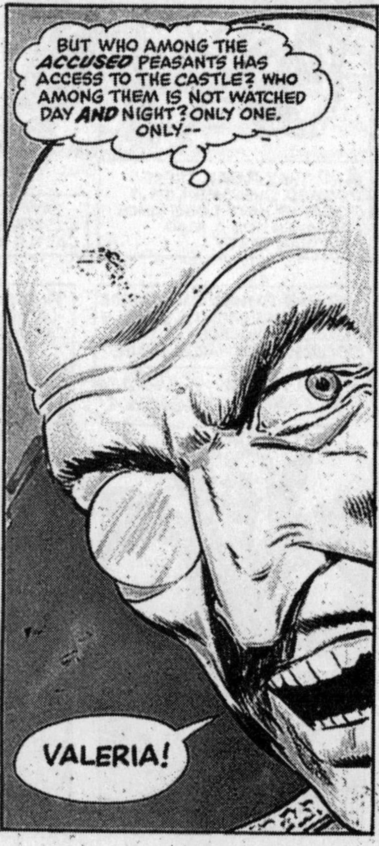
BUT WHO AMONG THE ACCUSED PEASANTS HAS ACCESS TO THE CASTLE? WHO AMONG THEM IS NOT WATCHED DAY AND NIGHT? ONLY ONE. ONLY--
VALERIA!

TELL ME, VALERIA. ARE YOU CONTENT WITH YOUR PRESENT STATION IN LIFE?
WHY SHOULD I BE UNHAPPY? MEIN HAUPTMAN GIVES ME FINE CLOTHES, FINE FOOD...I AM TREATED AS A QUEEN IS TREATED.

YOU HAVE GIVEN ME... COMPANIONSHIP... VALERIA, AND YET I WONDER--
--GIVEN THE CHANCE, WOULD YOU KILL ME?
YES, MEIN HAUPTMAN. SLOWLY... AND WITH GREAT PLEASURE.

I FEAR I SHALL NOT FIND ANOTHER LIKE YOU IN ALL THESE HELL-FROZEN HILLS, MY DEAR, DEAR VALERIA.
OHHH--!
KRAK!

STRANGE. SOMEHOW I FELT CERTAIN YOU WOULD CRUMBLE TO DUST BEFORE MY EYES, VAMPIRESS. NO MATTER...
THE DEED IS DONE, THE CASTLE SAFE.

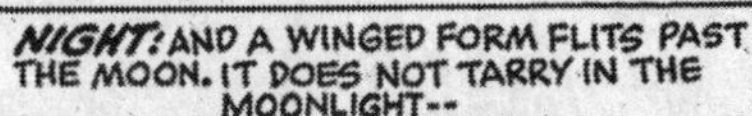
NIGHT: AND A WINGED FORM FLITS PAST THE MOON. IT DOES NOT TARRY IN THE MOONLIGHT--

FOR, IT HAS DEEDS TO DO--

--DEATHS TO DELIVER.

AGAIN, MORNING: AND HAUPTMAN KRISS IS ANGRY!
LEUTNANT, WE CAN AFFORD NO MORE DEATHS! THE MEN DO NOT REST AT NIGHT ANYMORE. THEY ARE WEAK FROM LACK OF SLEEP!
WE MUST ACT!

WE KNOW THE VAMPIRE IS A GYPSY. THEREFORE, YOU WILL TAKE SIX OF OUR MEN--
--OUR BEST MARKS-MEN!

"YOU WILL TAKE THEM TO THE GYPSY CAMP AT THE MOUTH OF THE RIVER ARGES.
"APPROACH QUIETLY. GIVE THEM NO WARNING.

"FOR, I WANT TO BE SURE THAT EVERY SINGLE GYPSY IS IN CAMP AT THAT MOMENT-- EVERY MAN, WOMAN, AND CHILD AMONG THEM.
"AND, WHEN YOU ARE CERTAIN THEY ARE ALL THERE--

"--YOU WILL STEP FROM YOUR COVER INTO THE BLAZING LIGHT OF THE NOONDAY SUN! YOU WILL LET THEM SEE THE MIGHT OF THE THIRD REICH, THE MIGHT THEY HAVE DARED TO CHALLENGE!

"DOUBTLESS THEY WILL TRY TO FLEE INTO THE WOODS... FLEE FROM THE WRATH OF THE MASTER RACE!

"DO NOT LET THEM!

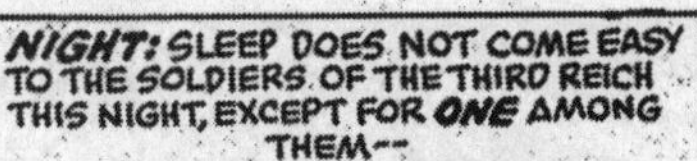
NIGHT: SLEEP DOES NOT COME EASY TO THE SOLDIERS OF THE THIRD REICH THIS NIGHT, EXCEPT FOR ONE AMONG THEM--

--ONE WHO FINDS SLEEP OF A SORT--
--A PERMANENT SORT.

MORNING: AND THOSE WHO IGNORED A HALF-CHOKED SCREAM IN THE DARK NOW STARE AWKWARDLY IN THE SUNLIGHT AT A BLOOD-DRAINED CORPSE.
THE VAMPIRE HAS STRUCK AGAIN!
THEN WE KILLED THE GYPSIES FOR NOTHING!
SMALL LOSS, IF ANY.

IT APPEARS WE MUST STILL FIND OUR VAMPIRE.
WHO WILL YOU KILL THIS TIME, HAUPTMAN? PERHAPS THERE IS A GYPSY LEFT SOMEWHERE!
HMM... I NEVER REALIZED YOU WERE SO EXCITABLE, MY DEAR LEUTNANT HANSON. I DO NOT LIKE EXCITABLE PEOPLE.

BUT WE WILL DISCUSS THAT ANOTHER TIME. IT OCCURS TO ME THAT THERE IS STILL ONE GYPSY AMONG US. KAA SE!
HE'S ONLY A BOY!
NO MATTER.

GUARDS! SEIZE THAT GYPSY WHELP!
EVEN IF HE IS A VAMPIRE, WHAT'S TO STOP HIM FROM RETURNING FROM THE DEAD AGAIN?
THERE'S ONE SURE WAY TO KILL A VAMPIRE--

--YOU MUST DRIVE A WOODEN STAKE THROUGH ITS HEART!

YOU DON'T EXPECT ME TO... HE'S JUST A BOY!
YOU'RE GETTING EXCITABLE AGAIN, LEUTNANT!
PLEASE, SIR. DON'T...

ARRGGGGH!

YOUR "VAMPIRE" IS DEAD, HERR HAUPTMAN!

EXCELLENT. PERHAPS I WAS MISTAKEN ABOUT YOUR EXCITABILITY, LEUTNANT. AT ANY RATE, THE AFFAIR IS ENDED.

IS IT, HAUPTMAN KRISS? OR WILL THE VAMPIRE CLAIM ANOTHER VICTIM TONIGHT?

AND WILL YOU CLAIM ANOTHER VICTIM THE FOLLOWING MORNING?

NIGHT: A BAT SWOOPS LOW OVER A CERTAIN WINDOW AND, AS IT DOES, CHANGES INTO SOMETHING MORE THAN A BAT, PERHAPS MORE THAN A MAN--

--A VAMPIRE!

THE VAMPIRE HAS TIRED OF LETTING A DUTY ROSTER SELECT ITS VICTIMS.

THIS NIGHT, THE VAMPIRE SEEKS SPECIFIC PREY--

LEUTNANT WILLI HANSON!

AND THEN IT HEARS THE HEAVY BREATHING... NOT FROM THE BED... BUT FROM ACROSS THE ROOM.

THE VAMPIRE WHIRLS--

MEIN GOTT!
THE VAMPIRE WEARS THE UNIFORM OF-- HAUPTMAN KRISS!
YES, FOOL! WHY DO YOU NOT SALUTE YOUR COMMANDING OFFICER AS IS HIS DUE? HAHAHAHAHAHAHAHA

YOUR VOICE-- THEN, YOU ARE MEIN HAUPTMAN-- YOU MUST BE!
BUT-- IT'S IMPOS-SIBLE!

IMPOSSIBLE? NOT AT ALL, MY DEAR LEUTNANT.
BUT I FEAR YOU SHALL NEVER LEARN THE HOW OF THIS--

--FOR NOW, YOU DIE!
NO!

"THERE IS ONE SURE WAY TO KILL A VAMPIRE--

"--YOU MUST DRIVE A WOODEN STAKE--
"--THROUGH ITS HEART!"

THEY SAY DRACULA IS *DEAD*, SLAIN BY A VAMPIRE-HUNTER ON THIS VERY ROAD. LT. HANSON DOES NOT BELIEVE THAT.

HE KNOW THAT *SOMEWHERE*...DRACULA LIVES! HE KNOWS THAT *SOMEDAY*....THE FULL FORCE OF DRACULA'S EVIL SHALL RETURN!

FOR THE NONCE, HE TRIES NOT TO THINK OF DRACULA, ONLY OF MOVING HIS WEARY MEN *ONWARD*, EVER *ONWARD*.

THEY HAVE NOT SLEPT IN MANY DAYS.

BUT THEY MARCH *ON*. BEFORE THIS MORNING'S END, THEY WANT TO BE FAR FROM THE CASTLE OF *DRACULA*--

--A CASTLE THAT REMAINS *INVIOLATE* THROUGHOUT THE REMAINDER OF THIS GLOBE-SPANNING *WAR*--

--*INVIOLATE*, SAVE FOR A RICH LAUGHTER ECHOING FROM DEEP WITHIN THE CASTLE ITSELF!

FINIS

A POISON OF THE BLOOD

NIGHT OVER MANHATTAN:

SMOG LIES HEAVY ON THE ISLAND METROPOLIS, A DINGY BROWN SMUDGE THAT DOES POOR SERVICE TO THE GLEAMING TOWERS AND TWINKLING LIGHTS.

THOSE LIGHTS SEEK TO BREAK THE EVENING MANTLE--TO SHATTER THE DROOPING SHROUD OF DARKNESS--

--AND PERHAPS PUSH BACK THE CHAOTIC FORCES OF THE UNCIVILIZED--THE UNNATURAL--THE SUPERNATURAL--

--SYMBOLIZED, THIS EVE, BY THE HAUNTING PRESENCE--OF A VAMPIRE BAT!

1

STORY BY GERRY CONWAY * ART BY GENE COLAN AND TOM PALMER

AT LAST--I HAVE RETURNED TO THIS ACCURSED CONTINENT.
PERHAPS THIS TIME--THE AFFAIR WILL END MORE TO MY LIKING.

I HAVE BEEN TOLD THAT MUCH HAS CHANGED SINCE LAST I STOOD UPON THESE ALIEN SHORES--
--AND, IT SEEMS I HAVE BEEN TOLD THE TRUTH--

--FOR, WHERE ONCE STRETCHED QUIET FOREST, THERE NOW LIES A CITY TO RIVAL LONDON--
PERHAPS ALL OF EUROPE, AS WELL!

BUT SUCH IS NOT MY CONCERN!
SCANT HOURS REMAIN UNTIL DAWN--WHEN I MUST RETURN TO THE SHIP WHICH BEARS MY COFFIN--

--AND I MUST SPEND THOSE HOURS PROFITABLY.
HE WHOM I SEEK LIVES WITHIN THIS CITY--
--FOR, UNLESS THIS REPORTER LIES--

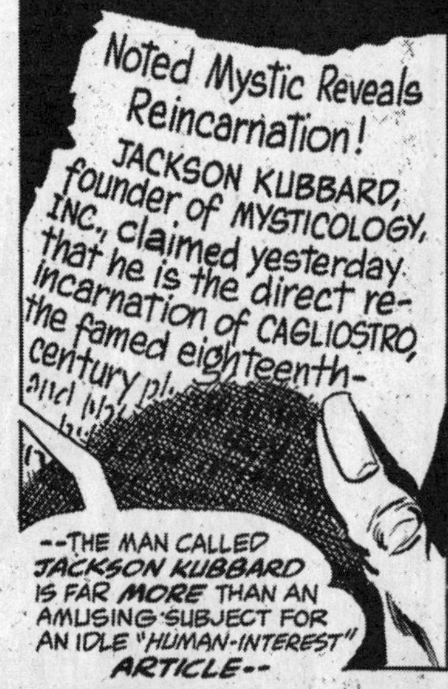
Noted Mystic Reveals Reincarnation!
JACKSON KUBBARD, founder of MYSTICOLOGY, INC., claimed yesterday that he is the direct re-incarnation of CAGLIOSTRO, the famed eighteenth-century
--THE MAN CALLED JACKSON KUBBARD IS FAR MORE THAN AN AMUSING SUBJECT FOR AN IDLE "HUMAN-INTEREST" ARTICLE--

--HE MIGHT TRULY BE THE REINCARNATION OF THE SORCEROR, CAGLIOSTRO--AN OLD ENEMY--
--ONE WHO WILL BE UNPLEASANTLY SURPRISED TO FIND HIMSELF GREETED BY A MAN HE THOUGHT LONG DESTROYED--
--COUNT DRACULA!

BUT--SUCH MEETINGS LIE IN THE NEAR FUTURE.
FOR THE MOMENT, I MUST BE SATISFIED WITH FAR MORE MUNDANE MATTERS--
--SUCH AS THE QUENCHING OF A BITTER THIRST-- A BURNING DESIRE FOR BLOOD!
FOOTSTEPS SOUND IN COUNTERPOINT TO THE MORE MUNDANE NOISES OF THIS LOWER EAST SIDE STREET--
--FATEFUL FOOTSTEPS, THE HESITANT TREAD OF A MAN DOOMED--
--A PALE MAN WHO SHALL REMAIN NAMELESS--NOW ONLY A TREMBLING FIGURE WHO GROPES FOR SUPPORT FROM A CONVENIENT LAMP-POST--HIS EYES RIMMED IN RED, HIS FOREHEAD WET WITH COLD SWEAT--
--SIGNS THAT GO UNNOTICED, AS--
CRIPES-- WHAT--?
SILENCE, MY FRIEND--
YOUR LAST MOMENT WILL BE PAINLESS--
THAT MUCH, I PROMISE YOU!
AAAAKKK

HE RISES FROM THE DYING FORM OF HIS VICTIM--
--AND PAUSES, EYES WIDENING AT A NEW SENSATION--
THIS PAIN--LIKE NOTHING I'VE EVER FELT BEFORE!
WHAT IS IT-- WHAT IS IT?
ONLY THEN DOES HE SEE THE NEEDLE FALLEN FROM THE DEAD MAN'S POCKET.
ONLY THEN--AS HE BLACKS OUT-- DOES DRACULA REALIZE--
A DRUG ADDICT! HE WAS AN AAAAAA--

...HEY, MAN, YOU AWAKE YET?
THEY BROUGHT YOU IN HERE, I THOUGHT YOU WERE GONE!
WHERE-- WHERE AM I--?

THE TOMBS, MAN--YOU KNOW, JAIL?
THEY LET ALL OF US COOL HERE AWHILE-- GO COLD TURKEY.
GUARD SAID THEY FOUND YOU PASSED OUT--
--SAID YOUR BUDDY DIDN'T MAKE IT. D.O.A.

AND YOU, MY FRIEND...?
THEY GOT ME RIGHT AFTER I SHOT IT, FRIEND.
I'M COOL ANOTHER DAY--BUT, WHO CARES, Y'KNOW?

I CARE, "FRIEND".
MY BLOOD IS TAINTED-- IT NEEDS REPLENISH-MENT.
FOR NOW-- YOUR OWN DRUGGED BLOOD MUST DO--
AAARRH!

--THOUGH IT ONLY PERPETUATES MY MISTAKE--
--AND OFFERS ME NO CURE!
A WHISPER OF WINGS-- A BRIEF SHADOW ACROSS THE MOON--AND THE ROOM IS EMPTIED-- BY ONE.

COFFEE SHOP
AN HOUR PASSES--TWO--AND THEN OUR STORY PICKS UP AGAIN, IN A QUIET GREENWICH VILLAGE COFFEE SHOP--

--WHERE A GIRL NAMED MADELINE ROGERS SITS--LISTENING TO SOFTLY-PLAYED MUSIC--
--SITS LISTENING, AND UNCONSCIOUSLY AWAITING--HER DESTINY!

PARDON ME, MISS--YET I COULD NOT HELP BUT NOTICE--
--THAT PENDANT--

ITS DESIGN IS RATHER UNUSUAL--THE STANDARD OF THE MYSTICOLOGISTS, IS IT NOT?
YOU--KNOW ABOUT US?
MY DEAR GIRL--I'VE BEEN SEARCHING FOR ONE OF YOU FOR SOME TIME!

I WAS TOLD THIS PLACE IS OFTEN FREQUENTED BY MEMBERS OF YOUR--SECT.
SURE--WE COME HERE A LOT.
SIT DOWN... PLEASE.

I WAS WONDERING--HOW COULD I MEET YOUR MR. KUBBARD?
THERE'S A GATHERING TONIGHT--WHY DON'T YOU COME ALONG?
YOU'LL LOVE IT--YOU REALLY WILL.

I AM SURE OF IT, MY DEAR...
QUITE SURE.

NOW THE MOMENTS PASS QUICKLY, AS THE PAIR STROLL UPTOWN THROUGH THE SHIFTING THRONGS--THRONGS FILLED WITH CURIOUS PEOPLE--WHO OCCASIONALLY CAST AN APPRAISING GLANCE, AND THEN TURN SWIFTLY AWAY.

I FIND THE INHABITANTS OF THIS CITY MOST AMUSING, MISS ROGERS.

THEY SEEM TO FIND ME FASCINATING--AND YET, REFUSE TO ACKNOWLEDGE THAT FASCINATION!

WELL, THAT'S NEW YORK, I GUESS.

YOU'RE NOT FROM AROUND HERE, ARE YOU?

I'M FROM IOWA, MYSELF.

LOOK--IF YOU DON'T WANT AN AMBULANCE, MAYBE WE'D BETTER TAKE A CAB THE REST OF THE WAY.
YOU'RE JUST NOT WELL.
THE BLOOD OF THAT ADDICT--IT SEEMS TO HAVE INFECTED ME--

NOW--HIS CURSE IS MY CURSE! HIS CRAVING FOR DRUGS--MY CRAVING!
AND THESE PAINS--OF COURSE! I SEEM TO BE--WHAT IS THE PHRASE?
WITHDRAWING FROM THE DRUG--!

ARE YOU OKAY NOW?
IN A MOMENT, MY DEAR.
FOR NOW--LET ME REST.

HIS EYES CLOSE, AND HIS MIND GOES BACK--BACK TO THE BEGINNING OF THIS DARK QUEST--
TO LONDON, WHERE HE FIRST READ OF JACK KIMBAL'S CLAIM.
YES, LONDON, AND THE COFFIN HE NEEDS FOR HIS DAYTIME REST--THE COFFIN HE HAD SHIPPED TO THE NEW WORLD, TO AMERICA, IN ANTICIPATION OF HIS JOURNEY THERE--

--A JOURNEY HE BEGAN LATE THAT NIGHT, IN THE FORM OF A BAT--
--A FORM HE WISHES HE COULD NOW ASSUME.

HERE YA ARE, LADY. EAST AVENUE.
THAT'S A DOLLAR TEN ON THE METER.

BE CAREFUL, NOW.
YOU STILL SEEM A LITTLE UNSTEADY.
I ASSURE YOU--I AM QUITE WELL NOW, MISS ROGERS.
SHALL WE PROCEED?

REGINA, THIS IS A FRIEND OF MINE. HE'S INTERESTED IN THE FRATERNITY--
I THINK HE'D LIKE TO MEET MISTER KUBBARD.
EVERYONE WOUL MADELINE. BUT PERHAPS MR. KUBBARD WILL MAKE AN EX-CEPTION IN THE CASE OF MISTER--AH--?
DRAKE, REGINA. MR. DRAKE.

MYSTICOLOGY
JACKSON KUBBARD: ARE YOU THE REINCARNATION OF CAGLIOSTRO?
PERHAPS... PERHAPS.

MR. DRAKE-- WILL YOU COME THIS WAY?
THERE'S A MEETING IN PROGRESS--

--AS I'M SURE YOU'LL BE ABLE TO SEE!

CAGLIOSTRO! AT LAST WE MEET--AT LAST, WE MAY RENEW OUR AGELESS BATTLE!
CAGLIOSTRO-- GREATEST MYSTIC OF THE MIDDLE AGES--
EXIT
--AND I, DRACULA-- PRINCE OF DARKNESS!

STRIKE, CAGLIOSTRO-- OFFER THE WOMAN'S SOUL TO YOUR NAME-LESS GODS--

STRIKE, SORCERER-- FOR WHAT DO YOU WAIT?

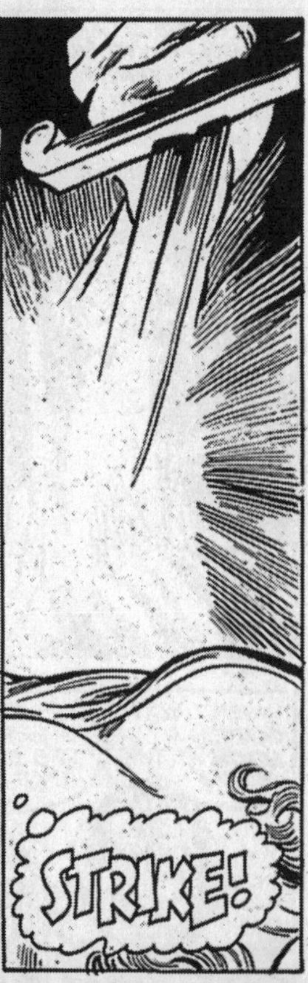
STRIKE!

BUT ENOUGH OF THIS PRETENSE. THE POINT SHOULD BE OBVIOUS, MY FRIENDS.
SORCERY IS ALIVE IN THE WORLD AROUND US. OCCULT FORCES AWAIT THE BLOW WHICH SHALL FREE THEM.
WHO AMONG YOU COULD NOT FEEL THE TENSION-- LURKING IN THIS VERY CHAMBER?

WHO AMONG YOU COULD NOT TASTE THE NEARNESS OF DEATH--AND WANTED IT TO COME?
SUCH IS THE STRENGTH OF MYSTICOLOGY, MY FRIENDS--
--AYE, AND THE STRENGTH OF CAGLIOSTRO, AS WELL!
DO YOU SEE?
THE WAY HE COMMANDS?

"YES," THE CLOAKED MAN ADMITS, "HIS POWER IS GREAT. THE AUDIENCE APPLAUDS--THEY APPROVE.
"BUT--OF WHAT DO THEY APPROVE?"

THAT IS WHAT CONCERNS ME NOW!
WELL, MR. KUBBARD'S PRIVATE SUITE IS DOWN THIS WAY.
MAYBE HE WILL SEE YOU--!
DON'T BET ON IT, SISTER.
NO JUNKIE'S GONNA SEE MR. KUBBARD--NO WAY.
JUNKIE?

HAVEN'T YOU GOTTEN A LOOK AT THIS BIRD?
IT'S FREEZIN' IN HERE--AND HE'S SWEATIN' LIKE A PIG.
YOU BELABOR THE OBVIOUS, YOUNG MAN--

--BUT I THINK, UPON CONSIDERATION--YOU WILL ALLOW ME ENTRANCE--
WON'T YOU?
Y-YES...
I... WILL... LET... YOU... IN.

THIS... WAY
EXCELLENT.
I WILL NO LONGER REQUIRE YOUR ASSISTANCE, MADELINE ROGERS.
YOU MAY LEAVE.

WAIT!
AREN'T YOU GOING TO TAKE ME--

--WITH YOU?
SLAM!

THE SOUND OF THE SLAMMING DOOR IS ALL TOO FINAL.
CONFUSED--HURT--MADELINE ROGERS TURNS AWAY--
--UNAWARE HOW CLOSE SHE'S COME TO DEATH--AND HOW CASUAL HER REPRIEVE!

APPARENTLY, THIS CULT HAS BEEN MOST GENEROUS TO JACKSON KUBBARD--HE LIVES AS WELL AS ANY EUROPEAN PRINCE.
I SHALL FIND OUR CONVERSATION--INTERESTING!
DANIEL, I TOLD YOU NOT TO DISTURB ME AFTER A-- eh?

WHO THE HELL ARE YOU? HOW DID YOU GET IN HERE?
I HAVE COME TO MEET THE SOUL OF CAGLIOSTRO, JACKSON KUBBARD...

AND MY NAME IS... DRACULA.
DRACULA? WHAT SORT OF NONSENSE IS THIS? I ASKED YOU, HOW YOU--
OH DEAR GOD--THAT MIRROR! YOU HAVE--NO REFLECTION--!

CRACK!
ENOUGH! YOUR WORDS BORE ME.
I CAME FIVE THOUSAND MILES TO SEE CAGLIOSTRO--A MAN I CALL MY BLOOD-SWORN ENEMY--

--AND INSTEAD, I FIND YOU. A SHAM--A CHARLATAN. CAGLIOSTRO WOULD NEVER HAVE FREED THAT GIRL--
HE WOULD HAVE STRUCK--AND FELT THE WARMTH OF HER SWEET BLOOD.
IT WAS JUST A GAME--
A HARMLESS LIE--TO--TO DRAW CROWDS! THAT'S ALL THEY WANT--AN--AN ESCAPE!

I NEVER--EXPECTED--ANY OF IT TO BE REAL!
WHAT--WHAT ARE YOU GOING TO DO?

DO, MR. KUBBARD?
I BURN FOR CLEAN BLOOD, MR. KUBBARD--
--THAT WITHIN ME IS POISONED--AND MUST BE REPLACED!

AND, SINCE IT WAS YOU WHO DREW ME TO AMERICA, AND SO INVOLVED ME IN THIS DISEASED MADNESS--
--THE BLOOD MUST COME FROM YOU!
AAAAAAGGHHHH
LIKE THE TRILL OF A DISTANT BIRD--
--THE SCREAM DRIFTS DOWN TO THE STREET BELOW, AND THERE LIFTS THE HEAD OF A WALKING GIRL...
...A GIRL WHOSE STORY IS NOT YET OVER.
I KNEW THOSE NUTS WOULD GO TOO FAR SOME DAY, FRED.
IT'S THIS CRAZY CITY!
POLICE
SOMETIMES IT MAKES EVEN ME A LITTLE BIT BUGABOO!
KEE-RIPES! WILL YOU GET A LOOKIT THAT?
THE WAY THAT GUY'S COMIN' AT US-- MUST BE DOPED TO THE SKULL!
HOLD IT RIGHT THERE, MISTER!
I SAID HOLD IT!
BUT THE MAN WITH THE BRIGHT EYES DOES NOT "HOLD IT"--
BAM!
--HIS FACE, SUFFUSED WITH A RUDDY GLOW, HE SNARLS IN ANGER--
--AND THE POLICE FIRE!
BAM!

OH SWEET LORD!
THE BULLETS ARE GOING RIGHT THROUGH HIM!

IT-IT ISN'T TRUE!
I-I LIKED YOU-- YOU CAN'T BE--
YOUR DESIRES HAVE NO EFFECT ON THE FORM OF REALITY, MY DEAR--

NOR, IT SEEMS, DO MINE.
ALREADY--THE DAWN BREAKS! AND IF I DO NOT SOON RETURN TO MY COFFIN--
--DRACULA WILL DIE!

AS FOR YOU, CHILD--
CONSIDER YOURSELF FORTUNATE.
YOU MUST LIVE WITHIN ITS BOUNDS--
YOU HAVE LEARNED--NO PRAYER OR INCANTATION CAN AFFECT YOUR WORLD--
--FOR THERE IS NOT NOW-- OR EVER-- AN ESCAPE!

QUICKLY, THE BLACK SHAPE FLITS ACROSS A DAWN-STREAKED SKYLINE.
AT LAST, ITS DESTINATION LOOMS--

--AND THE PRINCE OF EVIL READIES HIMSELF-- FOR HIS LONG AND FRUSTRATING JOURNEY--HOME!

AS FOR THE GIRL, MADELINE ROGERS:
SHE, TOO, TURNS HOMEWARD.
PERHAPS SHE HAS LEARNED--THERE CAN BE NO ESCAPE THROUGH THE WORSHIP OF MAGIC--
--BUT THE WORSHIP OF EVIL--AND OF EVIL'S PRINCE--NOW THERE IS ROOM FOR THOUGHT.
FINIS

THE VOODOO QUEEN OF NEW ORLEANS!
...GROUND BURIALS, YOU SEE, WERE QUITE IMPOSSIBLE UNTIL RECENTLY IN N'ORLEANS, BECAUSE THE EARTH HERE IS FAR TOO SWAMPY FOR GRAVE-DIGGING.
THAT IS WHY THESE MORE COLORFUL ABOVE-THE-GROUND TOMBS WERE ORIGINALLY CONSTRUCTED.
SOMEWHERE IN THIS VERY CEMETERY, IT IS SAID THAT THE BONES OF MARIE LAVEAU--THE MOST FAMOUS VOODOO WOMAN OF THEM ALL--LIE ENTOMBED!
OR THEN AGAIN, THEY MAY NOT--FOR THE REMAINS OF POOR PEOPLE WERE OFTEN REMOVED WHEN THEIR FAMILIES FAILED TO PAY THE, AH, RENT.
OH DEAR! HOW PERFECTLY REVOLTING!
YES, QUITE--THOUGH NOT NEARLY SO REVOLTING AS THE FAILURE TO MEET ONE'S FINANCIAL OBLIGATIONS
...AS I'M SURE YOU'LL AGREE, MA'AM.
STORY BY ROY THOMAS / ART BY GENE COLAN & DICK GIORDANO

BUT, IT'S GETTING LATE, AND SOON THIS YEAR'S MARDI GRAS WILL COMMENCE ELSEWHERE IN OUR FAIR CITY.
I TRUST YOU ALL HAVE ENJOYED THIS BRIEF GLIMPSE OF--
IT COULDN'T BE TOO BRIEF FOR FOR THE LIKES OF US, HUH, CHERRY?..
RIGHT ON, LOVER-DOLL!
WE'RE THE QUICK --NOT THE DEAD!

AS I WAS ABOUT TO SAY:
THE CEMETERIES OF N'ORLEANS HOLD SPECIAL BEAUTY AND MEANING FOR PERSONS OF TASTE...
...AND DISCRETION.

FOR THIS AFTERNOON, HOWEVER, I FEAR OUR TOUR IS ENDED...

...AND I MUST ASK YOU ALL TO PLEASE FOLLOW ME...

FOR, A CITY ORDI-NANCE REQUIRES THAT THESE GATES BE CLOSED BY SUNSET...

SCLOSEDAN ...
...AND LOCKED!
CLANNG

SHADOWS: FIRST THEY GROW LONG, THEN WIDEN AND CLASP HANDS TO BECOME A SWOLLEN, SILENT MASS... BLOTTING OUT ALL BUT THE DISAPPROVING MOON.

THIS IDEA OF YOURS IS A GAS, CHERRY. MAKIN' IT IN A CEMETERY-- WILD!
BUT TIME'S A-WASTIN', GIRL! LET'S--.

FREDDY--PLEASE! I JUST MET YOU THIS AFTERNOON!
WHAT KIND OF GIRL DO YOU THINK I AM?
THAT KIND, BABY. AM I RIGHT?

ARE YOU EVER!
LET'S GET IT ON, LOVER-DOLL--

--NOW!
KLUNK!

WHAT WAS THAT?
I TELL YOU I HEARD SOMETHING! IT WAS--
... MERELY THE TRIFLING SOUND OF YOUR OWN UNIMPORTANT DEATH.
HUH? WHERE THE HELL DID YOU--?
FANGS! MY GOD, FREDDY-- HE'S GOT FANGS!!
KEEP BACK, BABY! I'M GONNA--
YOU WILL DO NOTHING...
...BECAUSE YOU ARE NOTHING TO ME.
THWAK!
FREDDY--!
IT IS YOU I WANT, WOMAN...
...AND IT IS YOU I SHALL HAVE!
NO!! NNOOOO

THE GIRL'S CRIES ARE CUT SHORT, AS SHE RESPONDS TO A HYPNOTIC GAZE ... A CURT, COMMANDING VOICE...
...UNTIL SHE IS CAUGHT IN AN IRRESISTIBLE WHIRLPOOL OF SHIMMERING, SHUDDERING ECSTACY...

...CAUGHT...AND DROWNED!

AND NOW THE VAMPIRE RISES FROM HIS GRISLY REPAST...
...LEAVING THE HAPLESS PAIR TOGETHER, TO SHARE THE LONG DARK SLEEP OF DEATH.

FOR, OTHER THINGS CONCERN HIM THIS NIGHT.
SUCH AS THE MEMORY THAT THAT HE ENTERED HIS COFFIN IN THE CITY CALLED NEW YORK...
...AND AWOKE IN A DANK TOMB ...IN ANOTHER PLACE.

HE WOULD LEARN WHERE, BY FLYING OVER THESE ACCURSED GATES WITH EASE...
...BUT FINDS HE CAN TURN NEITHER INTO BAT ...NOR INTO EERIE MIST...

AND HIS STRENGTH SEEMS HALVED, AS WELL.
STILL, SOMETHING CALLS HIM, FROM BEYOND THESE WALLS...
...SOMETHING HE CANNOT NAME...

SOMETHING HE CANNOT RESIST...

...SOMETHING WHICH CANNOT BE DENIED!

PERHAPS HE COULD FIGHT BACK--FOR, THE WILL OF COUNT DRACULA IS A FAR FIRMER THING THAN HARD-WROUGHT IRON.
BUT HE MUST KNOW WHO HAS THE SHEER AUDACITY TO TOY THUS WITH THE KING OF VAMPIRES.
IN SHORT, HE IS CURIOUS.
!

AND HIS CURIOSITY LEADS HIM BLINDLY THRU THE NARROW STREETS OF THE VIEUX CARRÉ... THE FAMOUS FRENCH QUARTER...
FOR, ONLY NOW IS NEW ORLEANS COMING ALIVE WITH THE SOUNDS OF MEN...

MEN... AND THEIR MUSIC.
OTHERS MAY FIND THE SOUNDS MELODIC, UPLIFTING... GIVING RISE TO FLIGHTS OF UNFETTERED FANCY, TO AN UP-WINGING OF SPIRIT.
EWS
BUT DRACULA'S IS THE SOULLESS SOUL OF THE UNDEAD... THE LIVING TOMB THAT ADMITS NO BEAUTY.
SUCH IS THE VAMPIRE'S CURSE, THAT HE HEARS ONLY... NOISE.

AND, THERE IS ONE OTHER IN THE MILLING THRONG WHO IS LIKEWISE DEAF TO MELODY, BLIND TO BEAUTY. ONE OTHER MORE AT HOME IN A GRAVE THAN IN A CROWD...
ONCE HIS NAME WAS SIMON GARTH. NOW HE IS MERELY ...THE ZOMBIE.*
*AND YOU CAN READ HIS SINISTER STORY IN THE PREMIERE ISSUE OF HIS OWN MAGAZINE... NOW ON SALE. -- Roy.
FOR AN INSTANT, DRACULA SEEMS TO FEEL THE NEARNESS OF A KINDRED SPIRIT.
HE PAUSES.
BUT THEN HIS DIMMED SENSES FAIL HIM...
AND HE WALKS ON, THRU WINDING STREETS, TILL ALL SOUND OF FRIVOLITY AND HUMAN FRAILTY IS LEFT BEHIND...
Shoba
STEA
...EVEN AS LIFE ITSELF WAS LEFT BEHIND BY DRACULA, SO MANY CENTURIES AGO.
THE CALL IS STRONGER NOW.
IT BECKONS, COMPELS HIM DOWN A DARK ALLEYWAY, KNOWN TO FEW OF THE CITY'S INHABITANTS...
...AND, AT LENGTH, TO A DARKENED HOUSE AT ALLEY'S END.
SO! HERE IT IS THAT I SHALL LEARN WHO BROUGHT ME HERE...
AND HOW ...AND WHY.
ALL THESE THINGS I WISH TO KNOW...
...BEFORE I CARE TO EXACT MY REVENGE!
SKRIKKKKKKKKKK

KKKKKKKKT
ENTER... COUNT DRACULA...
ENTER FREELY ...AND OF YOUR OWN WILL.
A WOMAN'S VOICE... WEAK, RASPY... YET GENTLY MOCKING HIM WITH THE VERY WORDS HE ONCE SPOKE TO A MAN NAMED JONATHAN HARKER...

STILL, HE IS DRACULA... SO HE ENTERS.
THEN--
HE KNOWS, SUDDENLY, THAT SOMEONE ELSE HAS STEALTHILY ENTERED THE ROOM BEHIND HIM!

YOU! WHY DO YOU FOLLOW ME?
HOW DARE YOU--?
THE WHY OF IT, YOU'LL LEARN IN TIME.
AND I DARED, BECAUSE I HAVE--
--THIS!

YARRR!
A BLACK CROSS: SYMBOL OF DARK, FORBIDDEN VOODOO...
...YET STILL A CHARM AGAINST THE VAMPIRE!

HE IS ALL BUT HELPLESS, MADAME LAVEAU... JUST AS YOU SAID HE WOULD BE.
NOW-- SHALL I TELL HIM?
YES...YES... BUT HURRY, GASTON...
I FEEL MY TIME ...GROWS SHORT.
NOT NEARLY SO SHORT AS HIS, IF YOUR PLAN FAILS!
AND NOW, A THOUSAND PARDONS, MADAME...

.....BUT, YOUR LOCKET..!

DO YOU SEE, DRACULA? MADAME'S SKIN IS WRINKLED NOW ...HER BEAUTY FADED...
BUT THIS IS HOW SHE LOOKED--OVER ONE HUNDRED YEARS AGO!
THEN...SHE IS ONE OF THE FEW?
THE FORTUNATE FEW WHO KNOW THE SECRET OF IMMORTALITY--THE SECRET I BECAME A VAMPIRE TO LEARN!
AH, BUT TO CONQUER DEATH, YOU HAD TO DIE--WHILE MARIE LAVEAU LIVED!
OF COURSE, THE YEARS HAVE NOT BEEN KIND.
"SHE WAS THE MOST FAMOUS, MOST POWERFUL VOODOO WOMAN OF ALL TIME! FOUR GENERATIONS OF MEN SAW HER DANCE NAKED ON THE SHORES OF LAKE PONCHARTRAIN, THE SERPENT-GOD DAMBALLAH COILED AROUND HER MOON-GLEAMING BODY.
"MEN SAY, EVEN IN NEW ORLEANS, THAT THERE WERE A LEAST TWO MARIE LAVEAUS--MOTHER AND DAUGHTER--AND THAT BOTH LIE BURIED IN THE CEMETERY WHERE YOU AROSE AT SUNSET.
"BUT--THEY ARE WRONG!
"AND ALL THE FINE SOUTHERN LADIES--THEY CAME FROM ALL OVER DIXIE TO PURCHASE LOVE POTIONS THEY PRAYED WOULD HELP THEM HOLD THEIR MEN.
"HAD THEY BUT KNOWN THAT MARIE LAVEAU HAD FAR, FAR GREATER SECRETS TO IMPART!

"FOR SHE HAD DISCOVERED--HOW, WE SHALL NEVER KNOW, FOR SHE WILL NEVER SAY--THE FORMULA FOR ETERNAL LIFE!
"AND SHE HAD DRUNK DEEP OF THAT CUP!
"BUT, THOUGH SHE LIVED LONG PAST HER TIME, THE FORMULA WAS SOMEHOW INCOMPLETE. EVEN..."
"AND SO --SHE-- AGED..."
"SHE GREW OLD--WEAK--TILL SOON SHE COULD BARELY MOVE, OR EVEN FEED HERSELF.
"MY FATHER--AND HIS FATHER BEFORE HIM --CARED FOR MARIE LAVEAU, OUT OF CURIOUS BUT UNREWARDED DEVOTION.
"EACH OF US KEPT HER SAFE FROM DISCOVERY ALL THESE YEARS--AND EACH OF US KILLED FOR HER!
"UNREWARDED, I SAY--BECAUSE EACH OF THEM DIED IN TIME--WHILE SHE LIVED ON!
THE LEGEND OF MARIE LAVEAU HAS REACHED EVEN THE SHADOWED FORESTS OF TRANSYLVANIA, MY FRIEND.
BUT HOW DID YOU COME TO BRING ME HERE--WITHOUT MY KNOWLEDGE?
I WAS IN NEW YORK CITY A FEW DAYS AGO, TO INVESTIGATE A NEWSPAPER ITEM.
IT TOLD OF A MAN WHO CLAIMED TO BE A REINCARNATION OF THE GREAT SORCERER CAGLIOSTRO.
THEN, YOU SOUGHT HIM OUT--EVEN AS I DID!? BUT WHY?

BECAUSE I SUSPECTED THAT **HE** MIGHT BE... WHAT **YOU** ARE!

"UNFORTUNATLY FOR US **BOTH**, THE MAN PROVED TO BE A **CHARLATAN**... A **FAKE**.

EXIT

"BUT, I SAW **YOU** THERE.

"SPELLS OF MADAME'S CAUSED ME TO **KNOW** YOU.

I **FOLLOWED** YOU AFTER YOU SLEW THAT IMPOSTER.

"I SPRINKLED CERTAIN **HERBS** OVER YOU, IN YOUR **COFFIN**...

"THEN, WHILE YOU SLEPT LONG AND DEEP, I HAD YOU **REMOVED** FROM ONE SHIP--

"--AND PLACED ONTO **ANOTHER**, BOUND FOR **NEW ORLEANS**!

YOU **DARED** TREAT THE LORD OF THE UN-LIVING LIKE SOME PIECE OF **PROPERTY**?

YOU'LL **PAY** FOR THAT AFFRONT, CREOLE!

I THINK **NOT**.

FOR, WHEN MADAME LAVEAU AND I HAVE QUAFFED THIS **POTION OF IMMORTALITY** WHICH SHE HAS DIRECTED ME TO BREW...

...I SHALL BE-COME HER **LOVER**, WHILE YOU SHALL TRULY **PERISH** AT LAST!

NOW, HOLD OUT YOUR ARM, MY GOOD FRIEND!
WE HAVE NEED OF IT--AND OF THAT WHICH LIES BENEATH YOUR PUTRID WHITE SKIN!
HARSHLY, GASTON GRASPS HIS NOW-UNRESISTING FORE-ARM...!

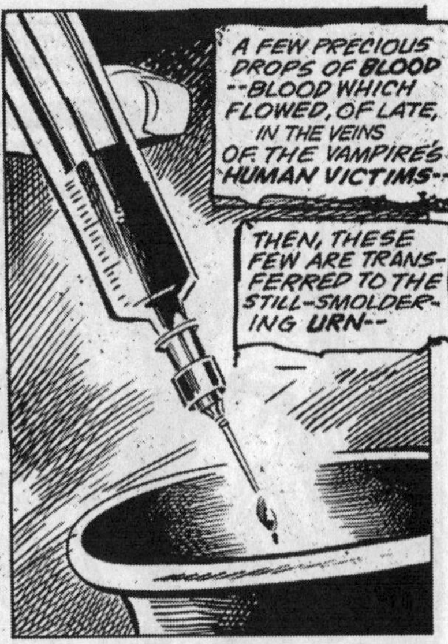
A FEW PRECIOUS DROPS OF BLOOD --BLOOD WHICH FLOWED, OF LATE, IN THE VEINS OF THE VAMPIRE'S HUMAN VICTIMS--
THEN, THESE FEW ARE TRANS-FERRED TO THE STILL-SMOLDER-ING URN--

--FROM WHICH FIRST THE YOUNG CREOLE DRINKS--

--AND FINALLY THE WITHERED, UNSPEAKING CRONE--

--WHILE DRACULA WATCHES HELPLESS-- IVA...
--YET SOMEHOW, STRANGELY SMILING.

--AS MARIE LAVEAU SHEDS HER MANY-SCORE YEARS, ALONG WITH HER MOTH-EATEN SHAWL, AND STANDS PROUD, AND ERECT BEFORE THEM!
THEN IT BEGINS: THE CHANGE--
ONCE MORE, SHE IS THE REAL, THE TRUE MARIE LAVEAU--
--ONCE AND FOR ALL TIME, THE VOODOO QUEEN OF NEW ORLEANS!

YOU ARE BEAUTIFUL, MADAME! BUT I --
WHAT IS WRONG WITH ME? I -- FEEL -- SO --
YOU PITIFUL FOOL! LOOK INTO THAT MIRROR YONDER --
--AND ANSWER YOUR OWN MAD QUESTION!
OH MY GOD! EVEN AS YOU BECAME YOUNGER WHEN YOU DRANK THE POTION...
...I HAVE BECOME OLDER!
NO! NO! THE TRUTH IS MORE HORRIBLE YET!
EVEN AS I LOOK -- I... BECOME OLDER STILL-- MOMENT BY MOMENT!
YOU TRICKED ME, MADAME! YOU--
NOOOOOO
HIS GNARLED LIMBS NOW TOO WEAK TO SUPPORT HIM, GASTON COLLAPSES ... AND DIES.
YOURS WAS A CRUEL JEST, MARIE LAVEAU.
BUT A NECESSARY ONE, DEAR COUNT.
THE REAL FINAL INGREDIENT OF MY POTION-- WAS GASTON'S LIFE-ESSENCE.
AND NOW-- ABOUT THAT GARLIC--
DO NOT TOY WITH ME, WOMAN! WHATEVER YOUR POWERS, I AM STILL DRACULA!
WHILE I AM MARIE LAVEAU...
...AND HAVE NO FURTHER NEED OF THESE TRIFLES!
MY OWN SPELLS ARE AMPLE TO PROTECT ME, NOW THAT I'VE REGAINED MY YOUTH.
BUT HEAR ME, COUNT-- FOR I'VE A PROPOSAL TO MAKE YOU.
SAY ON, THEN.

A MARRIAGE OF VOODOO AND VAMPIRISM, DEAR COUNT.
BECOME MY MATE, AND WE'LL LIVE FOREVER, YOU AND I...
...TILL ALL THE WORLD BOWS BENEATH OUR TWIN HEEL!

WELL? WHAT SAY YOU?
YOUR OFFER DOES ME CREDIT, MARIE LAVEAU, AND I MOST HUMBLY ACKNOWLEDGE IT.
IN ANOTHER TIME, ANOTHER PLACE... IT MIGHT BE AS YOU WISH.
BUT I MATE WITH NO ONE WHO HAS SOUGHT TO BIND ME WITH FORCE.

FOR, DRACULA HAS HIS OWN DARK DESTINY TO PURSUE, TILL TIME AND TIMES ARE DONE.
AND, PURSUE IT I SHALL...

--ALONE!
A MOMENT BEFORE, AND A MAN STOOD HERE. NOW THERE IS BUT THE HOVERING FORM OF A HUGE VAMPIRE BAT.
IN ITS AWESOME PRESENCE, EVEN THE VOODOO WOMAN CAN SCARCELY REPRESS A VISIBLE SHUDDER.

THEN SHE STEPS ASIDE... AND, WITH A FLUTTERING OF NIGHT-BORN WINGS, THE CREATURE IS GONE.
AND MARIE LAVEAU KNOWS THE LONELINESS WHICH ONLY THOSE MAY KNOW WHO TREAD THE WAYS OF LIFE-IN-DEATH FOREVER...
ONLY SHE... AND THE MAN CALLED DRACULA!
FINIS

PROLOGUE:
PARIS: THE CAPITAL OF FRANCE, SITUATED ON THE SEINE RIVER, 375 KILOMETERS UPSTREAM FROM ITS ENTRY INTO THE ENGLISH CHANNEL.
ON THE QUAYS IN ITS EASTERN DISTRICT, COUNTLESS SHIPS UNLOAD VARIED AND INTERNATIONAL FREIGHT.
ONE SUCH SHIP HAS JUST COMPLETED A JOURNEY FROM NEW ORLEANS, U.S.A...
... AND ITS CARGO IS SOMEWHAT... UNUSUAL.
AT LAST THE DAY ENDS: TIRED LONGSHOREMEN RETURN TO THEIR HOMES; THE FIRST MOMENTS OF DUSK CREEP UP THE RIVER SEINE...
...ACCOMPANIED BY THE SOUND OF FURTIVE FOOTSTEPS AND THE APPEARANCE OF A DETERMINED YOUNG WOMAN.
A WOMAN...
...WITH A MISSION...
A MISSION... AGAINST DRACULA!

FOR AN INSTANT, TIME SEEMS TO FREEZE. ALL OF REALITY FOCUSES ON THIS ONE MOMENT. THEN, AS AN UPRAISED MALLET PAUSES BEFORE BEGINNING ITS DEADLY DESCENT--
--THE SUN TREMBLES ON THE BRINK OF DARKNESS--
--AND IS SWALLOWED.
TOO LATE, GIRL! THE MOMENT OF CHOICE IS NO LONGER YOURS.
IT'S NIGHT-- AND ONCE MORE I MAY TAKE MY PLACE AMONG THE LIVING. ONCE MORE COUNT DRACULA MAY STRIDE THE EARTH!
ONCE MORE HE MAY TAKE WHAT HE NEEDS... AND GIRL, I NEED BLOOD!
SHADOW IN THE CITY OF LIGHT!
STORY: GERRY CONWAY
ART: ALFONSO FONT

BUT FIRST... I MUST KNOW HOW YOU KNEW MY COFFIN WOULD BE HERE. AND MORE...
I MUST KNOW WHY YOU WISH ME DESTROYED...YOU, WHO ARE A STRANGER TO ME. CAN IT BE THE VAN HELSINGS HUNT ME EVEN HERE?
I KNOW NOTHING OF THAT.
AHH, BUT YOU KNOW SOMETHING, DON'T YOU, CHILD? SPEAK!
I COMMAND YOU ...TELL ME WHAT I WANT TO KNOW!
LIKE A VIPER'S GLANCE, DRACULA'S EYES SEEM TO RIVET THE YOUNG GIRL'S ATTENTION... DRAINING HER VERY WILL, UNTIL...
MY NAME IS HÉLÈNE DUBO I HAVE A COUSI IN NEW ORLEAN HE HEARD RUMOR THAT YOU WERE THERE* ...THAT Y WERE RETURNING TO EUROPE...TO PARIS.
FRIENDS IN THE SHIPPING OFFICE TOLD ME ...WHEN SHIP WAS ARRIVING. I MADE ...PREPARATIONS... CAME HERE. BUT THE SUN...!
THAT EXPLAINS THE HOW, GIRL. NOW ...TELL ME WHY.
*LAST ISSUE -- RT.
AS THOUGH THIS LAST QUESTION IS A SIGNAL, THE GIRL SUDDENLY STIFFENS-- HER FACIAL MUSCLES WORKING IN ABRUPT SPASMS AS SHE TRIES TO SPEAK--
-- AND FINDS SHE CAN'T!
SEVERAL SECONDS PASS AS THE INWARD BATTLE RAGES.
FINALLY, AS QUICKLY AS IT BEGAN... THE BATTLE ENDS.
UNCONSCIOUS.
IT SEEMS HER WILL IS STRONG. RATHER THAN TELL ME WHAT SHE WISHED KEPT HIDDEN... HER MIND FORCED HER TO FAINT.
AN INTERESTING GAMBIT... BUT SADLY, A FUTILE ONE.

VAMPIRE: CREATURE OF DARKNESS, MERCILESS IN HIS NEED FOR FRESH BLOOD.
IT HAS BEEN DAYS SINCE LAST DRACULA FED. HIS NEED IS GREAT, AND YET...
NO. I HAVE A MUCH MORE INTERESTING USE FOR THIS YOUNG WOMAN.
SHE SHALL AMUSE ME WITH HER SECRETS... AND I WILL PLAY WITH A GAME OF CAT... AND MOUSE.
SHE WILL DIE WHEN IT SUITS ME--NOT BEFORE!
ELSEWHERE IN THE CITY OF LIGHT, ON THE FAMED ÎLE DE LA CITÉ, THE CATHEDRAL CHURCH OF NOTRE-DAME BECOMES THE SCENE OF A MYSTERIOUS CONFRONTATION QUITE RELEVANT TO OUR STORY...
WHO ARE YOU, MONSIEUR? WHAT ARE YOU DOING HERE--?
WAIT! YOUR FACE--
IN THE MEANTIME I SHALL FIND OTHER VICTIMS.
CAFE TABAC
PALAIS DU BON VIN
905
NEVER SHALL IT BE SAID THAT DRACULA WAS A SLAVE TO HIS APPETITES!
MON DIEU! I HAVE HEARD LEGENDS--WHISPERED BY MEN TOO DRUNK TO HOLD THEIR TONGUES!
BUT NEVER DID I SUSPECT THE LEGENDS COULD BE TRUE!
STAY BACK... COME NO CLOSER!
I WARN YOU... I WILL NOT HESITATE TO SHOOT.
KEEP BACK--I TELL YOU--
KEEP BACK!
KPOW

KPOW!
KPOW!

YYYYYYAAAA

AT THAT MOMENT, ON THE OTHER SIDE OF THE SEINE, A CERTAIN COUNT STANDS WAITING IN A FOG-MISTED ALLEYWAY, WATCHING THE APPROACH OF A YOUNG GIRL...

...AND WHEN THE GIRL HAS COME CLOSE ENOUGH...
ORISTE
DIPLOME

...HER MOMENT ARRIVES!
STE

THE SCREAM DIES ALMOST IMMEDIATLY... CHOKED OFF AS THE VAMPIRE'S VICTIM LOSES FIRST CONSCIOUSNESS AND THEN LIFE.
BUT THE CRY HAS LASTED LONG ENOUGH...
...FOR IT HAS AWAKENED THE WOMAN WHO NAMED HERSELF HÉLÈNE DUBOIS... AND IT HAS REKINDLED THE FIRE OF RED HATRED WITHIN HER!

HANDS UNCONSCIOUSLY GRASPING FOR A WEAPON, MARIE'S FINGERS CLOSE ON A PROVIDENTIAL CHAIR LEG IN THE RUBBISH NEAR HER...
...AND WITH A WILD, ALMOST ANIMALISTIC CRY..., SHE SPRINGS...!
FOOLISH CHILD... HAVEN'T WE PLAYED THIS SCENE BEFORE? IT BORES ME.
I AM YOUR SUPERIOR IN STRENGTH, HÉLÈNE DUBOIS...
...AND YOUR SUPERIOR IN WILL AS WELL! I HAVE BEEN PATIENT, GIRL... BUT YOUR RESISTANCE NO LONGER AMUSES ME
YOU WILL TELL ME WHAT I WISH TO KNOW... AND YOU WILL TELL ME NOW!
I... WILL... TELL YOU.
CAFE TAB
R
BAR
LES MEILLEURS VINS D'ALSACE
EXCELLENT, BUT LET US FIND MORE SUITABLE SURROUNDINGS FOR THE TALE.
THAT CAFE AHEAD SEEMS MOST PROPRIATE. IT HAS BEEN MANY YEARS SINCE LAST I TASTED A GOOD FRENCH WINE.
AND SO, WITHIN THE NEXT QUARTER HOUR, IN THE CAFE de la GORGE...
I'M NOT QUITE CERTAIN I COMPREHEND YOU, MADEMOISELLE. YOU SPEAK OF YOUR GREAT-GREAT-GRAND FATHER...
WHAT HAS HE TO DO WITH YOUR HATRED OF COUNT DRACULA?

EVERY-THING. IT IS HE WHOM I MUST REVENGE.
HE WHOSE SOUL I MUST FREE FROM THE HELL TO WHICH YOU CONDEMNED IT.
I?

OF COURSE. HIS NAME WAS JACQUES DUBOIS...
...AND HE FOUGHT AGAINST YOU AT THE SIDE OF COUNT CAGLIOSTRO, THE 18TH CENTURY MYSTIC WHO WAS YOUR MOST FEARED MORTAL ENEMY...!
ON THE HEELS OF THIS STARTLING REVELATION, LET US EXPOSE YET ANOTHER KNOT OF OUR UNWINDING PLOT, AS WE SHIFT OUR SCENE TO A CERTAIN BRIDGE LINKING THE ÎLE de la CITE WITH THE EAST BANK...
...WHERE A CURIOUS AGENT DE POLICE IS OBSERVING AN APPROACHING FIGURE WITH GRIM SUSPICION... AND FINALLY, SPEAKS:
MONSIEUR!
BUT THEN, AS THE SHADOWED FIGURE TURNS...

...THE GENDARME WISHES HE HAD REMAINED SILENT...!
OUT OF MY WAY.
HE IS HERE... AND I MUST FIND HIM... DESTROY HIM.

THEN, PERHAPS...I MAY BE FREE!
IT IS ALL I WISH! THAT... OR THAT I MAY TRULY BE STONE... WITHOUT SOUL TO TORMENT...

...OR MIND TO REMEMBER!

I BEGIN TO REMBMBER, HÉLÈNE DUBOIS. YOUR GREAT-GREAT GRANDFATHER WAS A STONE-CUTTER, WAS HE NOT?

A SCULPTOR... THE GREATEST SCULPTOR IN FRANCE.

I'M SURE. HE WAS ALSO A MADMAN. I RECALL IT NOW... SO LONG AGO...

"IT WAS A SPRING EVENING IN 1769. I HAD MADE THE AQUAINTANCE OF A MOST CHARMING PARISIAN LADY--I FORGET HER NAME--AND WE WERE RETURNING TO MY HOTEL IN A HANSOM CAB.

M'SIEU DRACULA... I AM NOT SURE I APPROVE OF THE WAY YOU ARE LOOKING AT ME...

WHAT WAY IS THAT, MADEMOISELLE?

IT IS YOUR EYES, M'SIEU THEY STARE SO...

I FEEL AS THOUGH YOU ...ARE PEERING ...INTO MY SOUL... MY VERY SOUL...

QUITE CORRECT, MADEMOISELLE.

AND NOW... THAT SOUL IS MINE!

...TO CLAIM!

EEEEEEEEEE

"THOUGH I WAS IN NO POSITION TO BE AWARE OF IT, AT THAT MOMENT A SHADOW WAS CROSSING THE MOON--

"--A MESSENGER FROM MY ENEMY, CAGLIOSTRO!

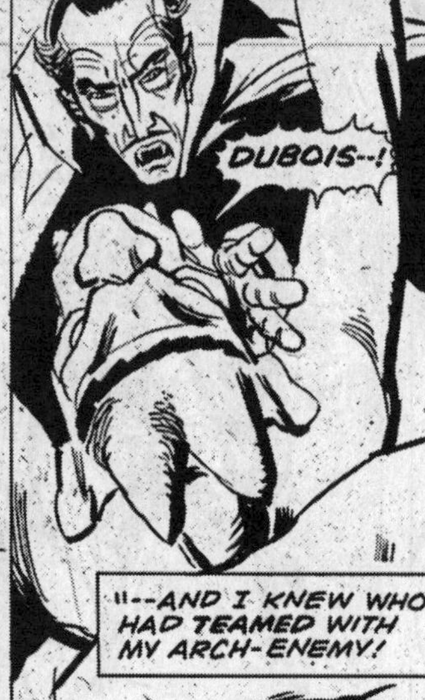

"... AND IT WAS OVER.

"I LEFT... AND AS EVER, I DID NOT LOOK BACK!"

YOU SHOULD HAVE, COUNT DRACULA.
IT MIGHT WELL HAVE SAVED YOUR FOUL LIFE!
THAT FACE! IT IS MY GREAT-GREAT GRANDFATHER!
YOU!!
YES-- BUT HE IS NOW BECOME A THING OF-- LIVING STONE!
WITH OUR END, WILL BE ADE FREE, CURSED VAMPIRE!
NO LONGER WILL I BE AS STONE--ALIVE ONLY DURING THE NIGHT'S BLACKEST HOURS, FROZEN INTO IM-MOBILITY DURING THE DAY!
I WILL BE FREE! FREE TO LIVE AS A MAN!
FREE!!
YOU MOUTH MADNESS, DUBOIS, --THERE IS NO REMEDY FOR YOUR CURSE.
YOU ARE WHAT YOU HAVE BECOME--AND WILL REMAIN SUCH TILL YOUR DESTRUCTION!
LIAR!!
CAGLIOSTRO TOLD ME: YOUR DEATH WOULD RELEASE FROM THIS UNHOLY HELL-- THIS LIVING PRISON!
HE TOLD ME IT WOULD CAST ME FREE!
AND YOU BELIEVED HIM? THE MASTER OF DECEIT?

LIES! LIES!
YOU SEEK TO BLUNT MY PURPOSE WITH THESE PETTY DISTRACTIONS--
BUT I WILL NOT BE DETERRED!
THE EIFFEL TOWER: COMPLETED IN 1889 BY ALEXANDRE GUSTAVE EIFFEL TO CELEBRATE THE PARIS EXHIBITION OF THAT YEAR, IT RISES TO A HEIGHT OF 1,056'...
WHUNK
GRAND-FATHER!
...LARGE ENOUGH FOR A SWOOPING BAT TO AVOID...
...BUT APPARENTLY NOT FOR A RAGING STONE MONSTER!
HE WAS A FOOL TO BELIEVE THE WORDS OF A MAN SUCH AS CAGLIOSTRO.
WHUMP!
AAAAAARRRR
AND YOU, HÉLÈNE DUBOIS-- YOU WERE ALSO A FOOL, TO COMMIT YOUR LIFE TO VENGEANCE FOR THE PAST.
BOTH OF YOU ALLOWED YOURSELVES TO BE-COME PAWNS... AND EVEN THE MOST ELEMENT-ARY CHESS-PLAYER KNOWS THAT, WHEN A PAWN MEETS A KING...
...EVEN THE MONARCH OF DARKNESS...
...THE RESULT CAN ONLY BE CHECK...
...AND MATE.
FINIS

STORY:
MARV WOLFMAN
FEAR STALKER
ART:
MIKE PLOOG & ERNIE CHUA
HOLLYWOOD: ONCE A BUSTLING, EVER GROWING WORLD OF FANTASY AND DREAMS, LIVING A TWENTY-FOUR HOUR DAY UNSTOPPED, UN-CHECKED, NOW RESTS NESTLED AND ALMOST SOMBER BENEATH THE HOT, MUGGY SOUTHERN CALIFORNIA SUN.
THE UNBRIDLED LAUGHS ARE GONE NOW; HAVING DESERTED TO OTHER WORLD PORTS AND COUNTRIES, LEAVING THIS ONCE-CITY OF INSTANT DREAMS AND SUCCESS A SOME-WHAT LONELY, SCARRED AND VERY SCARED TOWN-SHIP INDEED.
TONIGHT, THE HOLLYWOOD HILLS WILL HEAR ANOTHER CLARION CALL OF ITS VERY SLOW AND QUIET DEATH.
DIRECTOR

TO SET THE SCENE: AN OIL RIG FLOATING ONE HALF MILE FROM THE CALIFORNIA SHORES.
YOU CAN'T ESCAPE ME, DRACULA. I'LL RUN YOU THROUGH WITH MY WOODEN STAKE.
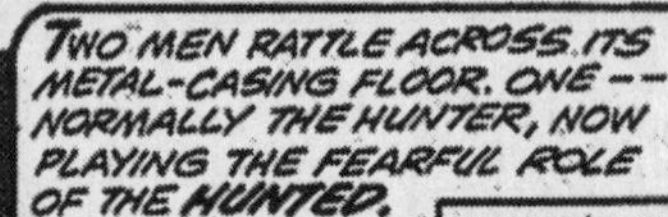
TWO MEN RATTLE ACROSS ITS METAL-CASING FLOOR. ONE -- NORMALLY THE HUNTER, NOW PLAYING THE FEARFUL ROLE OF THE HUNTED.

THERE'S NO PLACE TO HIDE, DRACULA-- AND YOU'RE TOO WEAK TO FLY AWAY.

AND A DEMON RUNS-- A DEMON WHO HAS LIVED FIVE HUNDRED YEARS, FACING PERHAPS HIS FINAL LIVING MOMENTS.
NO, MR. BRIGHAM DRACULA WILL (COUGH) NEVER DIE.

(COUGH) YOU CAN'T KILL ME-- I'LL JUST COME BACK AGAIN AND AGAIN.

WE'LL SEE ABOUT THAT, EVIL ONE. YOU MURDERED MY SISTER, MARIANNE-- AND I WANT MY REVENGE.

SHE'S NOT DEAD YET, BRIGHAM-- IN THREE NIGHTS SHE'LL RISE AGAIN --AS A VAMPIRE (COUGH).

DAMN YOU-- SHE DID DIE-- I THRUST THE STAKE IN HER MYSELF!
AND FOR HER, I'LL DO THE SAME TO YOU.
NNOOOOOOOOOOO

HA HA HA HA
HA

AND SO, ONCE AGAIN, THE VAMPIRE WHO TOOK SO MANY LIVES, HAS FALLEN TO HIS OWN MOST UNWELCOME DEATH.

LIGHTS FLICKER ON IN A ROOM FILLED WITH ALMOST DEADLY SILENCE-- A SILENCE THAT DAMPENS EVERYTHING SAVE FOR THE RAPID TURNING OF A PROJECTOR REWINDING FIVE REELS OF 35 MILIMETER FILM.
THEN, A VOICE BREAKS THE STILLNESS OF THE CRAMPED, STUFFY MINISCULE ROOM.
THE FANGS OF DRACULA!
THE END
WELL, M.G.--DID I NOT TELL YOU-- A COMEBACK ROLE IF EVER THERE WAS ONE, EH?
PRODUCER
IT STINKS-- DEAD, SMELLING-- SHOULD'VE BEEN BURIED WHEN THAT HACK WRITER FIRST CAME IN WITH IT.
AND WHERE DID YOU LEARN ACTING, BELSKI--? FROM FLIPPER?
DRACULA COUGHING? SWEATING? GARBAGE!
YOU'RE MAD, McGRUDER.
I AM THE FINEST ACTOR WHO HAS EVER PLAYED THE IMMORTAL COUNT.
WHY, MY PRESENTATION ON THE LONDON STAGE BROUGHT DOWN THE HOUSE.
YEAH--IT FELL DOWN-- CAUGHING AT YOU.
FACE IT, BELSKI-- YOUR ACT BELONGS IN A CRACKERJACK BOX--
AS FOR THIS FILM, IT'S BEING CANNED. WE'LL SELL IT AS A PACKAGE OVERSEAS--
--PREFERABLY TO SOME UNFRIENDLY NATION.
DOLT! MORON! CLOD! LOUIS BELSKI'S THE FINEST STAGE ACTOR THIS STUPID COUNTRY HAS EVER SEEN.
YOU SHOULD BE KISSING MY FEET FOR EVEN CONSENTING TO WORK WITH YOU, YOU FAT, BUMBLING JELLY-ROLL.

HOW DARE THAT DIRIGIBLE OF A DIRECTOR CRITICIZE MY CRAFT SIMPLY BECAUSE OF A, EH, FEW MINOR SETBACKS IN MY CAREER.
I SHOULD KNOW BETTER-- FOR A FEW YEARS YOU ARE HARD-PRESSED, OUT OF LUCK-- PERHAPS HIT THE BOTTLE TOO OFTEN--
--AND THEY NEVER LET YOU FORGET, DO THEY?
SCAVENGERS -- THEY'RE ALL SCAVENGERS.

LOOK-- THEY ALL LAUGH AT ME! WHY, NOT ONE OF THEM COULD ACT THEIR WAY OUT OF A B-WESTERN, LET ALONE SHAKESPEARE.
ONCE I WAS THE GREATEST--THE MOST SOUGHT AFTER ACTOR OF THEM ALL-- AND I SWEAR THE NAME LOUIS BELSKI WILL BE UP THERE IN LIGHTS AGAIN. BAH!

CUT TO: A SMALL, MOBILE DRESSING ROOM, ONE CURRENTLY POSSESSED BY A VERY SAD AND EMBITTERED MAN.
A MAN AS MUCH OUT OF HIS TIME AS THE CITY HE WORKS IN IS WITH THE WORLD.
LOUIS BELSKI-- A MAN WHO SHOULD NEVER HAVE SURVIVED THE THIRTIES. HE WOULD HAVE BEEN MUCH HAPPIER IN DEATH.
THEY ARE ALL FOOLS... ALL OF THEM.
FOOLS.

NO-- YOU ARE THE FOOL, LOUIS BELSKI-- AND THAT DAMNABLE EGO OF YOURS HAS PROBABLY COST YOU YOUR LAST JOB ANYWHERE.

ARE YOU HAPPY NOW, LOUIS BELSKI-- ARE YOU SO PROUD OF YOURSELF NOW?
WHY DON'T YOU JUST DIE? PERHAPS YOU WOULD, IF SOMEONE WOULD MOURN YOU.

GOD, IT'S TOO MUCH TO TAKE. I SHOULD NEVER HAVE HOPED IT WOULD BE DIFFERENT THIS TIME.
BUT IT WAS ONLY THE SAME--
--ONLY THE SAME.
A SHADOW FLICKERS IN THE MOONBEAMS WHICH DANCE OFF LOUIS BELSKI'S DRESSING TABLE--
--SHADOWS WHICH WILL SOON DO MORE THAN MERELY DANCE ON THE LIFE OF THIS RAPIDLY FADING MAN--
--THIS MAN WHO IS LITTLE MORE THAN A SHADOW HIMSELF.
DRACULA HAS TRAVELLED FAR TO FIND THIS MAN, BELSKI-- AND ALREADY HE IS SORRY HE MADE THAT LONG, HARROWING JOURNEY.
Johnny WALKER

ELEVEN P.M. AND WE SWITCH OUR SCENE TO ANOTHER SOUND STAGE ON THE LARGE SPRAWLING MOVIE LOT--
--ONE WHICH HAS NOT BEEN USED IN MANY MONTHS, AND ONE WHICH THE STUDIO HAS ALREADY DECIDED TO SELL.
STINKIN' TRAMP-- YA DO WHAT I SAY OR I'LL BUST UP YOUR FACE BAD.
SO BAD YOU CAN PLAY IN THEM HORROR MOVIES--WITHOUT MAKE-UP. SO STAY CLEAR O' THAT STINKIN' EXTRA.
YOU'RE MINE-- NO ONE ELSE'S-- JUST MINE.
I UNDER-STAND, MR. McGRUDER-- I UNDER-STAND.
DON'T GIVE IN, GIRL-- I'M HERE TO PROTECT YOU.
BELSKI? WHAT THE HELL ARE YOU DOIN'? YOU WANT YOUR FACE CAVED IN, YA STUPID DRUNK'N BUM? CLEAR OUT.
IF YOU VALUE YOUR LIFE, McGRUDER-- DON'T TOUCH THE GIRL.
SHE IS UNDER MY PROTECTION NOW, McGRUDER. BEFORE YOU MAY GET TO HER, YOU MUST FIRST DO BATTLE WITH ME.
YOU ARE DRUNK, YOU STINKIN' SOT.
GET THE HELL OUTTA HERE, BELSKI, AN' MAYBE I WON'T KICK YOU OUT ON YOUR CAN TOMORROW.
YOU DARE THREATEN ME, HUMAN? I'M LORD DRACULA-- KING OF THE VAMPIRES?
MY GOD-- HE'S FLIPPED HIS FREAKING FANGS.
YOU'RE LOUIS BELSKI, YOU DUMB POLISH HAM-- NOT DRACULA.
NO! I AM DRACULA...
...DRACULA!
NOW YOU WILL LISTEN TO ME AND KNOW I SPEAK THE TRUTH.
HE WON'T LISTEN TO ANYONE, LOUIS--
Y-YOU'VE KILLED HIM.

YOU'RE A MURDERER-- A MURDERER.
HOW COULD YOU KILL HIM?
N-NO--I WAS ONLY SAVING YOU. HE STRUCK YOU--HURT YOU.
ONLY 'CAUSE I BELONGED TO HIM. HE HAD THE RIGHT.
SO, I UNDERSTAND NOW--EVEN THOSE HUMANS WHOM I SAVE TURN AGAINST ME!
VERY WELL, THEN. I NOW DECLARE WAR ON HUMANS EVERYWHERE --BEGINNING WITH YOU, MY DEAR.
KEEP AWAY FROM ME, YOU MURDERER-- OR I'LL SCREAM.
SCREAM ALL YOU WANT, FEMALE--
--ONCE I'VE TASTED MYSELF OF YOUR BLOOD.
NOOOoooooooo
HMMM, SOMETHING IS WRONG. I CAN'T BREAK YOUR FLESH--?
LOOK-- OVER THERE. IT'S BELSKI--
--ATTACKING McGRUDER'S GIRL.
HE'S RUN OFF--ARE YOU ALL RIGHT, LIZA? WHAT DID HE DO TO YOU?
HE KILLED McGRUDER, AND THEN, OH GOD-- HE TRIED TO SUCK MY BLOOD.
SUCK YOUR WHAT?
H-HE THINKS HE'S A--A VAMPIRE!

W-WHAT DID I DO? I WENT CRAZY-- CRAZY.
MUST GET AWAY-- BEFORE THEY FIND ME-- BEFORE THEY LOCK ME AWAY SOMEWHERE.
I DIDN'T MEAN TO KILL HIM-- BUT NOBODY'D BELIEVE ME.
AS NONE WOULD BELIEVE THAT YOU ARE DRACULA, LOUIS BELSKI.
WHO--?
I AM DRACULA, HUMAN-- COME TO RECLAIM MY NAME-- THE ONE WHICH YOU HAVE SO READILY MOCKED.
YOU HAVE TAKEN MY TITLE AND DRAGGED IT THROUGH THE MOST STINKING GUTTER--AND NONE MAY HAVE THAT PRIVILEGE.
NO--IT CAN'T BE. YOU CAN'T BE-- DRACULA?
YOU DISBELIEVE THE LEGENDS YOU HAVE SO OFTEN PLAYED? DID YOU TRULY BELIEVE I WAS MERELY A PRODUCT OF SOME WRITER'S IMAGINATION--AND NOT TRUE FLESH AND BLOOD?
NO-- YOU'RE JUST AN ACTOR-- OUT TO TAKE OVER MY ROLE-- MY CHARACTER.
BUT I WON'T ALLOW IT. I'VE MADE THE NAME DRACULA FEARED BY MILLIONS. NO ONE WILL REPLACE ME-- NO ONE!
I TRAVELLED HERE TO SEE THE FOOL WHO DARED USURP MY NAME--AND NOW I SEE HE IS MORE THAN A FOOL-- HE IS A MADMAN!
THE STUDIO SENT YOU, I KNOW IT-- I CAN TELL. BUT IT WILL DO YOU NO GOOD, WHOEVER YOU ARE.
I WON'T GIVE IN. NO ONE CAN MAKE ME.
I'M THE ONLY VAMPIRE HERE-- NOT YOU--AND NOT EVEN MCGRUDER CAN CHANGE THAT.

BECAUSE I'LL KILL TO KEEP WHAT IS MINE.
YOU ARE ALMOST PITIABLE, HUMAN, TO THINK YOUR MERE WEAPON CAN END MORE THAN FIVE HUNDRED YEARS OF MY EXISTENCE.
BAM!
BUT YOU'LL SOON LEARN, LOUIS BELSKI-- YOU'LL SOON LEARN.
NO--YOU LIE-- I'M THE ONLY-- THE ONLY...
HE'S GONE-- DISAPPEAR-ED.
MAYBE HE WAS NEVER--

HA HA HA HA HA
--HERE--
--LAUGHTER-- GOD, NO--NO...
EXIT FOR A TIME ONE LOUIS BELSKI. A MAN, A VERY SORROWFUL MAN, WHO HAS CROSSED PATHS WITH A LEGEND AND, FOR THE MOMENT, HAS BEEN ALLOWED TO LIVE.

ONE WEEK MALLET STUDIOS IS CLOSED TO THE PUBLIC. ONE WEEK IN WHICH EVERY CALCITE MOUNTAIN, EVERY BALSA WOOD TREE, EVERY STAGE AND WARDROBE IS INSPECTED, PROBED AND DOUBLE-CHECKED FOR A MAN WHO STILL HIDES SOMEWHERE EVEN THE POLICE CAN NOT FIND.
FOR LOUIS BELSKI HAS WORKED HERE SINCE THE STUDIO WAS FIRST BUILT BACK IN 1927. AND THERE ARE FEW WHO KNOW AS MUCH ABOUT IT AS HE.
HI, SAMMY. ANY NEWS YET?
NAW. FUZZ 'RE STILL POKIN' 'ROUND, BUT NOW THEY THINK HE SNUCK OUT SOMEWHERE.

SOME LATE FILMING TONIGHT?
SOMETHING LIKE THAT, SAMMY. LOOK, IF ANYONE ASKS, WE'RE NOT HERE-- OKAY?
SURE, HA. I UNDERSTAND.

I DON'T LIKE IT, GARY! WHAT IF THAT NUT IS STILL AROUND--- HIDING?
DON'T KNOW WHAT IT IS, BUT EVERYTIME I EVEN THINK OF HIM, HE GIVES ME THE CREEPS.
DON'T WORRY, LOVE. I CAN TAKE CARE OF HIM. YEAH, DON'T WORRY AT ALL.

A MOMENT FROZEN IN TIME: FIRST COMES THE SHOCK AND HORROR--AND THEN--RECOGNITION.

AND WITH RECOGNITION COMES THE TERRIFYING REVULSION.

IT'S DONALDSON--OH GOD, GARY--HE'S KILLED HIMSELF.

N-NO, LIZA--HE'S BEEN--MURDERED.

M-MURDERED--? BY WHO--? GARY--?

GARY! WHERE ARE YOU GOING--? DON'T LEAVE ME HERE--PLEASE.

I'M GETTIN' SAMMY--AND THE COPS. YOU STAY HERE--YOU'LL BE SAFE--I SWEAR IT.

NO--DON'T LEAVE ME HERE--DON'T--!

TWICE IN FIVE MINUTES YOU'VE BEEN WRONG, GARY STONE--AND THIS TIME YOUR ACTIONS WILL RESULT IN TWO DEATHS...

THINK SOUNDLY OF THAT, YOUNG ACTOR--AS YOU RACE FROM THE GIRL YOU CLAIMED YOU CARED FOR.

HA! HA! HA! YOUR MAN'S RUN OFF, WOMAN--AND NOW YOU'RE MINE!

W-WHO'S UP THERE--?

THE NAME IS DRACULA, WOMAN --COUNT DRACULA --LORD OF THE UNDEAD--MASTER OF ALL VAMPIRES...
YOU'RE CRAZY-- YOU'RE LOUIS BELSKI --NOT DRACULA.
...AND I'VE COME TO SUCK YOUR MOST DELICIOUS BLOOD. HA! HA! HA!
NO, FOOL--NO LONGER AM I A MERE ACTOR --NOR EVEN A FRAIL HUMAN--
I HAVE TRANSGRESSED ALL MANKIND--FOR NOW I AM DRACULA--
--AND I COME TO WREAK VENGEANCE ON ALL WHO ONCE MOCKED ME.
YOU ALL THOUGHT YOURSELVES SO SUPERIOR THAT YOU COULD LAUGH AT A FOOL LIKE BELSKI AND BE DONE WITH IT--
--BUT I AM NOW MASTER OF YOUR FATE--AND YOU SHALL WITNESS WHAT POWER TRULY IS.
RUN IF YOU WISH-- SCREAM TILL YOUR MOUTH RUNS DRY WITH PAIN-- BUT YOU'LL NOT ESCAPE THE WRATH OF DRACULA!
Y-YOU DON'T KNOW WHAT YOU'RE SAYING, LOUIS. PLEASE--CALM DOWN-- WE CAN T-TALK IT OVER.
THE TIME FOR TALKING HAS LONG PASSED, WOMAN --YOU HAD YOUR CHANCE WHEN I SAVED YOU FROM THAT WALKING BUCKET OF SUET, McGRUDER--
--BUT YOU SIMPLY YELLED AT ME-- INSULTED ME-- AND THAT I COULD NEVER FORGET.
YOU SCARED ME THEN-- I DIDN'T KNOW WHAT I WAS SAYING OR DOING.
I-I MEAN I REALLY L-LIKE YOU--REALLY.
DON'T LIE TO ME, GIRL--YOU FIND ME REPULSIVE--WOMEN ALWAYS DID.
THEY WOULD LAUGH BEHIND MY BACK-- SNICKER AT ME EVEN AS THEY NERVOUSLY ASKED FOR MY AUTOGRAPH.

WHY, CHANEY. LUGOSI-- EVEN KARLOFF WITH HIS MAKEUP-- THE WOMEN CAME TO THEM IN BOTH HORROR AND SENSUAL FASCINATION--
--BUT NEVER TO ME-- THEY HATED ME--THEY DESPISED WHAT I WAS --WHAT I PORTRAYED ON THE SCREEN.
SO NEVER TELL ME THAT YOU FIND ME ATTRACTIVE, WOMAN-- FOR I KNOW YOUR TONE --AND IT IS ONE FRAUGHT WITH LIES.
LOUIS BELSKI--YOU WERE WARNED TO CEASE YOUR WAYS.
I HAVE OBSERVED YOU--AND YOU HAVE NOT EARNED THE RIGHT TO CALL YOURSELF DRACULA--
YOU--?
--YOU ARE NOT EVEN SUITABLE OF BEING CALLED A MAN.
THAT MY LIFE WAS PRESENTED ON THE STAGE HAS FOREVER AMUSED ME--BUT ALWAYS BEFORE THE HUMANS PLAYING ME HAVE HAD STATURE--A NOBILITY OF THEIR OWN.
LUGOSI SHOWED MY FEARSOMENESS. --CARRADINE MY NOBILITY --AND LEE PRESENTED MY STRENGTH.
BUT YOU--YOU ARE A CLOWN--A FOOL NOT FIT TO PLAY MY MOST LOWLY SERVANT, LET ALONE LORD OF THE VAMPIRES.
HOW DARE YOU TAKE THE NAME DRACULA AND TROUNCE IT THROUGH THE FILTHY MUDHOLES THAT YOU WALLOW IN?
HOW DARE YOU, HUMAN-- HOW DARE YOU??

I RECEIVE NO ANSWER, AND YET I EXPECTED NONE FROM ONE SUCH AS YOU.
BUT STILL YOU MUST BE PUNISHED FOR YOUR TRANSGRESSIONS AGAINST MY NAME--
--AND YOUR PUNISHMENT SHALL BE A MOST IRONIC ONE INDEED.
BUT FIRST I THIRST--FOR THE BLOOD YOU FOOLISHLY SOUGHT.
NOOOOO..
COME TO ME, WOMAN--AND ENJOY YOUR NEW-BORN FATE.
LIZA PYNE IS SCARED AND RIGHTFULLY SO; SHE HAS WATCHED THESE PAST MINUTES IN BEWILDERMENT --SEEING, AND YET NOT UNDERSTANDING WHAT SHE HAS SEEN.
FOR, INSTEAD OF TERROR, INSTEAD OF REPULSIVE HORROR --SHE FEELS AN ODD PLEASURE IN THE PAIN--AN ENJOYMENT IN HER DEATH, INDEED, FOR THE FIRST TIME IN HER SHORT, SHALLOW LIFE--SHE FEELS HAPPINESS.
BUT THOUGH SHE UNDERSTANDS SHE IS GOING TO DIE, SURPRISINGLY SHE OFFERS NO RESISTANCE AS DRACULA'S FANGS SINK THROUGH THE FIBERS OF HER FLESH, AND SUCKS THE THE LIFE-BLOOD FROM HER.

AND DRACULA FEELS THE PLEASURE, TOO--BUT FOR HIM IT'S A SENSATION HE'S FELT MANY TIMES BEFORE.
SO, HE CAN ONLY SMILE A VERY SATISFIED SMILE, AND ADD THIS GIRL TO THE NAMELESS NUMBERS HE HAS ALREADY ADDED TO HIS LEGIONS.
BUT...
NO! YOU'RE NOT TAKING ME FOR A FOOL, TOO--
I WON'T LET YOU.
AND, IF I MUST --I'LL KILL YOU AS I KILLED THE OTHERS WHO MOCKED ME.
YOU RIDICULED ME, HELD ME UP AS SOME PUBLIC JOKE-- BUT YOU'LL NOT GET AWAY WITH IT.
OH, I KNOW YOUR PLAN--AND I'M NOT ABOUT TO BE PUSHED AROUND BY SOME LOUSY TWO-BIT ACTOR TRYING TO TAKE OVER WHAT LOUIS BELSKI BEGAN.
I CREATED DRACULA--I BREATHED THE LIFE IN HIS VEINS--I GAVE HIM FEAR--POWER --AND NOW I AM DRACULA!!
I AM-- I--I-- UHHNHH...
YOUR EYES-- WHAT ARE YOU DOING TO ME--?
THEY'RE LOOKING RIGHT INTO ME--NO-- DON'T--DAMN YOU--DON'T LOOK AT ME THAT WAY.
--DON'T--PLEASE --YOU MUSTN'T --I'M SORRY-- GOD, I'M SORRY --SOB--I'M SORRY--
--I DIDN'T MEAN IT--I DIDN'T MEAN ANYTHING-- PLEASE--SOB --BUT PLEASE DON'T LOOK AT ME LIKE THAT...
...SOB...OH GOD... I'M SORRY... I'M SO SORRY...
RISE, LOUIS BELSKI--
--AND ACCEPT YOUR FATE AS BEFITTING A MAN.

THREE NIGHTS LATER AND DOWNTOWN LOS ANGELES IS AS QUIET AND MUGGY AS USUAL.
AND THOUGH THE WEATHER WILL NOT CHANGE FOR ALMOST TWO MORE WEEKS, THE SILENCE OF THE NIGHT IS ABOUT TO BE SHATTERED!
YEAH, THAT'S HER! FUNNY, I LEFT HER FOR JUST A FEW MINUTES--AND NOW SHE'S DEAD!
NOT TOO FUNNY TO ME, KID. TOO MANY YOUNG PEOPLE DIE IN THIS TOWN--MAYBE 'CAUSE HOLLYWOOD ITSELF IS LIKE SOME HUGE FANTASTIC FLAME--
--DRAWING HOPEFUL NEW MOTHS CLOSER TO IT EVERY YEAR.

IF IT ISN'T SUICIDE OVER FRUSTRATION, THEN IT'S SELF-DESTRUCTION ON ACID... OR MAYBE A JEALOUS BOY-FRIEND WHO DOESN'T LIKE THE IDEA OF A PRODUCER'S CASTING COUCH.
AFTER AWHILE YOU MAYBE GET USED TO SEEING A STACK OF KIDS LYING ON COLD SLABS, BUT IT'S NEVER FUNNY...
ANYTHING BUT FUNNY.
UNHHHH...

DON'T TRY EXPLAINING ANYTHING TO ME, KID. I'M TOO TIRED TO LISTEN ANYMORE.
WE JUST NEEDED YOU HERE FOR IDENTIFICATION...

...SO NOW YOU CAN GO FIND YOURSELF ANOTHER GIRL, IF YOU HAVEN'T ALREADY...
...AND MAYBE THIS TIME YOU'LL STICK A BIT CLOSER TO HER IF SHE'S EVER IN TROUBLE, HUH?
HELL, WHAT AM I TALKING ABOUT? IT'S BEEN A DAMN LONG DAY. DAMN LONG.
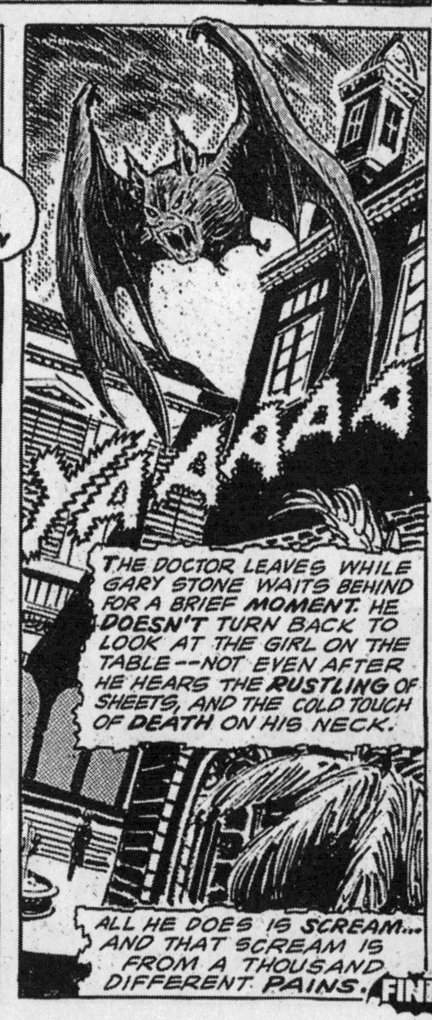
YAAAAA
THE DOCTOR LEAVES WHILE GARY STONE WAITS BEHIND FOR A BRIEF MOMENT. HE DOESN'T TURN BACK TO LOOK AT THE GIRL ON THE TABLE--NOT EVEN AFTER HE HEARS THE RUSTLING OF SHEETS, AND THE COLD TOUCH OF DEATH ON HIS NECK.
ALL HE DOES IS SCREAM... AND THAT SCREAM IS FROM A THOUSAND DIFFERENT PAINS.
FINI

THE DEPARTING 747 LINER CARRIES ANOTHER KIND OF HORROR--A DESPERATE MAN WHO HOLDS IN HIS HAND THE LIVES OF TWO HUNDRED PEOPLE LESS ONE.

THAT ONE IS CALLED DRACULA.

Tony Isabella
Writer

Gene Colan & Pablo Marcos
Artists

From an Idea by
Marv Wolfman

NIGHT FLIGHT TO TERROR!

DON'T STRUGGLE, BABY. MY THUMB MIGHT SLIP AND PRESS THIS DETONATOR.
PLEASE... WE HAVEN'T DONE ANY-THING TO YOU!..

YEAH? HOW ABOUT MAKING ME A KILLER, LADY?
AN' MAKIN' ME LISTEN TA GOOK WOMEN AN' KIDS SCREAMIN'?
SCREAMING NOT EVEN A HUNDRED BUCKS A DAY COULD SILENCE?
YOU'VE ALL DONE IT TO ME AND YOU'RE ALL GOING TO PAY!
AND NOT ONE OF YOU HAS THE NERVE TO TRY TO STOP ME!

TRY TO STOP A MADMAN? NOT ANGIE MALATUCCI...
..HE ONLY WANTS TO VISIT HIS PARENTS IN ITALY BEFORE THEY DIE.

NOT JANICE STEVENS. AFTER AN UNSUCCESSFUL SCREEN CAREER HERE...
...SHE ONLY WANTS TO FLEE BACK TO ALBANY... AND MARRY TOM BROOKS.
CERTAINLY NOT MARTIN TANITY, THE EXECUTIVE WHO ONCE ONLY WANTED TO BE A GREAT PAINTER...
BUT WHAT WOULD HIS BOARD OF DIRECTORS SAY?

YET, PERHAPS THERE IS ONE WITH SUCH NERVE ON THIS FATEFUL FLIGHT.
THIS YOUTH PUTS ME IN AN UNCOMFORTABLE POSITION.
I HAD HOPED THIS CRAFT WOULD CARRY ME TO NEW YORK SWIFTLY AFTER THAT DISTASTEFUL AFFAIR IN HOLLYWOOD.

I MUST REACH ONE OF MY COFFINS BEFORE DAWN. THE YOUTH IS AN OBSTRUCTION!
AND THOUGH I COULD SURELY OVER-POWER EVEN ONE AS MAD AS HE --

--MY UNFAMILIARITY WITH THIS MODE OF TRAVEL GIVES ME PAUSE.
AND YET, THE YOUTH'S FACE DISTURBS ME. I HAVE SEEN ITS LIKE BEFORE--
--ON MEN DETERMINED TO DESTROY THEMSELVES, AND WHO, IN DOING SO, BROUGHT DESTRUCTION TO OTHERS AS WELL.

CREAK!
WHAT-- WHO'S THERE ⁈

CALM DOWN, SON--JUST WANTED TO TELL YOU WE'VE BEEN CLEARED TO PROCEED TO NEW YOIRK.
WE'RE NOT GOING TO NEW YORK.
NONE OF US ARE GOING TO NEW YORK.

WE'RE GOING TO FLY INTO THE SUNRISE UNTIL OUR FUEL GIVES OUT, AND THEN--
--FLUTTER TO THE GROUND TO DIE IN THE FIRST, BLINDING RAYS OF MORNING'S GLORY!
IT WILL BE A MAGNIFICENT CLIMAX TO ALL OUR WORTH-LESS LIVES!

THE YOUTH HAS MADE MY CHOICE CLEAR. FOR WHILE I MIGHT SURVIVE SUCH A CRASH--
--THE DAWN'S LIGHT WOULD SURELY DOOM ME!

KLIK!

AM I TO BE INCLUDED IN YOUR VENGEANCE, TOO, YOUNG MAN? I HAVE DONE YOU NO WRONG.
I AM A FOREIGNER TO THIS COUNTRY. SURELY YOU ARE ABLE TO SEE THAT.

CAN'T YOU LOOK INTO MY EYES AND SEE THAT.

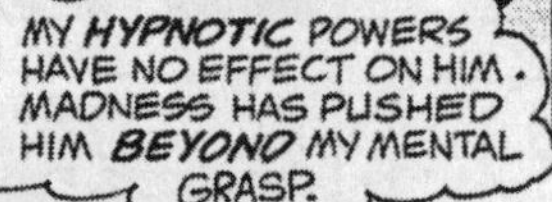
MY HYPNOTIC POWERS HAVE NO EFFECT ON HIM. MADNESS HAS PUSHED HIM BEYOND MY MENTAL GRASP.

GET BACK TO YOUR SEAT, MISTER--
--OR I'LL BLOW UP THIS PLANE NOW!
PLEASE, SIR--DO AS HE SAYS!
NONE MAY DICTATE TO ME, YOUNG LADY. BUT IF REASON WILL NOT SWAY OUR DEATH-SEEKING FRIEND--

YAAHH!
--THEN PERHAPS FORCE WILL!

PLUD!

BAROOMM!

THE WOUNDED 747 SPIRALS TOWARDS THE GROUND, THE FIRE IN ITS BELLY SHINING MORE BRIGHTLY THAN THE FULL MOON.
PILOT AND CO-PILOT FIGHT TO FREE MANUAL LANDING MECHANISMS THAT HAVE BEEN FUSED TOGETHER BY THE EXPLOSION.
AS FOR DRACULA AND HIS MAD FOE, THEY ARE UNCONSCIOUS, TORN APART BY THE INITIAL CONCUSSION OF THE BLAST.

THE PASSENGER JET TOUCHES DOWN ON THE ROCKY DESERT FLOOR, BOUNCING INSANELY.
KWAM!
MIRACULOUSLY, IT IS NOT CRUSHED ON IMPACT.
INSIDE: ANGIE MALATUCCI DUMBLY WONDERS IF IT IS RAINING IN ITALY AS SHRAPNEL PERFORATES HIS ALL TOO MORTAL FORM.

THE CRAFT SKIDS ACROSS THE DESERT WITH A SOUND BORN IN THE DEPTHS OF SOME BANSHEE'S BLACK SOUL ...
...BEFORE IT GRINDS TO A FLAMING HALT.
PAN AM
INSIDE: JANICE STEVENS THINKS NOT OF TOM BROOKS BUT OF CAMERAS AND FOOTLIGHTS, AS A WALL OF FLAME ENVELOPS HER.

IN THE DISTANCE, LAS VEGAS SPARKLES...
...WHILE THE FURY OF THE 747 IS SPENT, SAVE FOR A THICK, ACRID BLACK SMOKE THAT FILLS THE AIR.
INSIDE: MARTIN TANITY, TRAPPED IN THE WRECKAGE, THINKS THAT A STACK OF LEDGERS IS NO FIT MONUMENT TO A MAN'S WHOLE LIFE, BEFORE HE PASSES OUT.

BUT THE DEATH OF THIS AIRCRAFT HAS NOT GONE UNNOTICED.
A FULL THREE SCORE OF AMBULANCES RACE DOWN THE VEGAS NIGHT-CLUB STRIP...
GAMBL

...FOUR-WHEELED ANGELS OF MERCY WHOSE DRIVERS PRAY...
...THAT THEY ARE NOT TOO LATE.

THE DEATH-TOLL IS TRAGICALLY HIGH, BUT ITS NUMBERS LIE FORGOTTEN ON THE WARM SANDS.
THOSE STILL CLINGING TO LIFE MUST BE CARED FOR FIRST...
...BE THEY BROKEN, BURNED, OR...

...WEAK FROM LOSS OF BLOOD.

WEIRD COSTUME THAT GUY WAS WEARING, HUH?
MAYBE HE'S AN ACTOR WHO GOT A LITTLE CARRIED AWAY WITH HIS PART!
YOU THINK HE'LL MAKE IT?
LAS VEGAS GENERAL HOSPITAL

DON'T KNOW--ALMOST EVERY SURGEON IN TOWN ANSWERED THE CALL...
--BUT THERE'S SO MANY INJURED.
EMERGENCY ENTRANCE
LAS VEGAS GENERAL HOSPITAL
THEY TRY, THOSE DEDICATED MEN OF MEDICINE...

THERE ARE MANY VICTORIES AND MANY DEFEATS IN THAT OVERCROWDED OPERATING ROOM...
ANGIE MALATUCCI WILL NEVER SEE HIS PARENTS IN ITALY. HE DIES JUST BEFORE MIDNIGHT.
WHEN TOM BROOKS SEES JANICE STEVENS' FACE, HE WILL HEM, HAW, AND BREAK THEIR ENGAGEMENT. SHE WON'T CRY.
AND MARTIN TANITY WILL SEND A VERY RUDE LETTER TO THE BOARD OF DIRECTORS, THEN CHANGE HIS NAME TO SOMETHING AN ART CRITIC CAN REMEMBER!

WHY A PRIVATE ROOM FOR THIS GUY?
THE DOCS ARE WORRIED ABOUT 'IM! ASIDE FROM A FEW CUTS AND BRUISES, HE'S IN PERFECT HEALTH!

SO HOW COME HE NEEDED SUCH A MASSIVE BLOOD TRANSFUSION?

AWAY! AWAY, YOU DAMNABLE WRETCHES--
WHAAP!
UGNNNNN!
--AND THANK YOUR GODS THAT I DON'T SLAY YOU FOR WHAT YOU HAVE DONE!
OOOOF!!

THEY DARED GIVE ME BLOOD--
--AS A MOTHER GIVES MILK TO HER BABE?!

ACCHH!
THIS IS NOT HOW IT WAS MEANT TO BE!
BLOOD MUST NEVER BE MADE SO AVAILABLE!
THERE WAS NONE OF THE THRILL OF THE HUNT, THE GLORY OF THE CONQUEROR.
IF ONLY HE WHO CAUSED THIS IGNOMINY WERE NOT BEYOND MY VENGEANCE...

"WAIT-- SOMEONE COMES!"
WHERE DOES THIS ONE GO?
PRIVATE ROOM--SAME ONE THAT GUY IN THE CLOAK WAS TAKEN TO.

"IT IS HIM!"

LOOK OUT! HE'S GONE... OOOF!
SLAMM!
BACK, YOU MINDLESS CRETINS--
--NONE SHALL STAY THE HAND OF DRACULA!

THE FURY OF THE VAMPIRE-LORD IS AWESOME TO BEHOLD, HIS STRENGTH ENORMOUS...

CRASH!
...AND THOUGH THE YOUNG INTERNS WILL SURVIVE DRACULA'S ENRAGED ATTACK

...THEY WILL NEVER, NEVER FORGET IT.
NOT OFTEN DO MEN MEET DEATH AND LIVE TO SPEAK OF IT.

AND NOW, MY SUICIDAL FRIEND, YOU SHALL AT LAST GAIN THE DEATH YOU SOUGHT--
--ONLY TO RISE AS ONE OF THE UNDEAD! HA, HA, HA!

NO! THIS IS NOT THE WAY TO DEAL WITH THIS ONE!
HE WANTED A MAGNIFICENT DEATH--
VERY WELL THEN--
REAR EXIT

--HE SHALL HAVE IT!
DRACULA CALLS ON HIS POWER TO CHANGE HIS SHAPE AND SIZE, BECOMING A HUGE BAT...
...A BAT WHICH CARRIES A LIMP HUMAN FORM FROM THE HOSPITAL AND INTO THE HOT DESERT AIR.

DAWN FINDS THE CREATURE FLYING INTO A DEEP, DARK CAVERN WHERE NO LIGHT EVER PENETRATES.
THREE DAYS AND THREE NIGHTS PASS. THEN...

YOU'RE VERY LUCKY, YOU KNOW.
IMAGINE--DISAPPEARING FROM THE HOSPITAL AND TURNING UP THREE NIGHTS LATER IN PERFECT HEALTH--

--EXCEPT FOR THAT STRANGE LOSS OF BLOOD--

--AND THOSE WEIRD NECK WOUNDS. BUT THE TRANSFUSION WORKED AND NOW THE DOCTOR SAYS WE CAN GO TO A NICE PLACE TO RELAX WHILE YOU RECUPERATE!

HERE WE ARE--
--IN OUR BRAND-NEW SOLARIUM!

NOOOOOOOoo

SUNRISE IN LAS VEGAS!

A MAN WHO WANTED A MAGNIFICENT DEATH AT DAWN...
...FINDS INSTEAD A DIFFERENT KIND OF DEMISE...
...AT THE HANDS OF DRACULA!
FINIS

A DEATH IN THE CHAPEL!
STEVE GERBER WRITER
ART GENE COLAN ERNIE CHUA
ROME. THE ETERNAL CITY. FOUNDED BY THE TWINS ROMULUS AND REMUS, A PAIR OF PAGAN SAVAGES RAISED FROM INFANCY (ACCORDING TO LEGEND) BY WOLVES.
WHICH PERHAPS ACCOUNTS FOR THE CITY'S HISTORY OF GRANDEUR AND DEPRAVITY, EMPIRE AND RUIN, JUSTICE AND CORRUPTION, BEAUTY AND... DEATH.
REMUS HIMSELF WAS AMONG THE FIRST TO DIE HERE--SLAIN BY HIS WOLFISH BROTHER. BUT TONIGHT THE STALKERS OF PREY BARE NOT LUPINE CLAWS --
--BUT BATLIKE FANGS!
AND THEY THIRST NOT FOR POWER, ONLY FOR THICK, HOT BLOOD!
MY HOTEL'S JUST AROUND TH--HEY! YOUR EYES-- AND THOSE FANGS--!
SI, SIGNOR-- MARIA IS A VAMPIRE! AND YOU ARE A DEAD MAN!
OH, COME ON! THIS'S GOTTA BE A GAG! AND YET... YOUR GRIP... SO POWERFUL-- YOUR EYES, DARK, COMPELLING...
CAN'T... RESIST YOU... CAN'T...!

YOU ARE WRONG, MY AMERICAN FRIEND! AS OF THIS MOMENT, MARIA'S HUNT IS ENDED!
WHO--? NO! THE MONK--MONTES!!
TURN, BLOOD-SUCKER...!

AND THE ACCURSED CROSS!

AND THAT IS NOT THE ONLY WEAPON I WIELD, DEMON! LISTEN! LISTEN TO THESE WORDS!
WORDS FROM THE ARCANE LORE OF THE ANCIENT TEXT CALLED DARKHOLD!

WORDS THAT CALL FORTH THE POWER TO BANISH YOU TO OBLIVION!
HOLO ERASMA RABIS KATERAMA LUCEM DEI PARADOXIS SATANNICUS BELGREM!
THE LANGUAGE IS ONE UNHEARD ON THE EARTH FOR CENTURIES--AND THE MONK CANNOT EVEN BE CERTAIN OF THE PRECISE MEANING OF THE WORDS.
BUT AS HE SPEAKS, MARIA BURSTS INTO FLAME. AND WHEN HE IS DONE, ALL THAT REMAINS OF HER IS--

ASHES!

Y-YOU SAVED MY LIFE! HOW CAN I REPAY YOU?

YOU CANNOT, FOOL. HE HAS HAD HIS REWARD.
NO PAYMENT IS NECESSARY, MY SON. ONLY GO IN THE WAY OF THE LORD.
HE KNOWS HIS INCANTATION WORKS. HE KNOWS HE CAN DESTROY ALL MY MINIONS--AND ME.
HE KNOWS THAT, TO DRACULA, HE IS THE MOST DANGEROUS MAN ON EARTH!

"GO IN THE WAY OF THE LORD," INDEED! THE PIOUS OLD JACKASS!
HE REVELS IN HIS BRAND OF DESTRUCTION...
...FULLY AS MUCH AS I SAVOR MINE!
THUS FAR, MONTESI HAS BEEN CONTENT TO STALK SMALL GAME--NEW RECRUITS TO MY LEGIONS OF THE UNDEAD!
LET US SEE IF HE CAN SO EASILY VANQUISH THE PRINCE OF VAMPIRES!
I SHALL STAY ON HIS TRAIL THIS NIGHT--FOLLOW WHEREVER IT LEADS, AND--NO! NOT HERE!! IT MUSTN'T BE!
MONTESI HAS TAKEN REFUGE IN--THE VATICAN!
I CANNOT BEAR TO LOOK UPON THE PLACE! THE PAIN IT STIRS WITHIN ME--

SCREEE
THAT SCREAM! LIKE A WOUNDED BAT--!
HELLO, COUNT! I'VE BEEN EXPECTING YOU!

SCREEEEEEEE
"BUT I'M AFRAID I'M NOT QUITE READY TO DEAL WITH YOU-- YET.
"WE SHALL HAVE OUR RECKONING, DRACULA--SOON. BUT NOT NOW... AND I TRUST, NOT HERE, eh? DRACULA...?"

SOME DISTANCE AWAY--
--THE DARK LORD RESUMES HUMAN FORM, SPUTTERING CURSES AT THE WIND!

AND HE IS STILL CURSING AS HE STALKS OFF THROUGH THE NIGHT-DARK ROMAN STREETS...
HE LAUGHED AT ME! THAT SANCTIMONIOUS, SENILE OLD FOOL LAUGHED AT DRACULA!
AND, AS LONG AS HE ABIDES IN THAT FORTRESS— LIKE A MONUMENT TO GOODNESS AND LIGHT AND EVERYTHING NICE--
--I CAN'T TOUCH HIM!

BUT NEITHER DO I DARE ADMIT DEFEAT-- LEST MY EMPIRE CRUMBLE AS SURELY AS THAT WHOSE RUINS I TREAD!
I AM PRINCE OF EVIL-- MASTER OF ALL THE LIVING DEAD!

IF I AM TO REMAIN SO--IF MY MINIONS ARE TO INHERIT THE EARTH--
--I MUST BREACH THE WALLS OF THAT OVERGROWN COUNTRY CHURCH--

--AND DESTROY MONTESI'S COPY OF THE DARKHOLD INCANTATION! I-- WAIT! BEHIND ME!
THOSE TWO PRIESTS MAY BE THE ANSWER!
FOR A MOMENT, DRACULA HESITATES, CONTEMPLATING WHAT THE AWFUL CONSEQUENCES OF HIS DARING INSPIRATION COULD BE--SHOULD IT FAIL.

AND YES, HE CONCLUDES, THE STAKES ARE HIGH. THE STAKES ARE, IN FACT, HIS VERY EXISTENCE. AND YET, HIS NIGHTLY RISING WILL BE FRAUGHT WITH PERIL AS LONG AS MONTESI POSSESSES THAT SPELL. SO --
--AS THE TWO PRIESTS PASS, DRACULA LEAPS FROM THE SHADOWS AND LOCKS HIS POWER-FUL ARMS ABOUT THEIR NECKS.

HE HAS ALREADY RISKED TOO MUCH--
--TO LET THE SECRET ESCAPE NOW.

HE HAS PITTED HIMSELF AGAINST THE MAGIC OF THE WOMAN CALLED TOPAZ-- AND THE RAW POWER OF A WERE-WOLF..*
...JUST TO KEEP THE WORDS FROM OTHER EARS.
AND SO, THE STRANGLING OF THIS PRIEST--
*TOMB OF DRACULA #18 & WEREWOLF BY NIGHT #15.--RT.

--THE THEFT OF HIS ROBES--
--AND EVEN THE DIRE MISSION ON WHICH DRACULA NOW EMBARKS...

...ARE BUT MATTERS OF NECESSITY.
THE TIME FOR TURNING BACK HAS LONG SINCE PASSED!

HIS FACE HIDDEN BY THE WIDE BRIM OF THE PRIEST'S HAT-- HIS HEAD BOWED, EYES FIXED ON THE GROUND,--HIS HANDS FOLDED AS IF IN PRAYER--
--DRACULA ENTERS VATICAN CITY!

PERHAPS THIS ROLE SUITS ME.
THE GUARDS SUSPECTED NOTHING!
BUT THE QUESTION YET REMAINS: HOW CAN I MOVE ABOUT IN THIS PLACE--

--WHERE THERE ARE MORE CROSSES THAN FOOLS TO WORSHIP THEM?
DO I EVEN DARE LOOK UP...?
NO!!
THEY ARE EVERY-WHERE!

"I MUST HIDE MY EYES-- NOT EVEN LOOK AHEAD OF ME--"
--LEST I FIND MYSELF SURROUNDED BY THE DAMNABLE SYMBOLS!

SURROUNDED-- AND THUS PARALYZED! UNABLE TO ACT!

DEEPER INTO THE GREAT HALLS HE WANDERS, PAUSING NOT EVEN TO GLANCE AT THE THINGS OF BEAUTY AND NOBILITY WITHIN-- FOR FEAR OF CONFRONTING THE HATED CROSS.
GOOD EVENING, FATHER. I AM LOOKING FOR THE MONK-- MONTESI!
WHERE MIGHT I FIND HIM AT THIS HOUR?
IN THE ARCHIVES, I WOULD IMAGINE, FATHER, CONTINUING HIS RESEARCH.
YES. OF COURSE. THANK YOU.

THE ARCHIVES:
ALL OF THE DARKHOLD SAVE THESE WORDS WERE WRITTEN IN LATIN.
THE VOLUME ITSELF NO LONGER EXISTS-- ONLY THIS COPY OF THE INCANTATION.
BUT IF I CAN DECIPHER THE LINGUISTIC "CODE", WE MAY LEARN THE ORIGIN OF DARKHOLD--
--AND OF A LOST CULTURE WE NEVER KNEW OF BEFORE.
NOT TO MENTION RIDDING THE WORLD OF DRACULA AND HIS ILK!

MONTESI IS A MAN OF LETTERS--OF CONTEMPLATIVE REFLECTION--OF QUIET STUDY AND PHILOSOPHIC INVESTIGATION.
THUS, HE HAS NOT THOUGHT TO PREPARE-- NEVER ASKED HIMSELF WHAT HE WOULD DO--
HE IS NOT A MAN OF ACTION--NOT A VAMPIRE-SLAYER BY CHOICE, BUT OUT OF A SENSE OF DUTY TO HIS FELLOW MAN!
--IF THIS HAPPENED!

YOU SEEM SURPRISED, MONTESI--AS IF YOU THOUGHT ME INCAPABLE OF--!
BUT OF COURSE-- YOU ARE NO HARKER OR VAN HELSING OR BLADE!
YOU'RE AN AMATEUR-- A POMPOUS LITTLE GIANT-KILLER!

--WHO ONCE KNEW A MAGIC TRICK... THAT WENT UP IN SMOKE!

THAT'S RIGHT, MONTESI-- FLEE! AS ALL YOUR HOPES AND DREAMS BURN IN MY HAND!
FLEE-- FROM THE TRIUMPH OF THE LORD OF DARKNESS!

WAIT! I WAS GOING TO LET MONTESI LIVE-- TO SPEND THE REST OF HIS DAYS RELIVING HIS DEFEAT!
BUT HE MUST HAVE COMMITTED THE SPELL TO MEMORY!

AND SO HIS THREAT TO ME IS STILL REAL--AS LONG AS HE BREATHES! A PITY!!
BUT I LACK BOTH THE TIME AND THE INCLINATION FOR SENTIMENT.
THERE IS WORK TO BE DONE.
AND I SHALL NOT BE -- NO!
NO!
MY GAZE WAS TURNED DOWNWARD WHEN I ENTERED THIS HALL! I DID NOT SEE--! MUST TURN AWAY!
HOW COULD I HAVE BEEN SO STUPID? NOW, I MUST STALK THESE CORRIDORS WITH MY EYES EXPOSED!
AND I CANNOT AFFORD CAUTION OR STEALTH! I MUST FIND MY PREY--
--AND DESTROY HIM--BEFORE THE COMING OF DAWN!

BUT HE MIGHT HAVE GONE ANYWHERE! AND THERE MUST BE MILES OF HALLWAYS!
AND CROSSES-- CROSSES AT EVERY TURN!
AMID SUCH GRANDEUR AS TO TRANFIX THE MIND!

HOW SAD THAT ALL THIS BEAUTY SHOULD BE WASTED ON THESE RELIGIOUS MANIACS!
IF THESE WORKS OF ART COULD ADORN CASTLE DRACULA--!

I HAVE THE ARTISTIC SOUL TO-- AAGGH!

I MUST HAVE BEEN MAD TO UNDERTAKE THIS MIS-ADVENTURE!
I ALLOWED MY PRIDE, MY LUST FOR VEN-GEANCE--

--TO RULE MY JUDGEM--

YARRGH!

EEAUGH!
IT IS USELESS! FUTILE! THIS PLACE IS A DEATH TRAP FOR ME!

BUT NO SOONER HAS DRACULA DETERMINED TO ABANDON THE CHASE THAN--
MONTESI! I'VE FOUND YOU--AT LAST! AND IN THE SISTINE CHAPEL, NO LESS!
YES, COUNT-- YOU'VE FOUND ME--AND YOUR DOOM--IN GOD'S HOUSE!

HEAR ME, LORD: HOLORERASMA RABIS KATERAMA--
NO!! YOU SHALL NOT SPEAK THOSE WORDS!

BECAUSE DRACULA WILL SILENCE YOU-- FOREVER!

THAM!

HAHAHAHA
D-DO NOT... LAUGH... DRACULA..!

IT IS... NOT OVER. YOUR HELL... HAS JUST... BEGUN.
DAYS AGO... I... MAILED... COPY OF... INCANTATION... TO HARKER--!

NO! NO! YOU LIE!!
...EVEN AS THESE MEN ENTER!
MONTESI!
ALMOST INSANE WITH ANGER, DRACULA RACES FROM THE CHAPEL...

HE'S... DEAD, ISN'T HE? MURDERED BEFORE THE VERY FACE OF THE LORD!
THAT CLOAKED MAN-- SHOULDN'T WE CALL THE POLICE--?
IN TIME. A MAN THAT EVIL CANNOT HELP BUT BE CAUGHT-- OR BETRAY HIM-SELF.
FOR NOW, LET US ATTEND TO OUR BROTHER, AND PRAY FOR HIS SOUL...
...AND, YES, FOR HIS MURDERER'S AS WELL.
FINI

PROLOGUE: JANUARY 12th, 1974; WASHINGTON, DISTRICT OF COLUMBIA; RICHARD THOMAS GRANT AND DENNIS SMYTH; A MOMENT OF APPROACHING DESTINY...

AGAIN, DENNIS--BE SURE YOU CONTACT WILLIAMSON IN THE MORNING. I DON'T WANT ANY TROUBLE ON THOSE CONTRACTS. NOT THIS TIME.
I PROMISE YOU, SIR, THERE'LL BE NO TROUBLE.
SEE THAT THERE ISN'T, DENNIS...

IN THE PAST MONTH, I'VE FIRED TWO SECRETARIES FOR FAILING TO FOLLOW MY ORDERS-- I'VE NO QUALMS ABOUT FIRING A THIRD.
EH?
PARDON ME, SIR-- MAY I SPEAK WITH YOU?

IF THIS IS SOME KIND OF A "TOUCH"--YOU'RE WASTING YOUR TIME.
I THINK NOT. YOU SEE, I DON'T WANT YOUR MONEY, MR. GRANT--
I WANT YOUR LIFE.

MY WHAT? OH, I UNDERSTAND. THIS IS A JOKE, AND THAT CANE-- I SUPPOSE A KNIFE POPS FROM THE END WHEN YOU PUSH A BUTTON-- HMMM?
NOT QUITE, MR. GRANT. A KNIFE WOULD BE A CLICHÉ--

YAAAA!
--BUT, I THINK YOU'LL AGREE, A LASER-BEAM WOULD NOT!

HAHAHAHAHAHA
END OF PROLOGUE; BEGINNING OF STORY...
FOR THE LORD OF THE UN-DEAD, IT BEGINS HERE, ON A QUIET PATH IN A PARK IN BOSTON, TWO DAYS AFTER THE EVENTS IN WASHINGTON, D.C...
IT BEGINS ON AN EVENING LIKE MANY OTHERS, AN EVENING WHEN THE PRINCE OF DARKNESS HUNTS... AN EVENING WHEN DRACULA PREPARES TO FEED!
HERE COMES THE DEATH MAN
I ALMOST PITY THESE YOUNG FOOLS...ON A NIGHT WHEN MOST OF THIS CITY'S INHABITANTS COWER BEHIND LOCKED DOORS, FEARING DEATH AT THE HAND OF "THE VAMPIRE KILLER"...
...THESE YOUNG LOVERS CHOSE TO WANDER A DIM-LIT PARK, AS THOUGH THEY SEEK THE DEATH I BRING THEM!
BE THAT AS IT MAY, IT'S NONE OF MY CONCERN. DRACULA NEEDS BLOOD, AND SO THEY SHALL BE MY VICTIMS!

BUT, AS THE SALLOW-FACED VAMPIRE MOVES FORWARD, A STRAY BEAM OF MOONLIGHT TOUCHES A SHEET OF NEWS-PRINT, AND...
RICHARD GRANT... DEAD?
"WASHINGTON BUSINESSMAN DIES BIZARRE DEATH"... THEN IT'S TRUE. SOME-ONE WILL SUFFER FOR THIS...
...GRANT WAS THE LEADER OF MY EAST COAST FOLLOWERS... ONE OF THE FEW HUMANS I'VE EVER TRUSTED WITH THE GREATNESS OF MY PLAN.
SHINGT
DIES BIZ
WHOEVER KILLED HIM DE-STROYED MONTHS OF WORK... AND FOR THAT AND OTHER REASONS, HIS LIFE IS FORFEIT...
...FOR DRACULA CANNOT AFFORD TO HAVE HIS RULE UNDERMINED SO CASUALLY...
...NOT IF I'M TO REMAIN UNCHALLENGED... THE UNQUESTIONED LORD OF THE UNDEAD.
JANUARY 15, 1974: WASHINGTON, D.C.: AN ARCHERY RANGE JUST OUTSIDE THE CITY LIMITS; DR. THOMAS LEWIS AND FRIEND...
...A NEW BOW YOU WANT TO PATENT? WELL NOW, ARCHERY IS SOMETHING OF A HOBBY OF MINE, MR. --AH--?
MORTUS. I KNOW IT'S YOUR HOBBY, DOCTOR.
THAT'S WHY I CAME TO YOU... FOR YOUR SUPPORT.
WELL NOW, THAT'S AWFULLY KIND OF YOU, MR. MORTUS! I FANCY MYSELF A PARTIAL EXPERT ON THESE THINGS.
I'D BE HAPPY TO TAKE A LOOK AT THIS BOW, IF IT'S AROUND.
IT IS, DOCTOR LEWIS, IT IS. AS A MATTER OF FACT, IT'S IN THAT STOR-AGE BARN AHEAD...

WELL NOW, I GUESS YOU *KNEW* I'D BE *EAGER* TO SEE THIS BOW OF YOURS, DIDN'T YOU?

WELL NOW, I'M SURE I CAN'T *WAIT* UNTIL--

DEAR LORD, NO!

A *CALCULATED* GUESS.

IF YOU'LL LOOK IN FRONT OF YOU--YOU'LL *SEE* IT.

CLICK-BEEP

UH...WELL... IF YOU INSIST...
AND SO...
SEE HERE, I'VE TOLD YOU EVERYTHING. MR. GRANT HAD ENEMIES-- MANY ENEMIES. HOW AM I TO KNOW WHICH ONE KILLED HIM?
WARP
SILENCE. THAT REPORTER-- WHAT'S THAT HE'S SAYING?
"...AND THE THIRD BIZARRE KILLING IN FOUR DAYS, A SERIES WHICH BEGAN WITH THE DEATH OF BILLIONAIRE INDUSTRIALIST RICHARD GRANT, WAS FOLLOWED BY THE ACID-SLAYING OF JOSIAH HUNTINGCUT, AND NOW...
"...WITH THE DEMISE OF DOCTOR THOMAS LEWIS, SEEMS TO--"
HUNTING-CUT...LEWIS... WEREN'T THEY ASSOCIATES OF GRANT?
I BELIEVE SO.
YOU DON'T THINK THERE'S A CONNECTION?
THAT'S SOME-THING WE MUST DIS-COVER, DENNIS SMYTH. I'M AFRAID I MUST RE-QUEST YOUR CONTINUED ASSISTANCE...
WE'RE GOING TO YOUR FORMER EMPLOYER'S OFFICE, TO INVESTIGATE HIS FILES.
I TRUST YOU'VE NO OBJECTION?
NO--NO OBJECTIONS--
N-NO OBJECTIONS AT ALL!

JANUARY 15th, 1974--CONTINUED; THE GREGORIAN MUSEUM, A LITTLE KNOWN DEPOSITORY OF ARCHEOLOGICAL SPECIMENS; PROFESSOR CLINTON HALL, CURATOR OF THE SOUTH AMERICAN WING...
...A MAN ON THE VERGE OF BECOMING AN OBITUARY...
WHAT...? IS SOMEONE THERE?
YOU! WHO ARE YOU, SIR? DON'T YOU KNOW THE MUSEUM'S CLOSED?
YES, I KNOW... BUT I'VE SOMETHING OF GREAT IMPORTANCE TO SHOW YOU, PROFESSOR HALL...
...THIS.
I KNOW WHAT AN ENTHUSIAST YOU ARE FOR SPECTACULAR GEMS, PROFESSOR. YOU'VE SPENT YOUR LIFE STUDYING THEM IN THIS MUSEUM...
GOOD LORD! THAT JEWEL-- IT'S MAGNIFICENT!
...I THOUGHT IT ONLY FITTING THAT YOU STUDY THEM AT THE MOMENT OF YOUR DEATH, AS WELL!
EH? DON'T DROP IT, YOU FOOL-- DON'T--
KABOOM

INTERESTING. GRANT WAS IN INDUSTRIAL DESIGN--SPECIFICALLY, THE DEVELOPMENT OF LASERS FOR COMMERCIAL USE.
LEWIS WAS AN ARCHERY EXPERT--THIS HUNTINGCUT A CHEMIST--AND ALL THREE OF THEM WERE ASSOCIATED WITH SOMETHING CALLED THE BROADWAY PROJECT.
WHY, YES--I HANDLED THE CONTRACTS ON THAT ONE, SIR. AS A MATTER OF FACT, MR. GRANT WAS TALKING ABOUT THEM JUST BEFORE HE DIED.
THERE WERE TWO OTHER PEOPLE INVOLVED. A PROFESSOR CLINTON HALL, AND A WOMAN... MILDRED WILLIAMSON.
I SEE...
WHATEVER THIS BROADWAY PROJECT IS, IT SEEMS TO BE A COMMON DENOMINATOR OF THE THREE MEN WHO DIED--AND SO, OBVIOUSLY, OF THEIR KILLER.
GET IN TOUCH WITH THIS PROFESSOR HALL. I WANT TO TALK WITH HIM...
RICHARD T. GRANT
YES, SIR. I'LL PHONE HIM AT THE MUSEUM.
BUT, WHEN THE CONNECTION TO THE MUSEUM IS MADE...
OH. OH... YES...THANK YOU.
HALL IS DEAD, SIR--KILLED AN HOUR AGO--BY A BOMB HIDDEN IN A JEWEL.
BY THE GATES OF HELL! WHAT'S THE ADDRESS OF THE WILLIAMSON WOMAN?
10 EAST POTOMAC STREET... APARTMENT 12-6... BUT WHY...?
MEET ME THERE AS QUICKLY AS YOU CAN.
I'VE A FEELING WE'RE COMING TO THE END OF THIS LITTLE MYSTERY--

--AND I'VE NO TIME TO WASTE WITH CABS!
HE'S SEEN MANY CITIES, THIS COUNT DRACULA...AND MANY OF THEM ARE KNOWN AS THE GREATEST CITY IN THE WORLD...
...INCLUDING THIS CITY, THIS WASHINGTON, D.C...
PERHAPS IT IS; DRACULA NEITHER KNOWS, NOR CARES. A MAN WHO'S LIVED FIVE HUNDRED YEARS, HE KNOWS A BASIC TRUTH ABOUT CITIES...
LIKE GOVERNMENTS, THEY COME AND GO...
...AND ONLY EVIL IS ETERNAL.
WHAT--WHO'S THAT? WHO'S THERE?
ONLY I, WOMAN... DRACULA.
CREEEAK
DRACULA? DON'T BE ABSURD. HOW DID YOU GET UP HERE--WHAT DO YOU WANT? IF IT'S MONEY, I'M AFRAID YOU'RE TOO LATE...
I'VE NO MONEY LEFT TO GIVE ANYONE.
MONEY...?

--HE DIED, LEAVING ME NOTHING.

"THE BROADWAY PROJECT"--THEY WANTED MORE MONEY FROM ME, A RELEASE, FOR THE JEWEL'S INDUSTRIAL RIGHTS--BUT I GAVE THEM SOMETHING ELSE INSTEAD--

I GAVE THEM DEATH!

AAAAAAHHH

MISS WILLIAMSON! ARE YOU ALL RIGHT?
DEAR LORD--WHAT'S HAPPENING IN THERE?
AAAAAAHH!
THRUMP!
I'M COMING, MISS WILLIAMSON-- THAT DEATH MAN WON'T GET GET YOU AS WELL--DON'T WORRY, I'LL--
--SAVE YOU.
YOU NEEDN'T FEAR ME, DENNIS... YOU WERE A HELP IN SOLVING THIS MYSTERY, A HELP IN MY EFFORT TO GAIN REVENGE.
BESIDES... I'VE ALREADY FINISHED FEEDING..., AND I'VE NEVER HELD WITH GLUTTONY.
SO I TAKE MY LEAVE NOW, DENNIS--
YOU KILLED HER--YOU BIT HER NECK--
DON'T TAKE IT SO HARD, DENNIS. YOU'VE HAD A VALUABLE EXPERIENCE.
YOU'VE LEARNED, JUST A BIT, THE EXTENT OF EVIL IN THIS WORLD... EVIL WHICH MAY COME FROM ANY DIRECTION
HA... HAHAHA HA...
...AND ALWAYS, MY FRIEND... ALWAYS-- WHEN YOU LEAST EXPECT IT.
HAHAHAHAH
MORNING, JANUARY 15th, 197 A CORPSE AND A MAN DRIVE MAD; AND, OF COURSE, THE END
FINIS

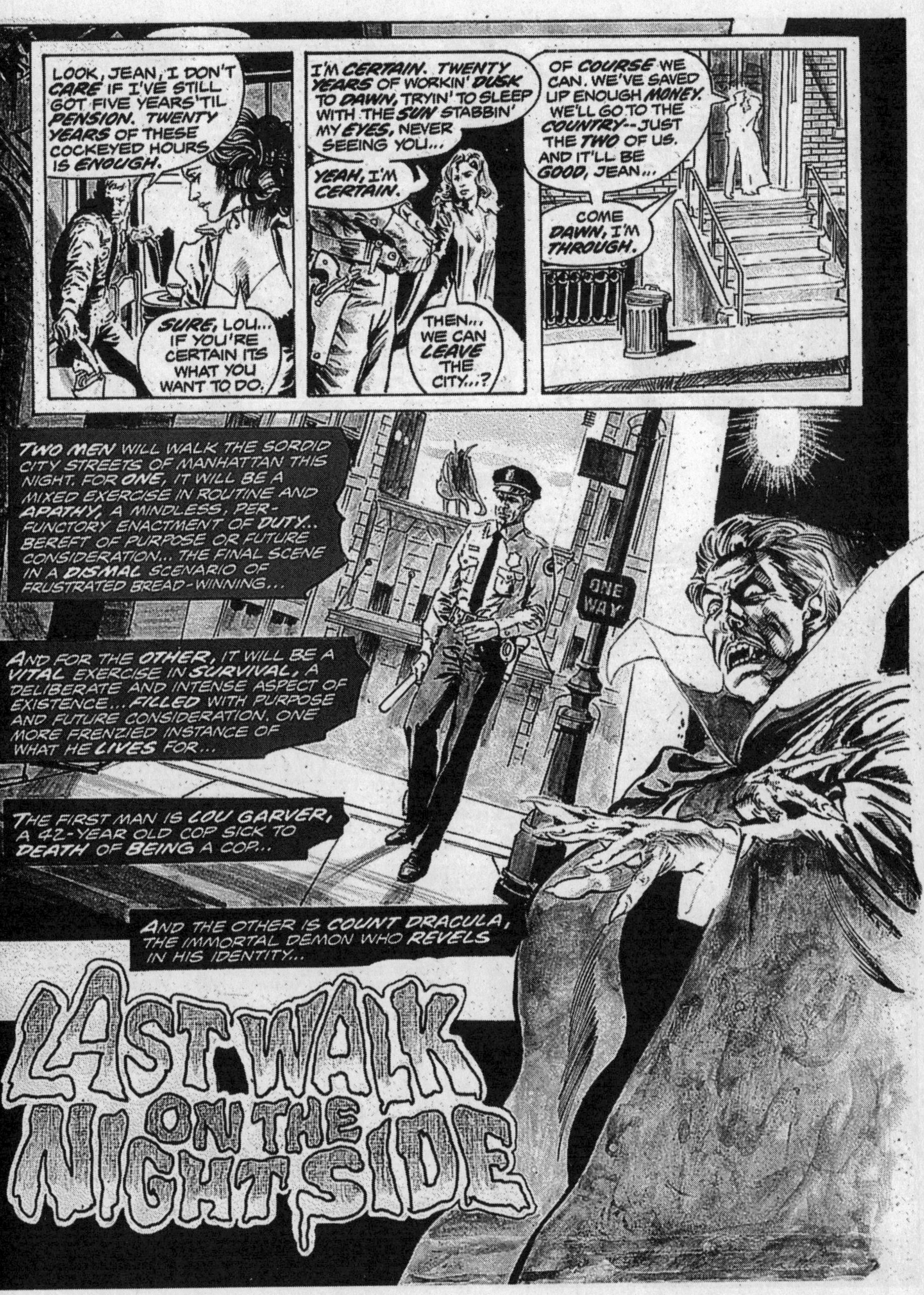

LOOK, JEAN, I DON'T CARE IF I'VE STILL GOT FIVE YEARS 'TIL PENSION. TWENTY YEARS OF THESE COCKEYED HOURS IS ENOUGH.
SURE, LOU... IF YOU'RE CERTAIN ITS WHAT YOU WANT TO DO.
I'M CERTAIN. TWENTY YEARS OF WORKIN' DUSK TO DAWN, TRYIN' TO SLEEP WITH THE SUN STABBIN' MY EYES, NEVER SEEING YOU...
YEAH, I'M CERTAIN.
THEN... WE CAN LEAVE THE CITY...?
OF COURSE WE CAN. WE'VE SAVED UP ENOUGH MONEY. WE'LL GO TO THE COUNTRY-- JUST THE TWO OF US. AND IT'LL BE GOOD, JEAN...
COME DAWN, I'M THROUGH.
TWO MEN WILL WALK THE SORDID CITY STREETS OF MANHATTAN THIS NIGHT. FOR ONE, IT WILL BE A MIXED EXERCISE IN ROUTINE AND APATHY, A MINDLESS, PERFUNCTORY ENACTMENT OF DUTY... BEREFT OF PURPOSE OR FUTURE CONSIDERATION... THE FINAL SCENE IN A DISMAL SCENARIO OF FRUSTRATED BREAD-WINNING...
ONE WAY
AND FOR THE OTHER, IT WILL BE A VITAL EXERCISE IN SURVIVAL, A DELIBERATE AND INTENSE ASPECT OF EXISTENCE... FILLED WITH PURPOSE AND FUTURE CONSIDERATION. ONE MORE FRENZIED INSTANCE OF WHAT HE LIVES FOR...
THE FIRST MAN IS LOU GARVER, A 42-YEAR OLD COP SICK TO DEATH OF BEING A COP...
AND THE OTHER IS COUNT DRACULA, THE IMMORTAL DEMON WHO REVELS IN HIS IDENTITY...
LAST WALK ON THE NIGHT SIDE

IT IS SAID THAT I HAVE BECOME A CULT-HERO TO THE MORTALS IN THIS CITY OF FESTERING EVIL...
...TO THE EXTENT THAT THE DECADENT RICH-- THE COLLECTORS--ARE PREPARED TO OFFER FANTASTIC SUMS FOR ANY OBJECT EVEN REMOTELY ASSOCIATED WITH ME.
AND WELL MUST IT BE TRUE... FOR HAVE NOT THE ARCHIVES IN MY CASTLE BEEN RANSACKED? BUT THIS CITY SHALL SOON LEARN THAT DRACULA DOES NOT RETURN TO AN EMPTY HOME... WITHOUT PUNISHING THE LOOTERS.
AND, TOO, SHALL IT LEARN THE TRUE MEANING OF EVIL... WHEN DRACULA PENETRATES ITS FACADE OF PETTY CORRUPTION.
BUT THE ART GALLERY ENTREPRENEUR SHALL BE SPARED MY RETRIBUTION ONE MORE NIGHT... FOR DRACULA REQUIRES MORE IMMEDIATE SATISFACTION...
DRACULA REQUIRES... BLOOD!
TWENTY YEARS ON THIS MISERABLE BEAT -- TWENTY YEARS OF MURDER AND RAPE, JUNKIES AND WHORES, GRAFT AND CORRUPTION, PERVERTS AND SICKOS...
TWENTY YEARS OF WALKING THROUGH A CARNIVAL OF HUMAN ATROCITY-- MAN'S WORST EXAMPLES OF DEGENERACY... AND NOW, ON MY LAST NIGHT... I COULDN'T CARE LESS...
OH NO, YOU AGAIN. MIGHTA KNOWN YOU'D COME WALTZIN' BY AT ABOUT THIS TIME, GARVER. I SUPPOSE YOU WANNA RUN ME IN TO THE STATION?
NO, GERDIE, I DON'T. IN FACT, I DON'T WANT TO HAVE ANYTHING TO DO WITH YOU.

SAY GOODBYE TO YOUR TRICKS FOR ME, GERDIE.
IT'S BEEN... NICE.
WELL THANK HEAVEN FOR LITTLE FAVORS.
WONDER WHAT'S BEEN BUGGIN' HIS--
EEEEE
EEEEEEE
WELL, THERE GOES THE FIRST SCREAM OF THE NIGHT...
...BUT IT'S PROBABLY JUST ANOTHER DOMESTIC SQUABBLE-- THE KIND TO WHICH COPS ARE NEVER INVITED.
BESIDES, THE NIGHT'S FULL OF SCREAMS-- LET ONE COME TO ME.
LOUSY BATS. THE CITY'S INFESTED WITH THEM-- YOU'D THINK THE COPS'D CLEAN THEM OUT.
TURN AROUND.

WH-WHAT--?!
COME HERE, WOMAN.

COME TO ME...
...YES...

AND, MESMERIZED, THE WOMAN OBEYS... HER ENTIRE REALM OF CONSCIOUSNESS FOCUSED ONLY ON TWO BURNING EYES...
...TWO DEMANDING EYES WHICH HAVE SEEN HELL.., AND BEYOND...

STILL BOUND IN A HAZY TRANCE OF SUBMITTANCE, THE WOMAN STOPS BEFORE THE GAUNT MAN COM-MANDING HER...
...AND FEELS NOTHING, SAVE THE FRIGID WARMTH OF HIS CLOAK-DRAPED EMBRACE...

...AND THE GENTLE CARESS OF HIS THIN, COLD LIPS AS THEY SLOWLY QUEST OVER THE SMOOTH CONTOURS OF HER THROAT...

THEN SHE SHIVERS, A DELICIOUS RIPPLE OF ANTICIPATION, AS SHE FEELS THE HEAT OF HIS FETID BREATH WHISPERING AGAINST HER THROAT...
...THE CARNAL STENCH PERMEATING HER FLARED NOSTRILS...
AND THEN SHE IS KISSED --KISSED AS SHE HAS NEVER BEEN KISSED BEFORE...
...KISSED BY DRACULA--
AAAA
EEEEEEEIIIIII
--A STRIDENT, UNHOLY SHRIEK WHICH SLICES THE NIGHT AIR FOR CITY BLOCKS...
--AND A SHRILL WAIL OF FOUL ECSTASY ERUPTS FROM HER VIOLATED THROAT--
...AND PIERCES THE EARS OF A COP WHO DOES NOT WANT TO LISTEN...
CHRIST, THAT'S A LOUD ONE--AND NOT YOUR TYPICAL DOMESTIC SQUABBLE SCREAM EITHER...
MORE LIKE A BLOODY BLUE MURDER SCREAM!
YEP-- EITHER A MUGGER... OR A RAPIST.
HALT--
POLICE!

I SAID, HOLD IT--!
--AND I MEANT IT!
KRATCH
FOOL! YOU WILL REGRET ATTACKING--
ARRHH
STOP-- OR I'LL SHOOT!
HUH?
A DEAD-END!
BUT HE'S GONE-- NOTHING HERE BUT MIST...

GOT AWAY, HUH?
YEAH... INTO A DEAD-END.
MUST'VE BEEN SOME PERVERT-- THIS GIRL'S THROAT IS TORN TO SHREDS...
PAL, YOU DON'T KNOW THE HALF OF IT...
I SAW THE GUY-- HE LUNGED FOR ME, IMPALED HIMSELF ON MY SPLINTERED NIGHT-STICK... AND GOD HELP ME, BUT HIS MOUTH WAS SMEARED WITH BLOOD.
HEY-- AREN'T YOU GOING TO MAKE OUT A REPORT?
I'LL MAIL IT IN... I JUST QUIT.
I AM HURT. AND THOUGH IT IS ONLY MY SHOULDER... AND WILL SOON HEAL...
...HE WILL PAY DEARLY FOR INFLICTING PAIN ON DRACULA!
DON'T EVEN KNOW WHY I BOTHERED GOING OUT TONIGHT...
JUST MORE OF THE SAME-- ALWAYS THE SAME.

THERE HE IS.
YEAH... AND HERE WE GO.
JEAN'S PROBABLY STILL ASLEEP. NO SENSE WAKING HER...
CLICK
MIGHT AS WELL JUST READ TILL MORNING. I'VE BEEN MEANING TO READ THIS--
BWAKK!
WHA--?!
'HELLO, COPPER. DON'T YOU REMEMBER US...? GUESS IT HAS BEEN A LONG TIME-- TEN YEARS, IN FACT.
TEN YEARS OF ROTTING IN STINKIN' PRISON--!
THAT'S A LOT OF TIME, COPPER. A LOT OF TIME TO HATE... A LOT OF TIME TO THINK ABOUT YOU, FREE ON THE OUTSIDE...
...WHILE WE WERE STUCK ON THE INSIDE, RUNNIN' THE SAME SCENE THROUGH OUR MINDS, OVER AND OVER. YOU WANNA KNOW WHAT THAT SCENE WAS, COPPER? YOU STARRED IN IT...
...AND WE WERE THE SUPPORTING CAST-- THE BAD GUYS WHO WON FOR A CHANGE... AND PINNED YOU TO THE WALL-- THROUGH YOUR HEART.
HEY, EDDIE-- LOOKIT THIS. A PLAQUE-- "AWARDED FOR 20 YEARS OF DISTINGUISHED SERVICE ON THE FORCE." REAL SILVER, TOO.

KWEESHH
WHAT IN THE--?!
TAKE 'IM EDDIE--HE MUST BE A COP!
WEIRDEST LOOKIN' COP I EVER--
--SUGHHH!
MORTAL FOOLS!
BLAM
BLAM
BLAM
YOU CAUSED ME PAIN ONCE, MORTAL... BUT NEVER AGAIN.

AND NOW... DRACULA WISHES YOU DEAD. DRINK DEEPLY, MORTAL, THESE LAST MOMENTS OF YOUR--
SILVER-- CURSED SILVER!
HSSSSSSS
?!
THIS SILVER PLAQUE AWARDED TO PATROLMAN LOU GARVER, COMMEMORATING 20 YEARS OF DISTINGUISHED SERVICE ON THE FORCE.
I DON'T KNOW WHAT KIND OF WHACKED BOZO YOU ARE... CALLING YOURSELF DRACULA...
...BUT IF THIS PLAQUE BOTHERS YOU, AND BULLETS DON'T--
--YOU'D BETTER BELIEVE I'M GONNA MAKE USE OF THE PLAQUE.
VERY WELL, MORTAL--DRACULA REALIZES THAT FATE DOES NOT FAVOR HIM THIS NIGHT... AND SO I WILL LEAVE.
BUT KNOW THAT I HAVE ALREADY EXACTED AMPLE REVENGE FROM YOU. I WILL BE SATISFIED WITH THAT.

BESIDES, I HAVE OTHER BUSINESS TO ATTEND... AT THE RIZZOLI ART GALLERY.

FAREWELL...

HOLY CHRISTMAS-- THERE REALLY IS A DRACULA--!

--AND THAT WAS HIM!

BUT WHAT DID HE MEAN ABOUT HE'D ALREADY GOTTEN REVENGE? THOSE TWO HOODS HE DEMOLISHED DIDN'T MEAN ANYTHING TO ME. IN FACT, HE SAVED ME FROM THEM...

OH GOD...

JEAN--

JEAN!

NO-- GOD, NO, NO, NO, NOOOOO!

Story: DOUG MOENCH Art: FRANK ROBBINS & FRANK SPRINGER

LOU GARVER HAS SPENT THE LONG NIGHT KNEELING IN A POOL OF HIS WIFE'S BLOOD... AND NOW SPENDS THE FOLLOWING MORNING TRYING TO EXPLAIN IT...
MAKE IT EASY ON YOURSELF, LOU, AND JUST TELL US WHY YOU DID IT.
I'M TELLING YOU I DIDN'T DO IT.
SURE -- JUST LIKE YOU DIDN'T LEAVE YOUR BEAT EARLY TO GO HOME TO HER...?
SHE WAS DEAD WHEN I GOT THERE.
THEN WHY IS IT THAT YOUR FINGERPRINTS WERE THE ONLY ONES SLAPPED ALL OVER THE MURDER WEAPON--?
AND WHY IS IT THAT THE MURDER WEAPON--THIS MALLET --WAS FOUND LYING ON THE FLOOR NEXT TO YOU...
...WITH THIS WOODEN SPIKE STICKING THROUGH THE HEART OF THE DECEASED?
BECAUSE I USED THE MALLET TO DRIVE THE STAKE THROUGH JEAN'S HEART. I ADMIT THAT.
BUT I ONLY DID IT BECAUSE SHE WAS ALREADY DEAD--
--SLAIN BY A VAMPIRE. I KNOW IT SOUNDS CRAZY, FRANK, BUT IT'S TRUE! I SWEAR IT!
AND IF YOU DON'T START BELIEVING ME--
--I'LL BE BEHIND BARS AND COUNT DRACULA WILL BE OUT LOOKING FOR NEW VICTIMS...
...MAYBE YOUR WIFE THIS TIME!
YOU SAW THE GASHES IN JEAN'S THROAT. WHAT MORE DO YOU WANT?
I WANT YOU TO GO HOME, LOU-- AND I WANT YOU TO STAY THERE.
I'M GOING TO KEEP THIS BUSINESS UNDER WRAPS... BUT IF I CATCH YOU OUT ON THE STREETS--
--YOU'RE GONNA FIND A MURDER-ONE RAP STENCILED ACROSS YOUR FOREHEAD.

NIGHT ENFOLDS MANHATTAN LIKE A SMOTHERING COBWEB WOVEN FROM STREAMERS OF VISCOUS FOG...
A SHARP SQUEAL PIPES IN THE DISTANT DARKNESS, AND THE DELICATE TAPESTRY OF LANGUID FOG IS SHREDDED BY THE SPURTING FLIGHT OF A HUGE BAT...
RIZZOLI AUCTION
...WHO BECOMES ONE WITH THE SWIRLING FOG AS IT SEEPS UNDER A DARKENED DOOR...

...TO BECOME COUNT DRACULA, LORD OF THE UNDEAD, BEYOND THAT DOOR.
NOW SHALL DRACULA DETERMINE WHETHER VENGEANCE WILL FLAVOR THIS NIGHT'S BLOOD.
MOVING WITH LIQUID GRACE, THE SPECTRE OF DEPRAVITY STEPS DEEPER INTO THE SHADOW-DRAPED GALLERY...UNTIL HIS BURNING EYES FILL WITH THE SIGHT OF DISPLAYED ARTIFACTS...
THEN IT IS TRUE--
-ARTIFACTS LAST SEEN IN HIS TRANSYLVANIAN HOME...
LOT # 102

IT IS THE MAN CALLED RIZZOLI WHO LOOTED MY CASTLE--!
BREATHE... AND YOU'RE DEAD.
LOT # 202

NOW TURN AROUND AND LET ME SEE WHO YOU ARE.
I AM DRACULA--
--AND I'M HERE TO SEND YOU TO HELL!

A GHASTLY HISS SLITHERS FROM DRACULA'S THROAT AS HE STEPS FORWARD--DIRECTLY INTO THE EXPLODING FORCE OF A CALMLY AIMED PISTOL.
FOOL!
BLAM!
YOU WOULD SLAY THE LORD OF THE UNDEAD WITH A MERE BULLET--?!

THEN YOU REALLY ARE DRACULA!
BUT YOU ARE ALSO A FOOL--
--TO THINK I WOULD BE UNPREPARED FOR YOU...

--AFTER PILFERING YOUR CASTLE OF ITS PRECIOUS OBJECTS.
SEARING BEAMS OF PRISTINE FORCE SEEM TO ERUPT FROM THE CRUCIFIX...

...FORCE WHICH FILLS THE VAMPIRE WITH SIZZLING AGONY.
KARAAASH!
RIZZOLI PROP.

...AND ANTON RIZZOLI SMIRKS AT THE RETREATING FORM OF A HUGE BAT... AS HE PLACES THE CRUCIFIX IN THE SHATTERED WINDOW OF HIS GALLERY...

LATER THAT NIGHT, ANTON RIZZOLI'S SMIRK MELTS INTO AN EXPRESSION OF SUAVE CHARM.... THE CHARM OF A GREEDY MAN WHO HAS A FORTUNE TO BARTER--
--AND WHO CAN AFFORD TO BE SUAVE.
EXIT
AN AUCTION ATTENDED BY A SELECT GROUP OF COLLECTORS PLUS ONE...

...LOU GARVER, A MAN WHO WISHES TO COLLECT NOTHING BUT VENGEANCE!
WHAT AM I BID FOR THIS PRICELESS CANDELABRA ONCE OWNED BY VLAD TEPES...?
...OTHERWISE KNOWN AS DRACULA.

FIVE-THOUSAND DOLLARS.

SOLD--ONCE AGAIN TO THE LADY IN BLACK!
WAP!

AND AFTER THE POST-AUCTION ARRANGEMENTS...
A C-NOTE FOR THE LADY'S NAME AND ADDRESS.

URSULA LENSKY... BUT HER ADDRESS IS YOUR PROBLEM.
SHE DID NOT WISH HER PURCHASES TO BE DELIVERED...

...PREFERRING TO PICK THEM UP HERSELF TOMORROW NIGHT.

BUT *URSULA'S* FASCINATION WITH THE DRACULA MYSTIQUE *TRANSCENDS* MERE TITILLATION...

INDEED, SHE IS GENUINELY *DEVOTED* TO THE LEGEND OF THE VAMPIRE-LORD...

...AND SECRETLY WISHES THAT HE ACTUALLY *EXISTED*.

WH-WHO ARE--?
DRACULA, WOMAN...
...THE ONE WHO PLACES A PRIOR CLAIM ON THE OBJECTS YOU HAVE UNJUSTLY PURCHASED THIS NIGHT.

...THE ONE WHO WOULD USE YOU TO REGAIN HIS POSSESSIONS...
...AND CARRY OUT HIS WRATHFUL VENGEANCE INTO THE BARGAIN.
YOU...YOU TRULY ARE DRACULA. SOMEHOW I CAN SEE THAT... IN YOUR EYES.

BUT WHAT DO YOU WANT ME TO DO...?
THE THIEF RIZZOLI WILL NOT THINK TO BRANDISH A CRUCIFIX TO YOUR APPROACH...

LOU GARVER HAS OCCUPIED THE LAST HALF HOUR TRYING TO TAG AN ADDRESS TO THE NAME URSULA LENSKY. HE HAS SUCCEEDED.
THIS IS IT-- 52 RIVERSIDE DRIVE.

AND SINCE THIS URSULA CHICK NOW OWNS THE STUFF DRACULA WILL KILL TO REPOSSESS...
...SHE'S DUE FOR A HELPING OF--
--DANGER.
THE CRIMSON SMEAR ON THE THICKLY-PILED CARPET HAS ALREADY BEGUN TO CONGEAL.

FRANK? THIS IS GARVER, AND DON'T GIVE ME ANY OF THAT BULL ABOUT STAYING OFF THE STREET.
I'M ON MY WAY OVER TO--
--RIZZOLI'S AUCTION GALLERY. A DARK AND SILENT PLACE AT THIS HOUR, BUT NEVERTHE-LESS, A PLACE WHICH EVEN NOW--
I'M AT THE PLACE OF A CHICK NAMED URSULA LENSKY. I THINK SOMETHING PRETTY HEAVY HAS JUST HAPPENED TO HER.
--RECEIVES A VISITOR.

MISS LENSKY-- WHAT A SURPRISE.
WON'T YOU COME IN?
THANK YOU, MR. RIZZOLI.

I ASSUME YOUR VISIT RELATES TO THE ITEMS I SOLD YOU THIS EVENING..?
YES, I HAVE COME TO SPEAK TO YOU ABOUT THE DRACULA ARTICLES...
...BUT I HAVE ALSO COME MERELY TO SPEAK TO YOU.

I'M AFRAID I DON'T QUITE UNDERSTAND...
OH, COME NOW, MR. RIZZOLI. YOU ARE A MAN OF THE WORLD...
SURELY YOU REALIZE WHEN A WOMAN FINDS YOU CHARMING.
YES...I AM BEGINNING TO GET THE PICTURE, MISS LENSKY.

LOU GARVER HAS KEPT HIS FOOT PRESSED TO THE *FLOOR* THROUGHOUT THE THREE-MILE DRIVE FROM URSULA LENSKY'S DESOLATE MANSION TO *RIZZOLI'S AUCTION GALLERY*...

THE MAN CALLED RIZZOLI HAS SILENTLY FALLEN *VICTIM* TO URSULA'S MESMERIZING GAZE...

HE FEELS NOTHING AS HIS BLOOD *SATIATES* THE WOMAN'S PERVERTED LUST...

...AND WHEN HIS WOULD-BE SAVIORS BURST THROUGH THE DOOR, HE IS NO MORE THAN THE BLOODLESS HUSK OF DRACULA'S VENGEANCE.
KRAASH

HISSING, SPITTING, THE HIDEOUS VAMPIRESS IS SLAMMED TO THE FLOOR...
HOLD HER DOWN WHILE I KEEP HER WEAKENED WITH THE CROSS--

--AND DRIVE THE STAKE THROUGH HER HEART BEFORE SHE TRANSFORMS TO MIST!
YIIEEEEEE!

LOU-- I WANT YOU TO KNOW I'M REINSTATING YOU TO THE FORCE IMMEDIATELY.
SURE... I ONLY QUIT TO BE WITH JEAN.
I MIGHT AS WELL REJOIN TO DEVOTE MYSELF TO--
--CATCHING THE FIEND WHO KILLED THOSE PLANS.

--SHIP A NUMBER OF HIGHLY VALUABLE CRATES TO TRANSYLVANIA.
EXPORT DEPT.

TRANSYLVANIA? YOU MEAN ROMANIA, DON'T YOU?

HAVE IT YOUR WAY. I AM AN EASY MAN TO DEAL WITH.

FINIS

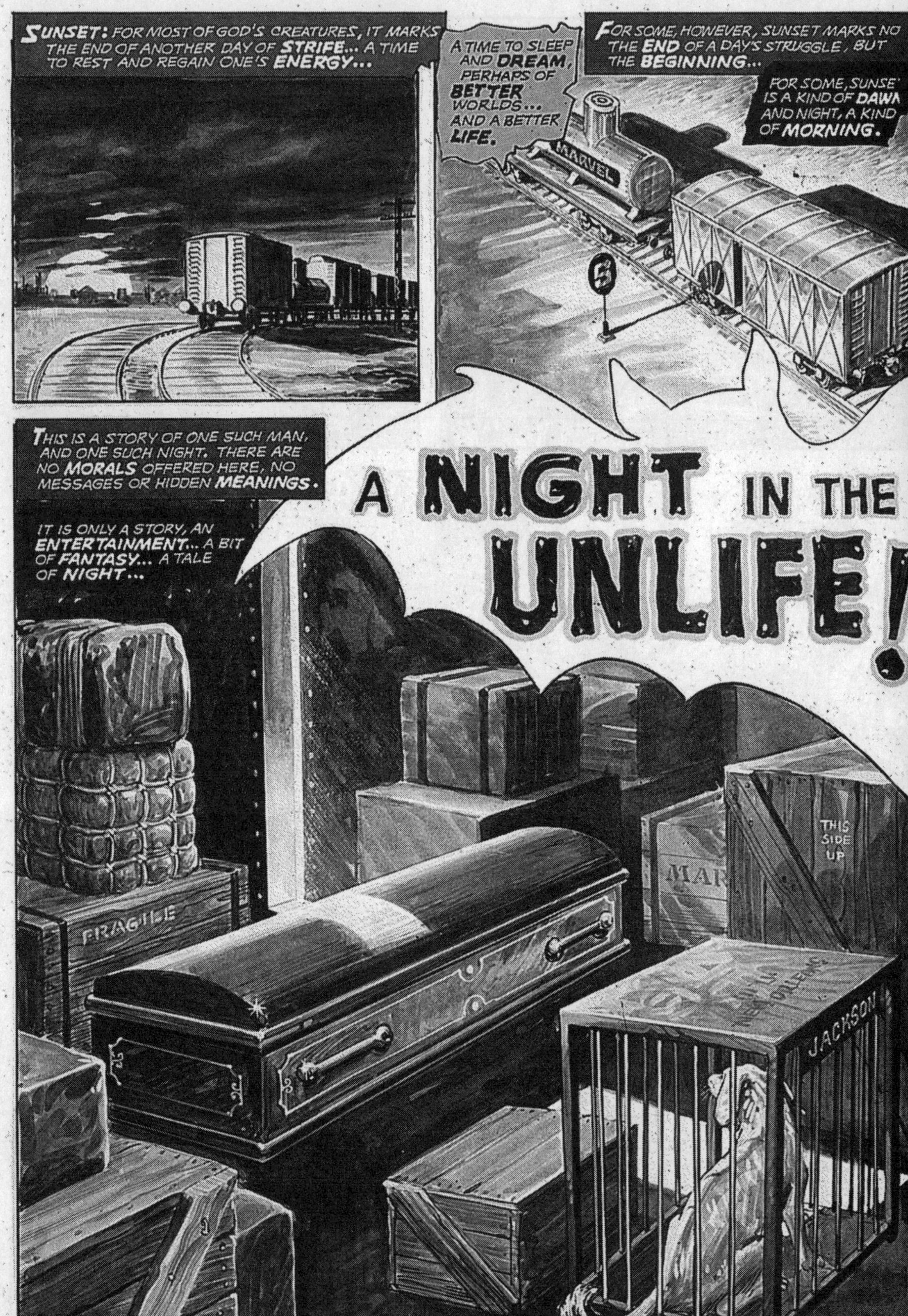
SUNSET: FOR MOST OF GOD'S CREATURES, IT MARKS THE END OF ANOTHER DAY OF STRIFE... A TIME TO REST AND REGAIN ONE'S ENERGY...
A TIME TO SLEEP AND DREAM, PERHAPS OF BETTER WORLDS... AND A BETTER LIFE.
FOR SOME, HOWEVER, SUNSET MARKS NO THE END OF A DAY'S STRUGGLE, BUT THE BEGINNING...
FOR SOME, SUNSE IS A KIND OF DAWN AND NIGHT, A KIND OF MORNING.
MARVEL
THIS IS A STORY OF ONE SUCH MAN, AND ONE SUCH NIGHT. THERE ARE NO MORALS OFFERED HERE, NO MESSAGES OR HIDDEN MEANINGS.
A NIGHT IN THE UNLIFE!
IT IS ONLY A STORY, AN ENTERTAINMENT... A BIT OF FANTASY... A TALE OF NIGHT...
FRAGILE
THIS SIDE UP
MAR
JACKSON

THE DOG'S NAME IS JACKSON, AFTER ANDREW JACKSON, AND HE'S BEING SHIPPED SOUTH TO HIS MASTER IN NEW ORLEANS...
HE'S THE FIRST TO SENSE THAT SOMETHING'S WRONG HERE...
WITH A SNARL BUBBLING UP FROM DEEP IN HIS THROAT, JACKSON HURLS HIMSELF AGAINST THE BARS OF HIS TRAVELING "CAGE"...
AGAIN AND AGAIN, HE TRIES TO SMASH FREE OF THE BAR'S RESTRAINTS...
FORTUNATELY FOR JACKSON, HE DOESN'T SUCCEED.
ONCE MORE, THE SUN HAS LEFT THE SKY--AND NO LONGER MUST I FEAR ITS BURNING RAYS.
DRACULA LIVES... AND TONIGHT, STALKS HIS PREY.
THE SIGHT OF THIS MAN, THE SMELL OF HIM, DRIVES JACKSON INSANE WITH RAGE; A FURY WHICH THREATENS TO EXPLODE WHEN THIS MAN GIVES THE DOG A DISDAINFUL SMILE...
YOU COULD DIE VERY EASILY, DOG.

HE SAYS NOTHING MORE, THIS TALL DARK MAN, BUT HIS WORDS ARE LIKELY A FIERY SWORD INSIDE THE DOG'S SMALL BRAIN...

--AND HE STARES, HIS DOG-MIND WHIRLING WITH WHAT HE SEES.
JACKSON KNEW THIS MAN WAS UNNATURAL AND STRANGE... BUT HE DIDN'T KNOW HOW STRANGE...

NOW THAT HE KNOWS... HE FEARS.
WHIMPERING, HE TRIES TO FIND A PLACE TO HIDE... BUT HIS CAGE IS SMALL...

...AND DRACULA IS ALREADY GONE!

CRAYTON IS A SMALL TOWN IN SOUTHERN ILLINOIS, THE COUNTY SEAT FOR WHAT'S BASICALLY AN AGRICULTURAL COMMUNITY. ITS PEOPLE ARE QUIET AND INDUSTRIOUS, WITH FEW DARK SECRETS, AND ITS YOUTH ARE EQUALLY QUIET AND INDUSTRIOUS...
...THOUGH WITH A FEW MORE SECRETS...
JIMMY, WE CAN'T. WE JUST CAN'T.
MOMMA WOULD JUST DIE IF SHE FOUND OUT... AND BESIDES, HOW WOULD WE LIVE?
HAMBURGER
ROY'S DRIVE-IN Restaurant

WHAT DO YOU MEAN "HOW WOULD WE LIVE"? LIKE EVERYONE ELSE.
YOU GOT A JOB I DON'T KNOW ABOUT, JIMMY? OR WERE YOU PLANNING ON SUPPORTING US BOTH ON YOUR HIGH SCHOOL SCHOLARSHIP?
AW, JULIE--WHAT DO YOU WANT ME TO DO ANYWAY?
YOU ORDERED BURGERS AND SHAKES? THAT'LL BE TWO-FIFTY, ALL TOGETHER.
I'LL GET IT, JIMMY. I KNOW YOU'RE DOWN TO YOUR LAST DOLLAR.
IF YOU HAD A JOB LIKE HANK JOHNSON, WE WOULDN'T ALWAYS HAVE TO GO DUTCH TREAT.
JIMMY HODGES STIFFLES HIS REPLY, AND WATCHES SULLENLY AS JULIE CHAMBERS PAYS THE BILL; THEN...
SO WHAT DO YOU WANT ME TO DO, JULIE? IF I'M GOING TO MAKE IT TO COLLEGE, I'VE GOT TO STUDY EVERY NIGHT--
--BUT IF YOU'RE GOING TO MARRY ME, YOU'VE GOT TO HAVE MONEY AND THAT'S THE BOTTOM LINE!
MONEY? WHAT'S SO IMPORTANT ABOUT MONEY WHEN YOU'RE IN LOVE, JULIE?
OH, BE REALISTIC, JIMMY. I WANT TO GET OUT OF CRAYTON, NOT STAY HERE ALL MY LIFE.
IF YOU WON'T GET A JOB-- THEN ROB A BANK!
WHAT?
YOU HEARD ME. A BANK, MAYBE A JEWELRY STORE-- THERE'S ONE OVER ON WINSTON STREET. YOU'VE GOT TO DO IT, JIMMY.
IT'S EITHER THAT --OR I WON'T SEE YOU ANYMORE.

IN A SILENCE SO THICK HE CAN HEAR A CAR GO BY ON THE HIGHWAY A MILE DISTANT, DRACULA STANDS AND WAITS...
AND, WAITING IS REWARDED...
WE'LL SEE YOU BOYS TOMORROW, OKAY? GOTTA GET HOME TO THE WIFE, OR SHE'LL HAVE MY HIDE!
BAR

I WISH SHE WOULD... THE WAY BARBARA'S BEEN ACTING LATELY, I MIGHT AS WELL NOT BE ALIVE.
HALF THE TIME, SHE'S SLEEPING WHEN I COME HOME FROM THE JOB...

...AND THE REST OF THE TIME, SHE COULDN'T CARE.
IT STARTED WHEN I FIRST TOOK ON AN OUT-OF-STATE HAUL. SHE SAID SHE DIDN'T LIKE ME GOING ON THE ROAD ALL NIGHT...

BUT, HECK--I'M A TRUCKER, RIGHT? I'VE GOTTA TAKE THE JOBS THE DISPATCHER GIVES ME, DON'T I?
BARBARA ACTS LIKE IT'S MY FAULT. CRAZY DAME. IF I JUST KNEW WHAT TO--

EEEEYOWWW
SOME SORTA MUGGER--!

JOE DON MAHONEY IS A VETERAN OF THE KOREAN WAR; AND EVEN IF HE WERE NOT, HE'S A VETERAN OF A ROUGH-AND-TUMBLE CHILDHOOD... WHICH IS POSSIBLY MORE IMPORTANT...
HE REACTS INSTANTLY, WITHOUT HESITATION...

IT IS THIS WHICH SAVES HIS LIFE...

CRASH

FOR THAT, YOUR DEATH WILL BE EVEN MORE UNPLEASANT THAN I HAD PLANNED IT TO-- EH?
HEY, JOE DON-- WHAT'S ALL THE RACKET?
YEAH, MAHONEY, THIS IS SUPPOSED TO BE A QUIET TOWN, NOT A-- SAY! WHAT'S GOIN' ON HERE?

THIS CREEP ATTACKED ME, THAT'S WHAT'S GOIN' ON.
WHAT IS HE, SOME SORT OF WEIRDO? LOOKIT THE WAY HE'S DRESSED... LIKE THE GUEST OF HONOR AT A FUNERAL!
IT SEEMS YOUR PITIABLE LIFE HAS BEEN REPRIEVED, MORTAL. I'VE NO DESIRE TO DEAL WITH A MOB--

--FOR THERE WILL BE OTHER VICTIMS IN THIS TOWN--
--VICTIMS WHO WILL BE DOUBTLESSLY ACCESSIBLE!

DID YOU--
WE SAW IT, JOE DON. WHAT I WANNA KNOW IS--WHAT ARE WE GONNA DO ABOUT IT?
ME... I WANT A DRINK.

FOR ALMOST THREE HOURS, JIMMY AND JULIE HAVE BEEN DRIVING VIRTUALLY IN CIRCLES... MIDNIGHT HAS COME AND GONE... AND ONLY NOW HAVE THEY MADE THE DECISION THEY KNEW THEY WOULD MAKE WHEN THEY STARTED OUT, THREE HOURS BEFORE...
MARVELLOUS J

I DON'T KNOW, JULIE--I MEAN, THIS IS A REALLY SERIOUS THING, YOU KNOW?
SO'S GETTING MARRIED, AND YOU'RE NOT SCARED OF THAT, ARE YOU?
ANYWAY, YOU WERE THE ONE WHO SAID YOU KNEW A WAY INTO TINEMAN'S JEWELRY STORE--

--I'M JUST ALONG FOR THE RIDE.
OKAY, OKAY. GIVE ME A CHANCE, WILL YOU? I'VE GOT TO BUILD UP TO THIS.
YOU GOT THOSE PLIERS FROM THE TOOLKIT?

RIGHT HERE. YOU GOING TO USE THEM--OR LOOK AT THEM? I'M WARNING YOU, JIMMY--
YOU BETTER MAKE UP YOUR MIND--OR I'M LEAVING.

JUST STAY BY THE CAR AND WAIT FOR ME.
ALL RIGHT, ALREADY... I'M GOING.

SHIVERING SLIGHTLY FROM THE COLD NIGHT AIR-- OR PERHAPS FROM FEAR-- JIMMY HODGES MOVES TO THE REAR OF THE JEWELRY STORE, AND...
JUST GOT TO CLIP THESE WIRES-- AND THAT'LL CUT OFF THE ALARM SYSTEM--
CLICK!

--AND THEN ALL I HAVE TO DO IS SMASH OPEN THE GLASS IN THE DOOR--
CRASH!

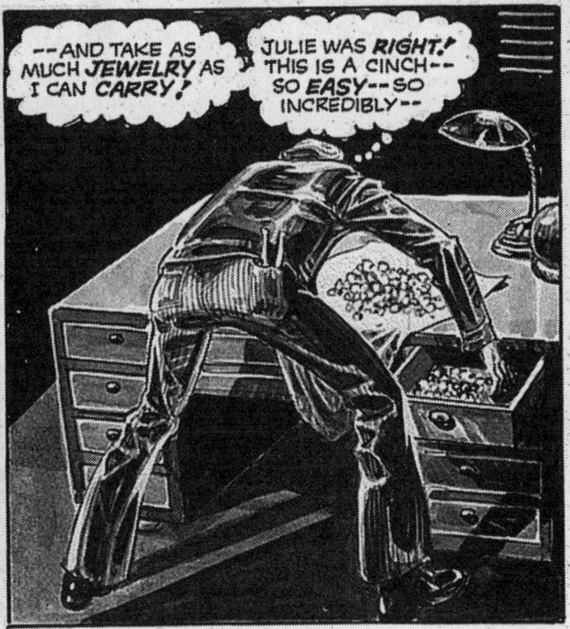
--AND TAKE AS MUCH JEWELRY AS I CAN CARRY!
JULIE WAS RIGHT! THIS IS A CINCH-- SO EASY--SO INCREDIBLY--

--EASY TO MANIPULATE HIM. I'VE BEEN WANTING TO GET OUT OF THIS FARM TOWN SINCE I WAS OLD ENOUGH TO READ, AND WITH JIMMY'S HELP--I'LL BE FREE!
AND ONCE WE GET TO CHICAGO OR NEW YORK, OF COURSE-- I'LL DUMP HIM. HE'S SUCH A CHILD, AFTER ALL...

...NOT WORTHY OF ME AT ALL. I NEED A MAN. A REAL MAN, WHO UNDERSTANDS WOMEN, AND--

EEEEEEEEEEEEEEE

HEART POUNDING, LUNGS LABORING FOR BREATH, JIMMY HODGES RUNS AT THE SOUND OF THE SCREAM--JULIE'S SCREAM. HE TRIPS, STUMBLES TWICE, FINALLY REACHES THE STREET, AND SEES--
JULIE!

WITHOUT THINKING, HE RACES FORWARD, AWARE ONLY OF THE LIMP FORM WHICH WAS ONCE THE GIRL HE LOVED--!
HE DOESN'T SEE THE HAND WHICH STRIKES HIM ALMOST IDLY.
ALMOST IMMEDIATELY, HE PASSES OUT.

TWO HOURS AFTER HE WAS ATTACKED, SHORTLY BEFORE TWO IN THE MORNING, JOE DON MAHONEY RETURNS HOME TO HIS PLEASANT, TWO-FAMILY HOUSE...
TO HIS SURPRISE, HE SEES LIGHTS IN THE WINDOWS...

BARBARA? ARE YOU STILL UP?
TOM HANDLY FROM THE BAR CALLED ME A WHILE AGO. HE TOLD ME YOU WERE ALMOST KILLED TONIGHT...

JOE DON... YOU WILL BE CAREFUL WITH YOURSELF, WON'T YOU?
SURE, HONEY. SURE.
PLEASE BE CAREFUL FOR ME?

AND SUDDENLY, ALL THE TENSION BETWEEN THEM IS GONE... WIPED AWAY BY A BRUSH WITH DEATH...
...FOR NOW, AT ANY RATE. AND FOR JOE DON MAHONEY... THAT'S ENOUGH.

AS FOR JIMMY HODGES: HE'S RECOVERED WHEN THE POLICE ARRIVE, SUMMONED BY AN ALARM HE ONLY THOUGHT HE'D DISCONNECTED-- RECOVERED, THAT IS, FROM THE PHYSICAL BLOW HE'S RECEIVED--
--BUT NOT QUITE RECOVERED FROM THE EMOTIONAL ONE--!

KID--DIDN'T YOU REALIZE THIS WAS JUST GLASS? NO JEWELER IN HIS RIGHT MIND LEAVES REAL STONES LYING AROUND--!
DOESN'T MATTER-- SHE LOVED ME, DON'T YOU UNDERSTAND?
JULIE LOVED ME...
...SHE LOVED ME... AND NOW SHE'S DEAD...

AND DRACULA? THE REST OF THE NIGHT IS SPENT QUIETLY ENOUGH... UNTIL IT'S TIME FOR SUNRISE, WHEN HE RETURNS TO THE FREIGHT CAR HE LEFT HOURS BEFORE...

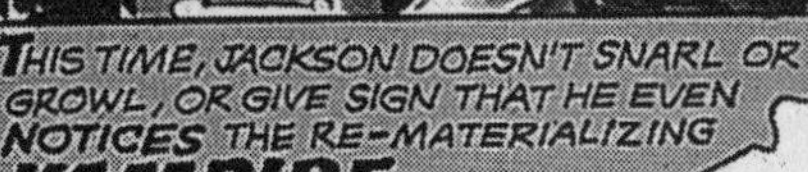
THIS TIME, JACKSON DOESN'T SNARL OR GROWL, OR GIVE SIGN THAT HE EVEN NOTICES THE RE-MATERIALIZING VAMPIRE...

FOR JACKSON IS ASLEEP...
...AND SOON, SO IS DRACULA, LORD OF THE VAMPIRES.

AND THEN ABRUPTLY, IT IS DAWN.
FINIS

Writer: RICK MARGOPOLOUS Artists: GEORGE TUSKA & VIRGILIO REDONDO

DRACULA ASKS--HIS VOICE DRIPPING WITH CHARM!
BON SOIR, MADEMOISELLE! MAY I JOIN YOU?
UH, YES, OF COURSE! BUT WHAT KIND OF ACCENT IS THAT? ARE YOU RUSSIAN?

MEMORIES:
SORRY TO WAKE YOU, KID... BUT I'VE GOTTA PUSH ON!
BUT MIKE... I I THOUGHT YOU PLANNED TO SPEND THE NIGHT!
YEAH, WELL, YOU KNOW THE WAY THINGS ARE, KID!
YES...I KNOW...

"NO! I AM OF EAST EUROPEAN EXTRACTION... ROMANIAN, TO BE PRECISE! YOU MAY CALL ME VLAD!"
"WILL DO, VLAD! AND YOU CAN CALL ME MARY! SAY, HAS ANYONE EVER TOLD YOU YOU'VE GOT REALLY INTENSE EYES?"

MEMORIES:
BILL--? THIS IS MARY! SINCE YOU HAVEN'T CALLED ALL WEEK...
...I TOOK THE LIBERTY OF RINGING YOU! HOPE YOU DON'T MIND...!

MEMORIES:
MIND?! LOOK, MARY...I TOLD YOU I'D BE BOGGED DOWN FOR A FEW DAYS! I'M UP TO MY NECK IN WORK!
YOU'RE A NEAT CHICK AND ALL THAT ...BUT JUST STAY OFF MY BACK, OKAY?
JEEZ! SOUNDS LIKE SHE'S CRYING AT THE OTHER END!

SOMEHOW, MARY KNOWS DRACULA WILL BE DIFFERENT FROM ALL THE COUNTLESS OTHERS!
SOMEHOW, AFTER AN HOUR OF SMALL TALK, SHE FINDS HERSELF LEAVING, LEANING IN HIS IRON EMBRACE!
AFFAIRE D'AMOUR (FRENCH), A LOVE AFFAIR!

MEMORIES:
HAW! YA CALL THAT FREAKIN' GARBAGE 'ART'?! LADY, YOU'VE GOT ONE FAR-OUT HEAD!
DON'T TALK LIKE THAT, JEFF... JUST COME OVER HERE... AND HOLD ME CLOSE!

MEMORIES:
MAN, WHAT A CLINGIN' VINE! DON'T YA EVER THINK OF NOTHIN' ELSE?
IF YA ASK ME, YOU'RE ONE SICK BROAD! I'M SPLITTIN!
JEFF... OH--!

TWO INDIVIDUALS... EACH WRAPPED IN THEIR OWN PERSONAL ILLUSIONS!
THE BLOOD-FIEND FEELS A SENTIMENT STIRRING HE THOUGHT LONG EXTINCT... THE AFFECTION HE ONCE HELD FOR A CERTAIN NAMELESS 'FRIEND' CENTURIES AGO.
RUE-
THE GOLDEN-HAIRED FEMALE MERELY SMILES AND TIGHTENS HER GRASP AROUND DRACULA'S WAIST! SHE THINKS SHE'S IN LOVE WITH THIS MAN!
THERE IS FANTASY HERE... AS WELL AS REALITY... BUT WHO CAN TRULY SAY WHERE THE ONE LEAVES OFF... AND THE OTHER BEGINS?

SCENE: AN APARTMENT-STUDIO ON THE LEFT BANK.
MARY SENSUALLY CASTS OFF HER COAT... AND SAYS BUT THREE SHORT WORDS!
TAKE ME, VLAD!
THE MASTER VAMPIRE TURNS SLOWLY ... EYES KEENLY ABLAZE... HIS BREATH COMING IN GUSTS THRU CLENCHED TEETH ... AS A FERAL FIRE SPARKS AN UNHOLY THIRST WITHIN HIM!

THERE IS NO NEED FOR WORDS BETWEEN THEM. THE RAVISHING GIRL SOFTLY SIGHS AS THE NIGHT LORD'S FINGERS GENTLY PROBE HER WARM NECK...

...AND HE SUPS DEEPLY!
THERE IS A BRIEF MOMENT OF ECSTACY... PLEASURE BEYOND SEXUAL FULFILLMENT... AS MARY TRADES HER LIFE'S LIQUID FOR A NEW IMMORTAL EXISTENCE!
ÂME DAMNÉE (FR.), A DAMNED OR LOST SOUL!

VLAD...! I-I FEEL... SO... WEAK...
SOON... A CHANGE WILL TAKE PLACE! DO NOT FIGHT THE TRANSFORMATION... BUT YIELD TO IT!
DO NOT MOVE. DO NOT EVEN ATTEMPT TO SPEAK!
THESIS: ACCORDING TO SCRIPTURE... CHRIST SHED HIS BLOOD WHILE NAILED TO A CROSS TO SAVE HUMANKIND!
ANTITHESIS: DRACULA FEASTS ON MANKIND'S BLOOD TO SAVE ONLY HIMSELF!

THREE NIGHTS COME AND GO... BEFORE THE LORD OF THE UNDEAD RETURNS TO MARY'S LOFT TO CHECK ON HER CONDITION...

...WHERE HE FINDS A FANGED FEMALE PHOENIX RISEN FROM COLD ASHES!
COME WITH ME PLEASE, VLAD! A MAD CRAVING IS ON ME! WE CAN FEED ...TOGETHER!

PARIS, FAR-FAMED "CITY OF LIGHTS", IS THEIR HUNTING GROUND THIS DARK-LING EVE...
...BUT AS THEY WHEEL AND DART UNDER THE PALE GIRTH OF AN EVER-WATCHFUL MOON... THEY SEEM TO BE MORE LIKE CHILDREN AT PLAY... RATHER THAN TWIN NIGHT-STALKERS SEEKING PREY!

IN A SENSE, THEY ARE CHILDREN OF A SORT!
MEDIEVAL MONKS CONSIDERED THEIR KIND "EX PATRE DIABOLO"...
..."CHILDREN OF THE DEVIL"!!

DOWN, SLAVE! BOW TO YOUR MASTER! STRUG-GLE AT THIS POINT IS USELESS!!
HURRY NOW, BELOVED! WHILE I HOLD THIS BESOTTED ONE... DRINK YOUR FILL!
ZUT ALORS--!!
BEING...

HA!
HA!
HA!
HA!
HA!
ONCE THE CORPSE HAD HELD THE PRECIOUS GLOW OF LIFE! NOW... IT IS ONLY A DRAINED HUSK... SO MUCH DROSS... LIKE THE BITS OF SCRAP PAPER AND DEAD LEAVES THAT SKITTER ABOUT IT IN THE WHIRLING MID-NIGHT WIND!
...AND NOTHINGNESS!

IT IS VERY LATE... ALMOST FOUR A.M... WHEN THE VAMPIRIC PAIR AGAIN REVERTS TO HUMAN FORM... IN THE NEAR-DESERTED "RED LIGHT" DISTRICT!
SOUNDLESSLY DRACULA POINTS AT THEIR NEXT INTENDED VICTIM! EQUALLY SILENT, MARY NODS IN INTUITIVE UNDERSTANDING!

TURN, SOW...TURN AND FACE ME! I HAVE NEED OF YOU!
AT FIRST, THIS WOMAN-OF-THE-EVENING IS TEMPTED TO SCREAM... BUT DENIAL-OF-REALITY TAKES HOLD... AND SHE FORCES A SMILE IN THE FACE OF DEATH!

OH, M'SIEU! I WAS ZO FRIGHTENED ZERE FOR A MOMENT!
EITHAIR YOU ARE A VERY DRUNK TOURIST ...OR YOU ARE COMING FROM A MASQUERADE, NO...??

NO--!!
IIIEEEEEEEEE!
SOMEONE MAY HAVE HEARD HER OUTCRY! DRINK QUICKLY...

...FOR I STILL MUST SATIATE MY OWN BURNING HUNGER!
AH, SHE IS RICH AND SWEET ...A MARKED IMPROVEMENT OVER THE BITTER TASTE OF OUR LAST WINE-REEKING KILL!

UNTIL YOU CAN BETTER DECIDE, ATTACK ONLY THE LOWEST ELEMENTS OF SOCIETY... BECAUSE THEY ARE LEAST TO BE MISSED!
CAFE

OBSERVE-- A WITLESS HUMAN!
ONE MOVE, MON AMI, AND YOU ARE A DEAD MAN!
LET ME 'AVE YOUR WALLET... AND PERHAPS YOU'LL LIVE TO SEE ZEE LIGHT OF DAY!

ON THE CONTRARY, PIG, IT IS YOU WHO WILL SUFFER A LOSS THIS NIGHT--
SACRE BLEU!!
--THE LOSS OF YOUR PHYSICAL BODY!!

MARY'S THOUGHTS STRANGELY STRIKE UPON THE TIME WHEN A NEW YORK ART CRITIC, REVIEWING HER WEIRDLY-GOTHIC PAINTINGS, REFERRED TO HER AS: BLOODY MARY!
NEVER HAS THAT NICKNAME PROVEN MORE APPROPRIATE THAN NOW!
REALIZATION SLOWLY AND PAINFULLY DAWNS... THAT THE INTEREST HE FEELS FOR MARY IS NOT EQUAL TO WHAT WAS ONCE FELT FOR THE OTHER WOMAN.
AND WHAT OF DRACULA? HE, TOO, IS THINKING BACK ...500 YEARS... BACK TO THE TIME OF A PREVIOUS ROMANCE.
THE PAST IS OVER! IT CAN NEVER TRULY BE RECAPTURED! THE VAMPIRE LORD KNOWS HE MUST RETURN TO THE PRESENT ...CONFRONT GRIM REALITY... AND END THIS MISLEADING ROLE HE'S BEEN ENACTING!

WHERE DRACULA WALKS... HE WALKS ALONE!

THE GAME MUST CEASE TONIGHT!
AT LAST... I'VE FINALLY FOUND THE EXCITEMENT I'VE ALWAYS BEEN LOOKING FOR!

I WANT TO BE WITH YOU FOREVER, VLAD!

BUT... SOME-THING'S WRONG! I CAN TELL BY THE WAY YOU'RE BEHAVING--!
YES, MARY... SOMETHING IS WRONG!

I AM DRACULA PRINCE OF EVIL... LORD OF THE UN-LIVING! NOT SOME FOPPISH SCHOOLBOY HOPELESSLY IN LOVE WITH A WILL O' THE WISP!
THERE CAN BE NO LOVE BETWEEN US... NEVER AMONGST THOSE OF OUR KIND!
SURELY YOU UNDERSTAND ALL THAT, DON'T YOU?!
TURPENTIN

BUT DRACULA CAN SEE BY THE PAINED LOOK IN HER EYE THAT SURELY SHE DOES NOT...

BIRTH IS PAINFUL... AND REBIRTH ESPECIALLY SO!
YOU ARE NOW BOTH APART AND ABOVE THE COLLECTIVE HERD OF HUMAN CATTLE!

"EMOTION" IS A WORD OF WEAKNESS, AND IT MUST MEAN NEXT TO NOTHING FOR A VAMPIRE!

YOU MUST THINK NEW THOUGHTS... STRONG THOUGHTS...
...BECOME "CAUSE" IN A WORLD OF TOTAL "EFFECT"!!

TO CONCEIVE OF YOURSELF AS HALF-DEFEATED, MARY, IS TO BE ALREADY BEATEN!
LEARN TO DEPEND ON YOUR OWN INNER-STRENGTH! YOU ARE AS POWERFUL AS YOU CHOOSE TO BE!

I LEAVE YOU WITH THESE WORDS OF MINE! REMEMBER THEM DEARLY..

...FOR I SHALL ALWAYS REMEMBER YOU!. FAREWELL!
GOODBYE, VLAD! I'LL NEVER FORGET YOU, EITHER!
...NEVER!!

HE'S GONE...

...JUST LIKE ALL...

POWER MAY HAVE BEEN CONTAINED IN DRACULA'S WORDS... AND, PERHAPS, A MEASURE OF WISDOM...
...OF THE REST!!
...BUT HERS WERE NOT THE EARS TO HEAR THEM ...AND SO SHE REMAINS DEAF TO THEIR TRUTH!

INSTEAD OF SUMMONING THE COURAGE UP FROM INSIDE OF HERSELF TO FORGE A NEW DESTINY...

...SHE FIXES A SHARPENED WOODEN STAKE TO THE FLOOR...

...AND LEAPS UPON IT... RENDING HER HEART...

...COMMITTING THE WORLD'S FIRST VAMPIRIC SUICIDE!
AND, AS SHE PERISHES THUS...

FINIS
... DRACULA, FAR AWAY DREAMS OF HER... AND SMILES SLIGHTLY! FEW, INDEED HAVE BEEN THE MORTALS HE'S DARED CARE FOR...
...AND, FOR A BRIEF TIME, MARY WAS NUMBERED AMONG THEM!

02187

DRACULA LIVES!™

TALES OF TERROR-- FROM THE COUNT'S OWN CRYPT!

THE WALKING DEAD IN NEW YORK!

WITCHCRAFT IN OLD SALEM!

PLUS: **DRACULA CAPTURED ON FILM!**

COMICS, FEATURES, AND **PHOTOS** OF THE MOST FAMOUS, MOST DEADLY **VAMPIRE** OF ALL!

BORIS

02187

DRACULA LIVES!™

SPECIAL *ORIGIN* ISSUE:
THE **BIRTH** OF
COUNT DRACULA

MIDNIGHT IN MYSTERIOUS
NEW ORLEANS
THE VAMPIRE
AND THE
VOODOO WOMAN

ILLUSTRATED STORIES AND FEARSOME PHOTO-FEATURES OF THE
Master of the Living Dead

DRACULA LIVES!™

PRINCE OF DARKNESS, CITY OF LIGHT

COUNT DRACULA STALKS THE STREETS— *TODAY!*

EXTRA BONUS:

DUEL OF THE UNDEAD

ALSO IN THIS UNEARTHLY ISSUE:

THE MAN WHO WAS DRACULA!

SOLOMON KANE, VAMPIRE-SLAYER

—AND A CREAKING COFFIN-FULL OF PHOTOS AND FACT-FEATURES ON THE KING OF THE LIVING DEAD

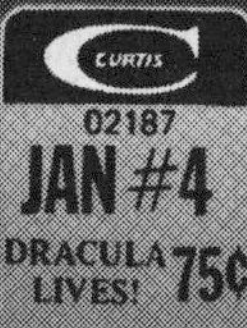

02187
JAN #4
DRACULA LIVES! 75¢

DRACULA LIVES!

VAMPIRE vs. VAMPIRE

IN THE HAUNTED BACK-LOTS OF HOLLYWOOD

MORE PHOTOS, FACT, AND FANTASY STARRING THE LORD OF THE UNDEAD

BONUS: THE COUNTESS OF BLOOD

DRACULA LIVES!

FANTASY, FEATURES, AND ACTUAL PHOTOS OF THE PRINCE OF DARKNESS

IN THIS ISSUE:

BRAM STOKER'S ORIGINAL HORROR-TALE OF THE LORD OF VAMPIRES --FIRST TIME EVER IN FULL SIZED ILLUSTRATED FORM

BONUS:
MONSTER-SIZE DRACULA PIN-UP!

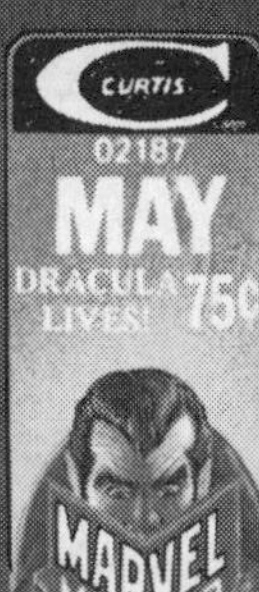

DRACULA LIVES!

TERROR LURKS... in the CHAPEL of BLOOD

ALSO: PHOTOS and FEATURES about the LORD of the LIVING DEAD

LUIS DOMINGUEZ

Pinup from *Dracula Lives #5* by Gene Colan

LORD OF THE VAMPIRES

Gene Colan

DRACULA™ LIVES!

THE DEATH-MAN COMETH

SPECIAL FEATURE: THE SHE-VAMPIRES OF CASTLE DRACULA

BONUS: FEARFUL PHOTOS OF CHRISTOPHER LEE AS THE LORD OF THE UNDEAD

DRACULA™ LIVES!

LAST WALK ON THE NIGHT SIDE

He Prowls the Streets... Today!

02187

NOV. Nº 9

DRACULA LIVES! 75¢

DRACULA LIVES!™

THE LORD OF VAMPIRES TURNS THE TABLES ON THE WOMAN WHO COLLECTED DRACULA

ALSO: "VENGEANCE!" CRIES THE VAMPIRE'S VICTIM

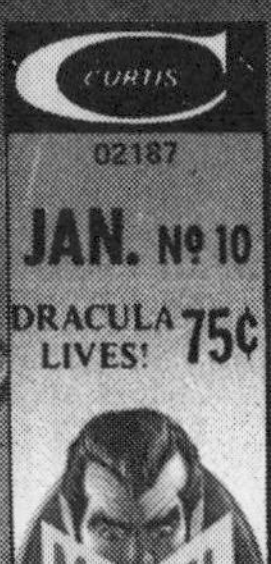

DRACULA LIVES!™

A WOMAN IN THE CLUTCHES OF THE LORD OF VAMPIRES

POLICE

A CITY IN THE GRIP OF TERROR...

Pinup from *Dracula Lives* #5 by Don Maitz and Duffy Vohland

DRACULA LIVES!™

TERROR LURKS BENEATH CASTLE DRACULA -- "PIT OF DEATH!"

CAN ANY MAN ESCAPE -- LILITH UNLEASHED!

Pinup from *Dracula Lives #11* by Bob Hall

CURTIS

02187
DRACULA
LIVES
MAY. Nº 12
75¢
MARVEL
MONSTER
GROUP
DRACULA
LIVES!
TM
SPECIAL
A NOVEL-LENGTH
TALE OF TERROR
PARCHMENT
OF BLOOD!

DRACULA LIVES!™

"BLOOD OF MY BLOOD!"
A DRACULA SOUL-SHOCKER!

FOUR TALES OF
VAMPIRIC TERROR

Pinup from *Dracula Lives #13* by Vicente Alcazar

CC
02956
AUG. Nº 6
$1.25

THE TOMB OF DRACULA™

THE MARVEL
MONSTER
GROUP™

SPECIAL
LAST
ISSUE!

Pinup from *Tomb of Dracula Magazine #6*
by Haim Kano

"BATTLE"

Pinups from *Tomb of Dracula Magazine* #6
by Gene Colan and Joe Rubinstein

I WILL RETURN!

A DRACULA PORTFOLIO

By Russ Heath

R HEATH

Tomb of Dracula #70 was originally intended to be spread over several issues, but when the decision was made to cancel the series, *#70* became a double-sized final issue. Marv Wolfman and Gene Colan had to excise pages that were already drawn in order to fit the new format. Presented here are copies of the unused pencil pages courtesy of Marv Wolfman.

Book Tomb of Dracula
Issue#
pg.#
WHO IS THE USURPER, DRACULA WONDERS. WHO DARES STEAL HIS WELL-DESERVED TITLE? WELL, WHOEVER THIS TORGO IS, THEY WILL MEET, THEY WILL BATTLE, AND THEN ONE WILL DIE.
DRACULA PAUSES FOR A BRIEF MOMENT. WHO WILL DIE? THE THOUGHT IS FLEETING, BUT IT STINGS THE VAMPIRE'S SENSES ANYHOW.
EVER SINCE HE MET THE ARCH-DEMON SATAN, DRACULA FINDS HIMSELF UNSTEADY... UNCERTAIN... UNSURE.
THIS NIGHT HE FOUGHT OFF THE SWARM OF VAMPIRES TO PROTECT HUMAN CHILDREN. BY ALL RIGHTS HE SHOULD HAVE JOINED THE OTHERS IN A BLOOD FEAST...
YET...
SO MANY QUESTIONS ASSAIL DRACULA'S MIND THAT HE DOESN'T KNOW HOW TO DEAL WITH THEM ALL. AND SO HE IS THANKFUL AS THE VAMPIRES SWOOP LOW TOWARD AN OLD AND DECAYING CEMETERY.
THEY ARE HOME AT LAST--
--AND IT IS HERE THAT DRACULA KNOWS TORGO AWAITS HIM.
TORGO, HE MUST DWELL WITHIN THE TALLEST OF THE MONUMENTS...
DRACULA SHUDDERS, THOUGH HE DOES NOT KNOW WHY.

DRACULA

Book *Tomb of Dracula* Issue *0* (6)

NOW, TAKE ME TO THIS TORGO FOOL. I DEMAND TO SEE THE FILTH WHO BELIEVES HE CAN REPLACE ME.

NO, DRACULA--TORGO HAS COMMANDED US TO SLAY YOU!

HE SAYS YOU ARE NOT WORTHY OF HIS ATTENTION.

THEN LET HIM TRY TO STOP ME FROM MARCHING RIGHT INTO HIS DAMNED 'PALACE' AND CRUSHING HIM LIKE AN OVERRIPE MELON.

NO! HE SAID KILL YOU!

THAT IS OUR ORDER!

ONLY DRACULA IS THE LORD OF VAMPIRES.

THEN YOU SHALL FIRST PERISH TRYING TO OBEY A MADMAN'S WISHES!

ONLY DRACULA--NO ONE ELSE!

THUD

KRAK

ACKKK!

NOW, IS ANY OTHER FOOL PREPARED TO PERISH BEFORE I PLUCK THE FOOL FROM HIS THRONE OF GLASS?

KNOWING THEY ARE ABOUT TO DIE, THEY NEVERTHELESS CLOSE IN ON THE FORMER LORD OF VAMPIRES...

THEY HAVE NO CHOICE. THEY MUST OBEY THE MAN WHO SITS UPON THE THRONE.

(DRAC STRIKES STILL ANOTHER WITH THE FORM OF A WILD BEAST)

DRACULA
Book TOMB OF DRACULA
Issue# 1/3
pg.# 14
HAH! WE SHALL SEE. KARLA-- FOLLOW DRACULA... MAKE SURE HE DOES NOT ESCAPE.
FIRST THERE MUST BE A FEAST... THEN OUR CHALLENGE MATCH BEGINS.
I SHALL OBEY YOU, DEAR TORSO... WITH PLEASURE.
KEEP YOUR HANDS OFF ME, SLUT. YOU DISGUST ME WITH YOUR PRESENCE.
IT IS PAST MIDNIGHT IN TRANSYLVANIA, THE STREETS ARE ALL BUT DESERTED AS A CLOUD OF BLACK SWARMS PAST A SILVER MOON.
ALL THAT CAN BE HEARD ON THE STREETS BELOW IS THE HARSH FLAP-PING OF LEATH-ERY WINGS.
THE CLOUD DECENDS AND SPLITS APART, AND THE FEW STRAGLERS OUT LATE AT NIGHT STARE UPWARDS IN WIDE-EYED HORROR.
THE DARK ONES HAVE RETURNED!
THEY MUST FLEE TO THEIR HOMES, BOLT THE DOORS BEHIND THEM.
HEY, EVERYONE... COME TO THE WINDOW. LOOK!
OH MY LORD. FRANK! QUINCY... COME HERE.
LOOK, LOOK! TELL ME I'M NOT SEEING WHAT I'M SEEING.
IT'S AS IF HELL ITSELF CONTROLS TRANSYLVANIA!

DRACULA

XEROX	STAN	DUE DATE	STATS NEG.	POS.	CODE
8					

Book Tomb of Dracula Issue# 70 pg.# 15

RACHEL VAN HELSING IS NOT GIVEN TO EXAGGERATION. USUALLY SHE IS A CALM, SOMBER, ALL-TOO-SERIOUS OBSERVER.

BUT WHAT SHE SEES IS NOT EXAGGERATION IF ANYTHING IT IS AN UNDER-STATEMENT.

HELL ITSELF HAS TAKEN OVER.

SLAVERING, DEMON-EYED HORDES SWEEP THROUGH THE VILLAGE WITHOUT MERCY. HUMANS FALL LIKE WHEAT UNDER A SCYTHE.

LORD, DON'T DO IT... PLEASE, T'GOD-- LEEME BE!

I'LL LET YOU BE, MAN... AFTER I'VE GIVEN YOU THE KISS...

...AND SUCH A GENTLE KISS... ONE YOU SHALL NEVER QUITE FORGET.

AND NO AMOUNT OF PLEADING CAN STOP THE HUNGRY VAMPIRES FROM SLAYING THEIR HORRIFIED VICTIMS.

HALT! DO NOT KILL HIM.

BUT TORGO--I THIRST!

I NEED THIS HUMAN... HE CAN DO THINGS A VAMPIRE CANNOT HOPE TO DO.

AND THAT IS WHY YOU WILL NOT KILL THE HUMAN.

NOW RISE, MAN. RISE!

(SHE PULLS AWAY AS THE NEW LORD SCREAMS OUT "HALT!")

("WE CAN USE ONE HUMAN UNDER OUR POWER BUT NOT A VAMPIRE - RISE!")

DRACULA
Book TOMB OF DRACULA
Issue# 70
PG.# 17
UPSTAIRS, IN ANOTHER ROOM, QUINCY HARKER AND HAROLD H. HAROLD HEAR A SUDDEN SHOUT. THEY RECOGNIZE THE VOICE INSTANTLY.
NO! DO NOT SLAY THEM.
THESE HUMANS ARE MINE!
Q-QUINCY--?
YES, HAROLD... THAT'S HIM--
I SAID CLEAR OUT, SCUM. DO NOT THINK YOU CAN DEFEAT ME BECAUSE TORGO SAYS HE IS NOW YOUR LEADER.
I CAN STILL SNAP YOU IN HALF.
OUT!
I COULD SLAY YOU NOW IF I WISHED TO, BUT I OWE YOU... OWE YOU FOR NOT ATTACKING ME THAT OTHER NIGHT.*
GO! HURRY TO YOUR DOOR. LOCK IT. PUT YOUR DAMNED CRUCIFIX IN PLACE AND YOU WILL BE SAFE FOR THE EVENING.
BUT WHEN I RETURN... WHEN I AM ONCE MORE THE LORD OF MY PEOPLE--
--THEN, DRAKE... THEN, VAN HELSING-- THEN WE SHALL SEE A BATTLE BETWEEN US THAT HAS BEEN LONG IN THE COMING!
*TOD #68 --MW
OUTSIDE, DRACULA CAN HEAR TORGO'S VOICE CALLING HIS LEGION. "IT IS OVER!" DRACULA TURNS ONCE MORE INTO HIS BAT SHAPE...
...HE WINGS INTO THE EBONY DARKNESS AND JOINS WITH THE OTHERS. HE WILL BE BACK... TOMORROW NIGHT. ONCE HE HAS BECOME LORD OF VAMPIRES...
AND ALL THE WHILE, TORGO CHUCKLES QUIETLY TO HIMSELF. HE IS CONTENT.
NEXT ISSUE: BEGINNING THE CLIMACTIC TWO-PARTER THAT WILL CHANGE EVERYTHING YOU'VE EVER KNOWN ABOUT DRACULA.
DEATH OF THE NIGHT STALKER

Book TOMB OF DRACULA Issue# 71 PG.# 3

DOMINI TURNS TO FACE TOPAZ WHO SAYS, "I KNOW WHAT HAPPENED TO DRACULA - AND SOMEHOW IT RELATES TO MY MAN--- JACK RUSSELL"

TOPAZ AND DOMINI WALK TOWARD A DIFFERENT ROOM

(IMAGES OF DRAC AND LEAD VAMPIRE APPEAR WITHIN THE SMOKE - THEIR HANDS ARE TIED TO EACH OTHER)

END

Book TOMB OF DRACULA Issue# 71 pg# 17

(DOMINI LEAVES - TOPAZ WATCHES)

DRACULA -MARV WOLFMAN

XEROX	STAN	DUE DATE	NEG.	CODE

Book TOMB OF DRACULA Issue# 72

(RACHEL AWAKENING IN A COLD SWEAT — SHE SCREAMS OUT "QUINCY!")

DRACULA

XEROX	STAN	DUE DATE	STATS NEG.	POS.

Book *TOMB OF DRACULA* Issue# 72 Page 6

(RACHEL OPENS DOOR TO QUINCY'S ROOM — AND FINDS HIM NOT THERE — HIS BED STILL MADE — HAS NEVER BEEN IN

XEROX	STAN	DUE DATE	STATS NEG.	STATS POS.	CODE

Book Tomb of Dracula DRACULA Issue# 72 Page 4

XEROX	STAN	DUE DATE	STATS NEG.	STATS POS.	CODE

Book DRACULA Issue# 72 Pg# 27

I Believe ending his life will not be as difficult as I once suspected

I intend to slay Dracula using a silver spike from my wheelchair, then I intend to destroy Castle Dracula after cutting off his head and stuffing it with garlic. There will be no way that Dracula shall survive.

QUINCY SYMBOLIC - "RACHEL - THAT IS NOT WHY I WRITE TO YOU - - I WRITE BECAUSE MY LIFE BECAME OBSESSED WITH THE VAMPIRE'S DEATH. I LOST ALL HOPE

Pinup from a Marvel calendar by Gene Colan and Tom Palmer courtesy Tom Palmer

COLAN & PALMER

THE BOYHOOD OF DRACULA

SCRIPT BY TONY ISABELLA ~ ART BY VAL MAYERIK

WAS DRACULA REALLY A SADISTIC RULER? OR WERE HIS IMPALING TACTICS MERELY PLOYS TO SCARE HIS ENEMIES AWAY AND PROTECT HIS PEOPLE? NO ONE CAN SAY. BUT REGARDLESS OF HIS MOTIVES, ONE THING IS CERTAIN...

IN GERMANY, SUSPECT CORPSES WERE BURIED WITH THEIR MOUTHS CRAMMED FULL OF MONEY, A KIND OF BRIBE TO PREVENT THE UNDEAD FROM DRAINING THEM DRY IN ANOTHER RESPECT.

Story: TONY ISABELLA Art: ERNIE CHUA

Pinup from *Dracula Lives #4* by Pablos Marcos